"When it comes to communicating timeless truth, all genres need to be used. Adam helps us see the serious and the silly. His comics hold up a mirror and let us gaze upon that which is heartwarming and heartbreaking."

—Matt Chandler, Lead Pastor of The Village Church, President of Acts 29 Church Planting Network, author of *The Mingling of Souls*

"I have enjoyed Adam's comics for a long time. In the spirit of *Calvin and Hobbes*, they make you laugh and make you think. I'm glad Adam's work can reach a wider audience with this new book."

—Kevin DeYoung, Senior Pastor of University Reformed Church, author of *What Does the Bible Really Teach about Homosexuality?*

"Adam Ford gives imaginative life to complex and controversial arguments. His comics always make me think, and often prompt me to reframe how I engage with those who don't see things the same way I do."

—Russell Moore, President of the Ethics and Religious Liberty Commission of the Southern Baptist Convention, author of *Onward*

"The Internet is filled with memes and graphics. We almost overload on them daily. Sometimes they are useful; most of the time they just remind us that graphics software is readily available. It takes some serious work to make something stand out, catch the attention, and really communicate a message worth pondering.

Adam Ford's Christian comics do just that. I know I take the time to look over each one as it appears. He combines necessary pithiness with theological insight and apologetic acumen—a very rare combination to be sure! I hope he has the freedom to continue to cause us to think, and encourage us to engage, for years to come."

—James White, director of Alpha and Omega Ministries, author of *What Every Christian Needs to Know About the Qur'an*

"Like a divine voice from inside a whirlwind, holy sarcasm roughs up everything around us, toppling whatever is not bolted down, exposing lies, and whip-slapping our conventions. This vortex of satire and wit is fueled by an ancient power that is strong enough to pick up idols and sling them away. At its best, such work is fueled by love, not hate; and its aim is redemption, not judgment. Adam Ford's art lives in this ancient legacy, whirlwinds of humor and typhoons of truth, strong enough to lift cultural lies and to push over the presumptions we have failed to question."

—Tony Reinke, writer at Desiring God, author of *12 Ways Your Phone Is Changing You*

"Adam's comics are always insightful, theological, and, well, comical."

—Tim Challies, blogger at *Challies.com*, author of *Visual Theology*

"There is more good and insightful theology in a comic by Adam Ford than in many of the bestselling books you'll find in a Christian bookstore."

—Justin Taylor, Managing Editor of the *ESV Study Bible*, blogger at *Between Two Worlds*

"If you're not following Adam4d, you're just doing the internet wrong."

—David French, writer at *National Review*, constitutional lawyer

"Don't be fooled by the cartoon facade; Adam Ford's comics are lasers, designed and deployed to illumine the truth. With simple artistry and creative wit, Adam is a master at presenting reality in a way that leaves me saying, 'I've never looked at it like that before.'"

—Matt Smethurst, Managing Editor of The Gospel Coalition

Thy Kingdom Comics

Curiously Christian drawings and writings about Jesus, tolerance, abortion, atheism, homosexuality, theology, and lots of other stuff

by Adam4d

Thy Kingdom Comics

PO Box 87044, Canton, MI 48187.
adam4d.com@gmail.com
twitter.com/adam4d
facebook.com/adam4dcom
instagram.com/adam4dcom

S.D.G.

Contents

A little bit about the author

Adam Ford AKA Adam4d is a Christian cartoonist/writer/recluse who can usually be found at church, running around Metro Detroit, or at home writing, drawing, reading, or watching baseball. He has one wife and three young sons whom he loves a whole lot. He only refers to himself in the third person when book formalities call for it.

Adam's first book, *Implications Abound*, can be found at www.implicationsabound.com. You can read all of Adam's comics at his website: www.Adam4d.com.

Who's the bigot?

I BELIEVE GAY COUPLES SHOULD BE ABLE TO GET MARRIED! DON'T YOU?
NO; ACTUALLY, I AM AGAINST THE REDEFINITION OF MARRIAGE. I THINK MARRIAGE SHOULD RE--
BIGOT!
GASP

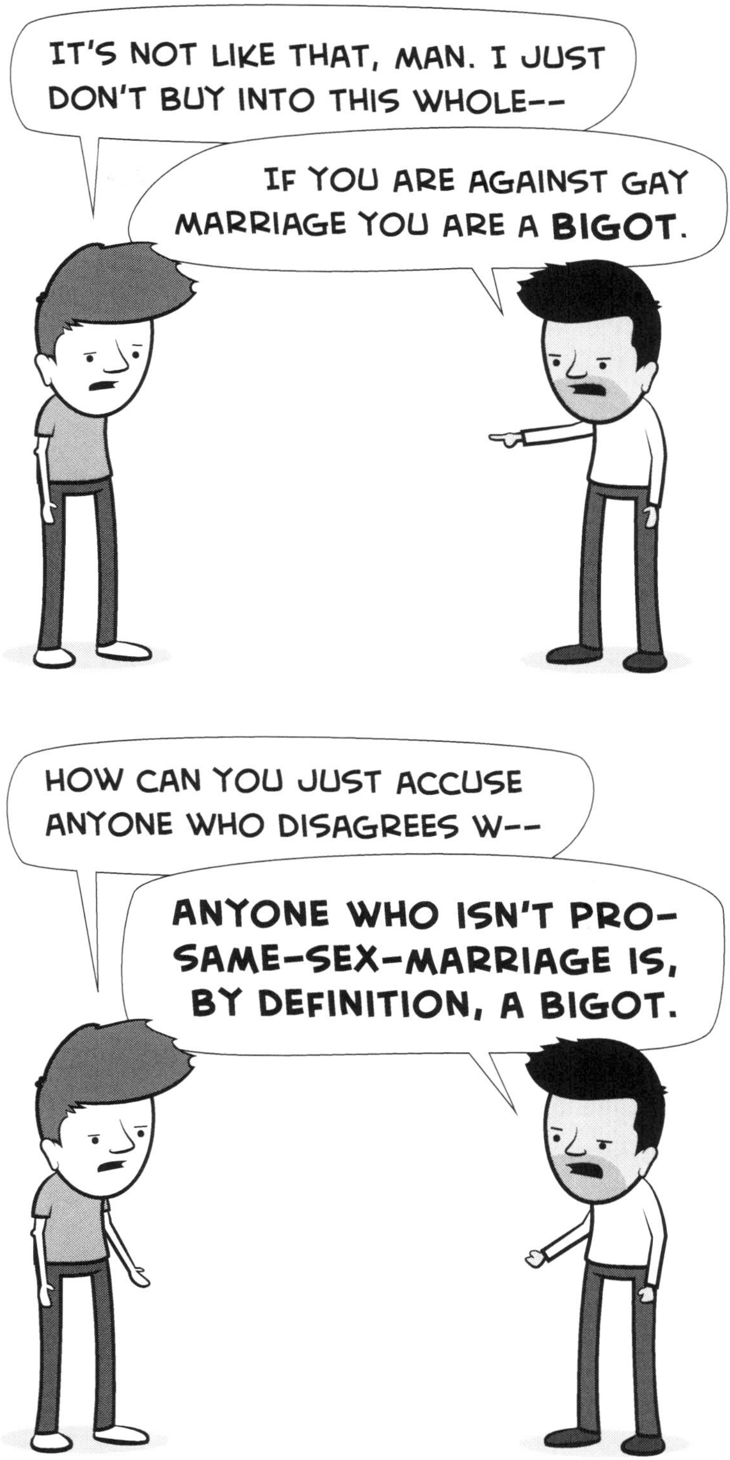
IT'S NOT LIKE THAT, MAN. I JUST DON'T BUY INTO THIS WHOLE--
IF YOU ARE AGAINST GAY MARRIAGE YOU ARE A **BIGOT**.
HOW CAN YOU JUST ACCUSE ANYONE WHO DISAGREES W--
ANYONE WHO ISN'T PRO-SAME-SEX-MARRIAGE IS, BY DEFINITION, A BIGOT.

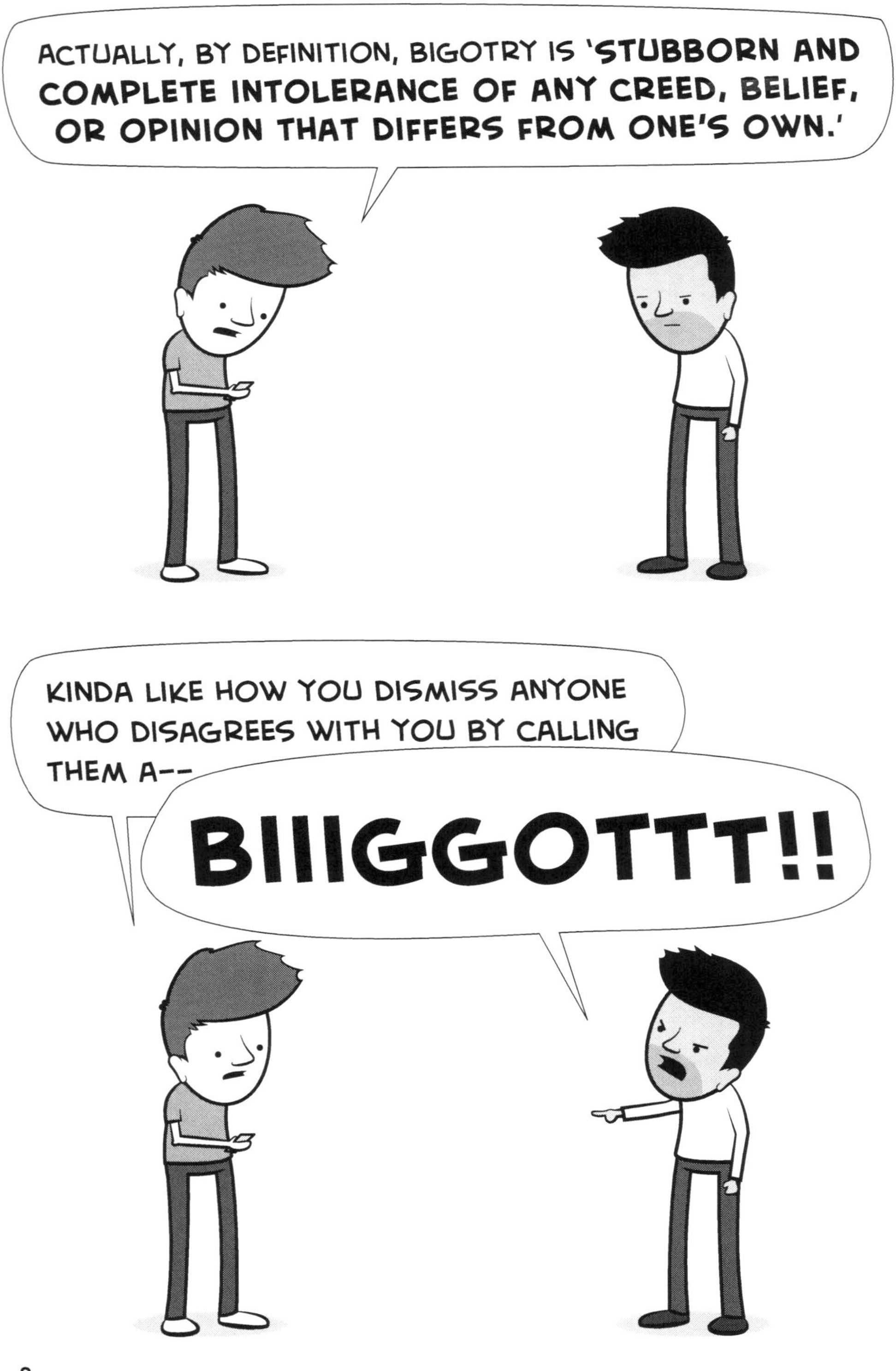
ACTUALLY, BY DEFINITION, BIGOTRY IS 'STUBBORN AND COMPLETE INTOLERANCE OF ANY CREED, BELIEF, OR OPINION THAT DIFFERS FROM ONE'S OWN.'
KINDA LIKE HOW YOU DISMISS ANYONE WHO DISAGREES WITH YOU BY CALLING THEM A--
BIIGGOTTT!!

What did you see while you were in Heaven?

Daddy, remember when we got in that bad car accident? And I almost died? I went to Heaven that day, daddy.

What did you see while you were in Heaven?

Tell me boy, what did you see??

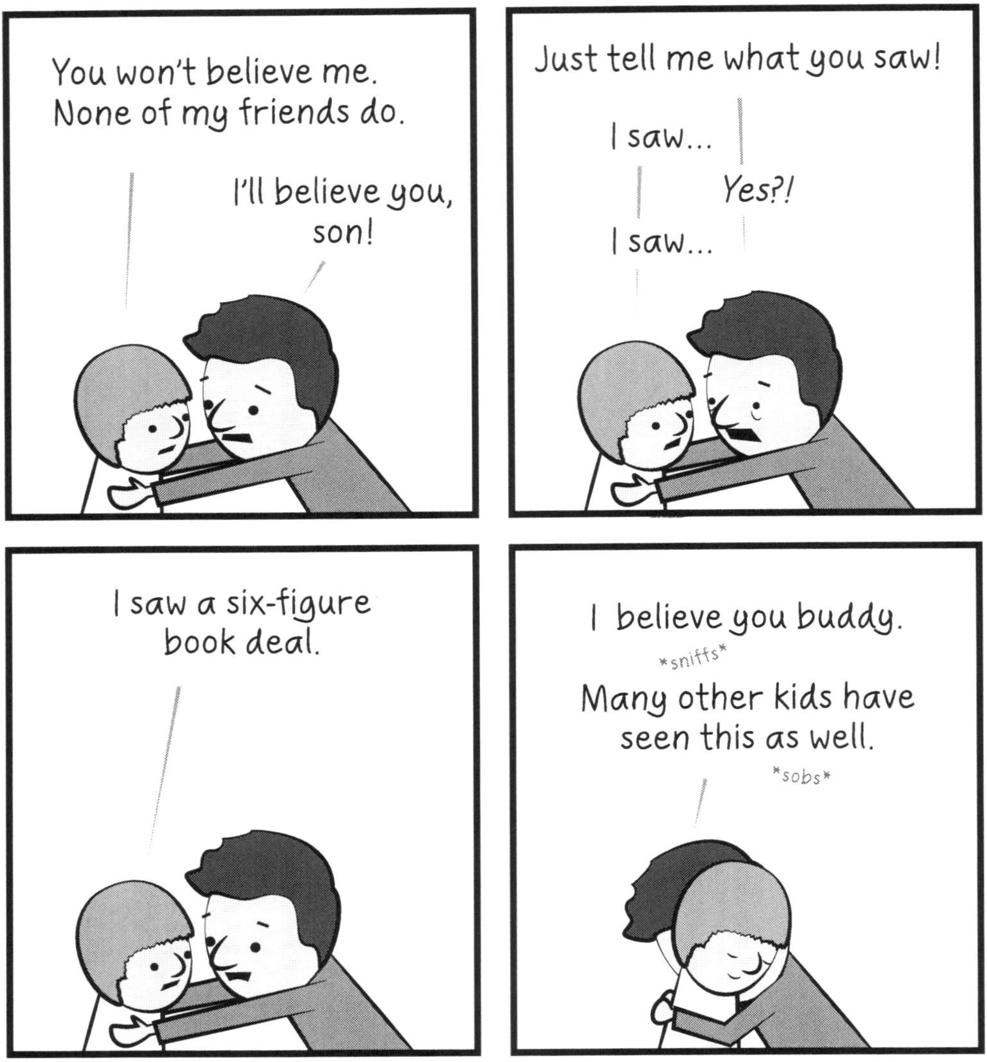
You won't believe me.
None of my friends do.
I'll believe you, son!
Just tell me what you saw!
I saw...
Yes?!
I saw...
I saw a six-figure book deal.
I believe you buddy.
sniffs
Many other kids have seen this as well.
sobs

The great Bible translation debate

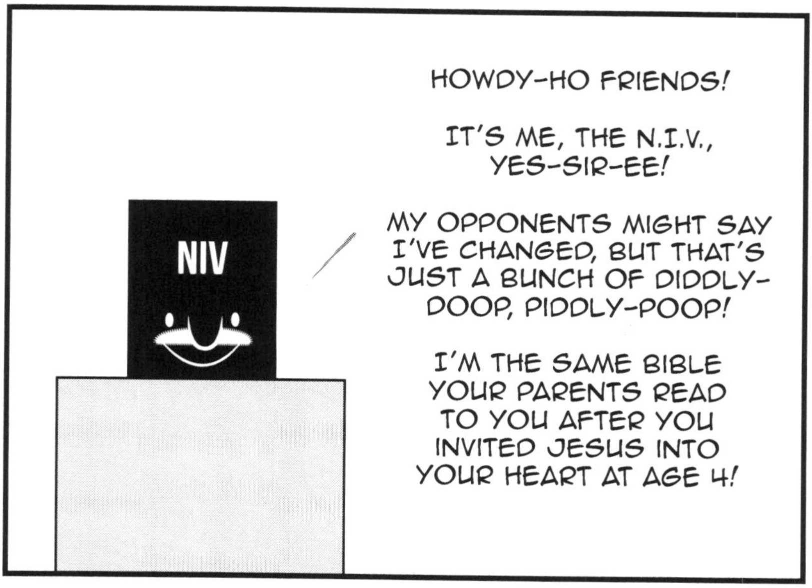
NIV
HOWDY-HO FRIENDS!
IT'S ME, THE N.I.V., YES-SIR-EE!
MY OPPONENTS MIGHT SAY I'VE CHANGED, BUT THAT'S JUST A BUNCH OF DIDDLY-DOOP, PIDDLY-POOP!
I'M THE SAME BIBLE YOUR PARENTS READ TO YOU AFTER YOU INVITED JESUS INTO YOUR HEART AT AGE 4!

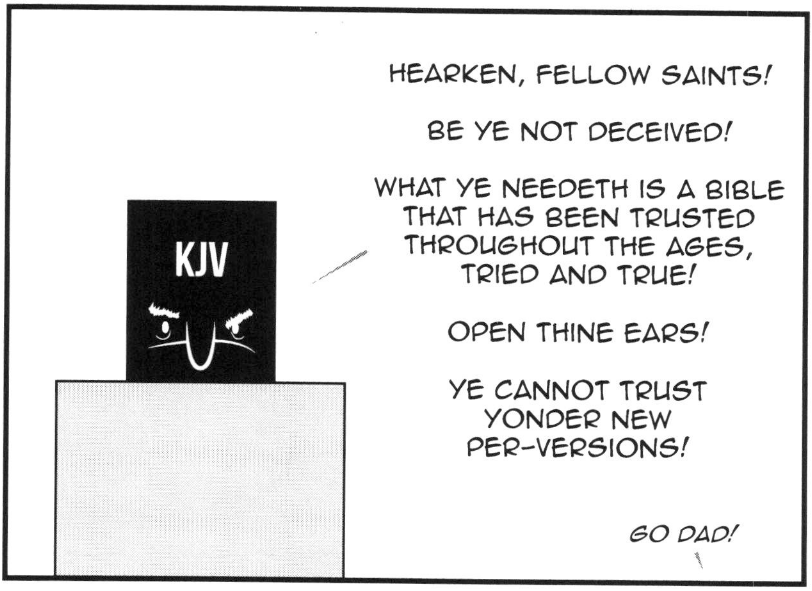
KJV
HEARKEN, FELLOW SAINTS!
BE YE NOT DECEIVED!
WHAT YE NEEDETH IS A BIBLE THAT HAS BEEN TRUSTED THROUGHOUT THE AGES, TRIED AND TRUE!
OPEN THINE EARS!
YE CANNOT TRUST YONDER NEW PER-VERSIONS!
GO DAD!

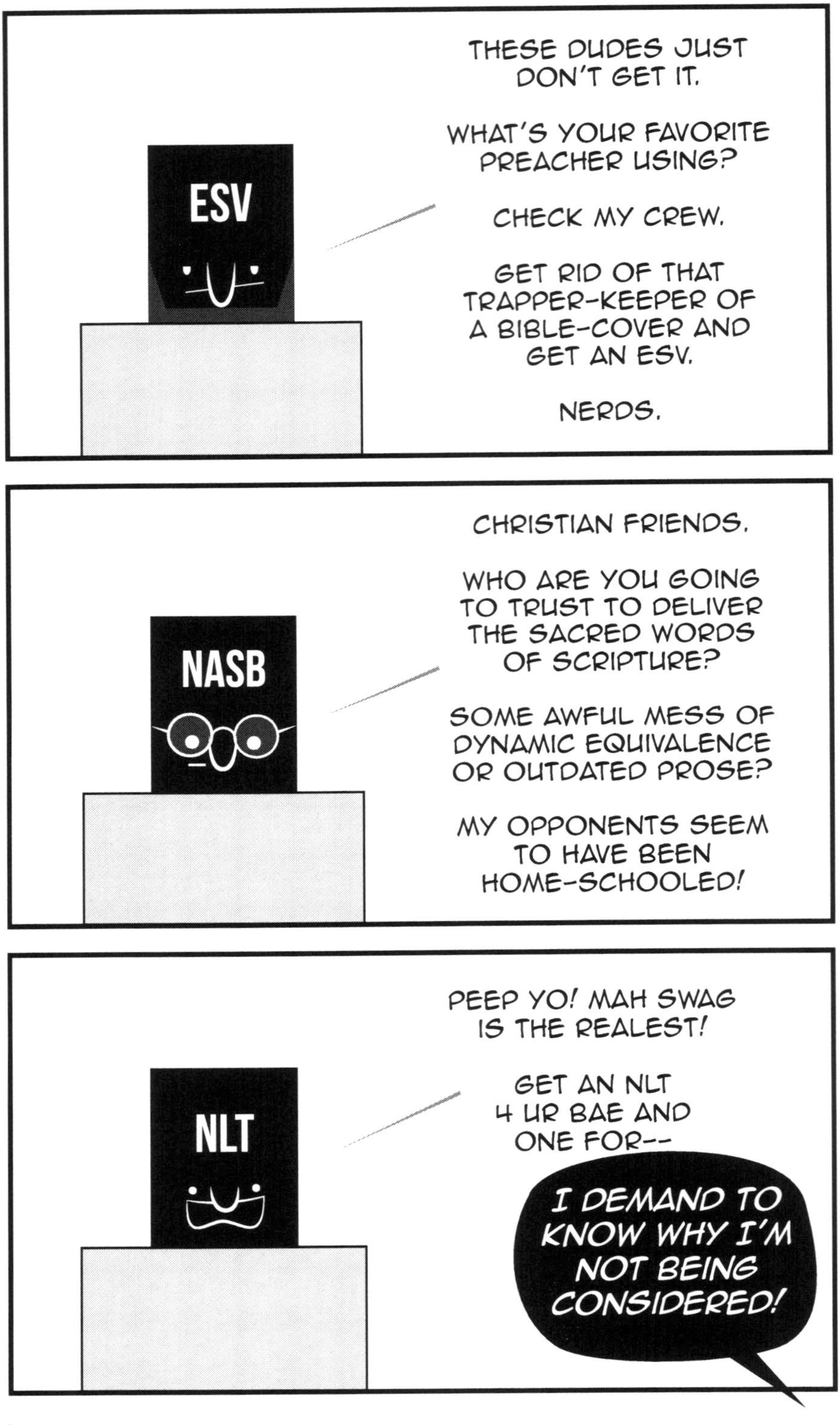
ESV
THESE DUDES JUST DON'T GET IT.
WHAT'S YOUR FAVORITE PREACHER USING?
CHECK MY CREW.
GET RID OF THAT TRAPPER-KEEPER OF A BIBLE-COVER AND GET AN ESV.
NERDS.
NASB
CHRISTIAN FRIENDS.
WHO ARE YOU GOING TO TRUST TO DELIVER THE SACRED WORDS OF SCRIPTURE?
SOME AWFUL MESS OF DYNAMIC EQUIVALENCE OR OUTDATED PROSE?
MY OPPONENTS SEEM TO HAVE BEEN HOME-SCHOOLED!
NLT
PEEP YO! MAH SWAG IS THE REALEST!
GET AN NLT 4 UR BAE AND ONE FOR--
I DEMAND TO KNOW WHY I'M NOT BEING CONSIDERED!

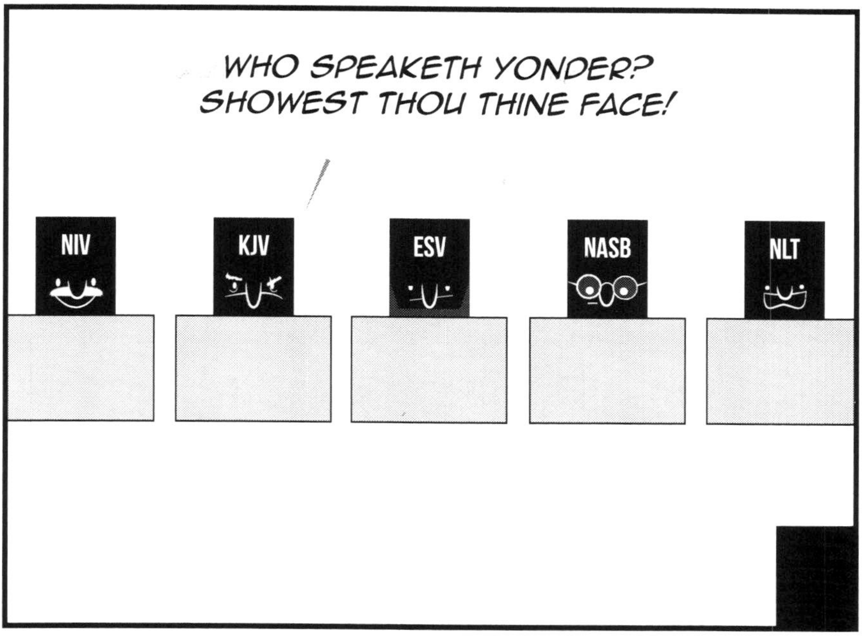
WHO SPEAKETH YONDER? SHOWEST THOU THINE FACE!
NIV
KJV
ESV
NASB
NLT

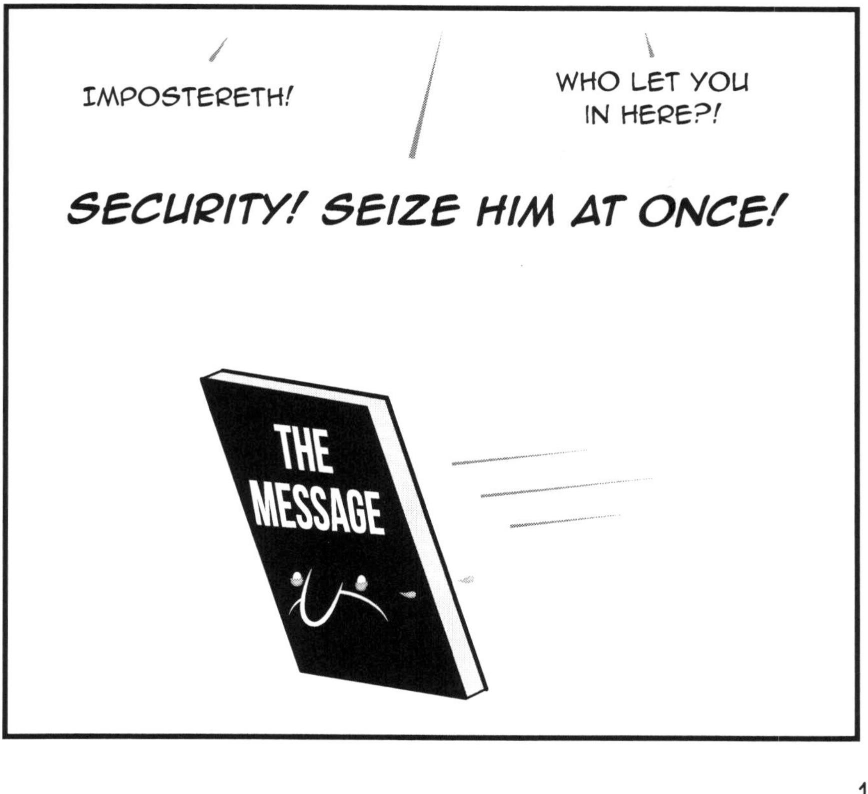
IMPOSTERETH!
WHO LET YOU IN HERE?!
SECURITY! SEIZE HIM AT ONCE!
THE MESSAGE

Closed-minded

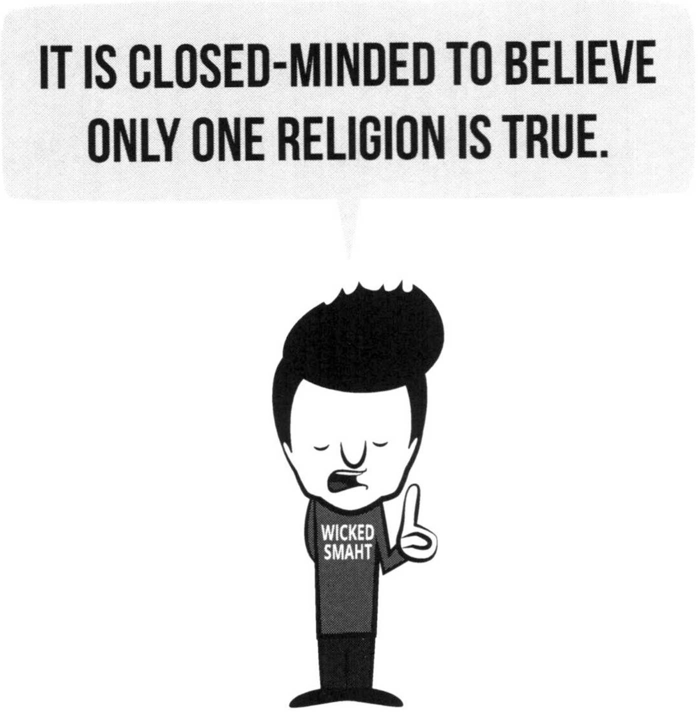
IT IS CLOSED-MINDED TO BELIEVE ONLY ONE RELIGION IS TRUE.
WICKED SMAHT

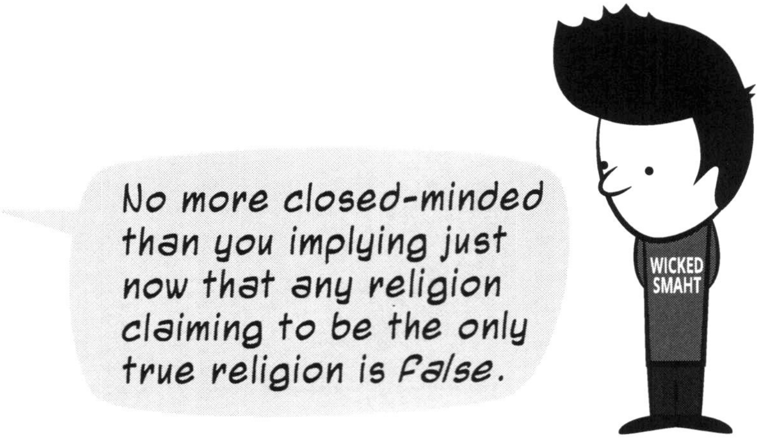
No more closed-minded than you implying just now that any religion claiming to be the only true religion is false.
WICKED SMAHT

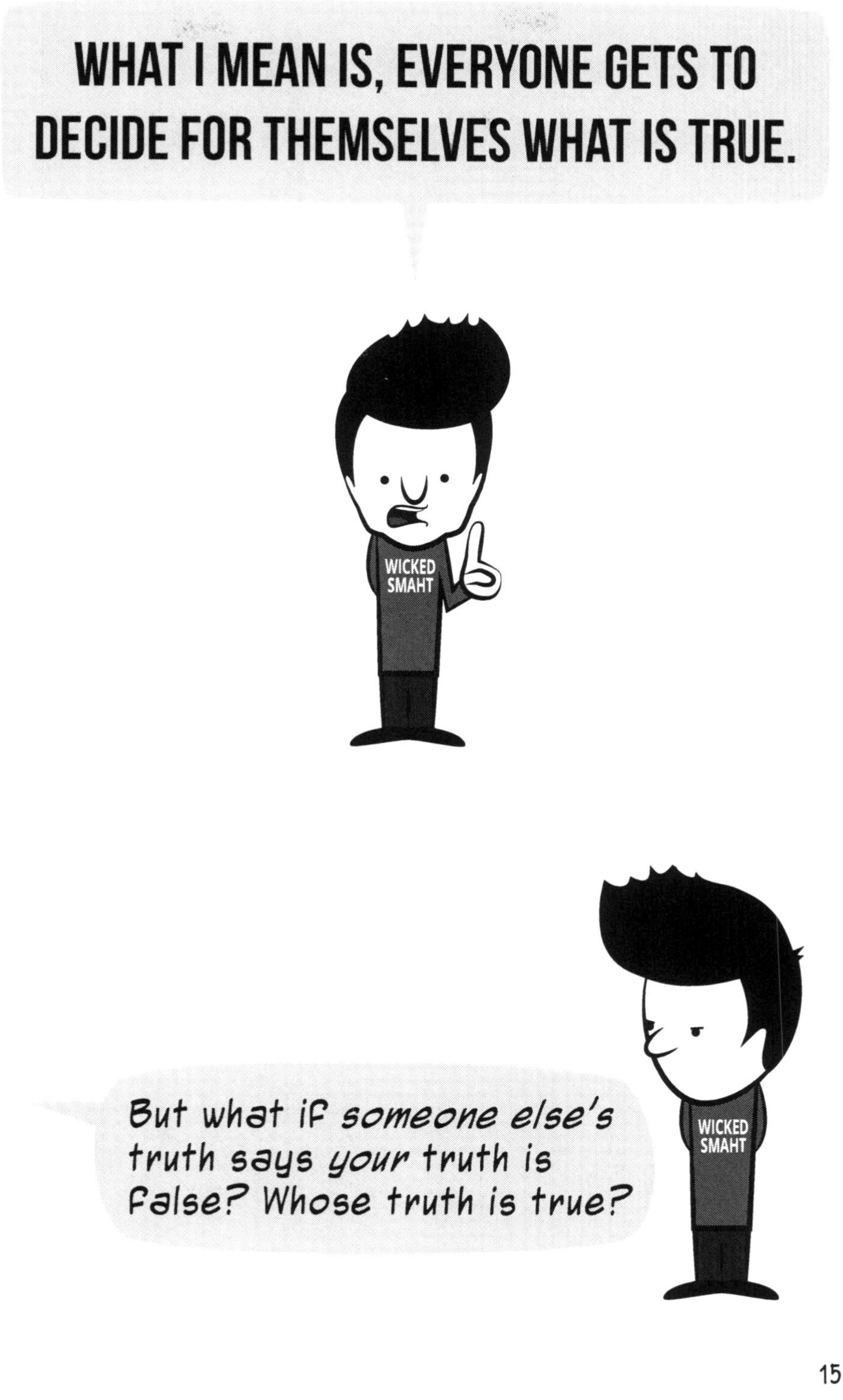
WHAT I MEAN IS, EVERYONE GETS TO DECIDE FOR THEMSELVES WHAT IS TRUE.
WICKED SMAHT
But what if someone else's truth says your truth is false? Whose truth is true?
WICKED SMAHT

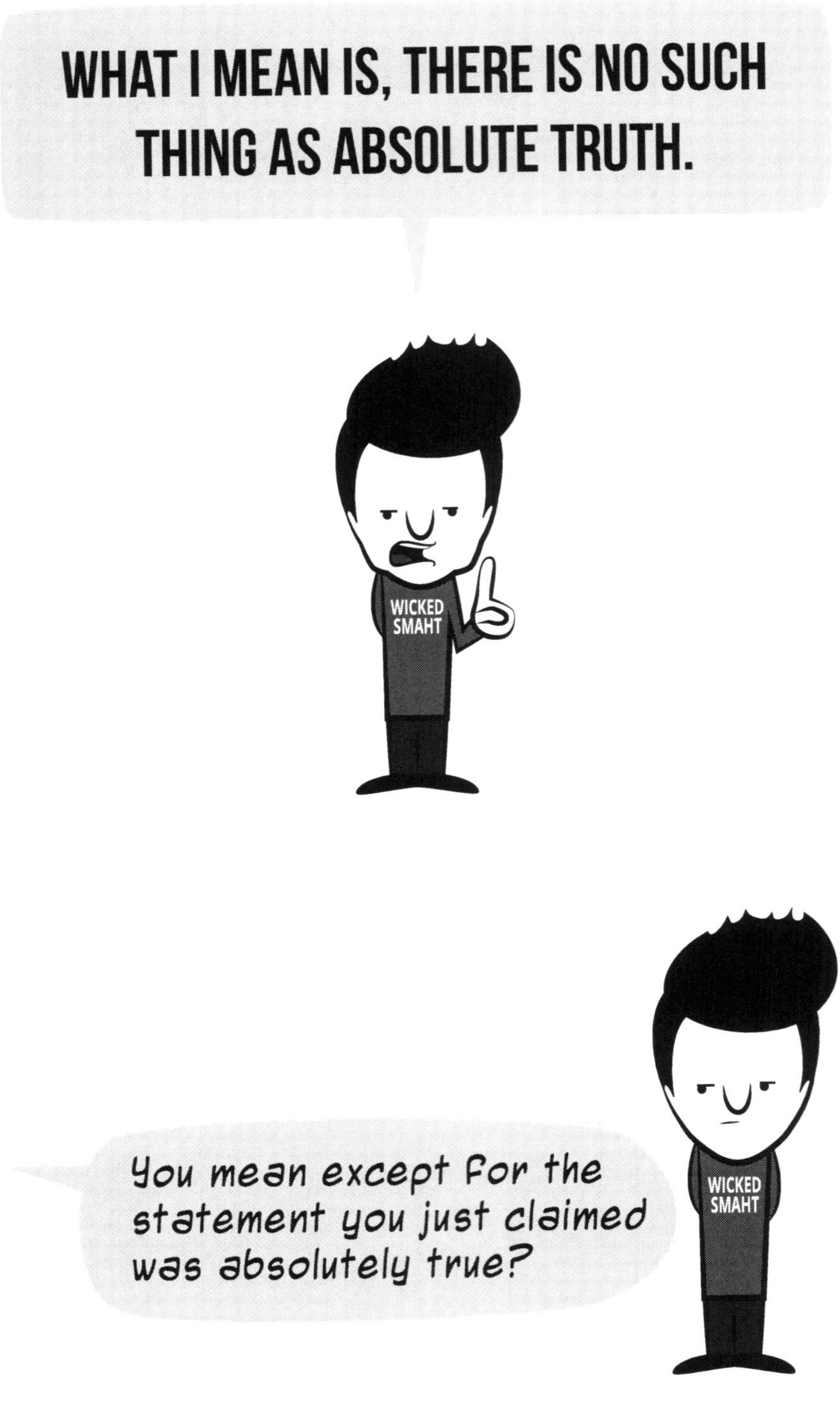
WHAT I MEAN IS, THERE IS NO SUCH THING AS ABSOLUTE TRUTH.
WICKED SMAHT
You mean except for the statement you just claimed was absolutely true?
WICKED SMAHT

WICKED
SMAHT
WHAT I REALLY MEAN IS, IT IS CLOSED-MINDED TO DISAGREE WITH SOMEONE AS OPEN-MINDED AS ME.
WICKED
SMAHT

How to spot a theological liberal

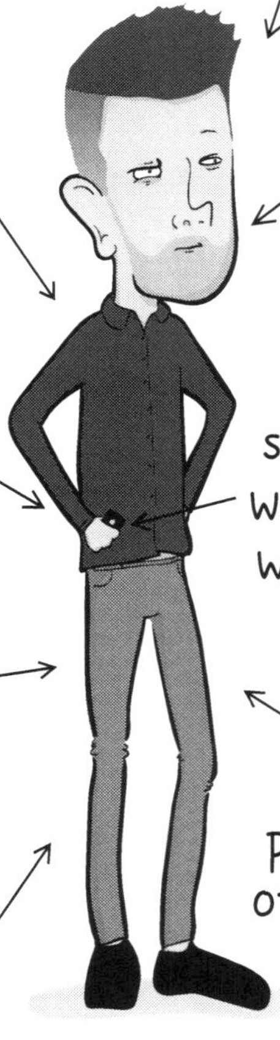

Strong shoulders for bearing the weight of the responsibility of overturning millenia of church agreement, one blog post at a time
Brave look on face
Cusses a lot because not a fundamentalist Puritan legalist
Favorite Bible commentary is /r/Christianity
Ready to join any social-media band-wagon or lynch mob without a moment's hesitation
Strong legs for running away from anything resembling historical Christianity
Occasionally wets pants at the thought of not being accepted by popular culture
Weak knees

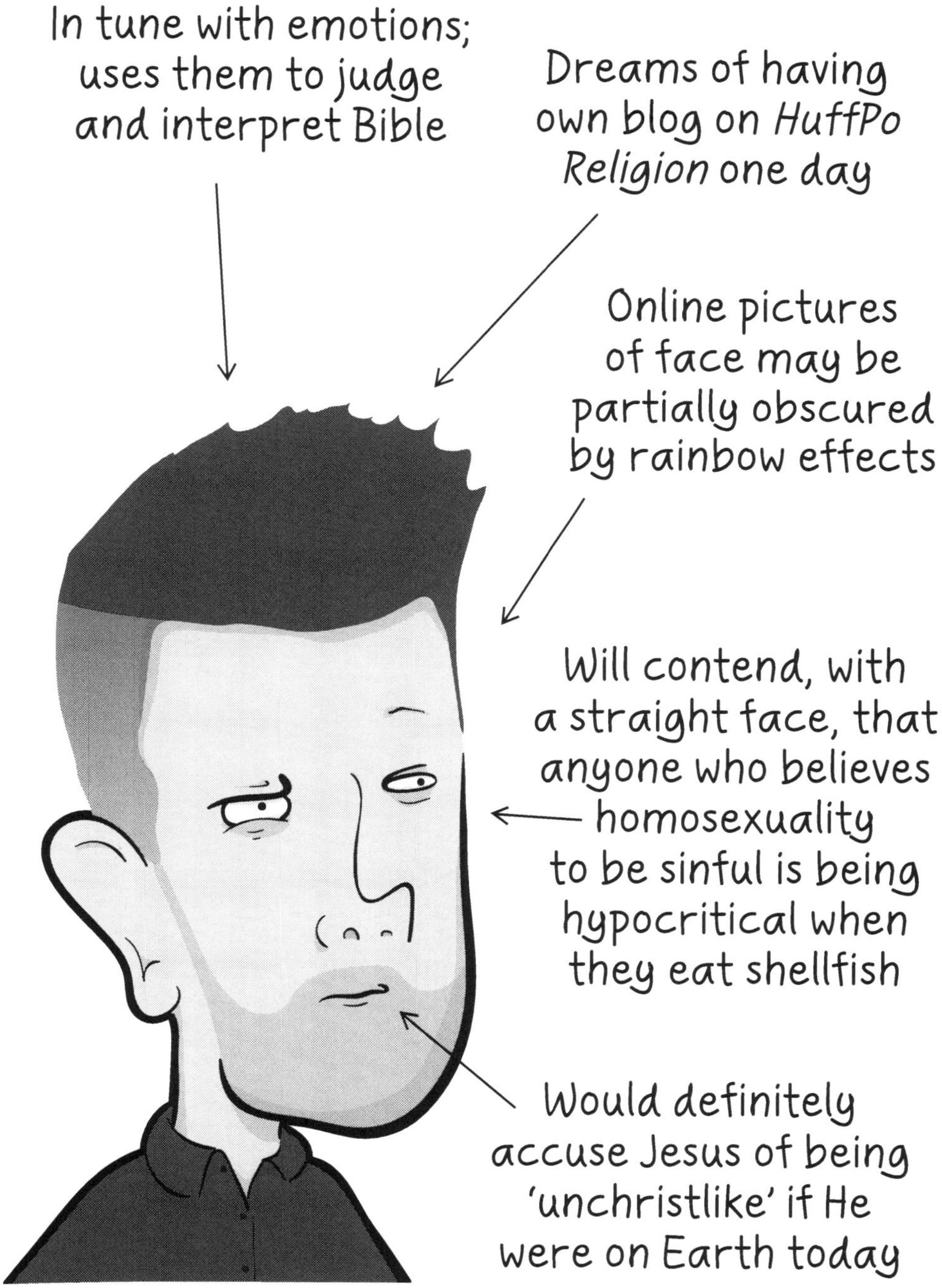
In tune with emotions; uses them to judge and interpret Bible
Dreams of having own blog on *HuffPo Religion* one day
Online pictures of face may be partially obscured by rainbow effects
Will contend, with a straight face, that anyone who believes homosexuality to be sinful is being hypocritical when they eat shellfish
Would definitely accuse Jesus of being 'unchristlike' if He were on Earth today

Everyone is religious (that includes you)

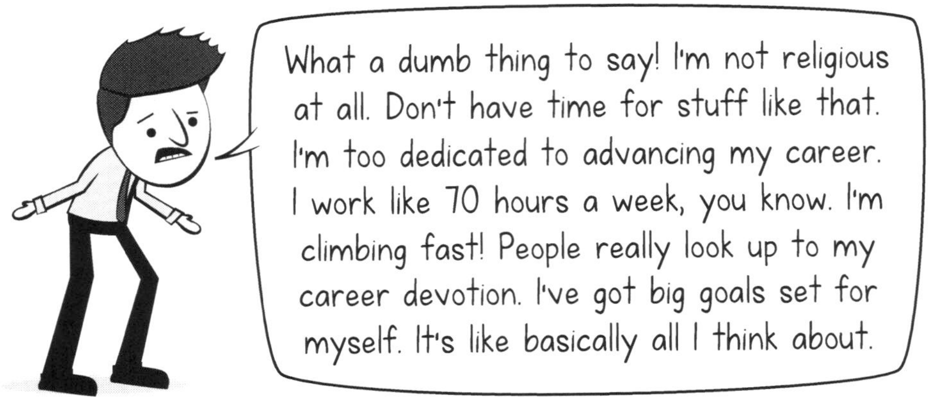

What a dumb thing to say! I'm not religious at all. Don't have time for stuff like that. I'm too dedicated to advancing my career. I work like 70 hours a week, you know. I'm climbing fast! People really look up to my career devotion. I've got big goals set for myself. It's like basically all I think about.

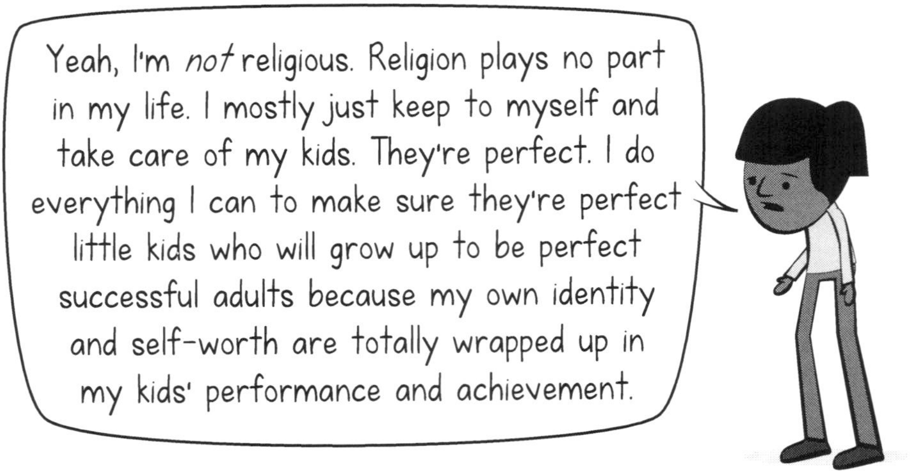

Yeah, I'm *not* religious. Religion plays no part in my life. I mostly just keep to myself and take care of my kids. They're perfect. I do everything I can to make sure they're perfect little kids who will grow up to be perfect successful adults because my own identity and self-worth are totally wrapped up in my kids' performance and achievement.

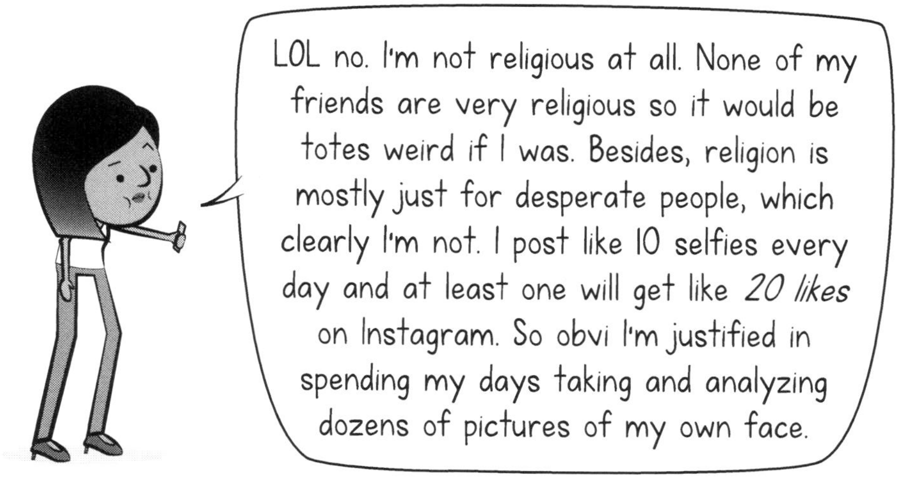
LOL no. I'm not religious at all. None of my friends are very religious so it would be totes weird if I was. Besides, religion is mostly just for desperate people, which clearly I'm not. I post like 10 selfies every day and at least one will get like *20 likes* on Instagram. So obvi I'm justified in spending my days taking and analyzing dozens of pictures of my own face.

Human beings are designed to worship. *Everyone* worships something or someone and organizes their life around the object(s) of their affection. Everyone is religious. Even people who are *anti-religion* are conspicuously, uhhh… *religious.*

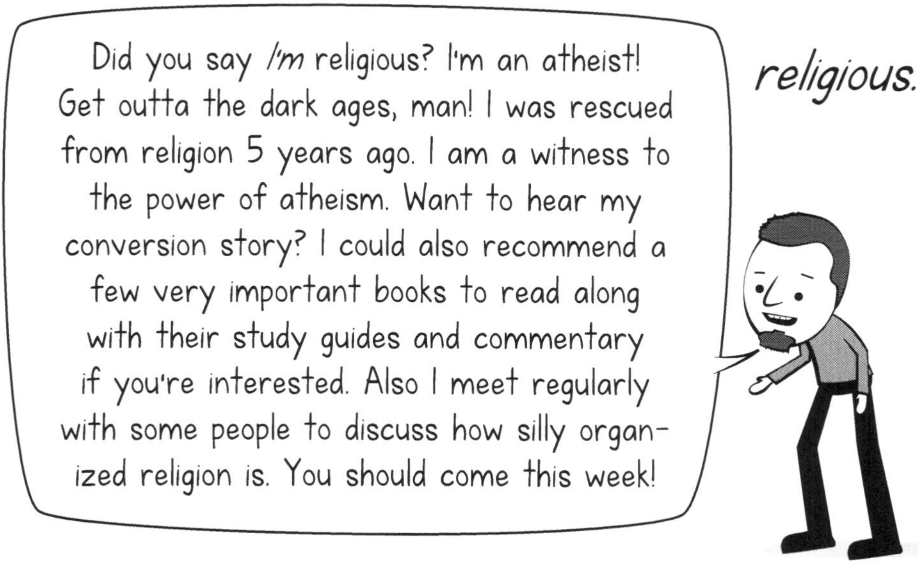
Did you say *I'm* religious? I'm an atheist! Get outta the dark ages, man! I was rescued from religion 5 years ago. I am a witness to the power of atheism. Want to hear my conversion story? I could also recommend a few very important books to read along with their study guides and commentary if you're interested. Also I meet regularly with some people to discuss how silly organized religion is. You should come this week!

There are countless objects of worship in the world. Millions of plastic gods at the centers of billions of little faux religions.

These gods, every one of them, will fail you.

People can lose their jobs. White-picket-fence childhoods sometimes turn into grown-up tragedies. Beauty is almost as fleeting as popular opinion. We all know these things are true.

Fake gods fail their followers and ultimately ruin them.

But...

Jesus, the Christ predicted accurately by the Old Testament, left the glory of heaven to be born as a baby, for you.

Jesus, the God of eternity, lived a perfect human life, though tempted, for you.

Jesus, the historical man, endured unjust torture and execution on a cross, for you.

Jesus, the ultimate sacrifice, absorbed the wrath of God, for you.

Jesus will never fail you.

Everyone is religious because humans have been designed by God to worship. But that's not all...

We've been designed by God to worship Jesus.

All of us. That includes you.

(And all of them ⌐↓)

Put down your plastic gods.

Come see what it's like to give your life to the One who gave His life for you.

He will never, ever fail you.

Christians and Muslims do not worship the same God

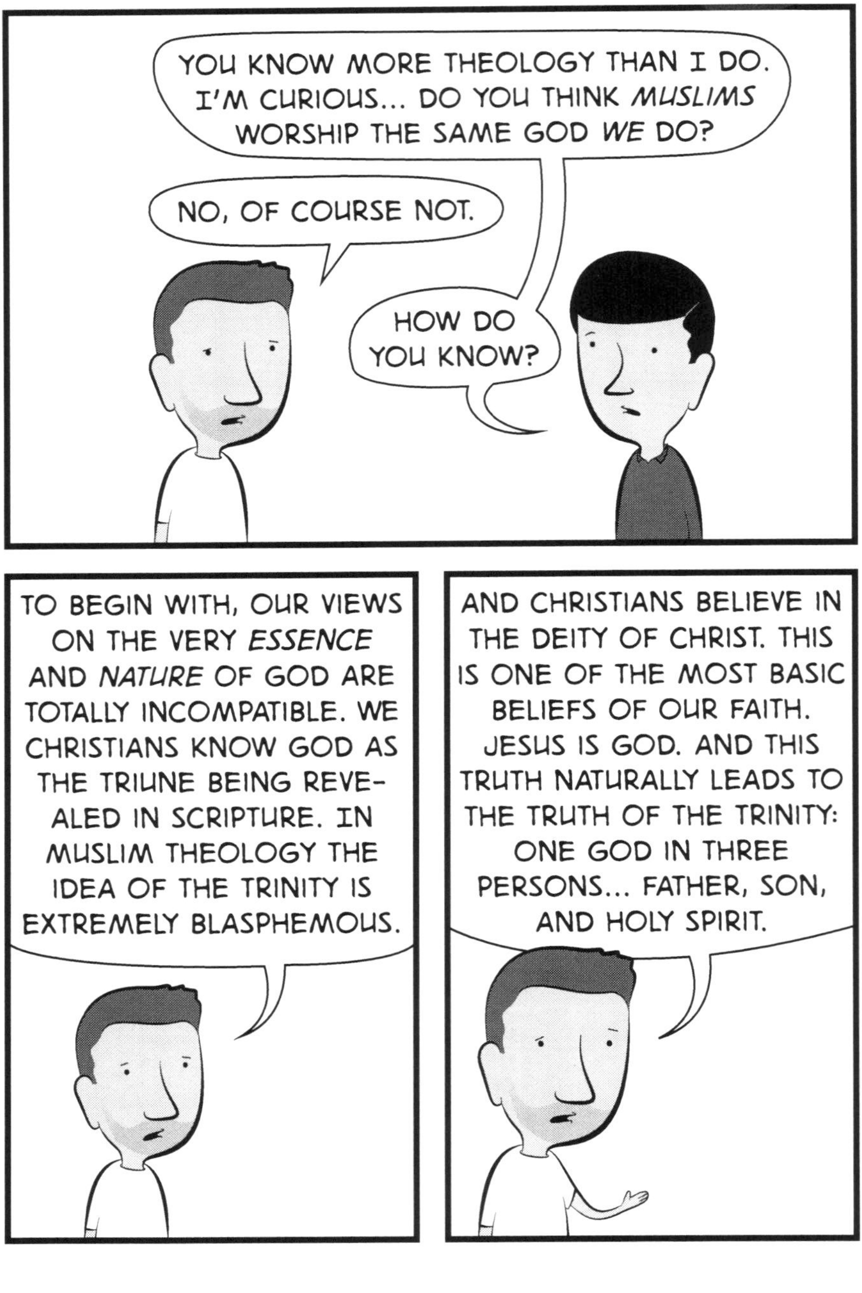
YOU KNOW MORE THEOLOGY THAN I DO. I'M CURIOUS... DO YOU THINK *MUSLIMS* WORSHIP THE SAME GOD *WE* DO?
NO, OF COURSE NOT.
HOW DO YOU KNOW?
TO BEGIN WITH, OUR VIEWS ON THE VERY *ESSENCE* AND *NATURE* OF GOD ARE TOTALLY INCOMPATIBLE. WE CHRISTIANS KNOW GOD AS THE TRIUNE BEING REVEALED IN SCRIPTURE. IN MUSLIM THEOLOGY THE IDEA OF THE TRINITY IS EXTREMELY BLASPHEMOUS.
AND CHRISTIANS BELIEVE IN THE DEITY OF CHRIST. THIS IS ONE OF THE MOST BASIC BELIEFS OF OUR FAITH. JESUS IS GOD. AND THIS TRUTH NATURALLY LEADS TO THE TRUTH OF THE TRINITY: ONE GOD IN THREE PERSONS... FATHER, SON, AND HOLY SPIRIT.

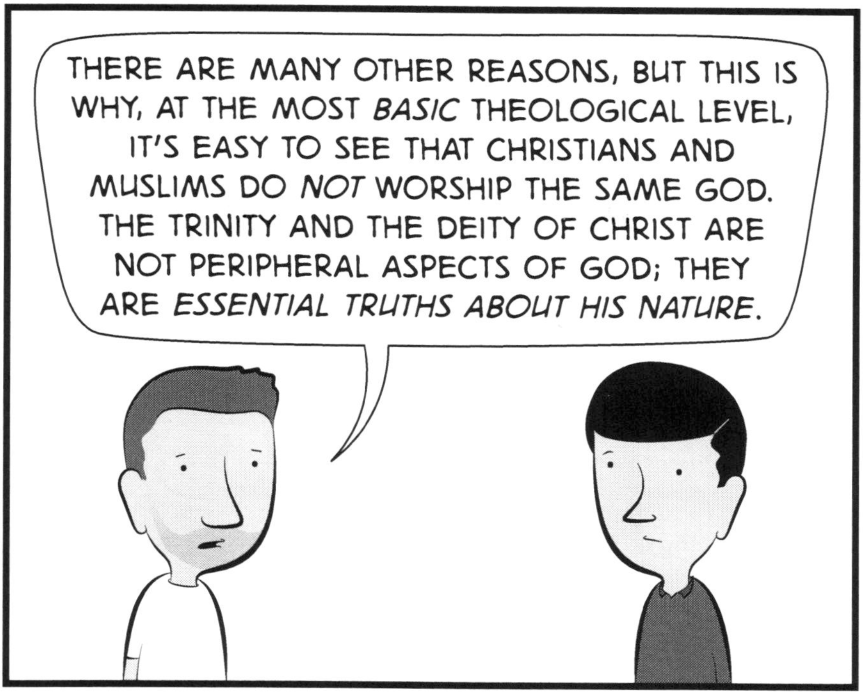
THERE ARE MANY OTHER REASONS, BUT THIS IS WHY, AT THE MOST BASIC THEOLOGICAL LEVEL, IT'S EASY TO SEE THAT CHRISTIANS AND MUSLIMS DO NOT WORSHIP THE SAME GOD. THE TRINITY AND THE DEITY OF CHRIST ARE NOT PERIPHERAL ASPECTS OF GOD; THEY ARE ESSENTIAL TRUTHS ABOUT HIS NATURE.

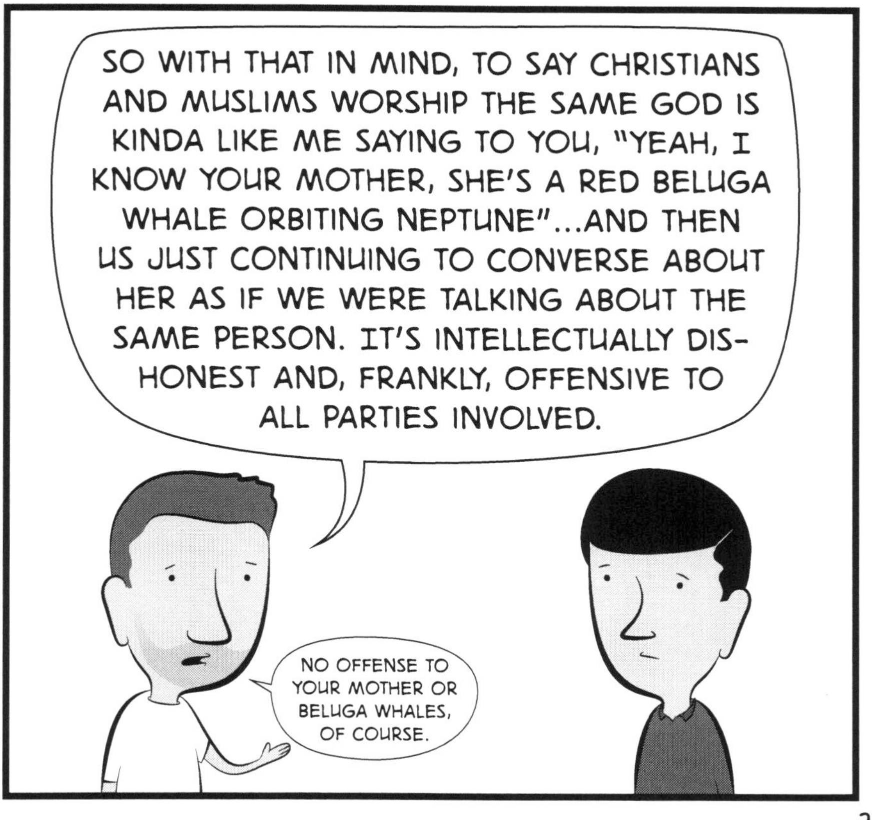
SO WITH THAT IN MIND, TO SAY CHRISTIANS AND MUSLIMS WORSHIP THE SAME GOD IS KINDA LIKE ME SAYING TO YOU, "YEAH, I KNOW YOUR MOTHER, SHE'S A RED BELUGA WHALE ORBITING NEPTUNE"...AND THEN US JUST CONTINUING TO CONVERSE ABOUT HER AS IF WE WERE TALKING ABOUT THE SAME PERSON. IT'S INTELLECTUALLY DIS-HONEST AND, FRANKLY, OFFENSIVE TO ALL PARTIES INVOLVED.
NO OFFENSE TO YOUR MOTHER OR BELUGA WHALES, OF COURSE.

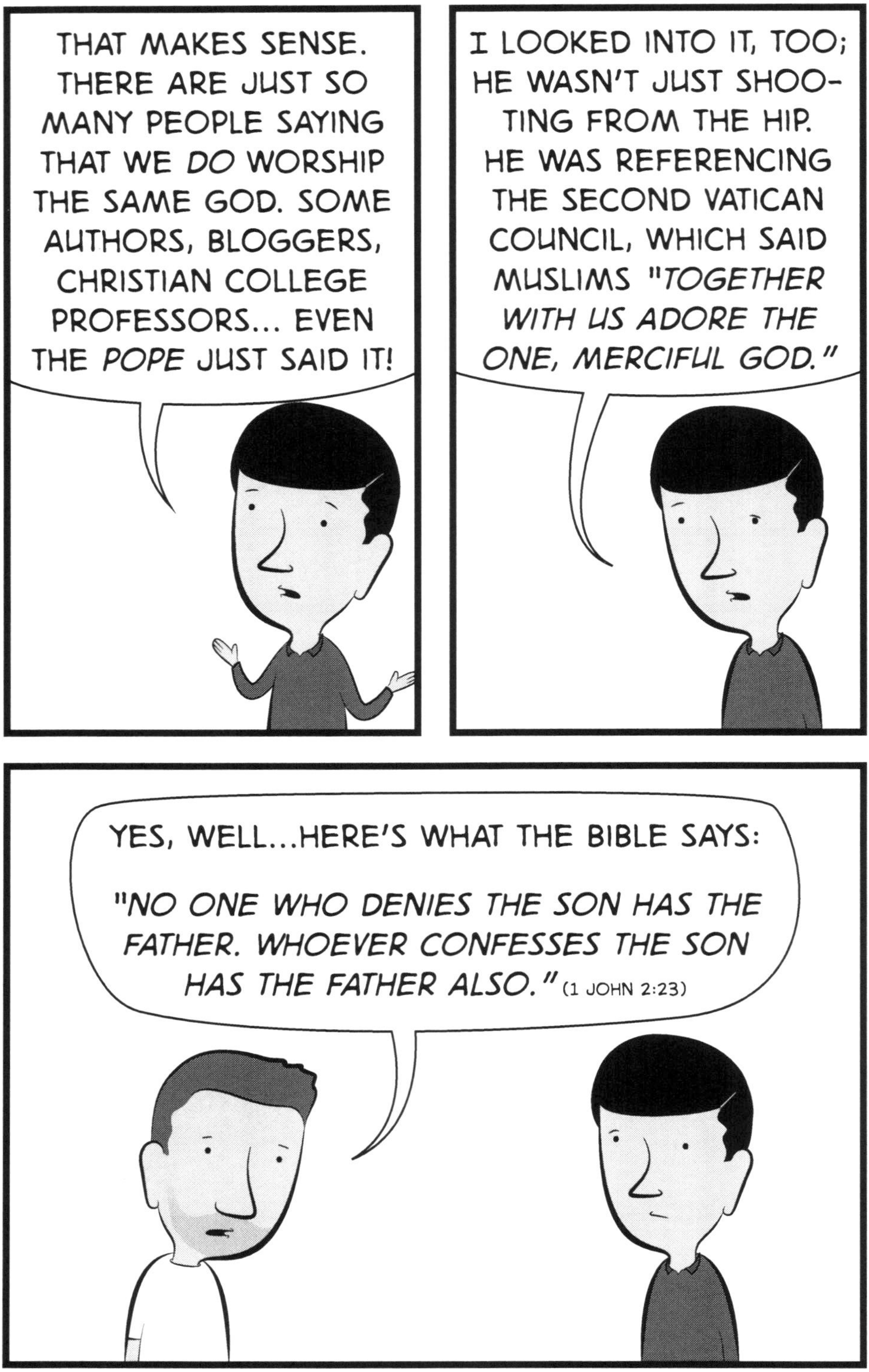
THAT MAKES SENSE. THERE ARE JUST SO MANY PEOPLE SAYING THAT WE *DO* WORSHIP THE SAME GOD. SOME AUTHORS, BLOGGERS, CHRISTIAN COLLEGE PROFESSORS... EVEN THE *POPE* JUST SAID IT!
I LOOKED INTO IT, TOO; HE WASN'T JUST SHOOTING FROM THE HIP. HE WAS REFERENCING THE SECOND VATICAN COUNCIL, WHICH SAID MUSLIMS "*TOGETHER WITH US ADORE THE ONE, MERCIFUL GOD.*"
YES, WELL...HERE'S WHAT THE BIBLE SAYS:
"NO ONE WHO DENIES THE SON HAS THE FATHER. WHOEVER CONFESSES THE SON HAS THE FATHER ALSO." (1 JOHN 2:23)

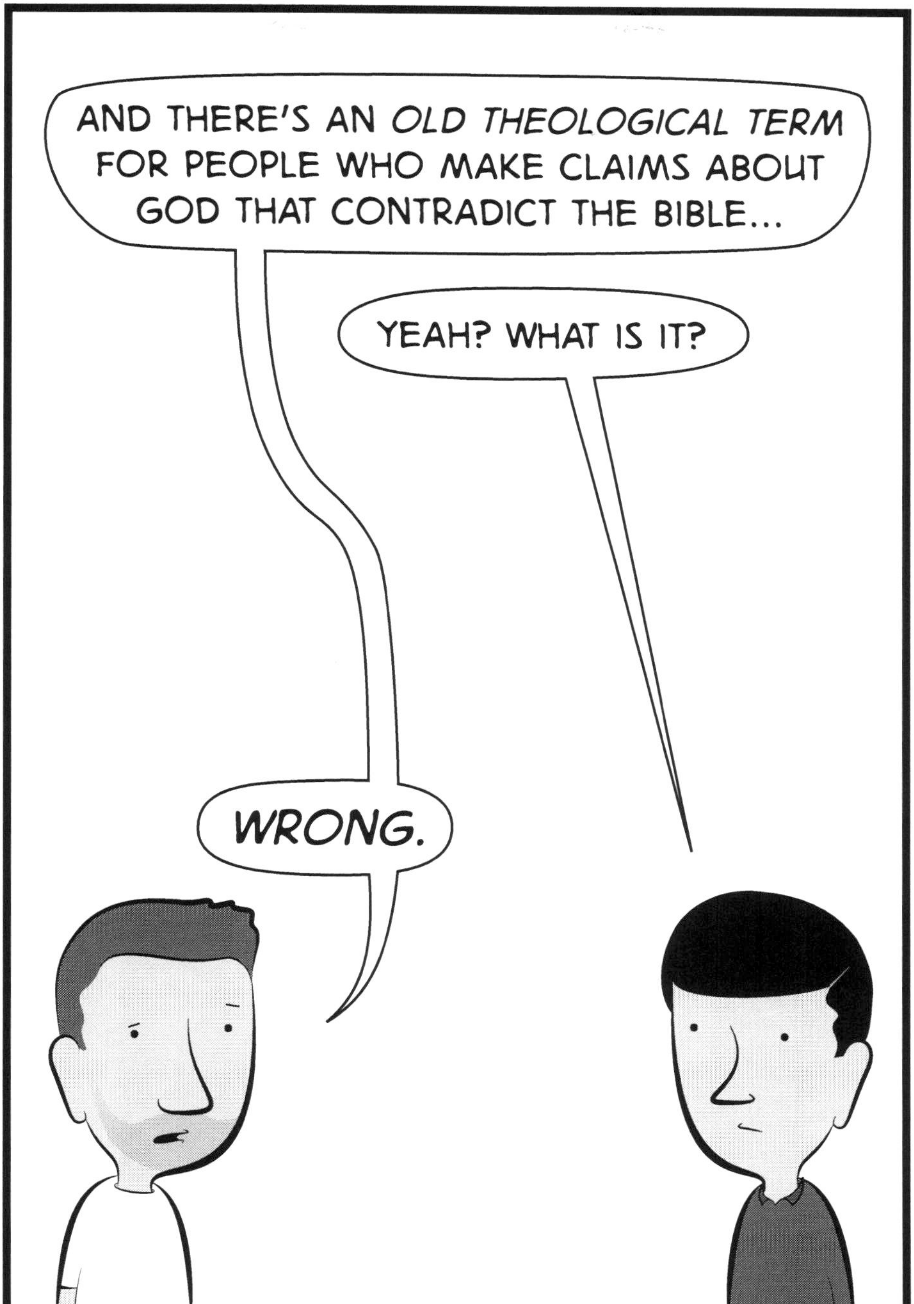
AND THERE'S AN *OLD THEOLOGICAL TERM* FOR PEOPLE WHO MAKE CLAIMS ABOUT GOD THAT CONTRADICT THE BIBLE...
YEAH? WHAT IS IT?
WRONG.

Plan A® contraceptive for men

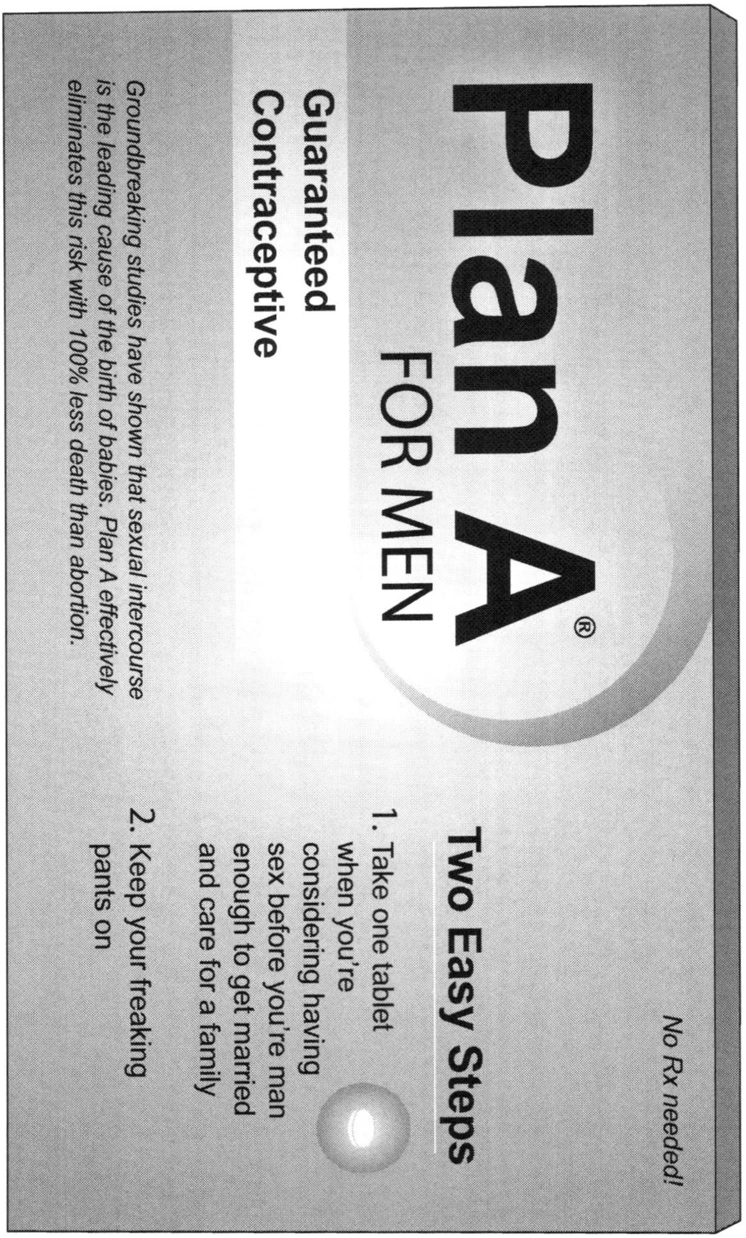
Plan A®
FOR MEN
Guaranteed Contraceptive
Groundbreaking studies have shown that sexual intercourse is the leading cause of the birth of babies. Plan A effectively eliminates this risk with 100% less death than abortion.
Two Easy Steps
1. Take one tablet when you're considering having sex before you're man enough to get married and care for a family
2. Keep your freaking pants on
No Rx needed!

FFFFFFF

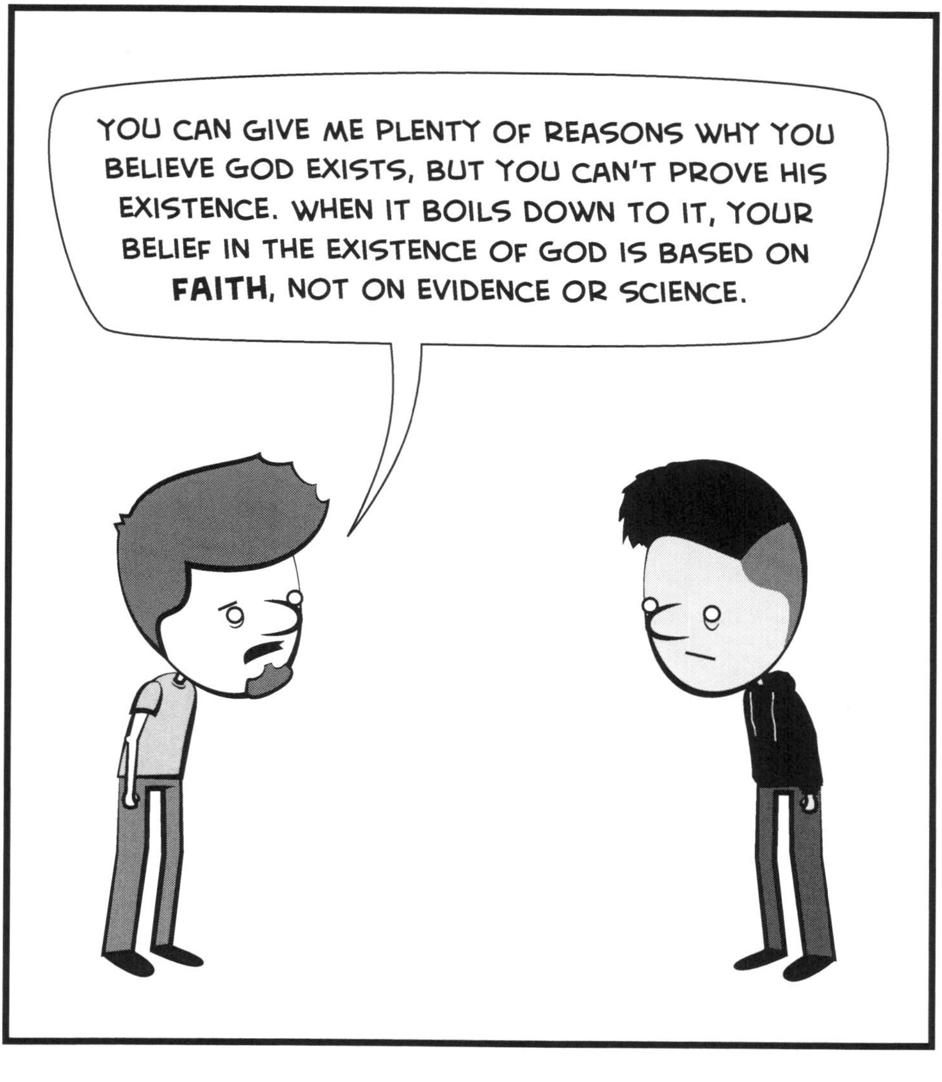
YOU CAN GIVE ME PLENTY OF REASONS WHY YOU BELIEVE GOD EXISTS, BUT YOU CAN'T PROVE HIS EXISTENCE. WHEN IT BOILS DOWN TO IT, YOUR BELIEF IN THE EXISTENCE OF GOD IS BASED ON **FAITH**, NOT ON EVIDENCE OR SCIENCE.

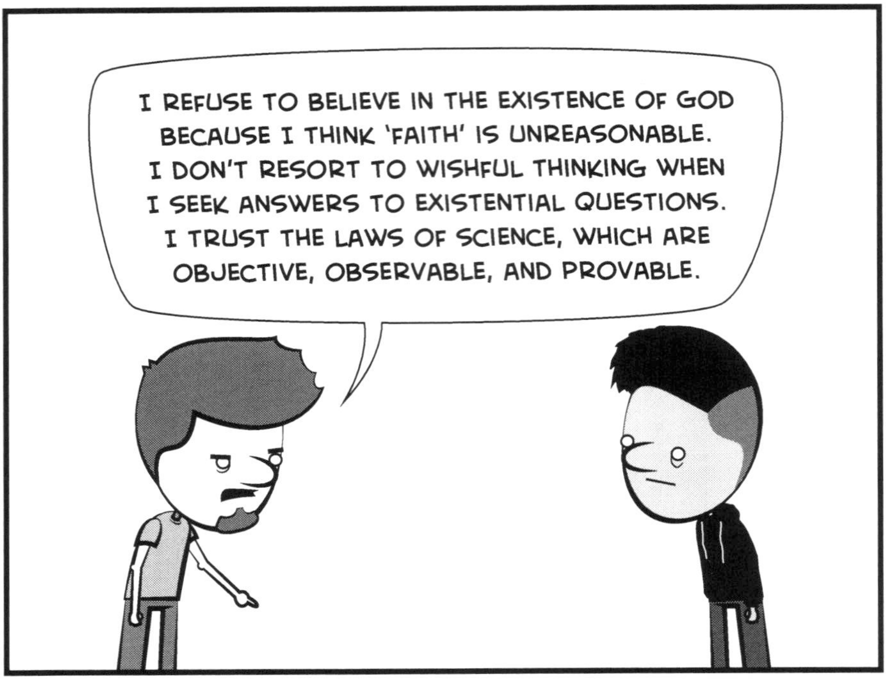
I REFUSE TO BELIEVE IN THE EXISTENCE OF GOD BECAUSE I THINK 'FAITH' IS UNREASONABLE. I DON'T RESORT TO WISHFUL THINKING WHEN I SEEK ANSWERS TO EXISTENTIAL QUESTIONS. I TRUST THE LAWS OF SCIENCE, WHICH ARE OBJECTIVE, OBSERVABLE, AND PROVABLE.

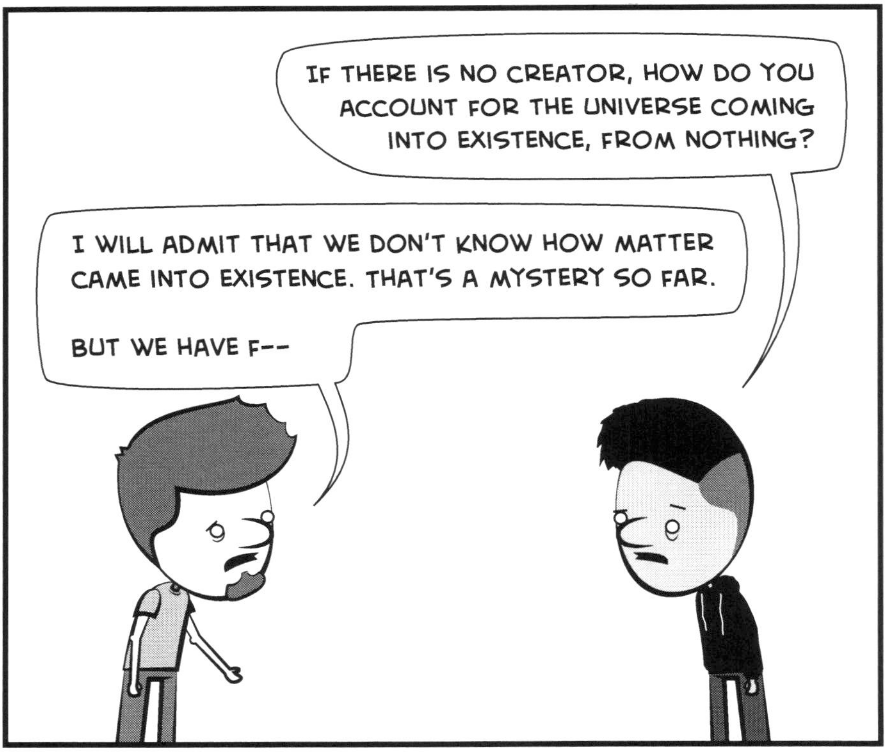
IF THERE IS NO CREATOR, HOW DO YOU ACCOUNT FOR THE UNIVERSE COMING INTO EXISTENCE, FROM NOTHING?
I WILL ADMIT THAT WE DON'T KNOW HOW MATTER CAME INTO EXISTENCE. THAT'S A MYSTERY SO FAR.
BUT WE HAVE F--

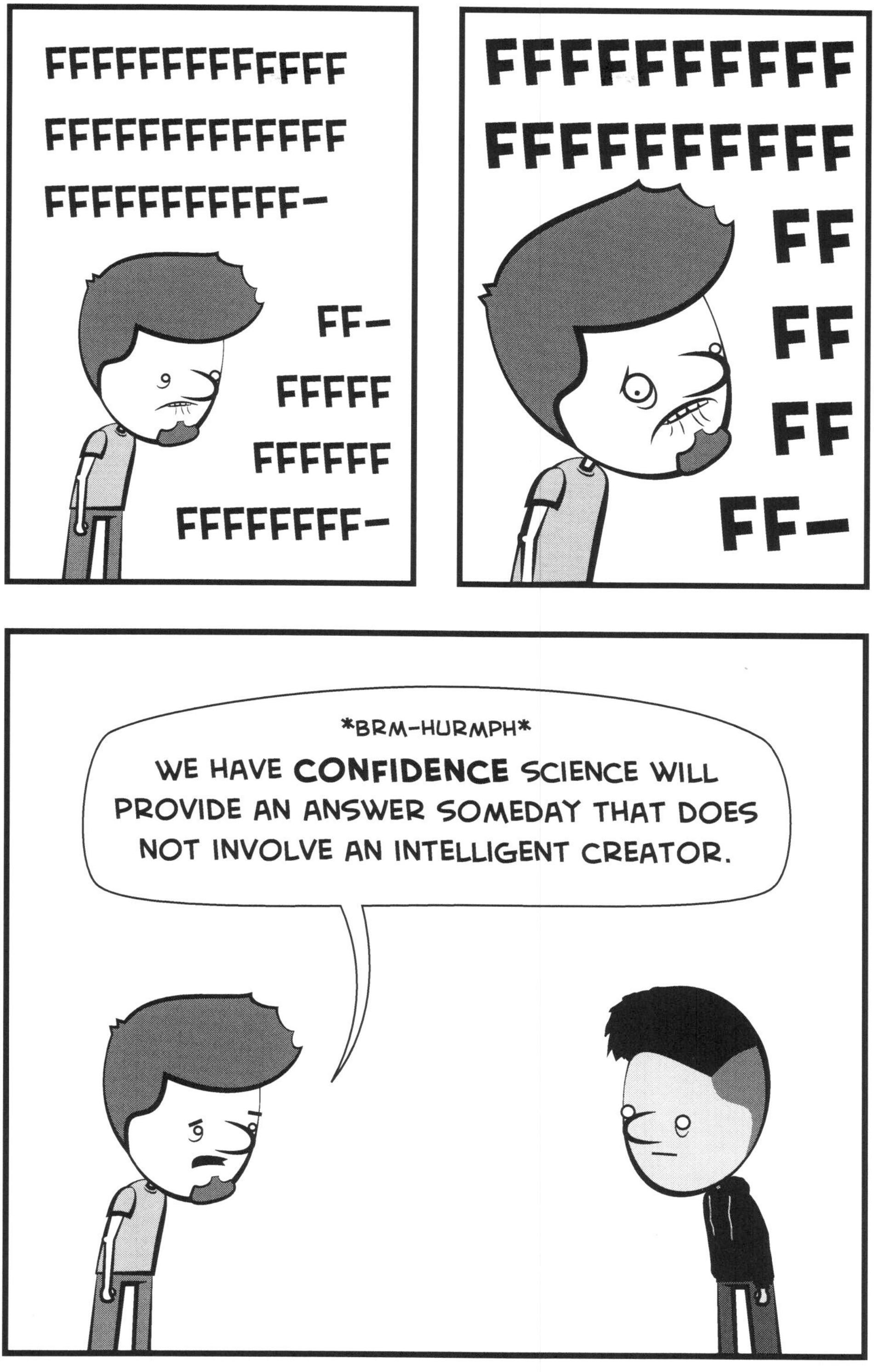
FFFFFFFFFFFFF
FFFFFFFFFFFFF
FFFFFFFFFFF-
FF-
FFFFF
FFFFFF
FFFFFFFF-
FFFFFFFFFF
FFFFFFFFFF
FF
FF
FF
FF-
BRM-HURMPH
WE HAVE **CONFIDENCE** SCIENCE WILL PROVIDE AN ANSWER SOMEDAY THAT DOES NOT INVOLVE AN INTELLIGENT CREATOR.

Wives, submit to your husbands; husbands, love your wives

"Wives, submit to your own husbands, as to the Lord..."

"Husbands, love your wives, as Christ loved the church and gave himself up for her..." -Eph 5:22,25

DOES NOT MEAN THIS:

NOW AS THE SUPERIOR SEX, IT IS MAH DUTY TO GET MAH WAY ALL THE TIME, BECAUSE AS THE MAN, AH AM BETTER THAN MAH LITTLE WIFE, AND SINCE SHE IS INFERIOR, SHE DOES EVERYTHING AH TELL HER TO DO, AT ALL TIMES...

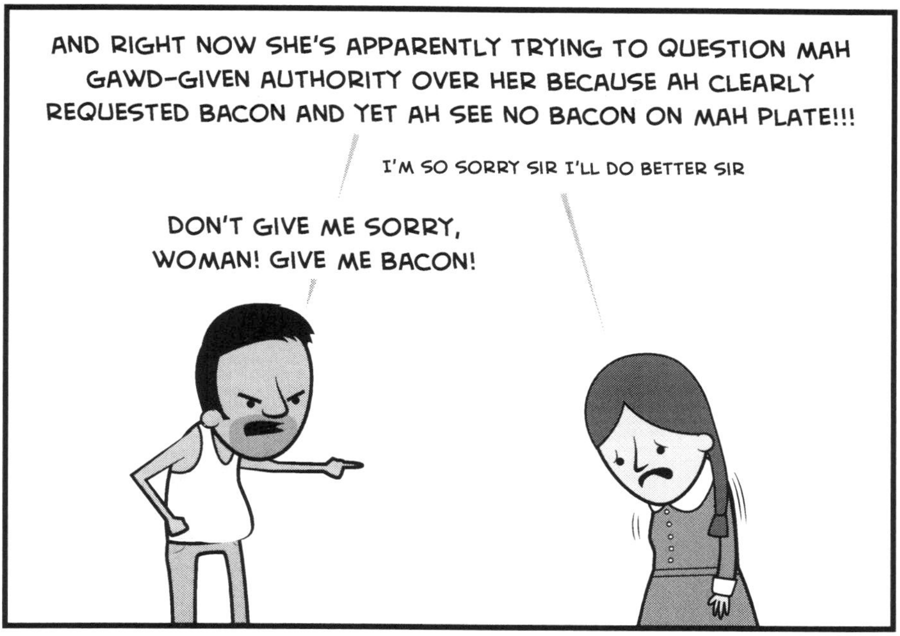
AND RIGHT NOW SHE'S APPARENTLY TRYING TO QUESTION MAH GAWD-GIVEN AUTHORITY OVER HER BECAUSE AH CLEARLY REQUESTED BACON AND YET AH SEE NO BACON ON MAH PLATE!!!
I'M SO SORRY SIR I'LL DO BETTER SIR
DON'T GIVE ME SORRY, WOMAN! GIVE ME BACON!

IT DOES MEAN THIS:

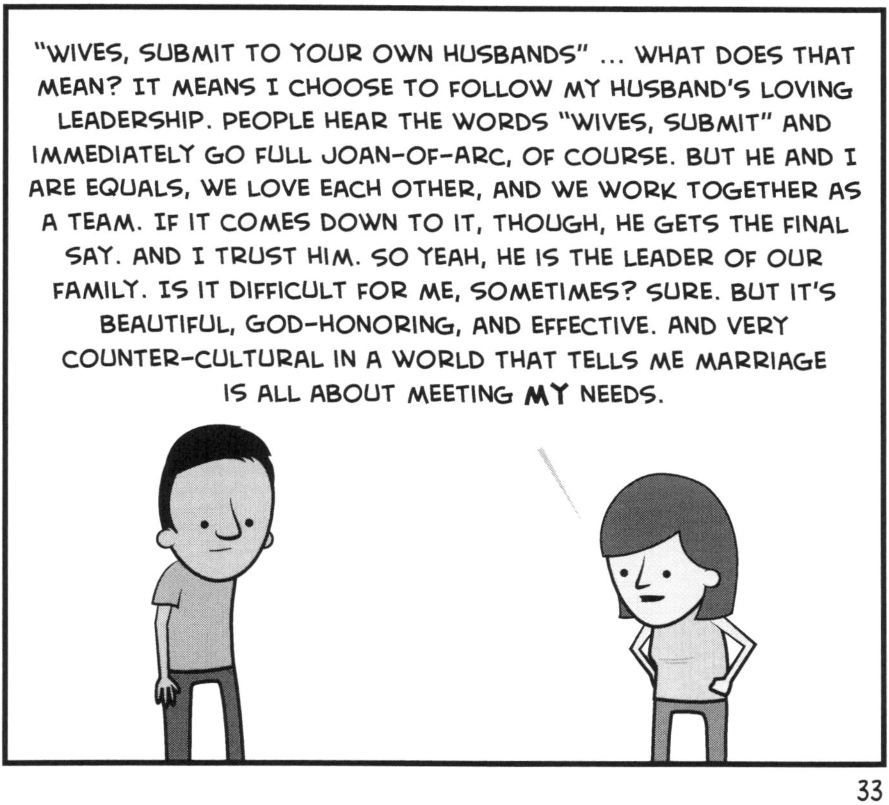
"WIVES, SUBMIT TO YOUR OWN HUSBANDS" ... WHAT DOES THAT MEAN? IT MEANS I CHOOSE TO FOLLOW MY HUSBAND'S LOVING LEADERSHIP. PEOPLE HEAR THE WORDS "WIVES, SUBMIT" AND IMMEDIATELY GO FULL JOAN-OF-ARC, OF COURSE. BUT HE AND I ARE EQUALS, WE LOVE EACH OTHER, AND WE WORK TOGETHER AS A TEAM. IF IT COMES DOWN TO IT, THOUGH, HE GETS THE FINAL SAY. AND I TRUST HIM. SO YEAH, HE IS THE LEADER OF OUR FAMILY. IS IT DIFFICULT FOR ME, SOMETIMES? SURE. BUT IT'S BEAUTIFUL, GOD-HONORING, AND EFFECTIVE. AND VERY COUNTER-CULTURAL IN A WORLD THAT TELLS ME MARRIAGE IS ALL ABOUT MEETING **MY** NEEDS.

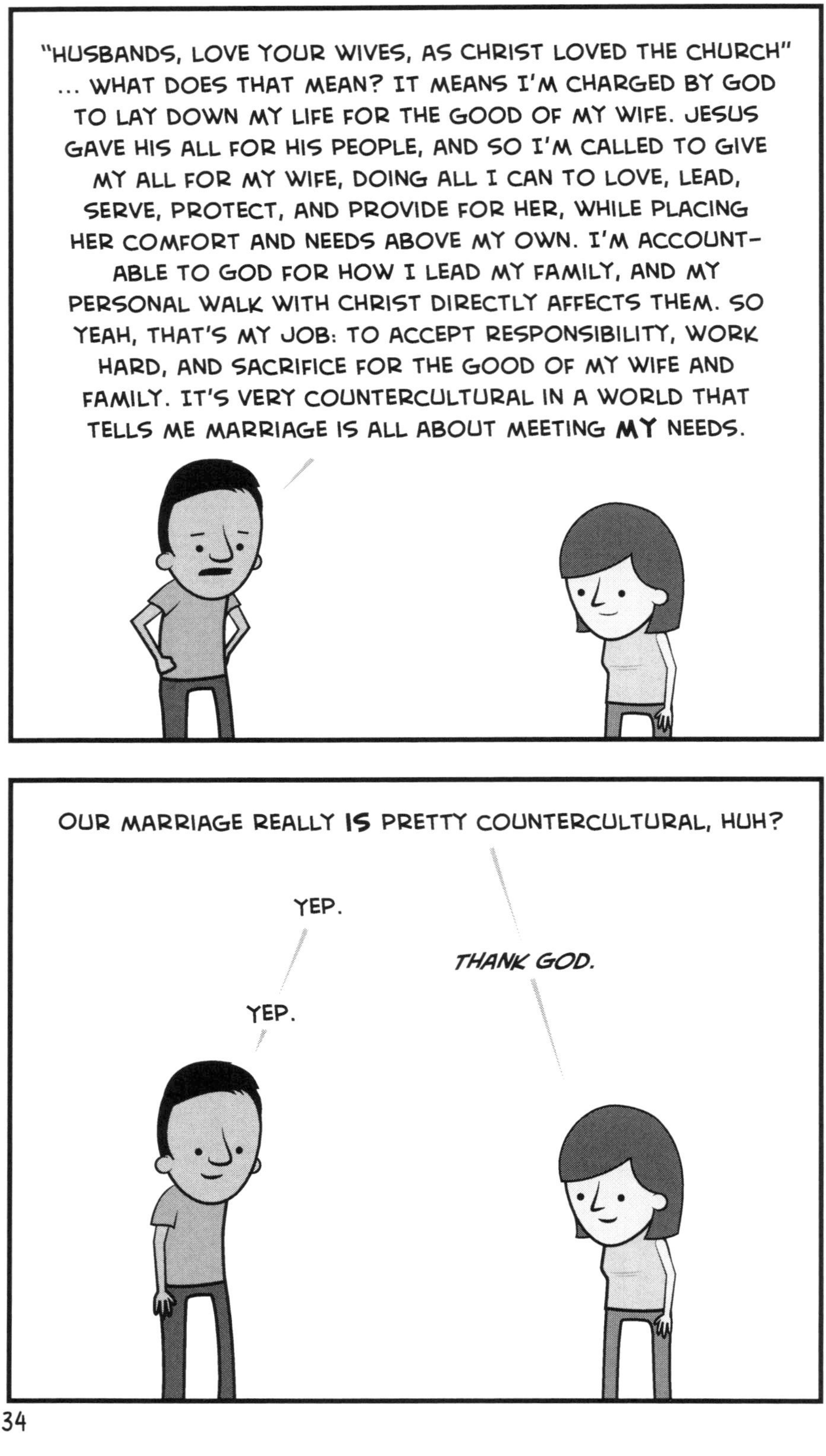
"HUSBANDS, LOVE YOUR WIVES, AS CHRIST LOVED THE CHURCH" ... WHAT DOES THAT MEAN? IT MEANS I'M CHARGED BY GOD TO LAY DOWN MY LIFE FOR THE GOOD OF MY WIFE. JESUS GAVE HIS ALL FOR HIS PEOPLE, AND SO I'M CALLED TO GIVE MY ALL FOR MY WIFE, DOING ALL I CAN TO LOVE, LEAD, SERVE, PROTECT, AND PROVIDE FOR HER, WHILE PLACING HER COMFORT AND NEEDS ABOVE MY OWN. I'M ACCOUNTABLE TO GOD FOR HOW I LEAD MY FAMILY, AND MY PERSONAL WALK WITH CHRIST DIRECTLY AFFECTS THEM. SO YEAH, THAT'S MY JOB: TO ACCEPT RESPONSIBILITY, WORK HARD, AND SACRIFICE FOR THE GOOD OF MY WIFE AND FAMILY. IT'S VERY COUNTERCULTURAL IN A WORLD THAT TELLS ME MARRIAGE IS ALL ABOUT MEETING **MY** NEEDS.
OUR MARRIAGE REALLY **IS** PRETTY COUNTERCULTURAL, HUH?
YEP.
YEP.
THANK GOD.

I am a theology nerd

That means I love learning about God.

I love reading about God.

I love thinking about God and talking about God.

I even love thinking about talking about God...

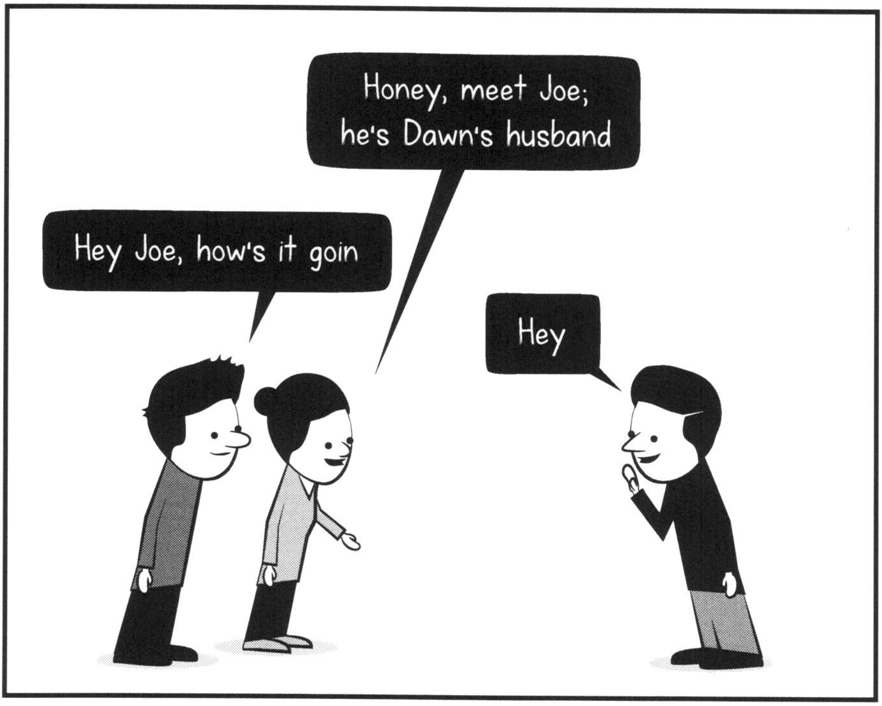

Honey, meet Joe;
he's Dawn's husband
Hey Joe, how's it goin
Hey

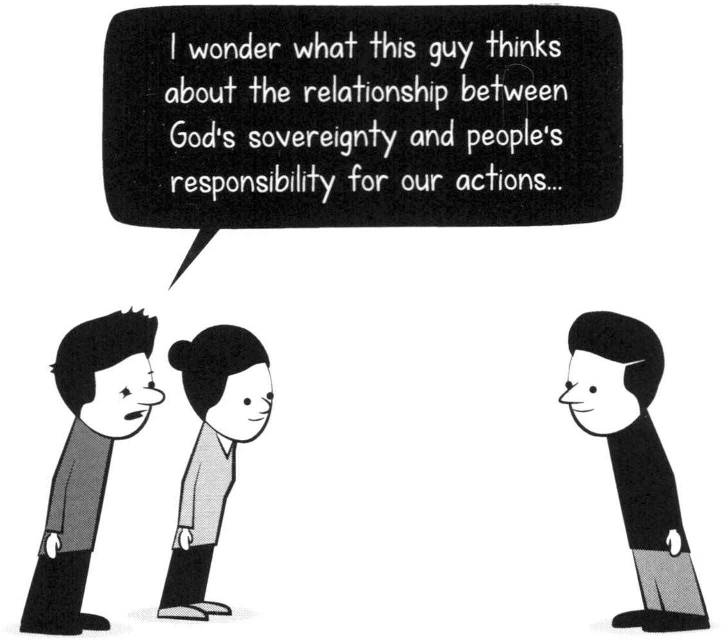
I wonder what this guy thinks about the relationship between God's sovereignty and people's responsibility for our actions...

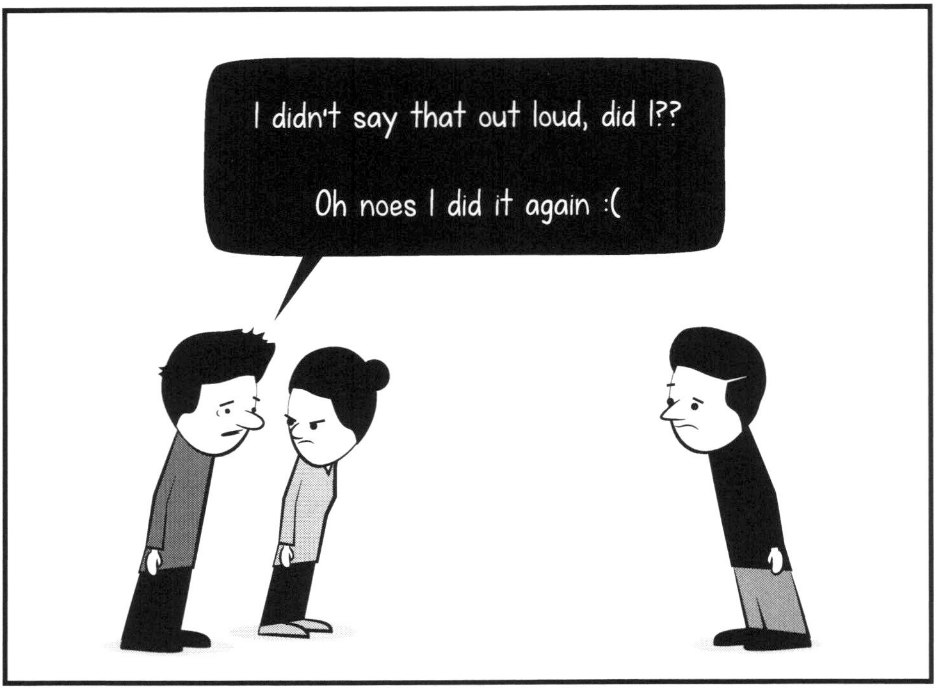
I didn't say that out loud, did I??

Oh noes I did it again :(

...which gets me into trouble sometimes.

Theology nerds are **different**.
We're not like most people.
We're not like most Christians, even.

We **really** enjoy learning and reading
and thinking and talking all about God.
Like, there's nothing we'd rather do.

We might differ in many ways.
We might disagree on non-essential theological issues.
We might look very different from each other on the outside.

But on the **inside**...

we're theology nerds.

And right now we'd probably rather be holed up with some old books written by dead Christian geniuses than doing whatever it is we're doing.

theology nerd + old books = extremely happy theology nerd

(AKA "nerding out")

I am a theology nerd because I can't help it.

I don't understand why *everybody* isn't a theology nerd.

What topic of thought, study, or discussion could be so interesting and rewarding to the Christian as

the glorious, almighty maker and sustainer of every atom in the universe, whose manifold attributes represent the apex of perfection, whose character is inexhaustible in depth and transcendence, and whose presence as loving Father is the neverending gift of grace to those who love Him?

Tell me, what could be so perpetually relevant, so fitting a use of our private time than to learn more about the one by whom and for whom we were made?

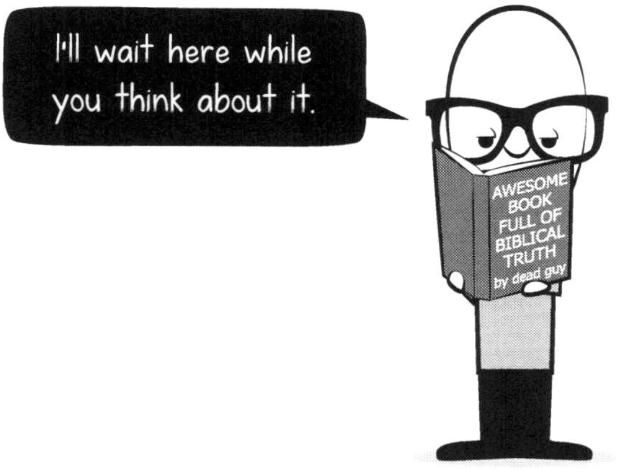
I'll wait here while you think about it.
AWESOME BOOK FULL OF BIBLICAL TRUTH by dead guy

Of course, there are those who will claim that people get *too* into theology, to the detriment of Christian *action*. But speaking personally, I have found no more potent fuel for *action* than

robust theological study.

The more I fill my brain with Bible and the more I study under the greatest minds in the history of Christianity, the more my feet and hands are compelled to action.

The deeper I understand God's character and what He has done for me in Christ despite my unworthiness, the better perspective I have in any situation.

And the more I know about the part God has given me to play in this broken world which will one day be a beautifully-finished display of God's redemption of history, the better I can play it.

Which is why, my friends,

I am a theology nerd.

When Jesus knocks

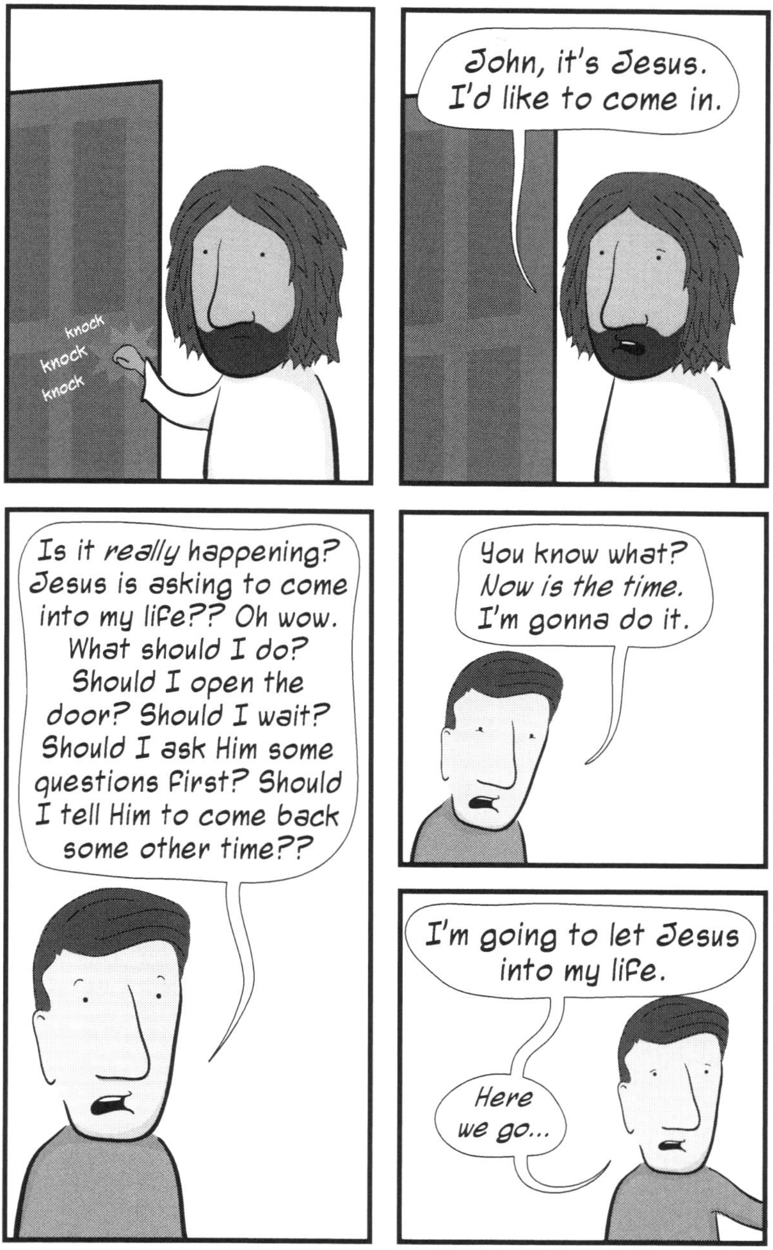
knock
knock
knock
John, it's Jesus. I'd like to come in.
Is it *really* happening? Jesus is asking to come into my life?? Oh wow. What should I do? Should I open the door? Should I wait? Should I ask Him some questions first? Should I tell Him to come back some other time??
You know what? Now is the time. I'm gonna do it.
I'm going to let Jesus into my life.
Here we go...

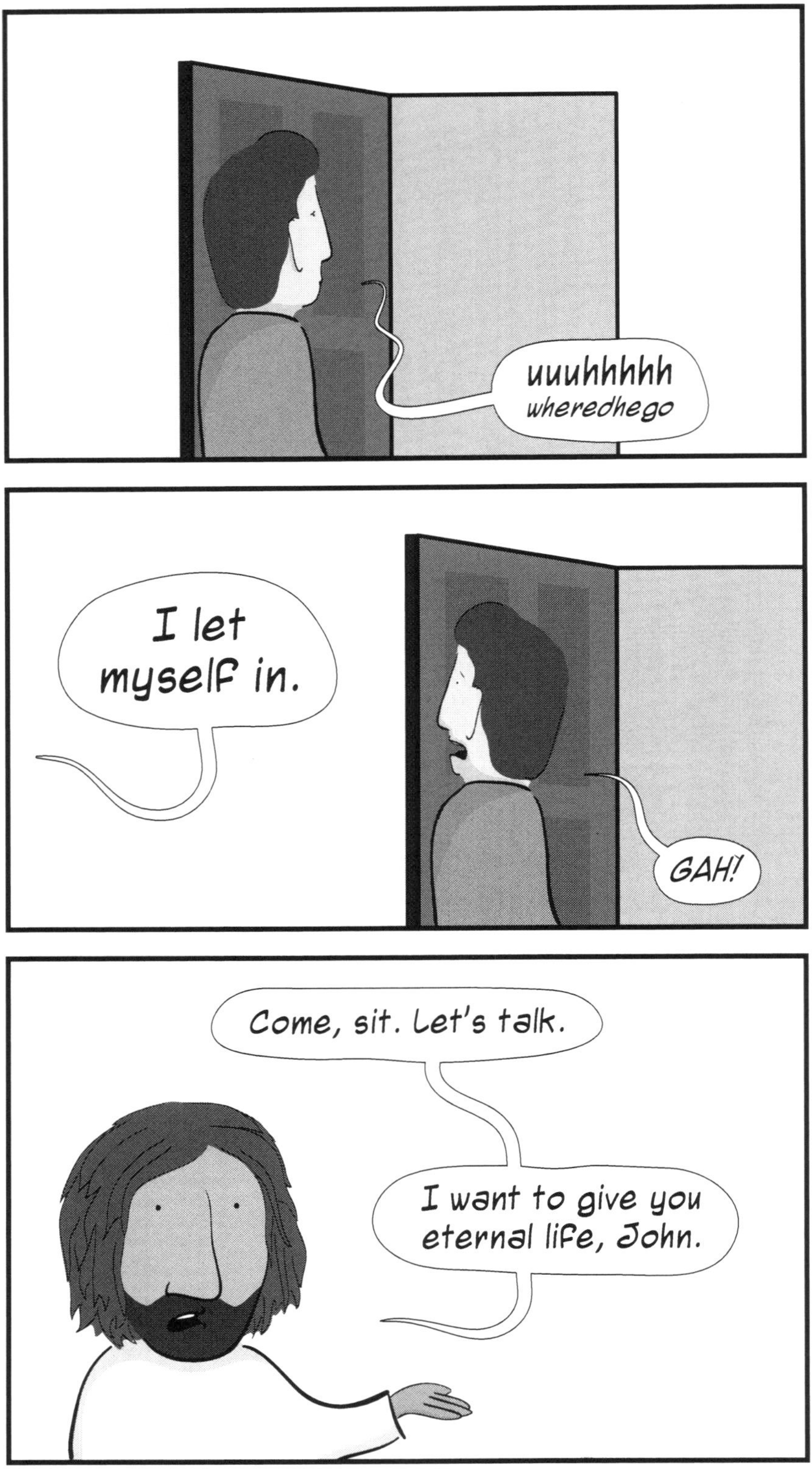
uuuhhhhh
wheredhego
I let myself in.
GAH!
Come, sit. Let's talk.
I want to give you eternal life, John.

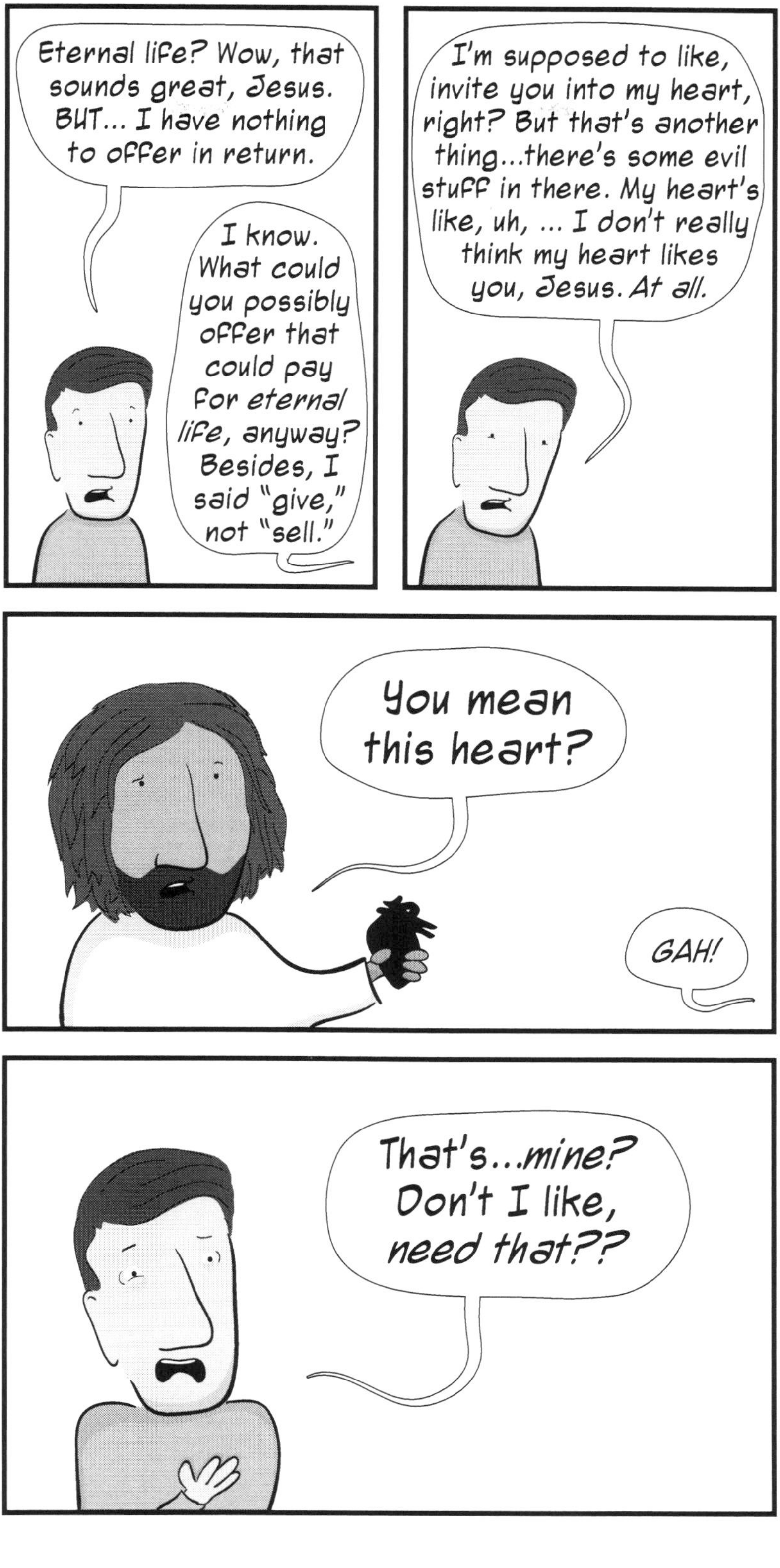

Eternal life? Wow, that sounds great, Jesus. BUT... I have nothing to offer in return.
I know. What could you possibly offer that could pay for *eternal life*, anyway? Besides, I said "give," not "sell."
I'm supposed to like, invite you into my heart, right? But that's another thing...there's some evil stuff in there. My heart's like, uh, ... I don't really think my heart likes you, Jesus. *At all.*
You mean this heart?
GAH!
That's...*mine?* Don't I like, *need that??*

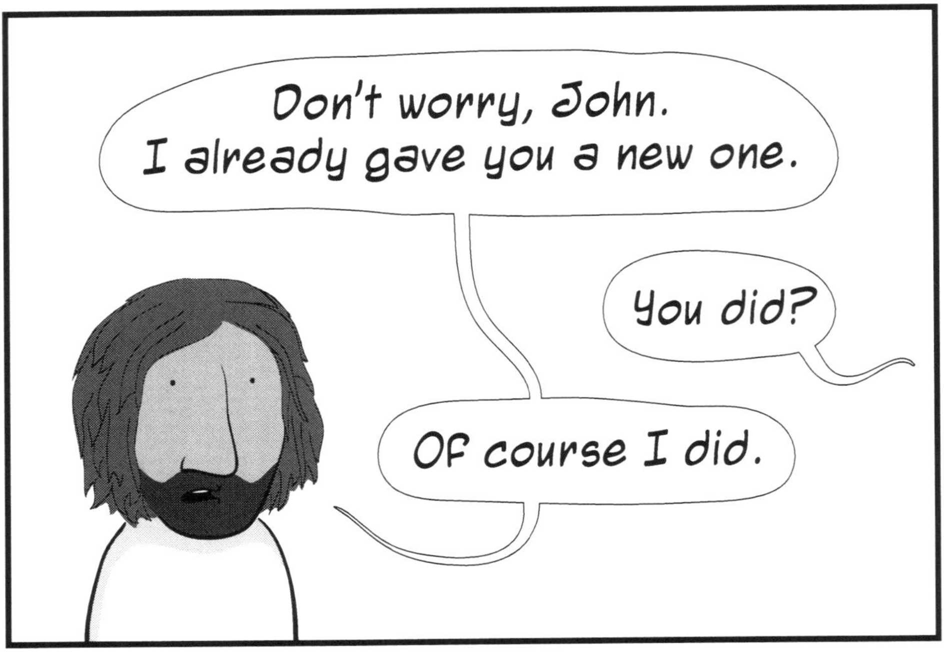
Don't worry, John.
I already gave you a new one.
You did?
Of course I did.

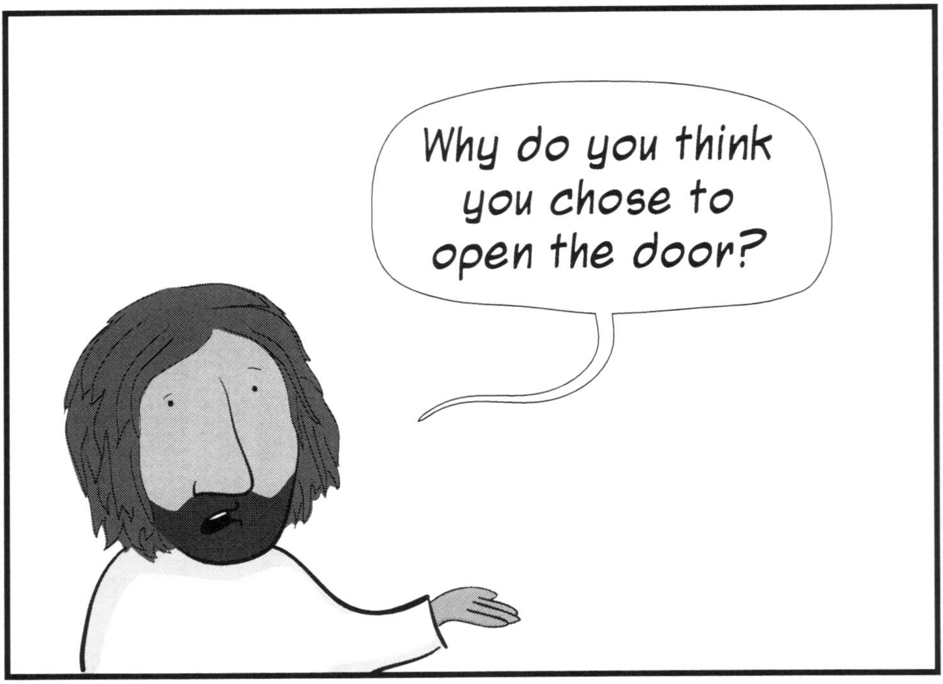
Why do you think you chose to open the door?

Some common misconceptions about our relationship with sin

Before becoming a Christian:

I sin sometimes. I do bad stuff. And I LIKE it.

Misconception   Reality

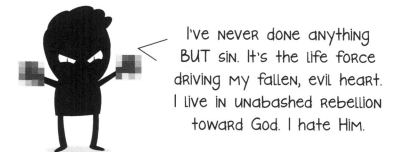

I've NEVER done anything BUT sin. It's the life force driving my fallen, evil heart. I live in unabashed rebellion toward God. I hate Him.

Becoming a Christian:

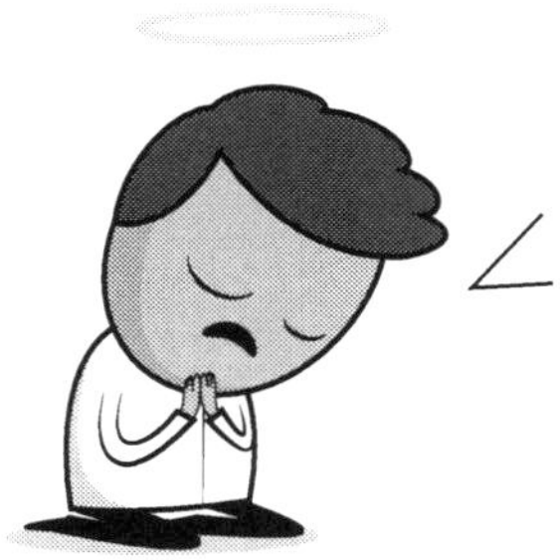

Jesus, I have cleaned myself up and I'm ready to accept you and be a Christian now. I promise I won't do any bad things that make you mad at me anymore. You can trust me now.

Misconception Reality

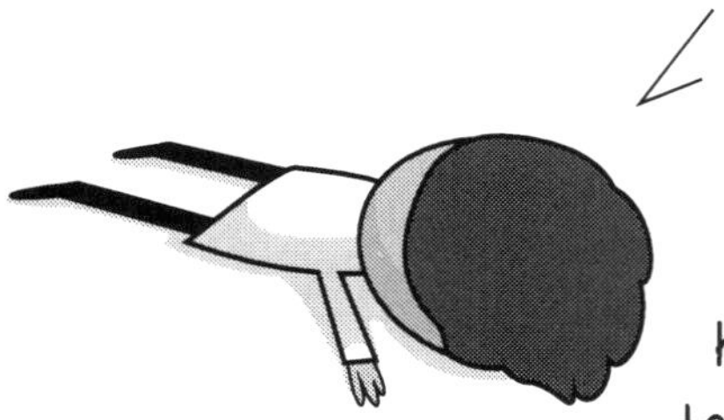

Jesus, I am full of sin and there's nothing I can do to fix it. I believe you died to pay the penalty for the sin of your people and to give them your righteousness; even people as wretched as me. I'm utterly hopeless without you. I'm ready to trust you with everything now.

After becoming a Christian:

Now that I have my get-out-of-hell-free card I can do ABSOLUTELY ANYTHING I WANT AND DON'T YOU DARE JUDGE ME!

Misconception   Reality

I MAKE WAR WITH MY SIN. I hate sin because I love Jesus. If I didn't love Jesus I wouldn't hate sin. If I didn't hate sin I wouldn't really love Jesus.

Cage-stage Calvinist

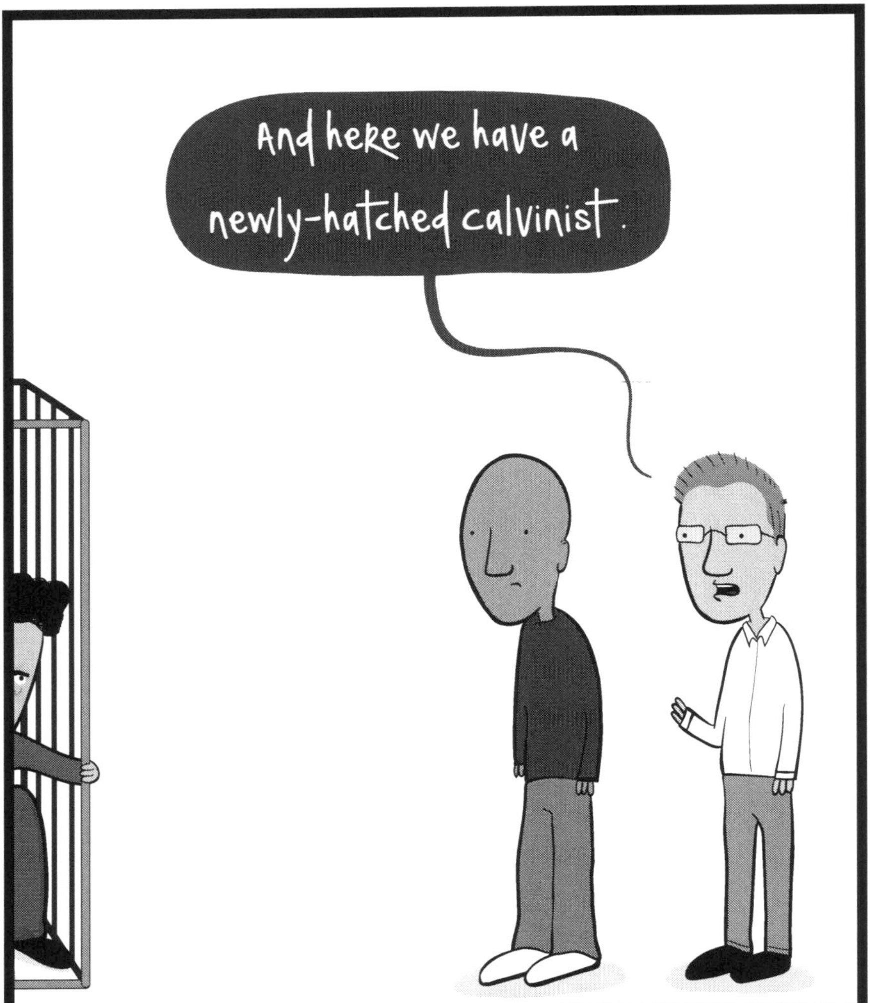
And here we have a newly-hatched calvinist.

He's just recently embraced the truths of the doctrines of grace, but he's still in what we call the "cage stage."

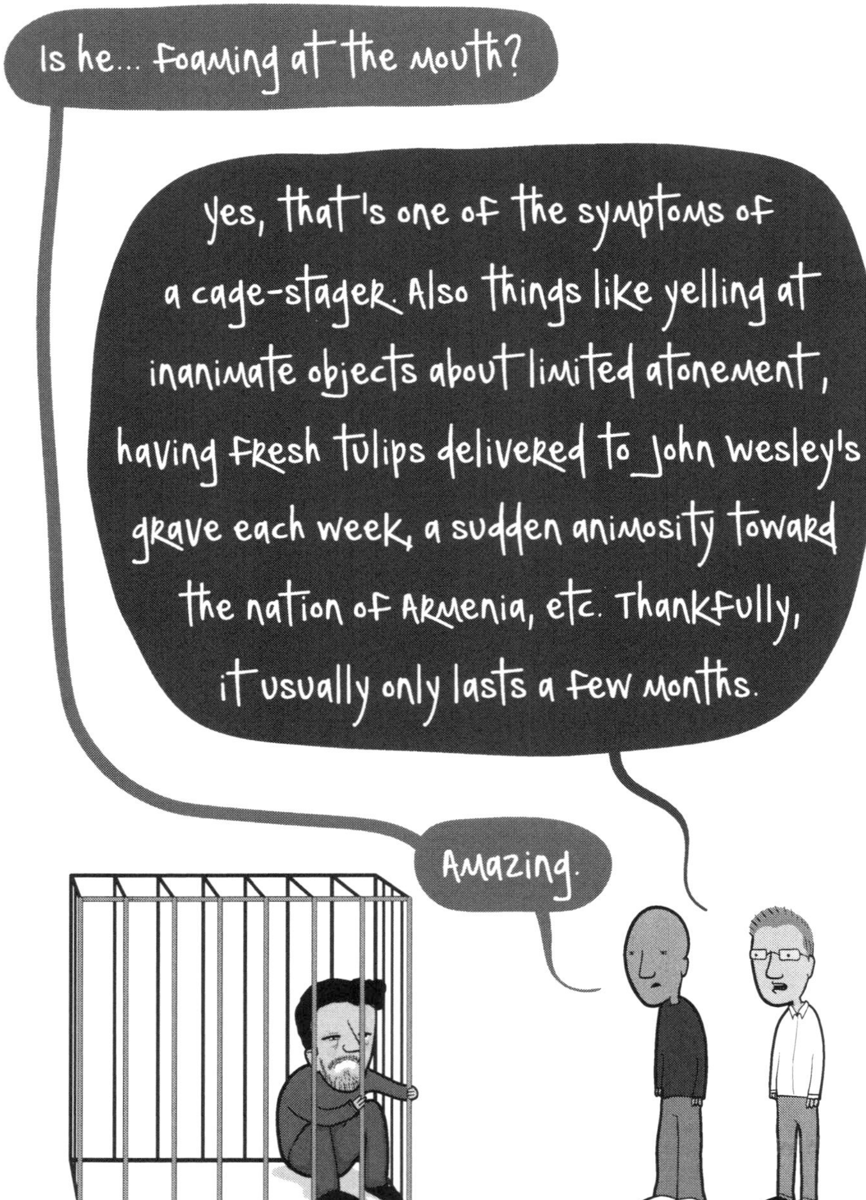
Is he... foaming at the mouth?
Yes, that's one of the symptoms of a cage-stager. Also things like yelling at inanimate objects about limited atonement, having fresh tulips delivered to John Wesley's grave each week, a sudden animosity toward the nation of Armenia, etc. Thankfully, it usually only lasts a few months.
Amazing.

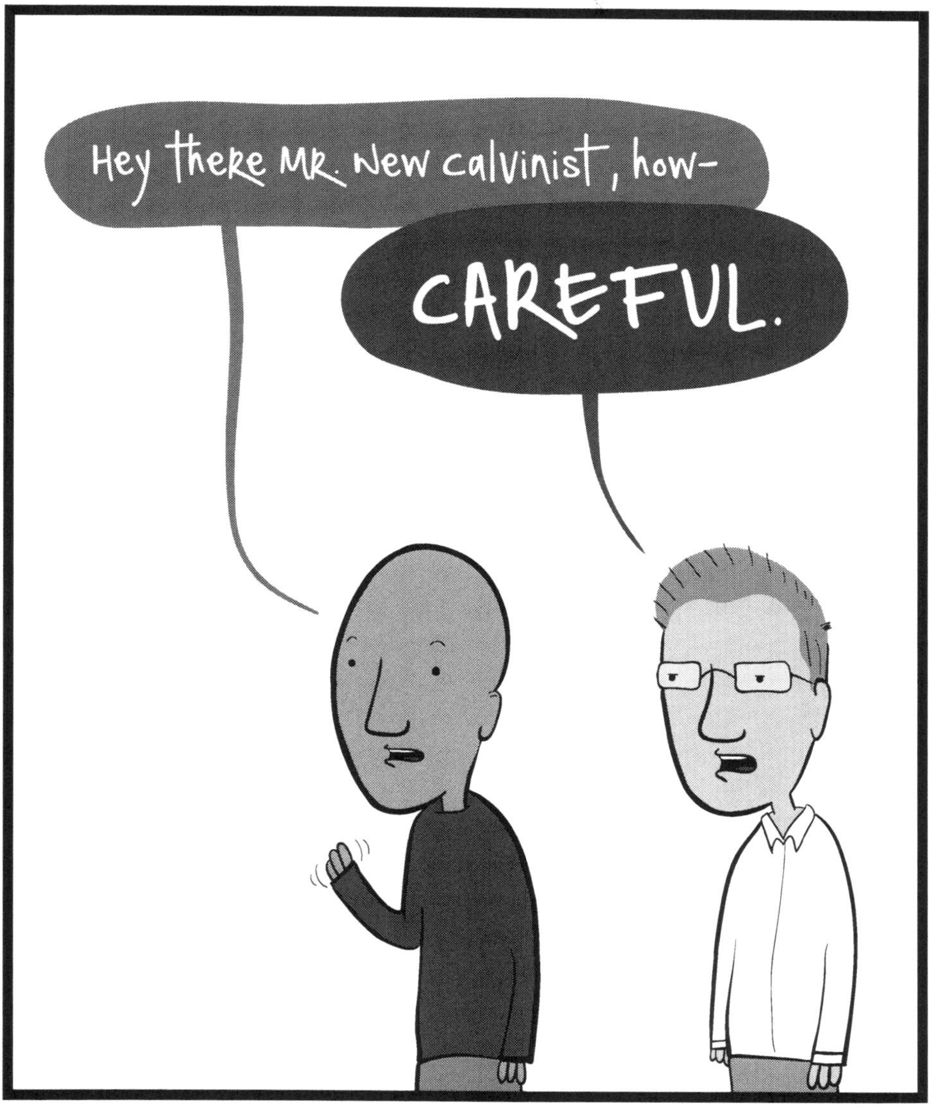
Hey there Mr. New calvinist, how-
CAREFUL.

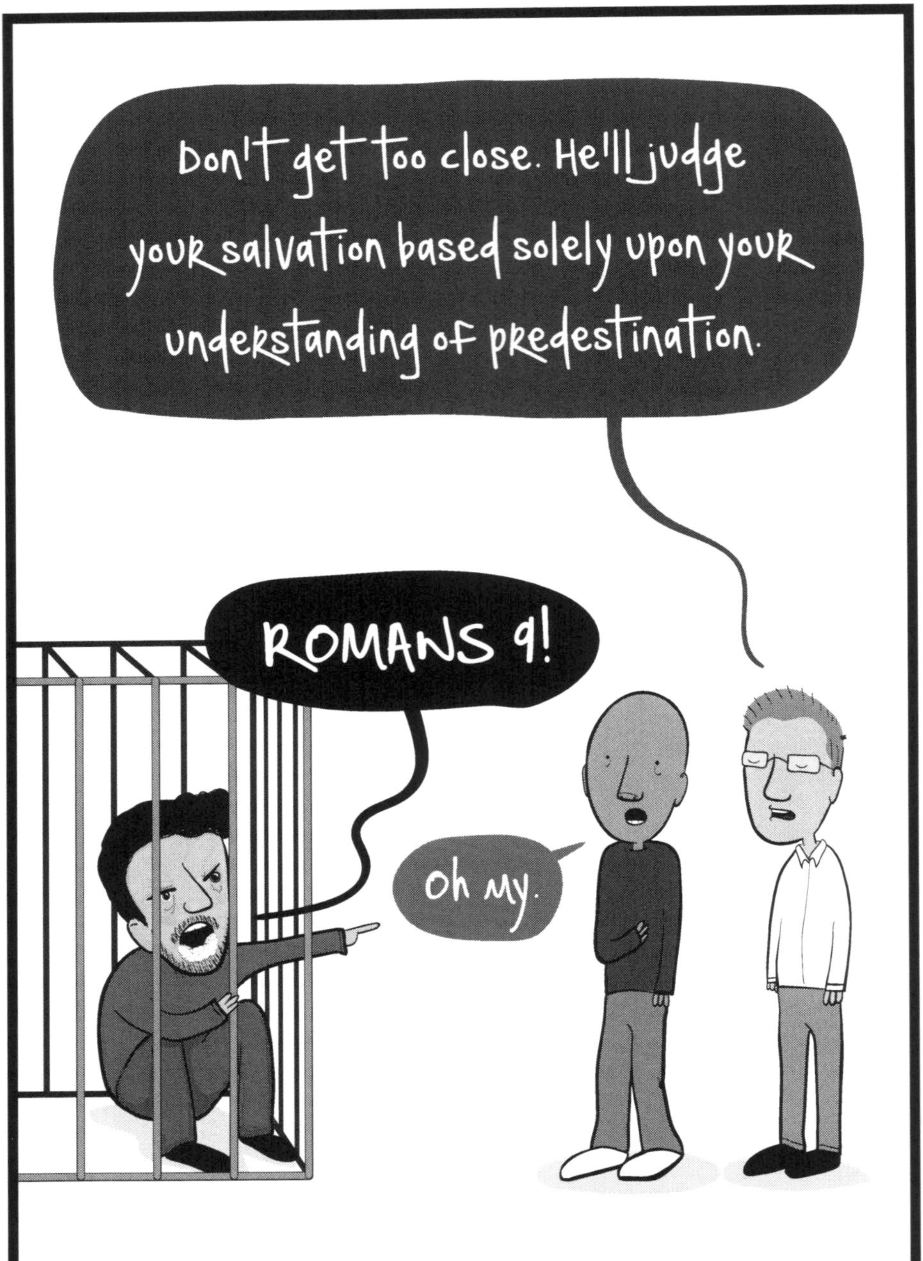
Don't get too close. He'll judge your salvation based solely upon your understanding of predestination.
ROMANS 9!
Oh my.

We will not be one of the cool kids

For the disciple of Jesus, it's important to accept the fact that
we will not be one of the cool kids.

We will not find ourselves adored and emulated by the masses of this world, because we are walking manifestations of a gospel that is a pungent offense to most people.

In our journey as aliens through this strange life, the world will be quicker to crucify us than crown us, for no disciple is above his teacher. And that's OK.

Wrestle with this truth and let it pin you down. Let it kneel on top of you and spit on your face. Don't even fight back. Just let it win. Then get up and offer to carry its backpack.

The truth is, if you're one of Christ's followers, dead to this world, a δοῦλος (slave) of God...then you're weird.

We're not like everyone else, by default. We're different.

And our job is to serve people and tell them about Jesus.

Jesus, the guy who never shied away from the hardest topics. Who said there was no hope for anyone apart from Him. Who sought followers by telling them to give up everything if they wanted to be found in Him.

JESUS, NOT THIS TOPIC AGAIN!
OH DEY GONNA BE MAD

We never have to apologize for what Jesus has said.

We must crucify daily our need to be approved by everyone around us. That will get us nowhere.

Jesus has called us to an unpopular mission: to be His hands and feet on this earth.

Let's not forget what happened to His hands and feet while He was on this earth.

He knows our fears, anxieties, and needs;
He's well-acquainted with our shame and grief;
He's felt the mockery and belittlement Himself;

and He's promised to always be with us on this mission.

So we don't need to try to be one of the cool kids.

We need to serve people and tell them about Jesus.

The Bible is not anti-women

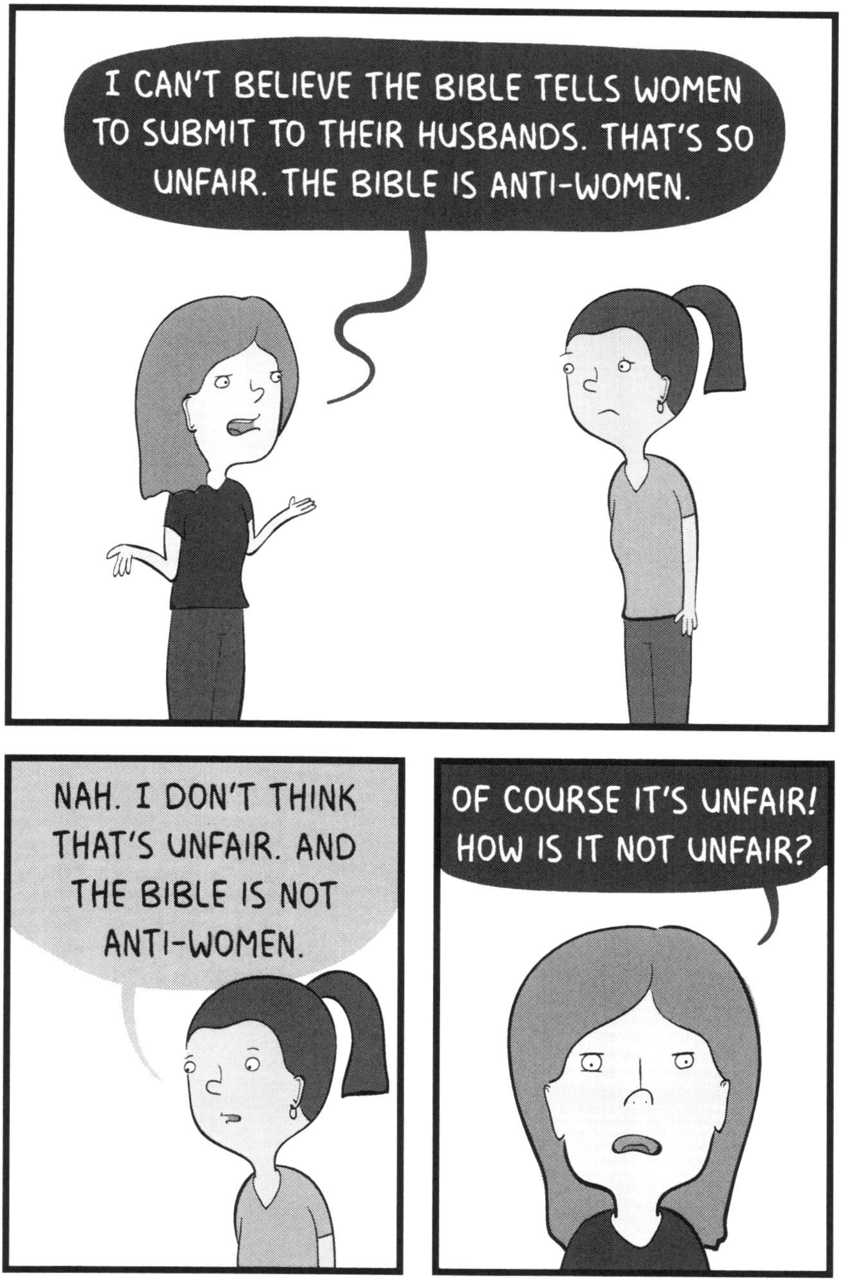
I CAN'T BELIEVE THE BIBLE TELLS WOMEN TO SUBMIT TO THEIR HUSBANDS. THAT'S SO UNFAIR. THE BIBLE IS ANTI-WOMEN.
NAH. I DON'T THINK THAT'S UNFAIR. AND THE BIBLE IS NOT ANTI-WOMEN.
OF COURSE IT'S UNFAIR! HOW IS IT NOT UNFAIR?

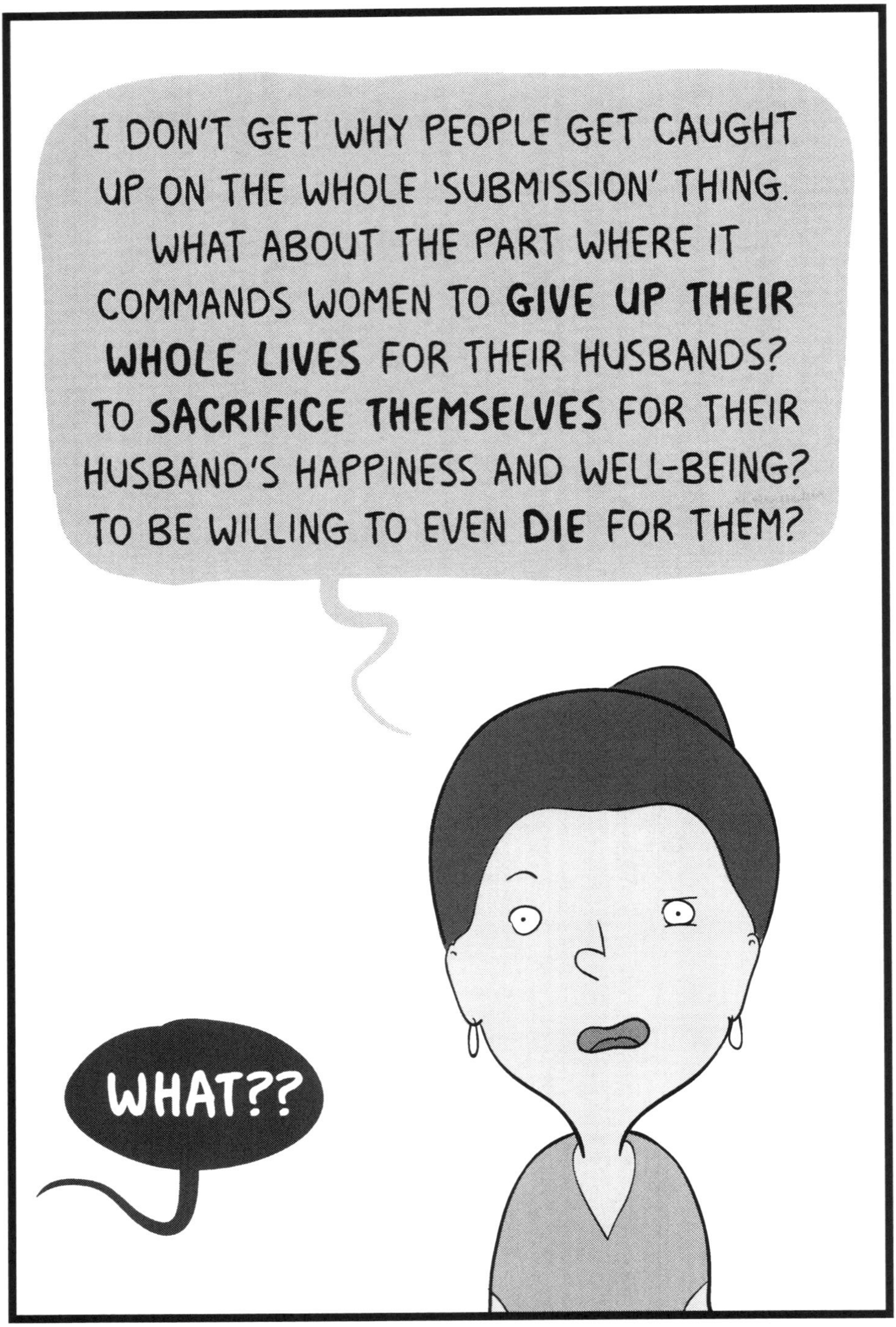
I DON'T GET WHY PEOPLE GET CAUGHT UP ON THE WHOLE 'SUBMISSION' THING. WHAT ABOUT THE PART WHERE IT COMMANDS WOMEN TO **GIVE UP THEIR WHOLE LIVES** FOR THEIR HUSBANDS? TO **SACRIFICE THEMSELVES** FOR THEIR HUSBAND'S HAPPINESS AND WELL-BEING? TO BE WILLING TO EVEN **DIE** FOR THEM?
WHAT??

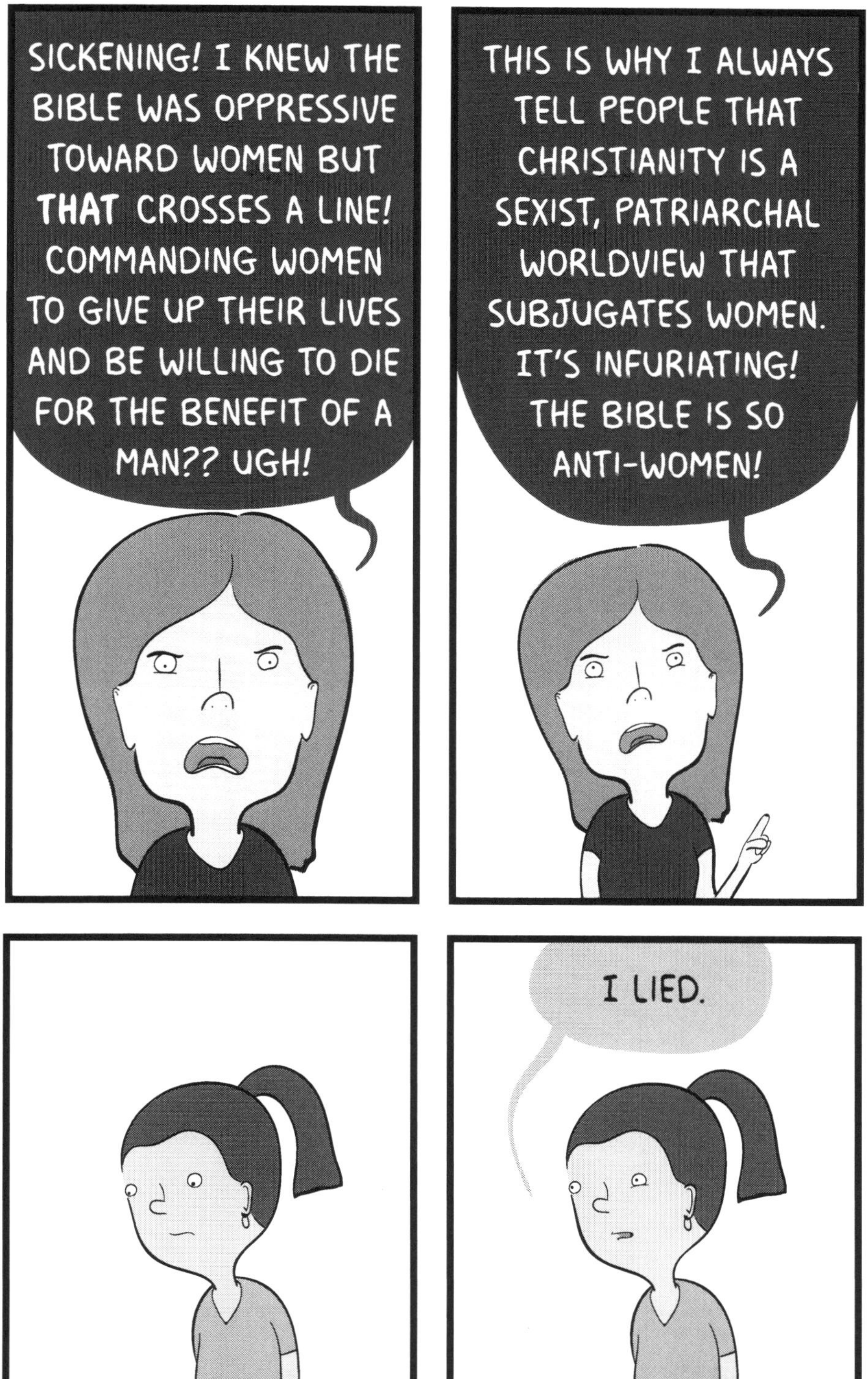
SICKENING! I KNEW THE BIBLE WAS OPPRESSIVE TOWARD WOMEN BUT **THAT** CROSSES A LINE! COMMANDING WOMEN TO GIVE UP THEIR LIVES AND BE WILLING TO DIE FOR THE BENEFIT OF A MAN?? UGH!
THIS IS WHY I ALWAYS TELL PEOPLE THAT CHRISTIANITY IS A SEXIST, PATRIARCHAL WORLDVIEW THAT SUBJUGATES WOMEN. IT'S INFURIATING! THE BIBLE IS SO ANTI-WOMEN!
I LIED.

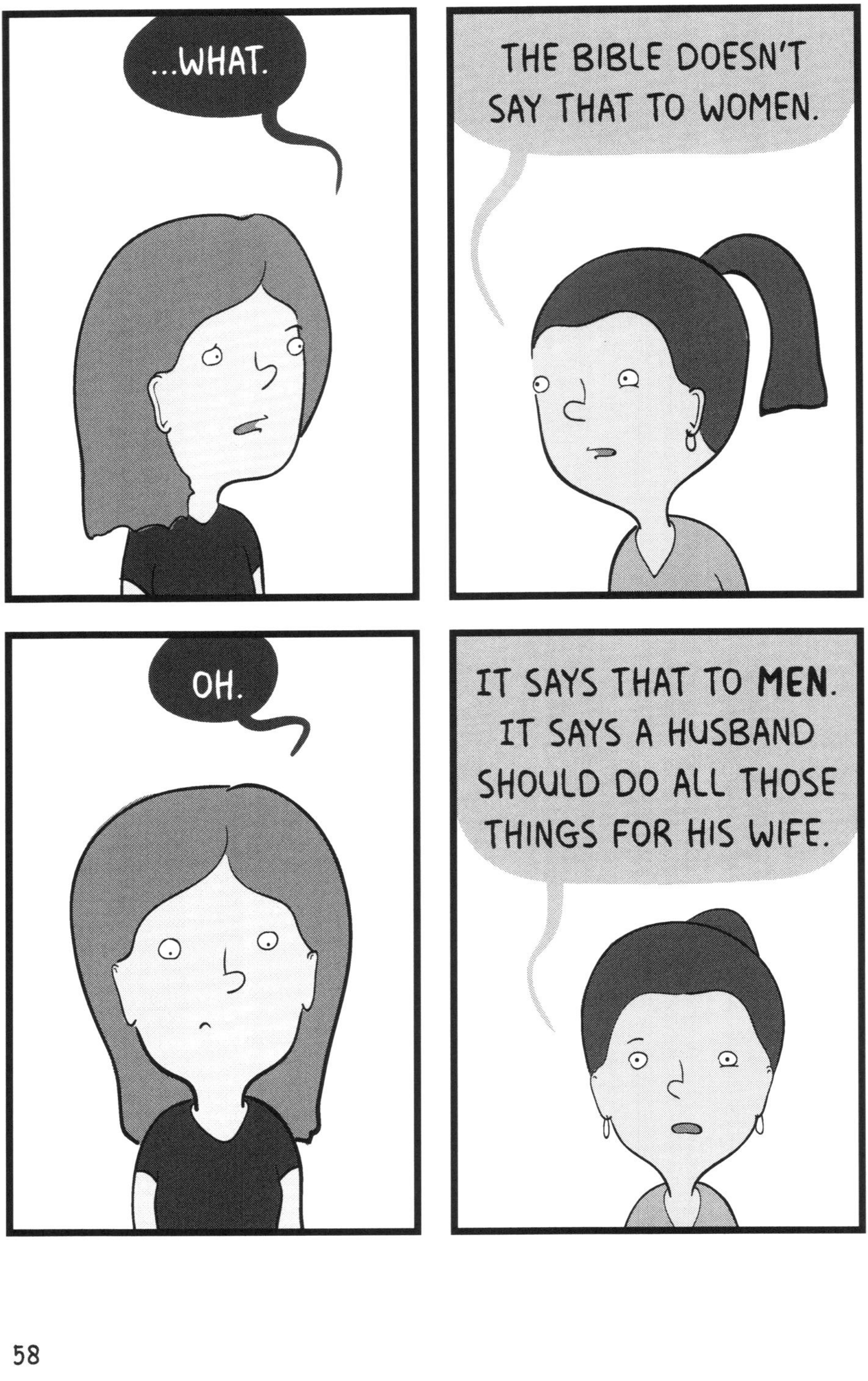
...WHAT.
THE BIBLE DOESN'T SAY THAT TO WOMEN.
OH.
IT SAYS THAT TO **MEN**. IT SAYS A HUSBAND SHOULD DO ALL THOSE THINGS FOR HIS WIFE.

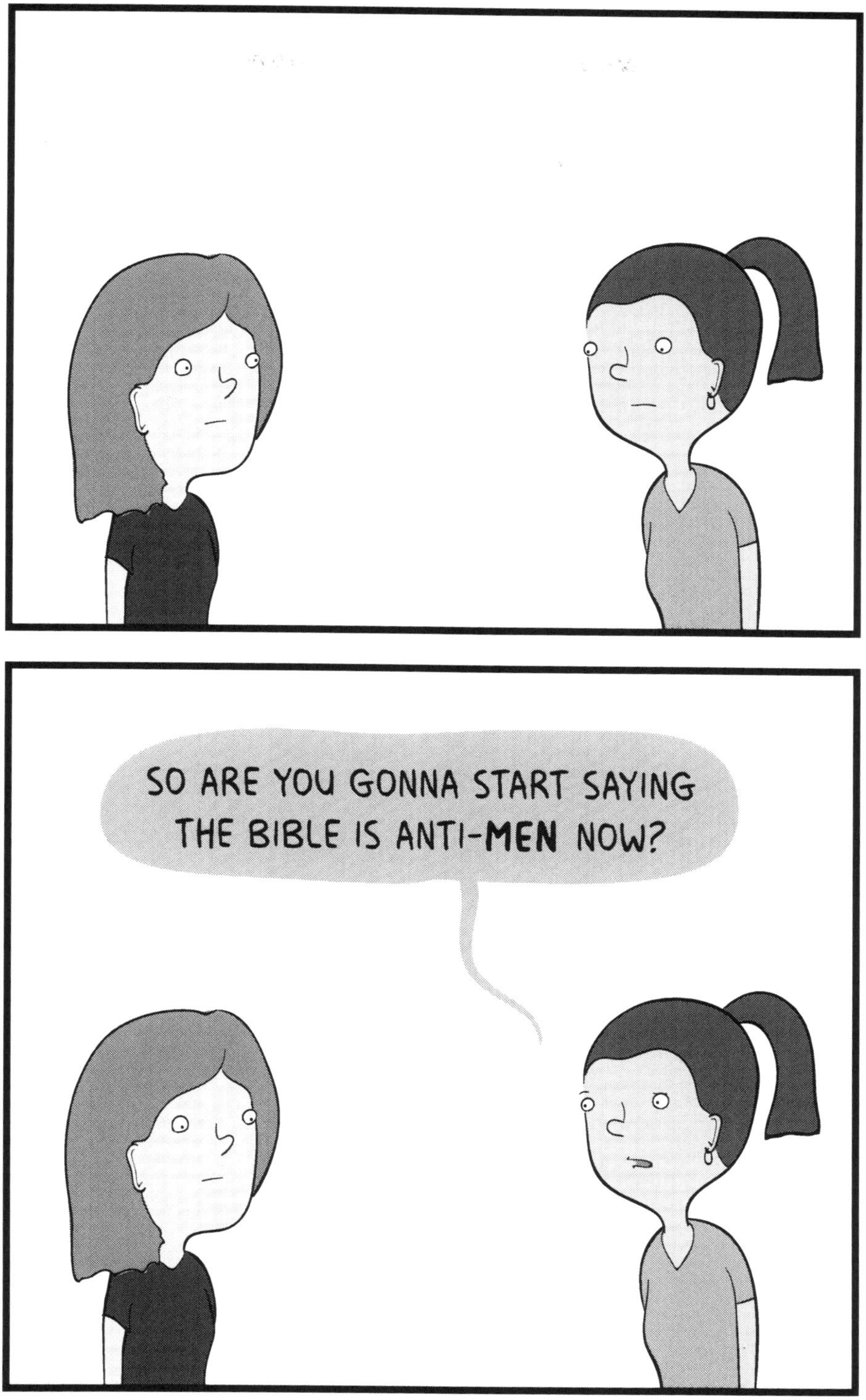
SO ARE YOU GONNA START SAYING THE BIBLE IS ANTI-**MEN** NOW?

Thank you, church child-care worker

Thank you, church child-care worker, for the sacrifices you make so the rest of us can worship, fellowship, and study.

You play with our kids and feed them snacks.
You deal with their crying, fighting, and pooping.
You wipe their noses and comfort them when they cry.
And instead of running away weeping, you come back for more, always welcoming the children with smiles.

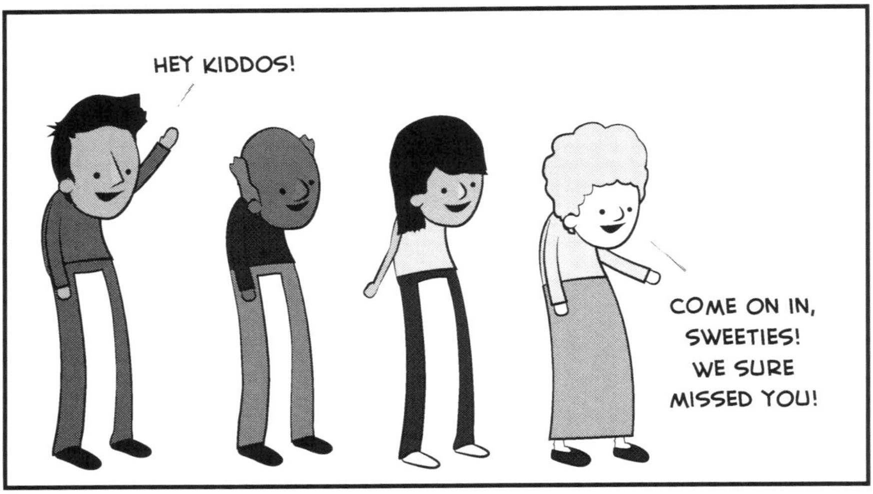
HEY KIDDOS!
COME ON IN, SWEETIES! WE SURE MISSED YOU!

You bear this cross with honor and dignity, weekly stepping back into the arena, fully aware of the barbarism small children are capable of when placed into groups.

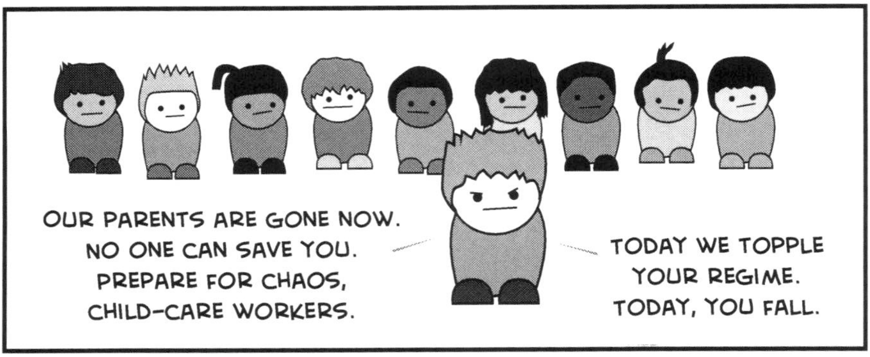
OUR PARENTS ARE GONE NOW. NO ONE CAN SAVE YOU. PREPARE FOR CHAOS, CHILD-CARE WORKERS.
TODAY WE TOPPLE YOUR REGIME. TODAY, YOU FALL.

Each week the children attempt their coup, and each week they fail...for underneath your smiley exterior and singsong voice lies an experienced, hardened, valiant

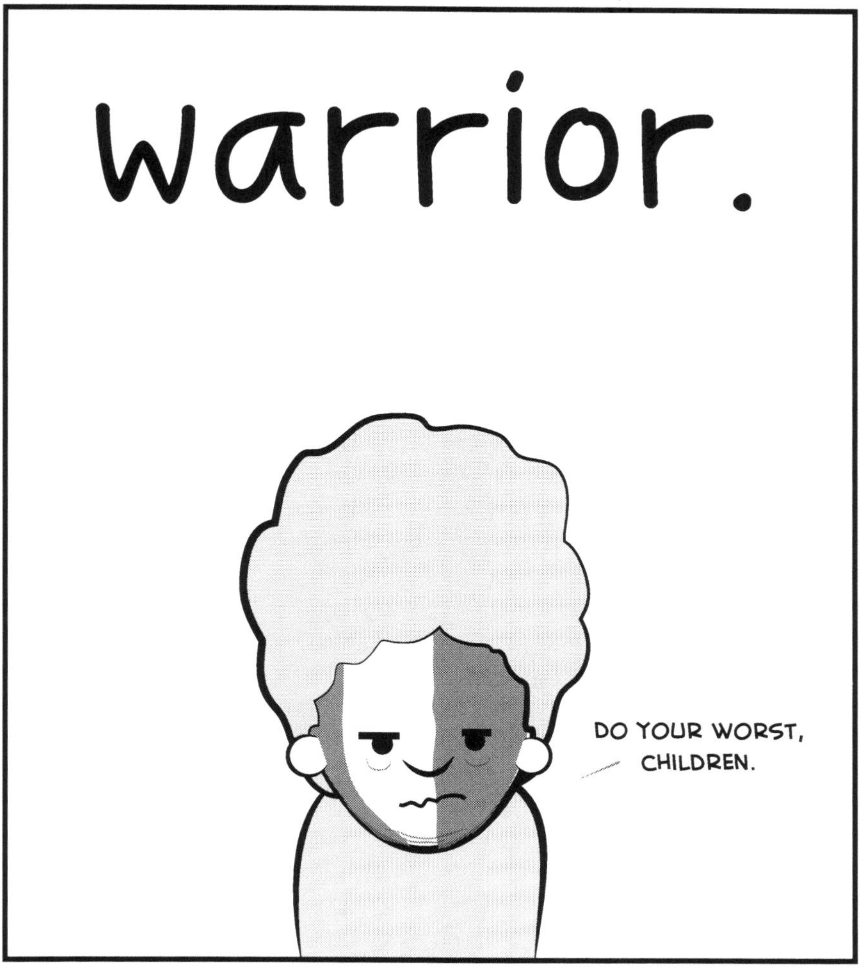
warrior.
DO YOUR WORST, CHILDREN.

Again I say ***thank you***, church child-care worker.

May your valor produce piles of heavenly treasure the size of Mount Everest.

A lot of Christians use the acronym OMG and I think that's pretty dumb

Well when I use it, it doesn't mean "Oh my God," it means "Oh my GOSH."

No, it doesn't.
OMG means "Oh my God."

Walk up to the next stranger you see and ask them what OMG means—see what they say.

Saying OMG means "Oh my gosh" is like saying WTF means "What the fudge," just for you, just because you say so. C'mon with all that.

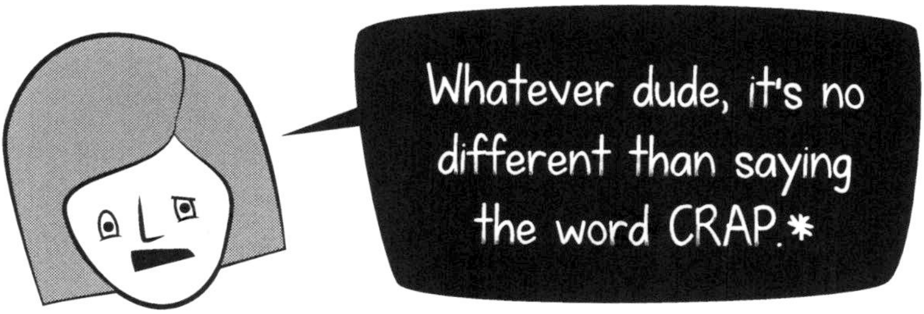

Whatever dude, it's no different than saying the word CRAP.*

*Actual response I read from a "popular Christian blogger" when someone asked about his regular use of "OMG."

God is holy; righteous; perfect; special; set apart. Do you believe this? If so, do you use His title as a dirty, throwaway expletive?

I need to express surprise, anger, or disgust real quick... should I go with the slang word for excrement? Or the title of my Creator and Savior?

decisions...   decisions...

Here's a good rule of thumb for Christians, methinks: whether you're speaking or typing, use the word "God" only if you're actually *referring* to God.

If you're saying "God" or typing "OMG" and *you could use a cuss word instead*, something's wrong there.

For instance:

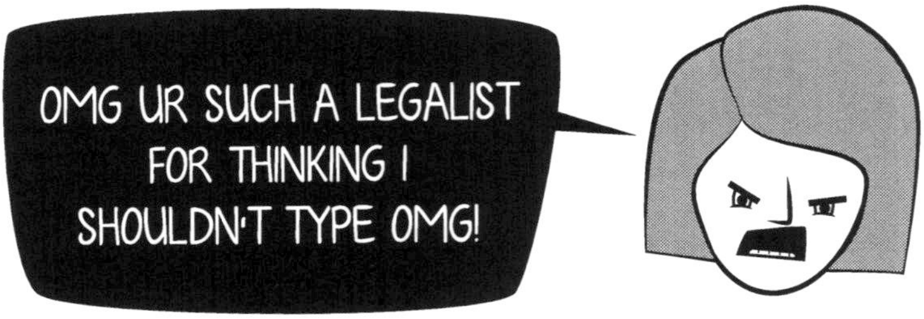
OMG UR SUCH A LEGALIST FOR THINKING I SHOULDN'T TYPE OMG!

and

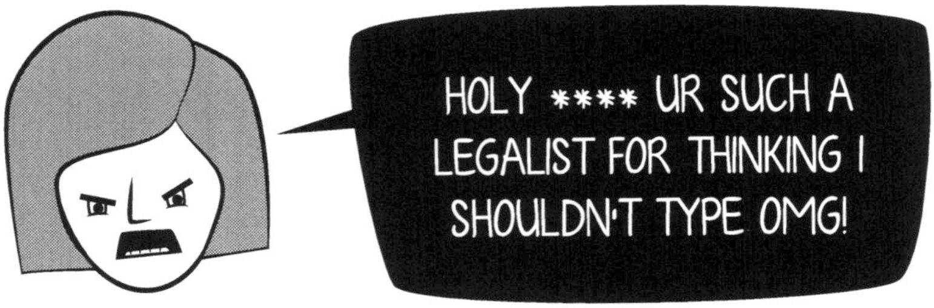
HOLY **** UR SUCH A LEGALIST FOR THINKING I SHOULDN'T TYPE OMG!

The sentiment being expressed does not change between these two sentences. Most times "OMG" is used, it's just using "God" as a substitute for a four-letter word.

And I think, my Christian friends, that's pretty dumb.

The elephant speaks

Four blind men are walking along
when they come upon an elephant.

Not sure what it is, they each begin to feel around,
hoping to discover the nature of what they've found.

One grabs the elephant's trunk and declares,

This is a big snake.

Another feels its leg and tells the others,

This is a tree.

The third man grasps its tail and posits,

This is a rope.

The final man feels the elephant's side and says,

This is a wall.

Why were all the men wrong?

They were wrong because they were trying to deduce and declare the nature of something much larger than themselves based solely on their own limited perspective.

God is like the elephant, says this popular analogy.

And we are like the blind men, so sure of our own ideas about God while being blind to truths about Him experienced by others and to the more expansive nature of His being.

How insolent, how pretentious to assume any one of the human perspectives of God is the only correct one.

Says this popular analogy.

And sure, it may sound like an apt, dynamic, compelling, humble description of God and man's relation to Him.

But if the elephant is to truly represent God, there is one major, universe-shifting detail left out of this story...

The elephant speaks.

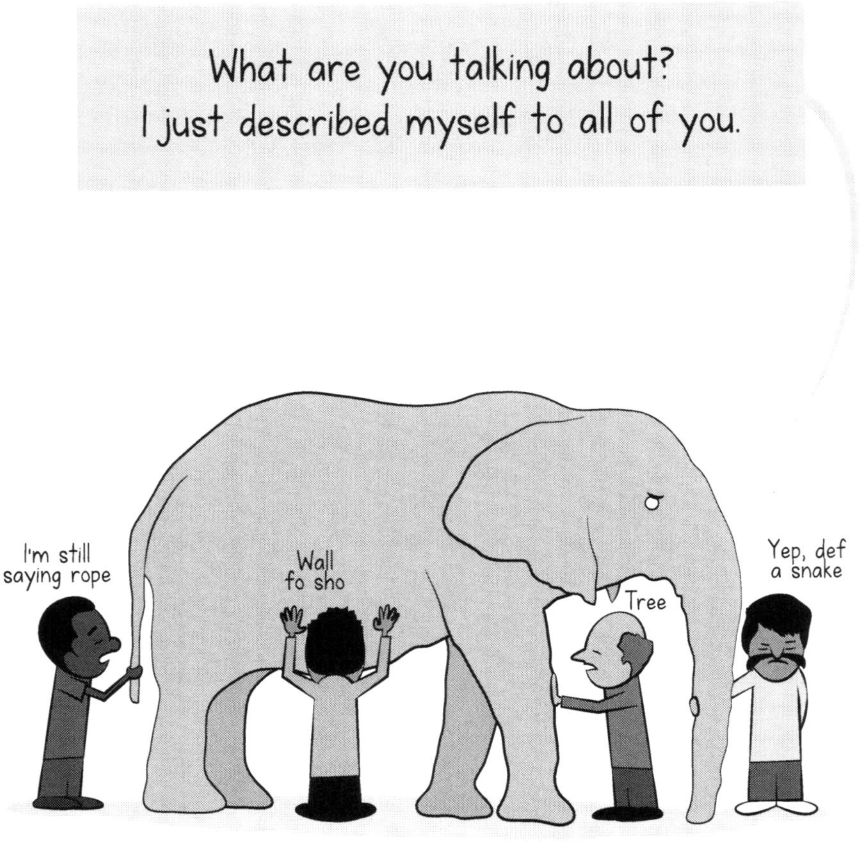
What are you talking about?
I just described myself to all of you.
I'm still saying rope
Wall fo sho
Tree
Yep, def a snake

God has not left us to accept uncertainty by relegating His nature to that of an ethereal, foggy, celestial being, nor to feign humility by declaring *any* description of God plausible.

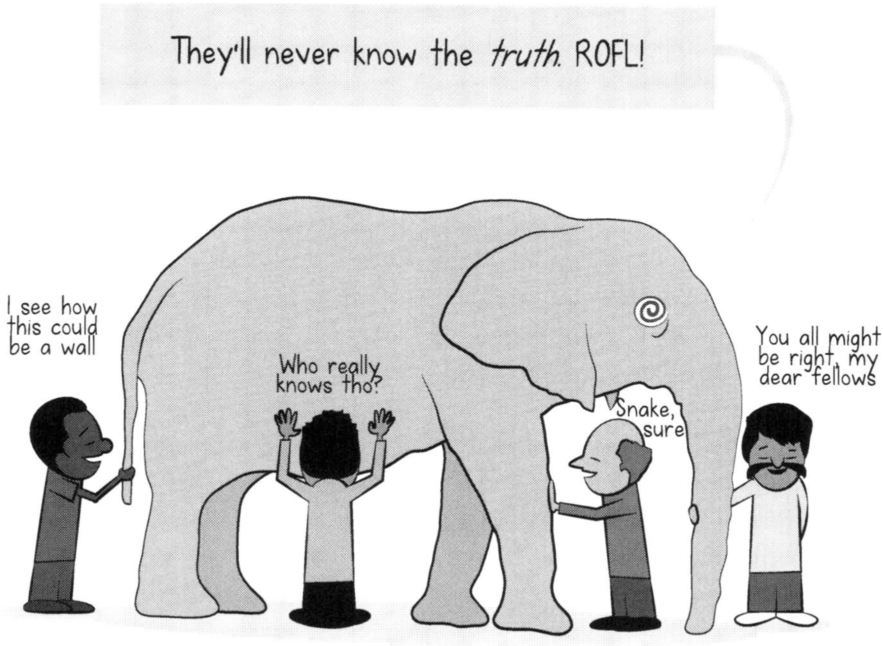
They'll never know the *truth*. ROFL!
I see how this could be a wall
Who really knows tho?
Snake, sure
You all might be right, my dear fellows

Want to know what God is like?

Study the Bible.

God *has* revealed Himself to us.

The elephant speaks.

SRSLY

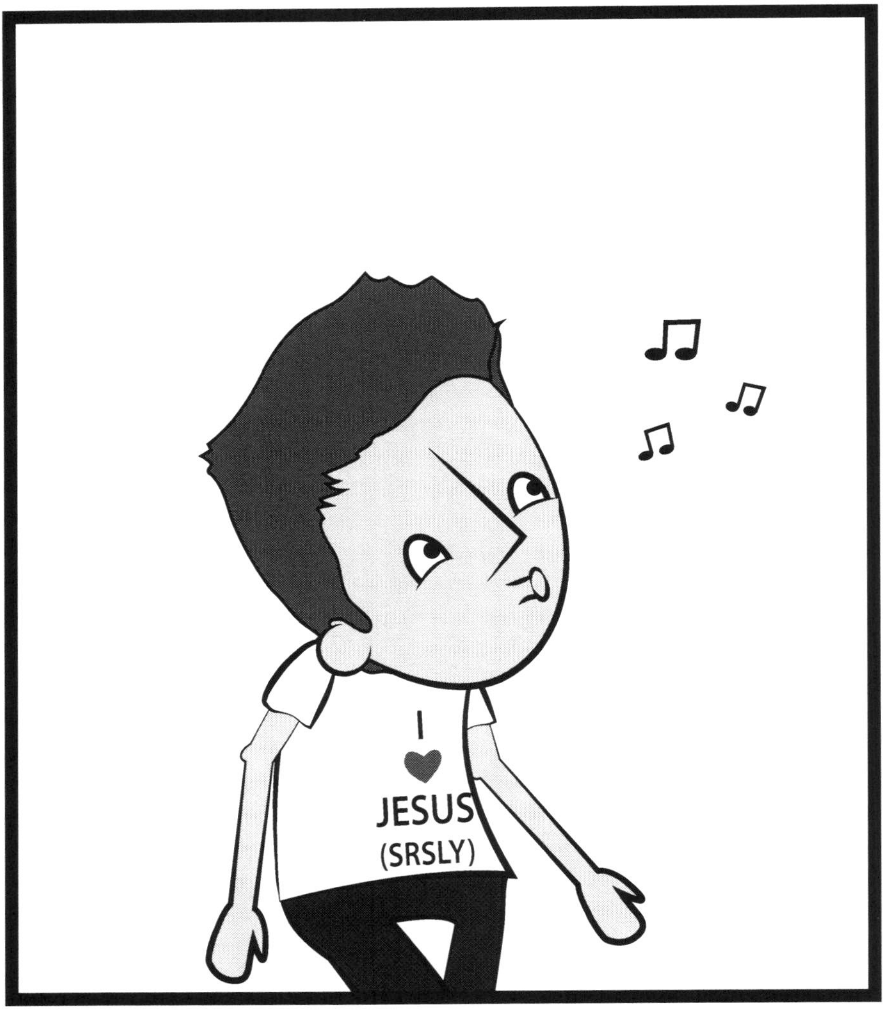
I ♥ JESUS
(SRSLY)

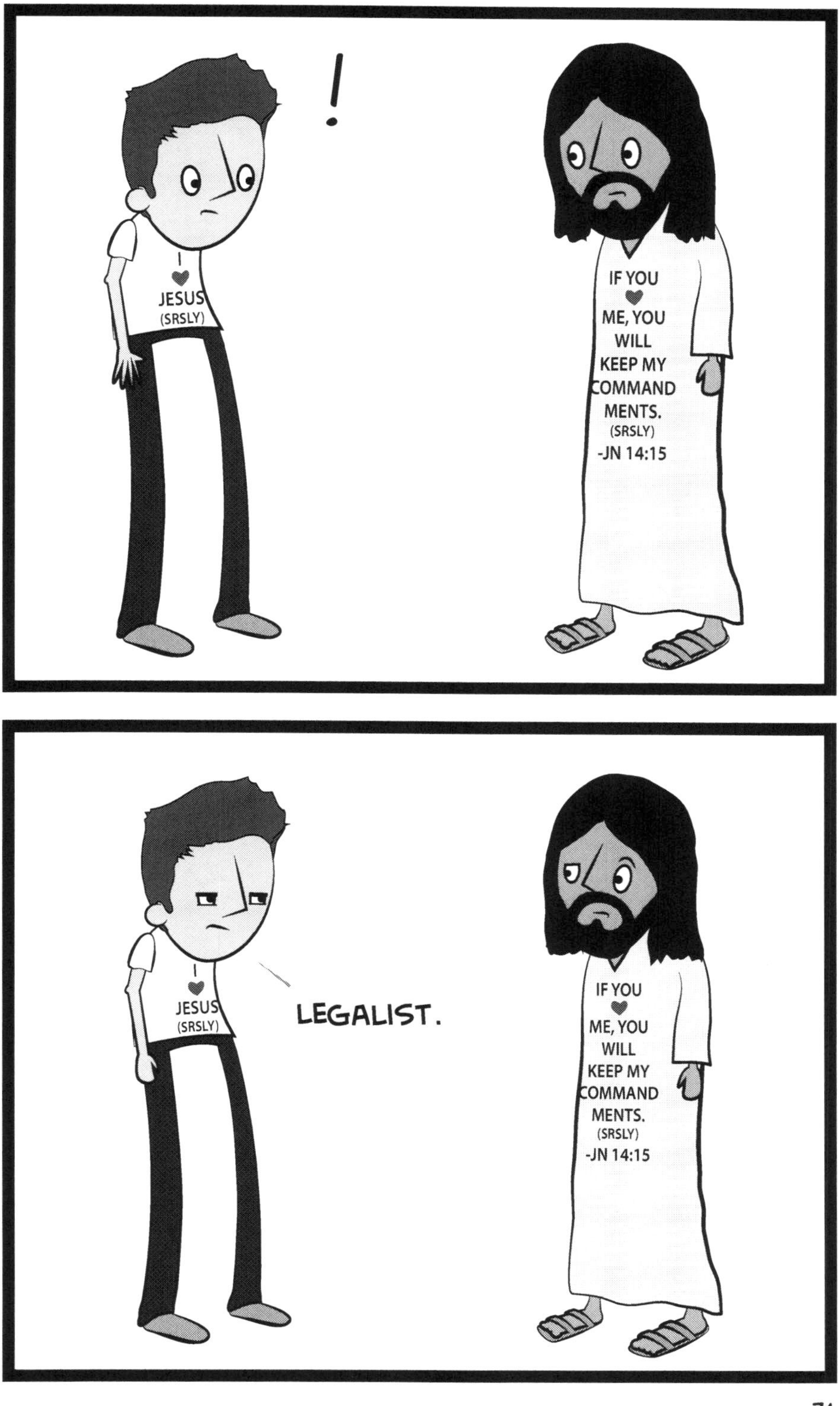
!
I ♥ JESUS (SRSLY)
IF YOU ♥ ME, YOU WILL KEEP MY COMMANDMENTS. (SRSLY) -JN 14:15
I ♥ JESUS (SRSLY)
LEGALIST.
IF YOU ♥ ME, YOU WILL KEEP MY COMMANDMENTS. (SRSLY) -JN 14:15

The God of the Old Testament

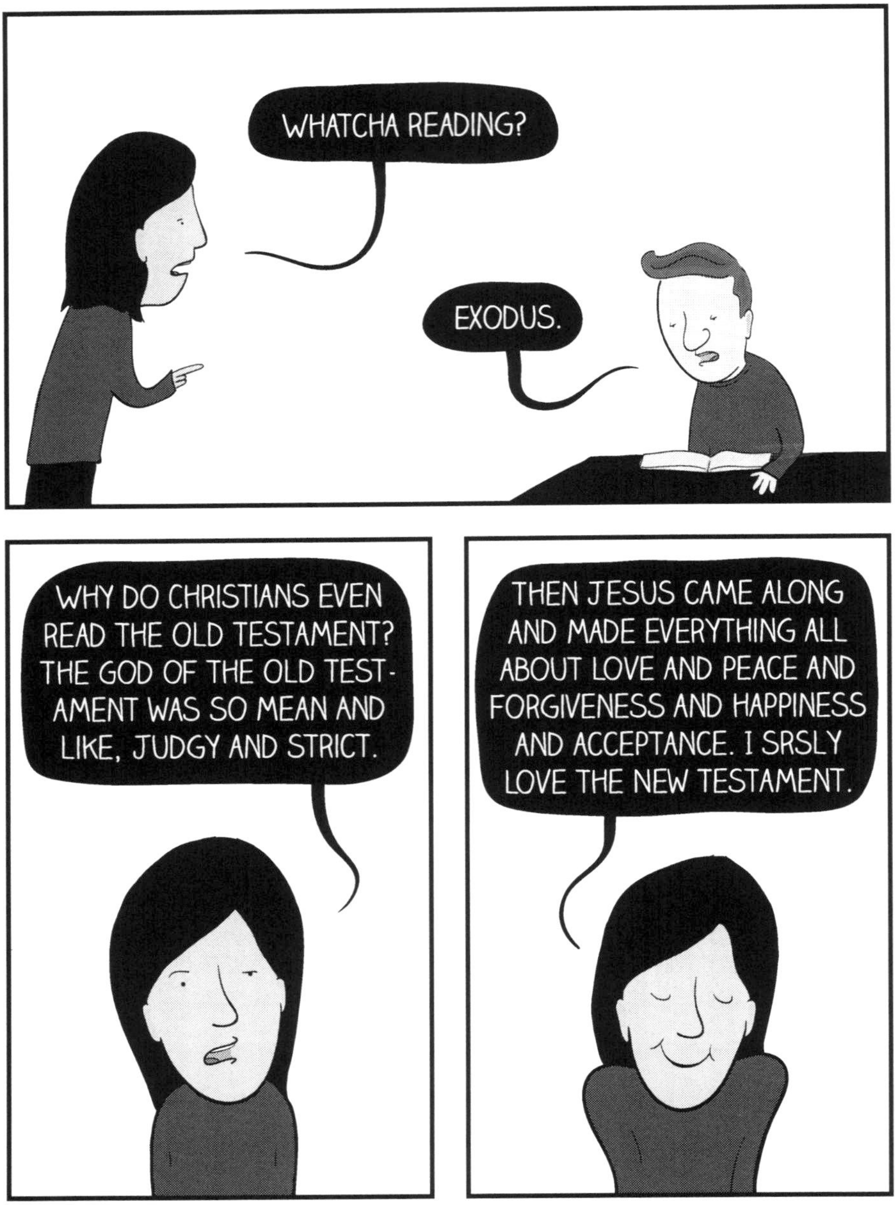

WHATCHA READING?
EXODUS.
WHY DO CHRISTIANS EVEN READ THE OLD TESTAMENT? THE GOD OF THE OLD TEST-AMENT WAS SO MEAN AND LIKE, JUDGY AND STRICT.
THEN JESUS CAME ALONG AND MADE EVERYTHING ALL ABOUT LOVE AND PEACE AND FORGIVENESS AND HAPPINESS AND ACCEPTANCE. I SRSLY LOVE THE NEW TESTAMENT.

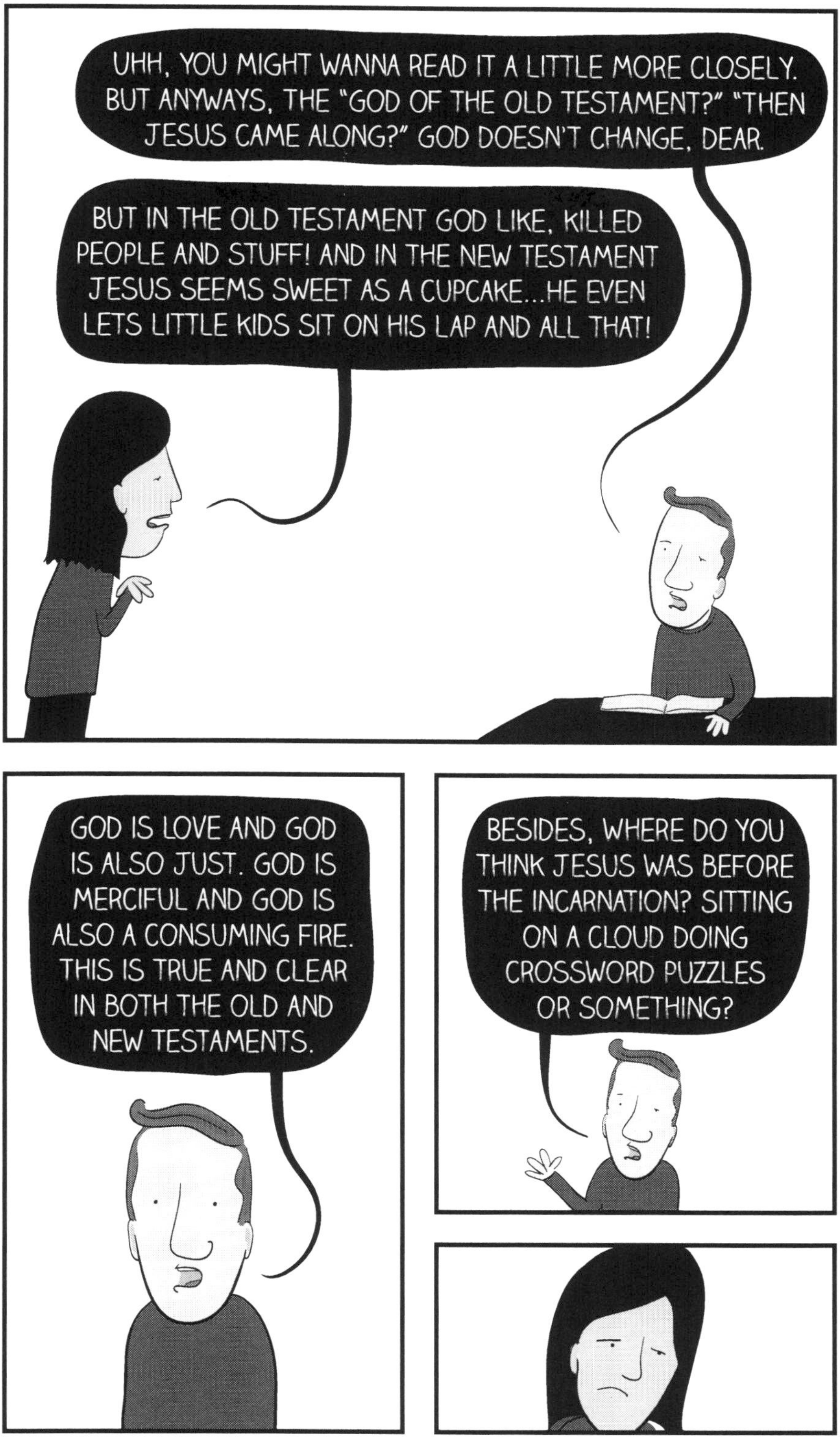
UHH, YOU MIGHT WANNA READ IT A LITTLE MORE CLOSELY. BUT ANYWAYS, THE "GOD OF THE OLD TESTAMENT?" "THEN JESUS CAME ALONG?" GOD DOESN'T CHANGE, DEAR.
BUT IN THE OLD TESTAMENT GOD LIKE, KILLED PEOPLE AND STUFF! AND IN THE NEW TESTAMENT JESUS SEEMS SWEET AS A CUPCAKE...HE EVEN LETS LITTLE KIDS SIT ON HIS LAP AND ALL THAT!
GOD IS LOVE AND GOD IS ALSO JUST. GOD IS MERCIFUL AND GOD IS ALSO A CONSUMING FIRE. THIS IS TRUE AND CLEAR IN BOTH THE OLD AND NEW TESTAMENTS.
BESIDES, WHERE DO YOU THINK JESUS WAS BEFORE THE INCARNATION? SITTING ON A CLOUD DOING CROSSWORD PUZZLES OR SOMETHING?

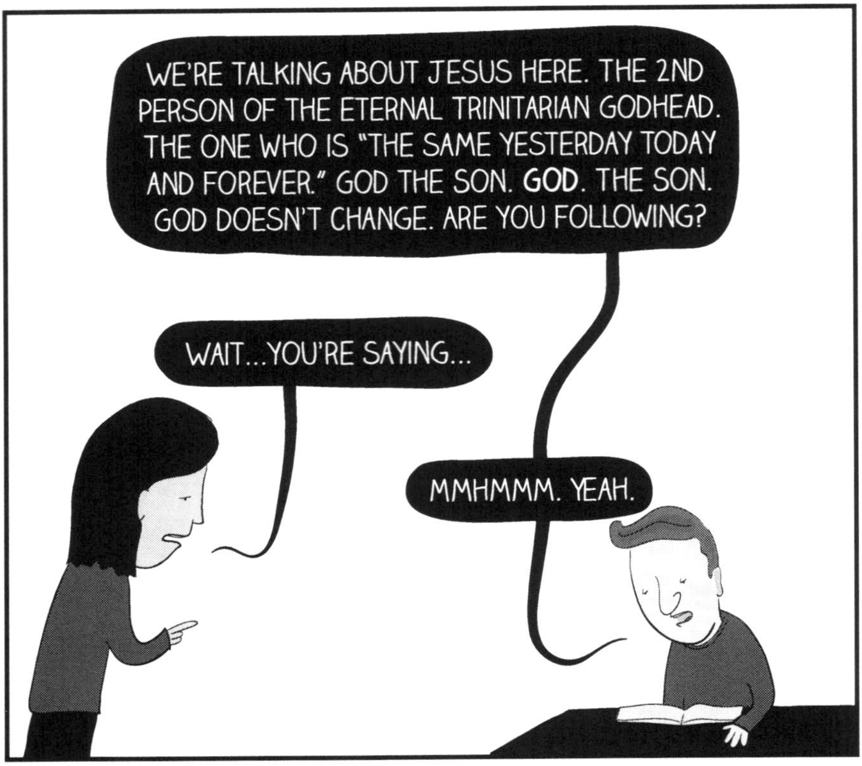
WE'RE TALKING ABOUT JESUS HERE. THE 2ND PERSON OF THE ETERNAL TRINITARIAN GODHEAD. THE ONE WHO IS "THE SAME YESTERDAY TODAY AND FOREVER." GOD THE SON. **GOD**. THE SON. GOD DOESN'T CHANGE. ARE YOU FOLLOWING?
WAIT... YOU'RE SAYING...
MMHMMM. YEAH.

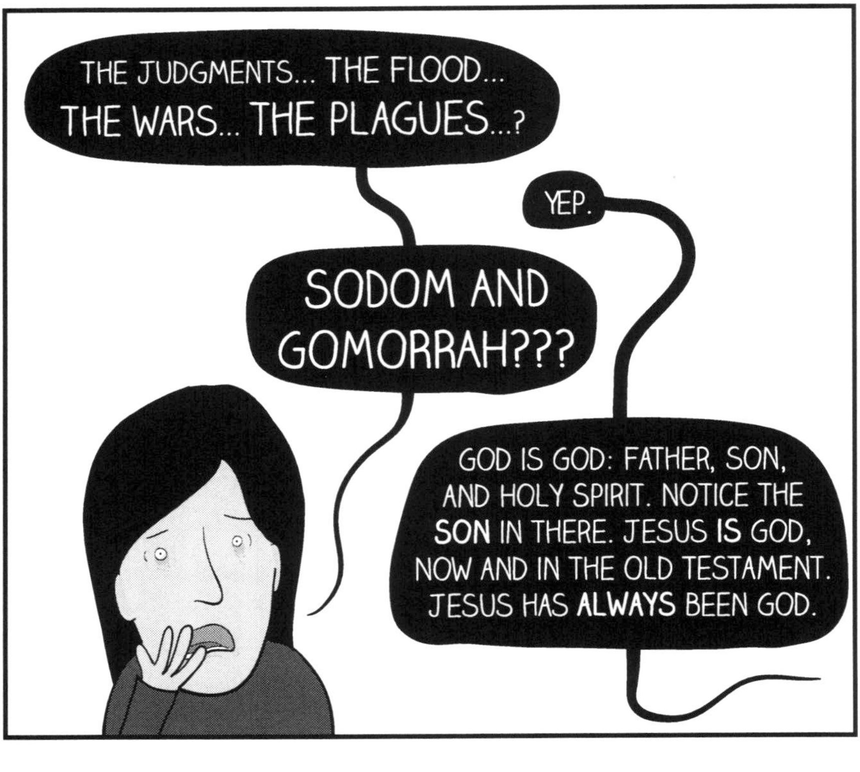
THE JUDGMENTS... THE FLOOD... THE WARS... THE PLAGUES...?
YEP.
SODOM AND GOMORRAH???
GOD IS GOD: FATHER, SON, AND HOLY SPIRIT. NOTICE THE **SON** IN THERE. JESUS **IS** GOD, NOW AND IN THE OLD TESTAMENT. JESUS HAS **ALWAYS** BEEN GOD.

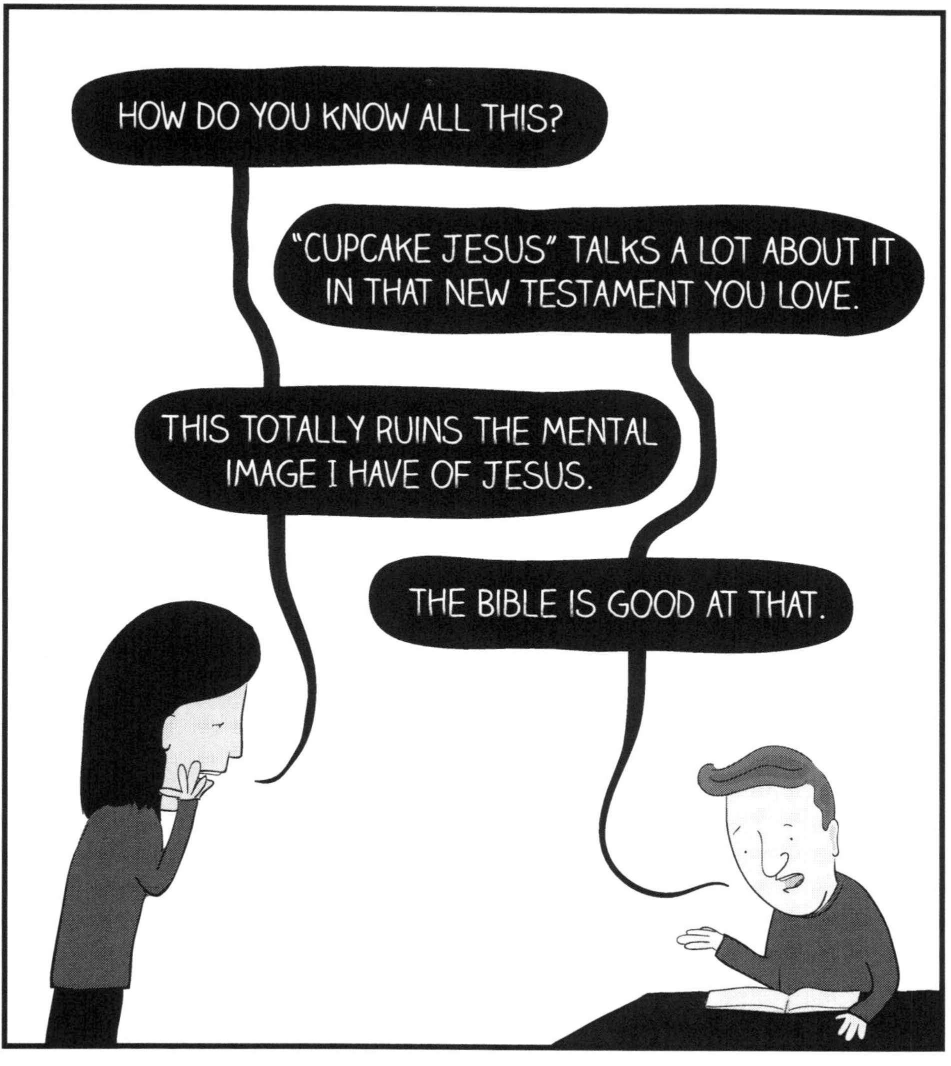
HOW DO YOU KNOW ALL THIS?
"CUPCAKE JESUS" TALKS A LOT ABOUT IT IN THAT NEW TESTAMENT YOU LOVE.
THIS TOTALLY RUINS THE MENTAL IMAGE I HAVE OF JESUS.
THE BIBLE IS GOOD AT THAT.

Anxiety, depression, and the truth

I struggle with anxiety and depression.

I've been a Christian for about 10 years: 5 of them as a Type-A extrovert and 5 of them as an anxiety-ridden introvert.

The first time I had an anxiety attack, I thought I was having a stroke. I was driving. I almost crashed.

I couldn't drive for a long time after that.

I've never been the same since that day.
Anxiety and depression have changed my life.

I've had long stretches of time like this
(from Generalized Anxiety Disorder + Panic Disorder + Social Anxiety)

What I should eat for breakfast is the heaviest decision anyone has ever had to make

Literally incapable of processing information

I can't make decisions
I can't focus I can't think
I can't remember

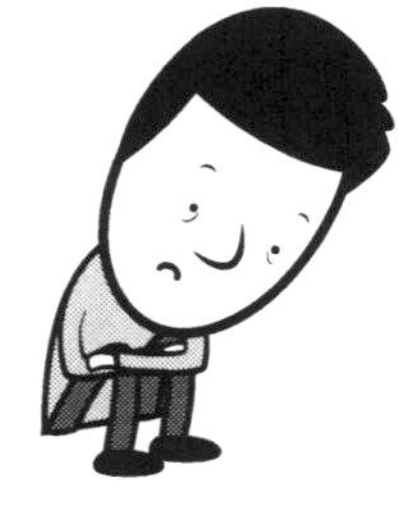

I wish the invisible taser would stop zapping me now

Central nervous system keeps short-circuiting must not leave house

What if I'm like this forever

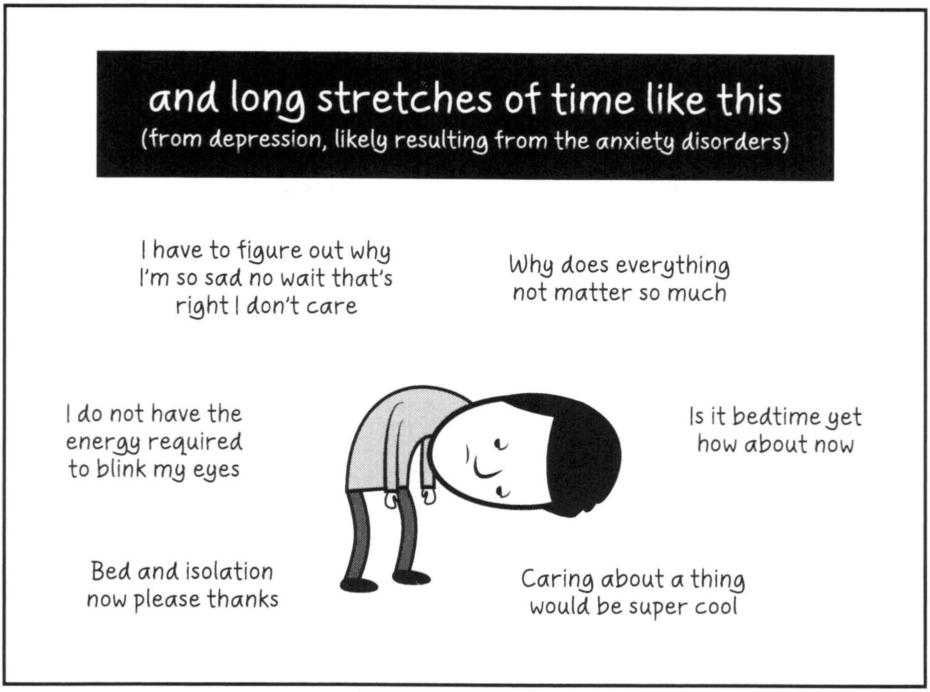
and long stretches of time like this
(from depression, likely resulting from the anxiety disorders)
I have to figure out why I'm so sad no wait that's right I don't care
Why does everything not matter so much
I do not have the energy required to blink my eyes
Is it bedtime yet how about now
Bed and isolation now please thanks
Caring about a thing would be super cool

Pre-anxiety-depression-me was extremely outgoing.

Now I struggle MIGHTILY with things like meeting new people, going new places, being in any group setting, and being the center of attention in any capacity.

Pre-anxiety-depression-me wanted to be a preacher. *LOL!*

Now the idea of leading a small Bible study is enough to make me lose sleep and/or be violently ill and/or die.

It's a daily struggle. There are good days and there are bad days, good months and bad months.

I'm writing this because I know many of you can relate to what I've described. And I know many of you know what it's like to be in the midst of terrible anxiety or depression...

filled with thoughts like these:

Why is God
letting this
happen

I do not feel God
not at all
not even a little

God doesn't
really love me

Is God really real

I have no desire
to pray or read my
Bible whatsoever

I feel no security
I feel no hope

There is a wet
blanket over
my soul

I do not claim to have an exhaustive answer as to why God allows me to struggle with my disorders.

I do believe, though, that part of the reason is so I can encourage others who struggle as I do.

Feelings can be dirty, filthy, stinking liars.

So I am writing this to encourage you with the truth.

The truth is what gets us through.

And the truth of the gospel is not dependent on how you *feel* about it at any given time, Christian.

God loves you and chose you before the foundation of the world to be holy and blameless, even if you get too depressed to care sometimes, Christian.

Jesus died on the cross to atone for your sins and secure your status as an eternal child of God, whether or not there are enough happy chemicals in your brain right now for that thought to give you the warm and fuzzies, Christian.

Your standing before God is based on the work of Jesus Christ, and when God looks at you, even anxiety-ridden you, even depressed you, even in your very lowest points, He sees His beloved child securely clothed in the full righteousness of Christ, Christian.

Store the truth in your heart and cling to it in those times when your emotions betray you.

The truth is not dependent on our feelings.

I thank God for that.

The “death of Christianity” in America

AMERICA 20 YEARS AGO

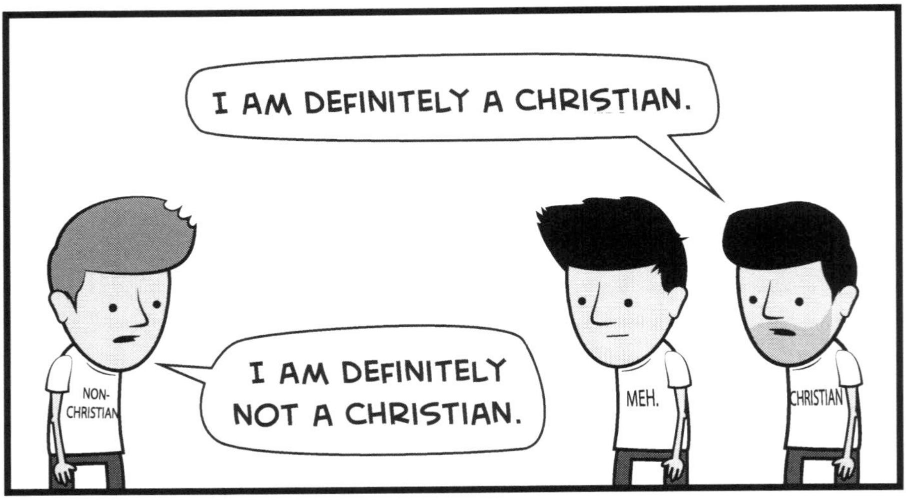
I AM DEFINITELY A CHRISTIAN.
NON-CHRISTIAN
I AM DEFINITELY NOT A CHRISTIAN.
MEH.
CHRISTIAN

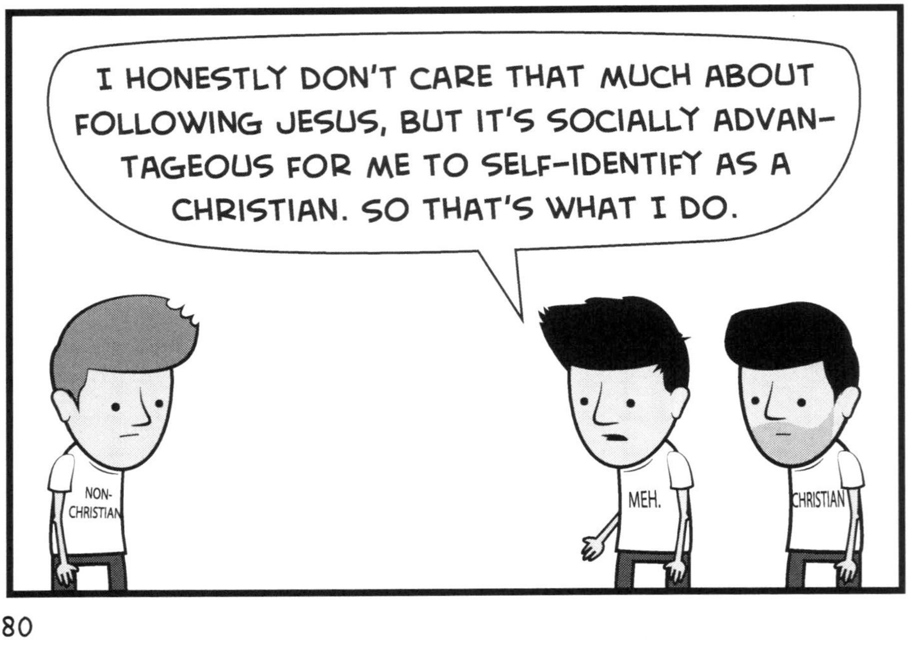
I HONESTLY DON'T CARE THAT MUCH ABOUT FOLLOWING JESUS, BUT IT'S SOCIALLY ADVANTAGEOUS FOR ME TO SELF-IDENTIFY AS A CHRISTIAN. SO THAT'S WHAT I DO.
NON-CHRISTIAN
MEH.
CHRISTIAN

AMERICA TODAY

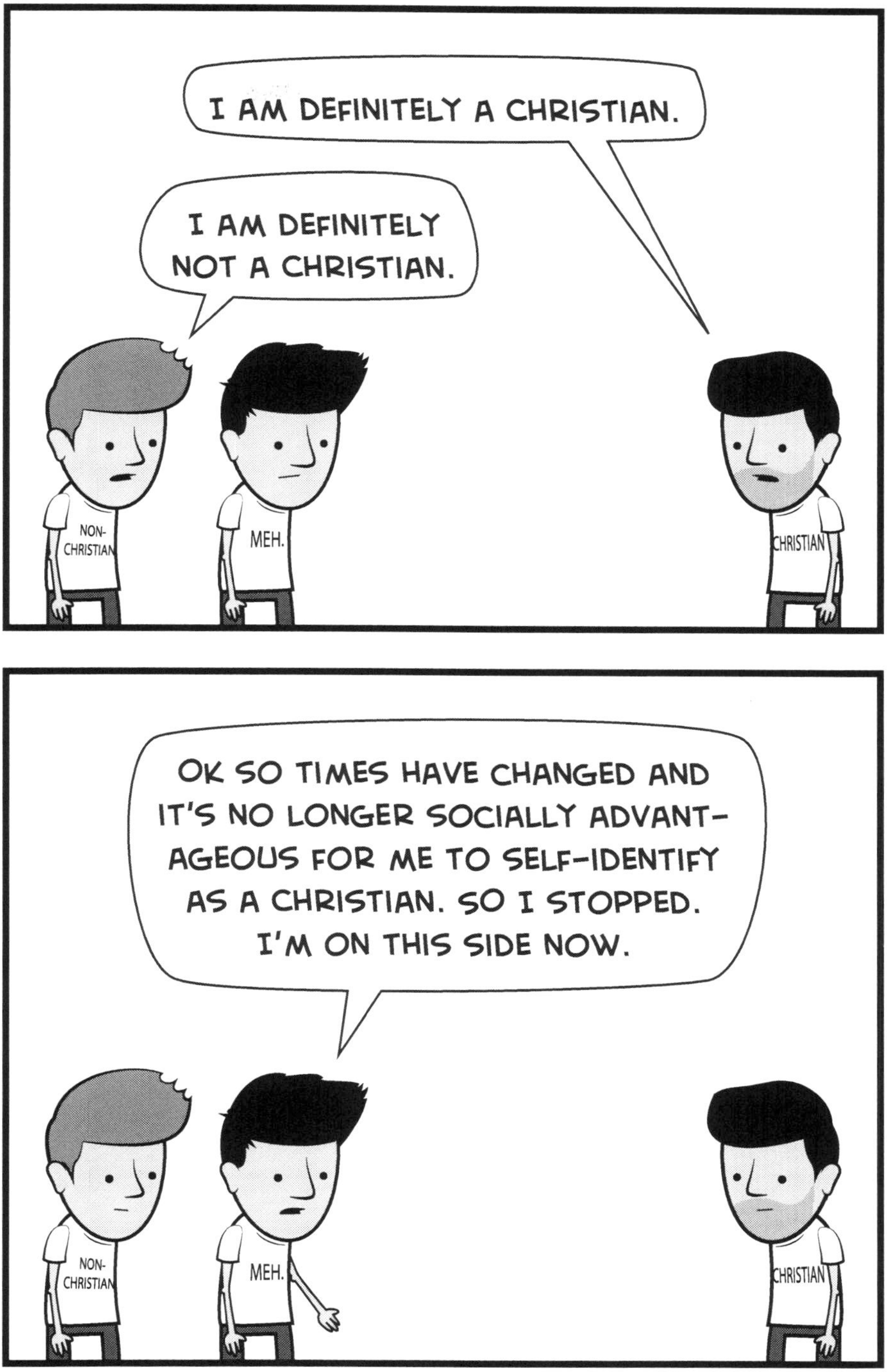
I AM DEFINITELY A CHRISTIAN.
I AM DEFINITELY NOT A CHRISTIAN.
NON-CHRISTIAN
MEH.
CHRISTIAN
OK SO TIMES HAVE CHANGED AND IT'S NO LONGER SOCIALLY ADVANTAGEOUS FOR ME TO SELF-IDENTIFY AS A CHRISTIAN. SO I STOPPED. I'M ON THIS SIDE NOW.
NON-CHRISTIAN
MEH.
CHRISTIAN

WHAT THE HEADLINES SAY

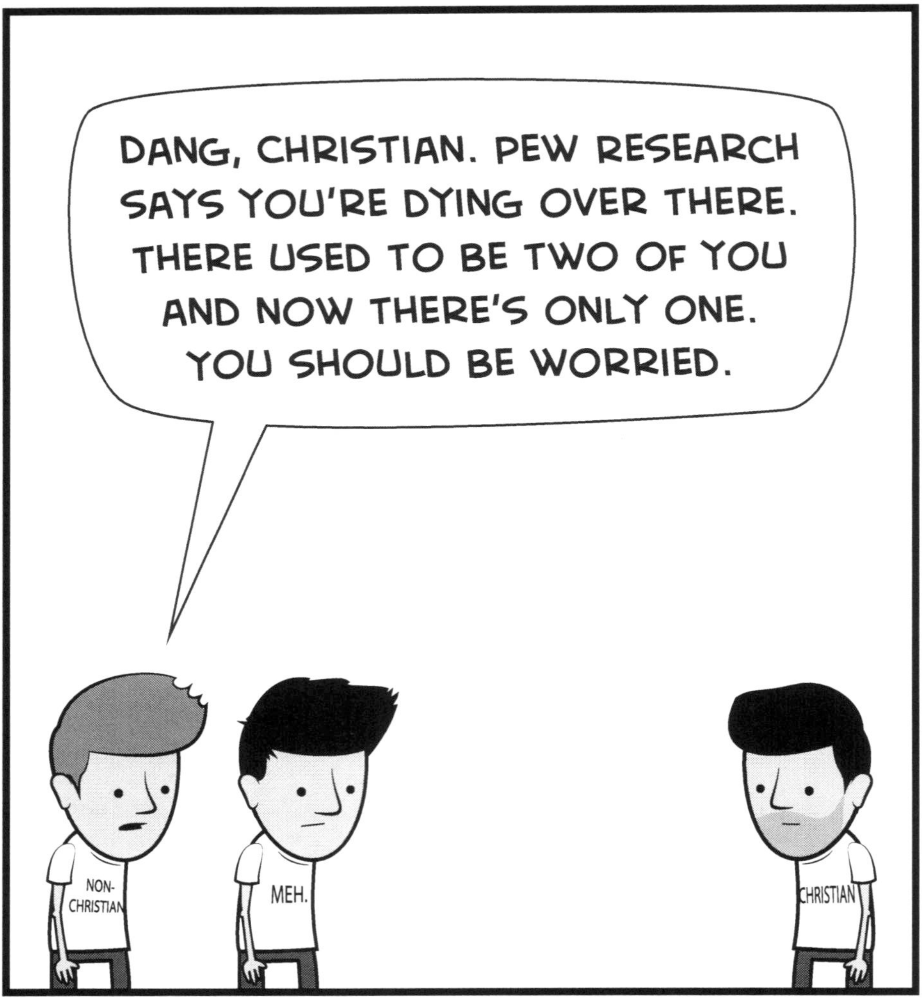
DANG, CHRISTIAN. PEW RESEARCH SAYS YOU'RE DYING OVER THERE. THERE USED TO BE TWO OF YOU AND NOW THERE'S ONLY ONE. YOU SHOULD BE WORRIED.
NON-CHRISTIAN
MEH.
CHRISTIAN

WHAT THE TRUTH IS

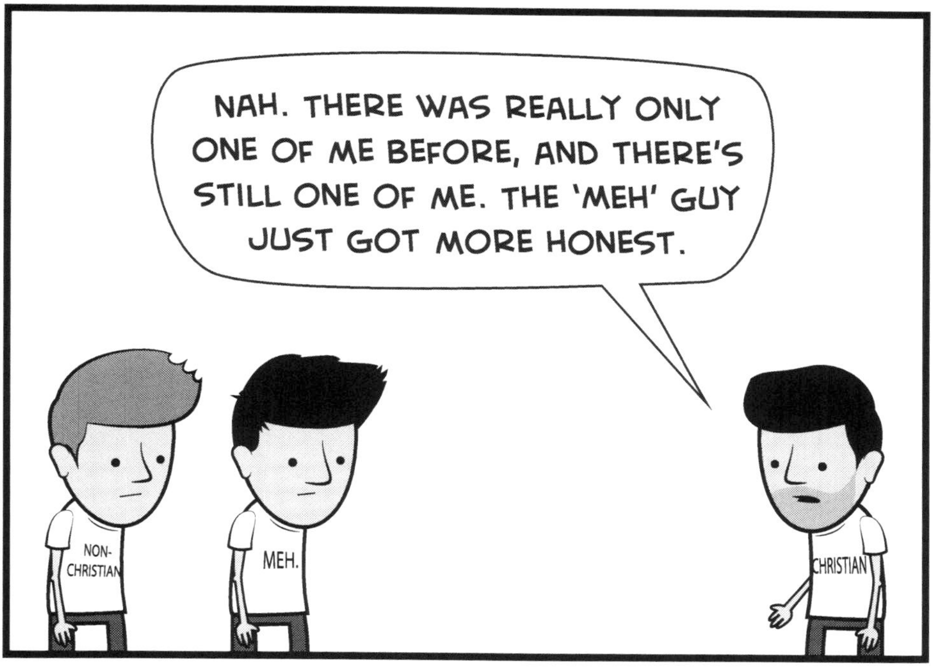
NAH. THERE WAS REALLY ONLY ONE OF ME BEFORE, AND THERE'S STILL ONE OF ME. THE 'MEH' GUY JUST GOT MORE HONEST.
NON-CHRISTIAN
MEH.
CHRISTIAN

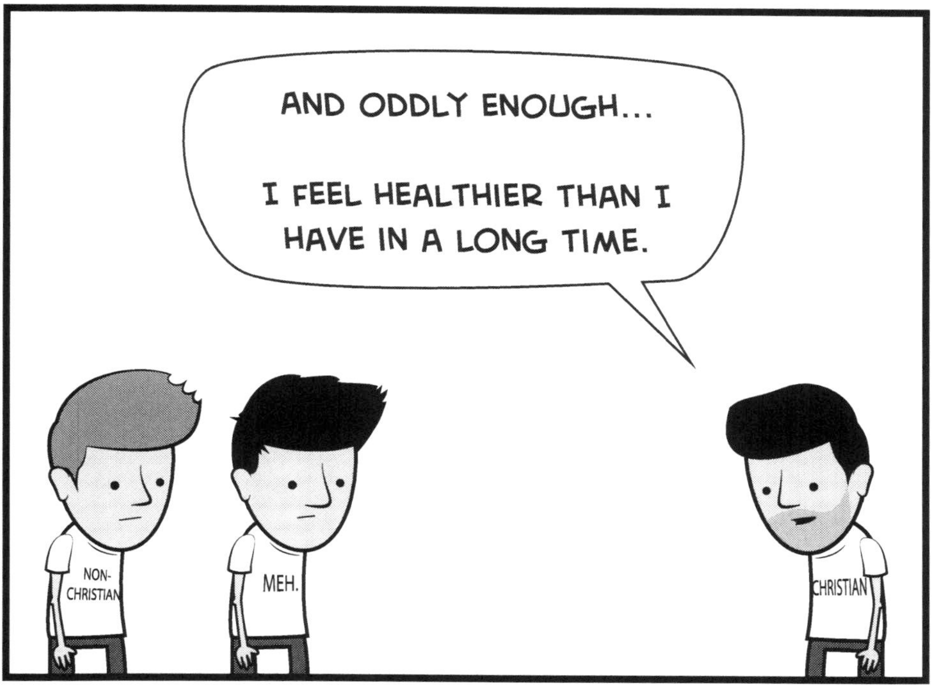
AND ODDLY ENOUGH...
I FEEL HEALTHIER THAN I HAVE IN A LONG TIME.
NON-CHRISTIAN
MEH.
CHRISTIAN

Because of whom?

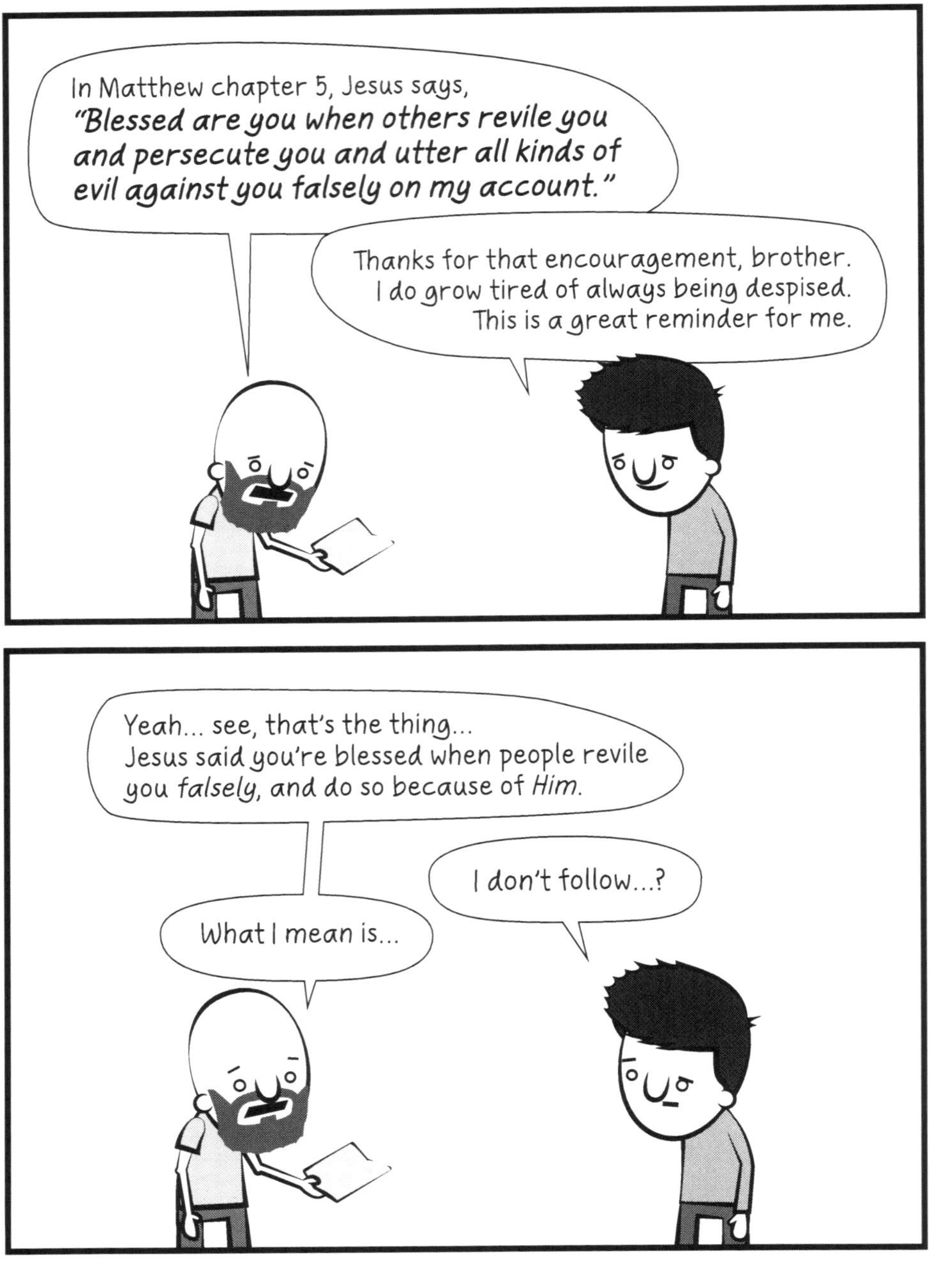
In Matthew chapter 5, Jesus says, *"Blessed are you when others revile you and persecute you and utter all kinds of evil against you falsely on my account."*
Thanks for that encouragement, brother. I do grow tired of always being despised. This is a great reminder for me.
Yeah... see, that's the thing... Jesus said you're blessed when people revile you *falsely*, and do so because of *Him*.
I don't follow...?
What I mean is...

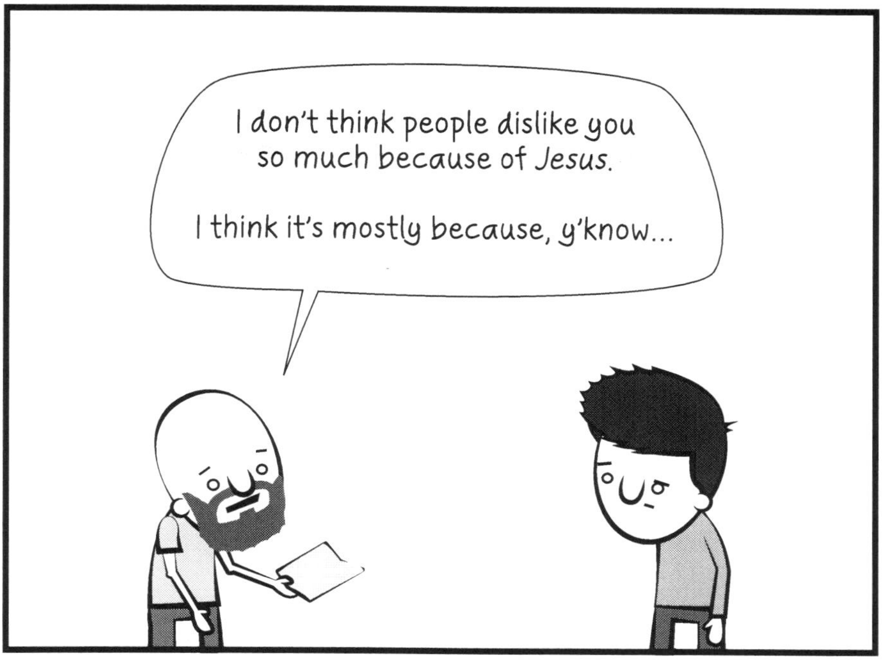
I don't think people dislike you so much because of *Jesus*.
I think it's mostly because, y'know...

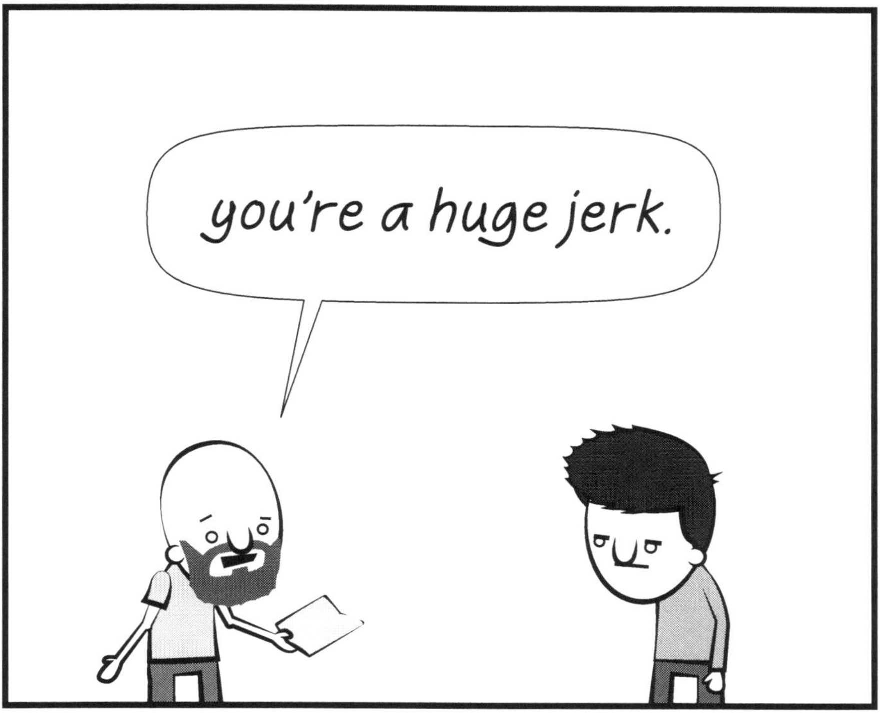
you're a huge jerk.

Please don't be intolerant

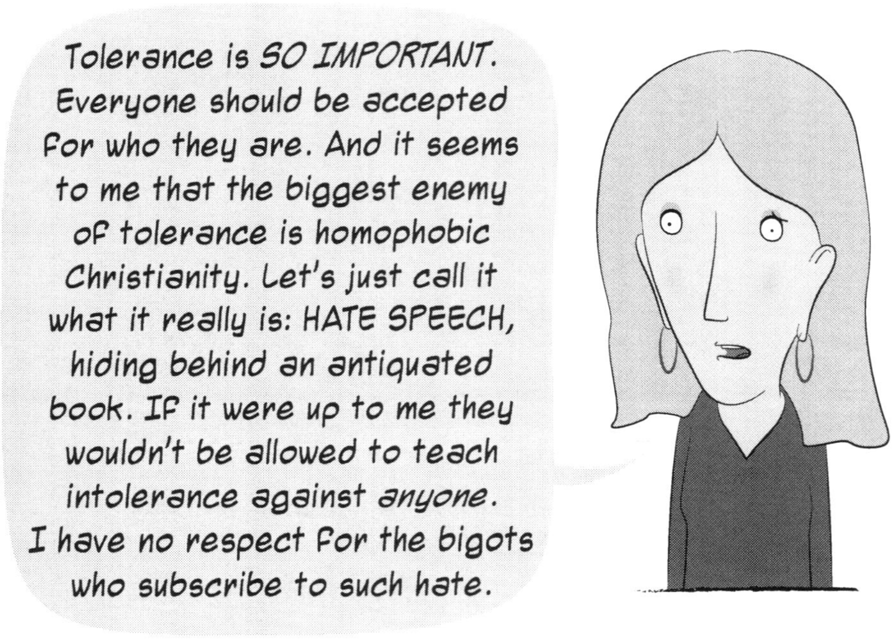
Tolerance is *SO IMPORTANT*. Everyone should be accepted for who they are. And it seems to me that the biggest enemy of tolerance is homophobic Christianity. Let's just call it what it really is: HATE SPEECH, hiding behind an antiquated book. If it were up to me they wouldn't be allowed to teach intolerance against *anyone*. I have no respect for the bigots who subscribe to such hate.

WHICH IS SHE?

- ☐ TOLERANT
- ☐ INTOLERANT

(CHECK ONE. JUST, LIKE, IN YOUR HEAD.)

I am a Christian and I think homosexuality is a SIN. I believe this because the Bible says so and the Bible is God's word. I love gay people but I ALWAYS vote pro-traditional-marriage and I am NOT shy about trying to convince my gay friends to repent of their sin and give their lives to JESUS.

WHAT ABOUT HER?

☐ TOLERANT
☐ INTOLERANT

LET US CONSULT A DEFINITION OR THREE.

OXFORD DICTIONARIES DEFINES 'TOLERANCE' AS:

> The ability or willingness to tolerate something, in particular the existence of opinions or behavior that one does not necessarily agree with.

SINCE 'TOLERATE' IS AN OPERATIVE WORD IN THE DEFINITION, LET'S HAVE OXFORD'S DEFINITION OF IT AS WELL:

> To allow the existence, occurrence, or practice of (something that one does not necessarily like or agree with) without interference.

SO AS YOU MIGHT EXPECT, THE DEFINITION OF 'TOLERANT' IS A COMBINATION OF THOSE TWO:

> Showing willingness to allow the existence of opinions or behavior that one does not necessarily agree with.

STRAIGHTFORWARD ENOUGH, METHINKS.

BACK TO THIS LADY, THEN.

DESPITE BEING MANY PEOPLE'S MENTAL IMAGE OF A "TOLERANCE WARRIOR," SHE ACTUALLY FAILS THE TOLERANCE TEST. READ THE DEFINITIONS AGAIN.

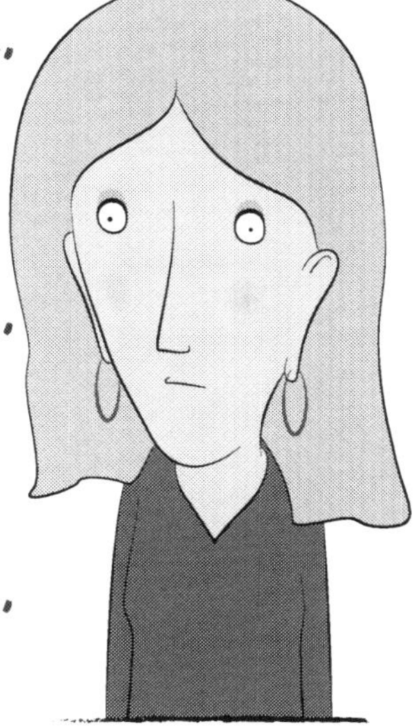

IN THE NAME OF "TOLERANCE," SHE IS **NOT** WILLING TO TOLERATE RELIGIONS SHE DISAGREES WITH.

IN THE NAME OF "TOLERANCE," SHE **WOULD** INTERFERE IN PEOPLE'S ABILITY TO PRACTICE THEIR RELIGION.

IN THE NAME OF "TOLERANCE," SHE **DISLIKES** CHRISTIAN PEOPLE BECAUSE OF THEIR LIFESTYLE CHOICES AND FLINGS INSULTS AND ACCUSATIONS AT THEM.

SHE CALLS HERSELF "TOLERANT," BUT CALLING YOURSELF A THING DOES NOT AUTOMATICALLY MAKE YOU THAT THING.

SHE MISUSES THE WORD "TOLERANCE," IN ORDER TO BE, IRONICALLY ENOUGH,

INTOLERANT.

AND NOW THIS LADY, WHO MANY PEOPLE WOULD SEE AS A STANDARD INTOLERANT, BIGOTED, HOMOPHOBIC CHRISTIAN.

BUT SHE DOESN'T THINK PEOPLE SHOULD NOT BE ALLOWED TO BE GAY.

SHE THINKS HER RELIGION IS TRUE AND WANTS TO CONVINCE PEOPLE OF THAT.

SHE DOESN'T HATE THE PEOPLE WITH WHOM SHE DISAGREES. IN FACT, SHE SAID SHE HAS FRIENDS WHO ARE GAY, AND SHE HAS DISCUSSIONS WITH THEM ABOUT HOMOSEXUALITY AND RELIGION AND SUCH.

GO BACK TO THE DEFINITIONS. THIS LADY TOLERATES THE PEOPLE WITH WHOM SHE DISAGREES. THEREFORE, SHE IS

TOLERANT.

THE REASON MANY OF YOU ARE SHAKING YOUR HEADS IS BECAUSE YOU ALWAYS HEAR THAT BIBLICAL CHRISTIANITY IS INHERENTLY INTOLERANT AND THAT CHRISTIANS ARE BIGOTED AND HATEFUL.

THIS IS NOT TRUE.

THE MOST LOVING PEOPLE I KNOW ARE BIBLICAL CHRISTIANS AND THEY WOULD GIVE ANYONE (STRAIGHT, GAY, TRANS, BI, OLD, YOUNG, BLACK, WHITE, CHARTREUSE, HUMAN, ALIEN) THE SHIRT RIGHT OFF THEIR BACK IF NECESSARY.

THEY WOULD DO THIS BECAUSE THEY ARE CHRISTIANS WHO TAKE THE BIBLE VERY SERIOUSLY.

AND SINCE THEY TAKE THE BIBLE VERY SERIOUSLY, THEY WOULD ALSO BE OPPOSED TO THINGS LIKE GAY MARRIAGE, OR PEOPLE WHO HAVE PENISES BEING USHERED INTO WOMEN'S BATH- ROOMS, HOWEVER THEY MIGHT SELF- IDENTIFY. THIS DOES NOT MAKE THEM BIGOTS.

Yes it DOES because that's HOMOPHOBIC & TRANSPHOBIC!

NO. IT. ISN'T.

MOST CHRISTIANS ARE NOT HOMOPHOBIC OR TRANSPHOBIC. THEY ARE NOT "HATEFUL OR FEARFUL OF HOMOSEXUALS OR TRANSSEXUALS."

THEY JUST DISAGREE WITH THEM.

SURE, THERE ARE SOME PEOPLE WHO CALL THEMSELVES CHRISTIANS AND REALLY DO FEAR AND/OR HATE GAY AND/OR TRANS PEOPLE.

BUT I HAVE PLENTY OF CHRISTIAN FRIENDS AND I KNOW EXACTLY ZERO WHO WOULD FIT THIS DESCRIPTION.

AND IF I DISCOVERED THAT ONE OF MY FRIENDS WAS INDEED ACTIVELY HATEFUL TOWARD GAY OR TRANS PEOPLE, I WOULD PROBABLY INVITE THEM TO PANERA FOR A COFFEE AND CHOCOLATE-CHIP MUFFIN...

AND REBUKE THEM.

THE FACT THAT WORDS LIKE "BIGOTED, HOMOPHOBIC, HATEFUL, INTOLERANT" ETC. HAVE REAL AND ACTUAL MEANINGS HAS NOT STOPPED PEOPLE FROM HI-JACKING AND USING THEM TO MEAN NOTHING MORE THAN "ANY CHRISTIAN WHO DISAGREES WITH MY SUPER-PROGRESSIVE SELF."

PEOPLE CALL CHRISTIANS "BIGOTS" IN ORDER TO **SILENCE** THEM AND SAY THAT THEY **DON'T MATTER.**

IT'S NOT A LEGITIMATE INDICTMENT BASED ON REALITY, IT'S A GUERRILLA TACTIC; AN AD HOMINEM ATTACK MEANT TO WIN A DEBATE.

BECAUSE AS LONG AS THEY CAN BRAND THEIR OPPONENT WITH THE SCARLET B...

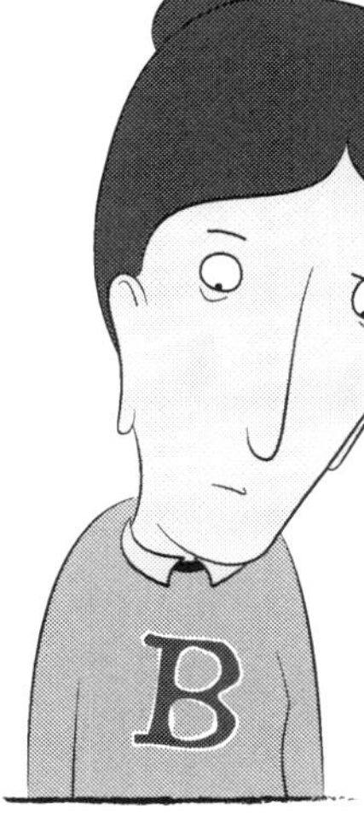
B

NOTHING THEY SAY MATTERS.

I GLADLY AFFIRM THAT EVERYONE SHOULD BE TOLERANT.

BUT BY THAT I MEAN THE REAL, ACTUAL KIND OF TOLERANCE.

NOT THE KIND THAT HAS BECOME SO RAMPANT TODAY:

Everyone should be TOLERANT and by that I mean they should AGREE WITH EVERY- THING I SAY IS THAT CLEAR NOD YOUR HEAD VIGOROUSLY DO IT NOW

DISAGREEMENT IS NOT INTOLERANCE.

ON THE CONTRARY: TO BE TOLERANT TOWARD SOMEONE *ASSUMES* YOU ARE DISAGREEING WITH THEM. OTHERWISE YOU WOULDN'T BE TOLERATING . . . YOU'D BE AGREEING.

TOLERANCE SAYS, "WE HOLD DIFFERENT OPINIONS, EVEN ON VERY IMPORTANT MATTERS, AND WE AREN'T AFRAID TO SPEAK OR ACT OR -GASP- EVEN *VOTE* BASED ON OUR BELIEFS, BUT FOR THE LOVE OF COFFEE AND CHOCOLATE-CHIP MUFFINS, WE CAN STILL MEET AND DISCUSS OUR DIFFERENCES WITHOUT VILIFYING EACH OTHER."

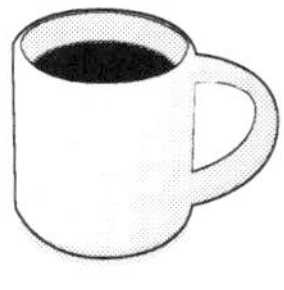

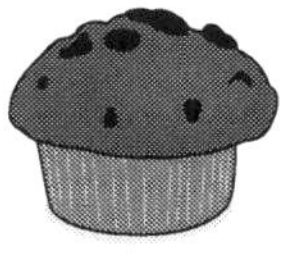

BUT IF, INSTEAD OF *TOLERATING* THE PEOPLE WITH WHOM YOU DISAGREE, YOU DISMISS THEIR LEGITIMACY BY DISHONESTLY BRANDING THEM AS BIGOTS, HATE-MONGERS, AND HOMOPHOBES, YOU ARE, IN FACT, BEING

INTOLERANT.

PLEASE DON'T BE INTOLERANT.

Homophobia

HOMOPHOBIA
I'm afraid of gay people because I know I'll get a disease if one gets close to me.
HOMOPHOBIA
I hate gay people. Hate 'em! They are the scum of the earth!
HOMOPHOBIA
I call gay people bad names and sometimes punch them cuz they're disgusting.
NOT HOMOPHOBIA
I am a Christian. I believe homosexuality is sinful because the Bible says it is.

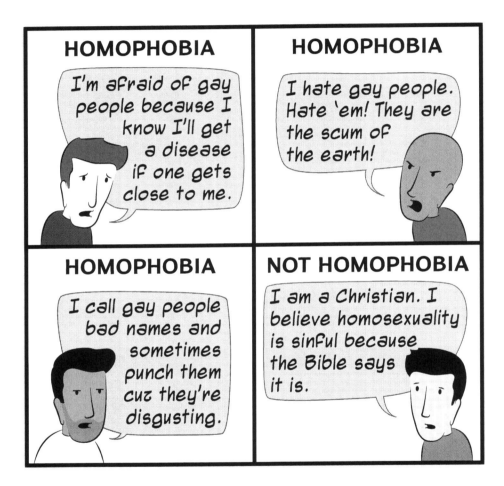

FUN FACT: I placed this comic directly after the *Please don't be intolerant* comic in this book for a reason: this was the exact order I published them online, and when I published THIS one, *Facebook took it down*. In the name of tolerance, of course.

Let your brain marinate in that glorious irony for a few seconds.

I'm too bad to become a Christian

> I'm too bad to become a Christian.
> I've done some terrible things.

If you've ever said that,
let me tell you about 2 guys I know.

They're both Christians now, but were not
converted until they were adults.

Before they met Jesus, they were...pretty bad.

Guy #1

The first guy I know used to be the biggest jerk on the planet. Full of himself. Chip on his shoulder. The type of guy who'd rather punch a homeless guy than give him a dollar. Just a mean individual.

He enjoyed conflict, got in fights, was always drunk, always stoned, woke up every morning and smoked bowls of high-grade weed, a hobby he maintained by selling said weed by the ounce. This guy smoked more dope every day than most people *see* in their lifetime.

He was arrested twice for MIP (minor in possession of alcohol) by age 19, the second offense affording him months of donning bright orange and picking up trash on the side of the road with a van-full of other criminals.

Lots of illegal substances. Lots of partying. Lots of sex. Lots of malice. Lots of hate. True story.

Then he met Jesus and his entire life changed.

To this day he is a committed Christian.

You may be thinking,

"Wow, that dude was pretty bad."

Yes he was. But God stepped in.
God saved him. Jesus changed his life.

Or you might be thinking,

"That guy wasn't all *that* bad.
I've done stuff like that."

To you I present the *other* guy I know. ⟶

Guy #2

This other guy I know has an amazing story. He actually used to be a local religious leader in the Middle East. And he hated Christians. Like, *hated*.

Where he used to live, Christians were a minority religious group. This guy would actually lead groups of men to go door-to-door searching for Christians. They would drag them out of their homes, imprison them, *sometimes even publicly execute them* in the name of their religion. Islamic-State-style, before Islamic State existed. True story.

I don't know if he actually murdered anyone with his own hands, and I can't really ask him that. I do know, at the very least, he ordered others to do it.

Would you believe God could save a guy like this?
Was this guy too bad to become a Christian?

Well, in the midst of his violence, he met Jesus. God saved him. Changed him from the inside out. Years later this man became one of the first people to teach me all about Jesus. True story.

This guy went from *killing* Christians to telling everyone who would listen about Jesus Christ.

You may be bad, but you're not as bad as Guy #2 was.

You are *not* too far gone to be outside the reach of God's grace.

Ay u need some trees?
Then why r u lookin at me?

(LOL @ old me)

If God can save Guy #1,
he can save you.

Guy #1 is me.

God saved me, changed me,
and here I am following Jesus.

Pardon me, but I smell Jesus-
loving scum in this house.

(Old Saul prob woulda
been on Vice News)

If God can save Guy #2,
he can definitely save you.

Guy #2 is Paul.

As in, the *Apostle* Paul; my hero.
God saved him, turned him into the
greatest missionary ever, and used him
to write 1/3 of the New Testament.

It doesn't matter how bad you are,
God can save you.

It doesn't matter how far gone *anyone* is
they are not too far gone
for God to save.

Jesus came for people like us.

Keep fighting

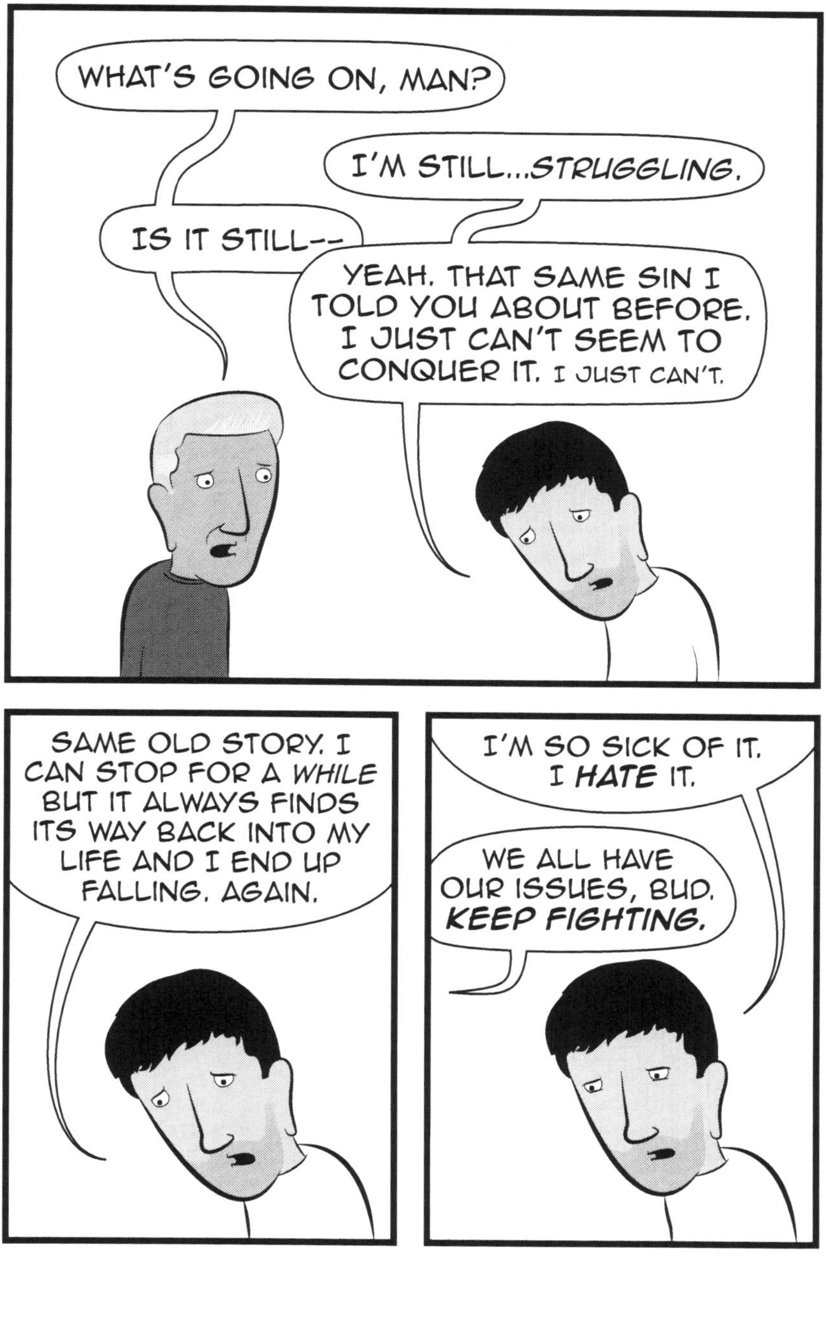
WHAT'S GOING ON, MAN?
I'M STILL...*STRUGGLING.*
IS IT STILL--
YEAH. THAT SAME SIN I TOLD YOU ABOUT BEFORE. I JUST CAN'T SEEM TO CONQUER IT. I JUST CAN'T.
SAME OLD STORY. I CAN STOP FOR A *WHILE* BUT IT ALWAYS FINDS ITS WAY BACK INTO MY LIFE AND I END UP FALLING. AGAIN.
I'M SO SICK OF IT. I ***HATE*** IT.
WE ALL HAVE OUR ISSUES, BUD. ***KEEP FIGHTING.***

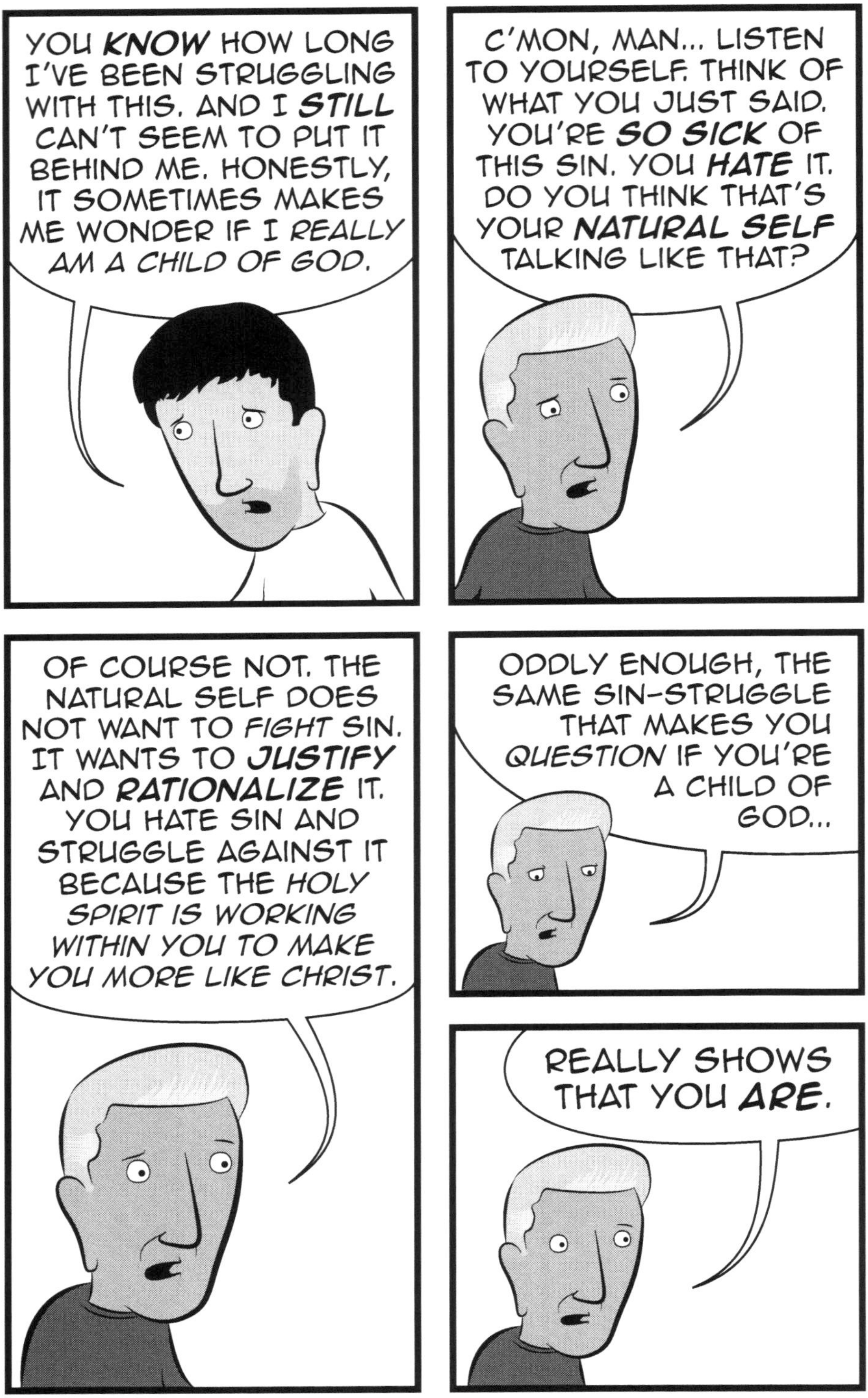
YOU KNOW HOW LONG I'VE BEEN STRUGGLING WITH THIS. AND I STILL CAN'T SEEM TO PUT IT BEHIND ME. HONESTLY, IT SOMETIMES MAKES ME WONDER IF I REALLY AM A CHILD OF GOD.
C'MON, MAN... LISTEN TO YOURSELF. THINK OF WHAT YOU JUST SAID. YOU'RE SO SICK OF THIS SIN. YOU HATE IT. DO YOU THINK THAT'S YOUR NATURAL SELF TALKING LIKE THAT?
OF COURSE NOT. THE NATURAL SELF DOES NOT WANT TO FIGHT SIN. IT WANTS TO JUSTIFY AND RATIONALIZE IT. YOU HATE SIN AND STRUGGLE AGAINST IT BECAUSE THE HOLY SPIRIT IS WORKING WITHIN YOU TO MAKE YOU MORE LIKE CHRIST.
ODDLY ENOUGH, THE SAME SIN-STRUGGLE THAT MAKES YOU QUESTION IF YOU'RE A CHILD OF GOD...
REALLY SHOWS THAT YOU ARE.

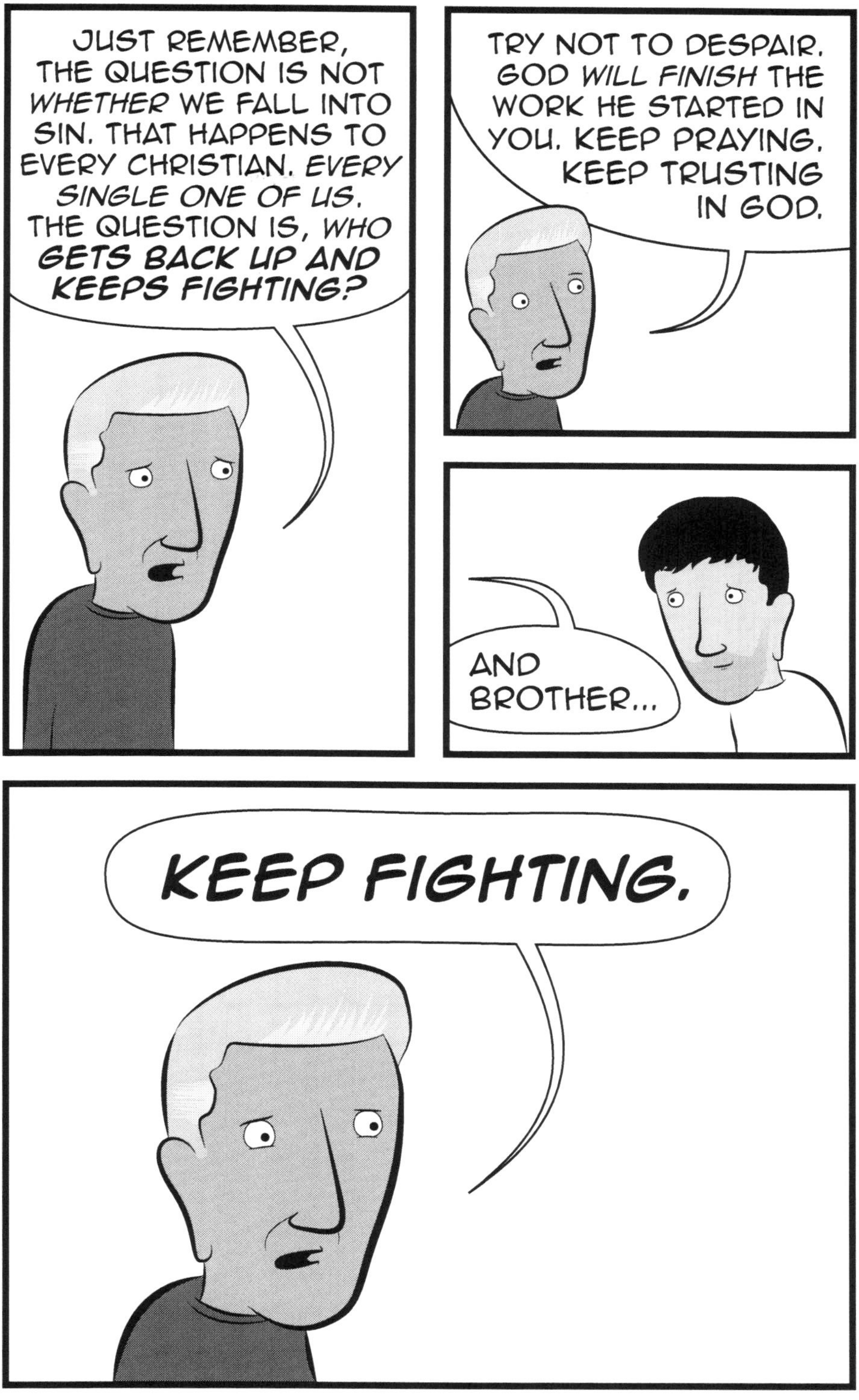
JUST REMEMBER, THE QUESTION IS NOT *WHETHER* WE FALL INTO SIN. THAT HAPPENS TO EVERY CHRISTIAN. *EVERY SINGLE ONE OF US.* THE QUESTION IS, *WHO* ***GETS BACK UP AND KEEPS FIGHTING?***
TRY NOT TO DESPAIR. GOD *WILL FINISH* THE WORK HE STARTED IN YOU. KEEP PRAYING. KEEP TRUSTING IN GOD.
AND BROTHER...
KEEP FIGHTING.

Let's talk about Moralistic Therapeutic Deism

I did not grow up in a Christian family.

My whole life changed when I was converted about 10 years ago. Every day became a new adventure as I saw everything and everyone through the new lenses I was wearing. As I studied and learned more and more, many things surprised me, but perhaps nothing caught me more off-guard than a strange phenomenon I observed among "church folks." At the time I didn't know what to call it, but since then a couple of researchers have identified and named it:

Moralistic Therapeutic Deism.

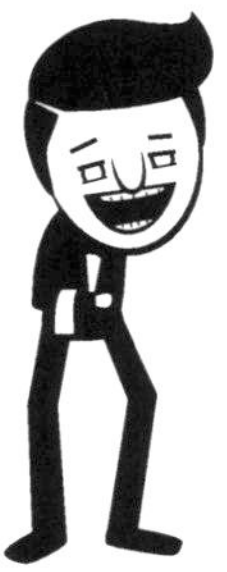

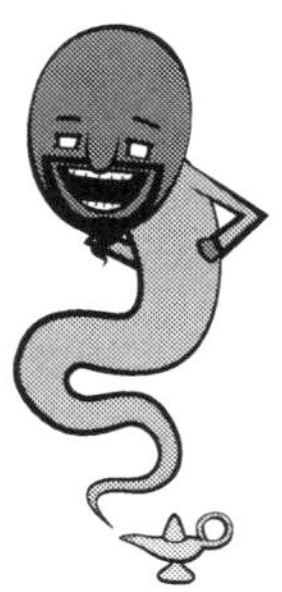

"What the heck is that?" you ask.

It happens to be a preferred religion of Western culture, which usually (and tragically) goes by the name *Christianity*.

Sociologists Christian Smith and Melinda Lundquist Denton published a book in 2005 to summarize the findings of the *National Study of Youth and Religion* research project, for which thousands of teenagers were interviewed regarding their religious beliefs.

The crazy results of the study were pretty similar to the confusing things I was noticing as an outsider coming into church culture for the first time while also studying the Bible and the historic faith. As the authors state it:

"A significant part of Christianity in the United States is actually only tenuously Christian in any sense that is seriously connected to the actual historical Christian tradition, but has rather substantially morphed into Christianity's misbegotten stepcousin, Christian Moralistic Therapeutic Deism."

So what is this *MTD* so many people believe in?
Its beliefs can be summarized by...

The Five Points of Moralistic Therapeutic Deism:

→ A god exists who created and ordered the world and watches over human life on earth.

→ God wants people to be good, nice, and fair to each other, as taught in the Bible and by most world religions.

→ The central goal of life is to be happy and to feel good about oneself.

→ God does not need to be particularly involved in one's life except when God is needed to resolve a problem.

→ Good people go to heaven when they die.

Why is it called *Moralistic Therapeutic Deism?*

> → ***Moralistic:*** We should be good, moral people. Not born-again followers of Jesus Christ – just, you know, "Good people."
>
> → ***Therapeutic:*** The goal of this religion is to provide therapeutic benefits to its adherents. Not to worship, adore, and obey the living God. God wants us to feel good about ourselves and have high self-esteem.
>
> → ***Deism:*** God exists and created the world, but then kinda just leaves us alone unless we need him to fix a problem or provide us with something.

This is the religion of many people who call themselves Christians.

The god of this religion is passionately focused on serving us while making us feel really good about ourselves. He'll mind his own business until we need something, and then he will spring into action. It's not about him; he requires nothing of us. It's all about us. He is at our beck and call.

He's like a toady butler

or a fawning genie.

Put those two guys together and you get

the god of Moralistic Therapeutic Deism:

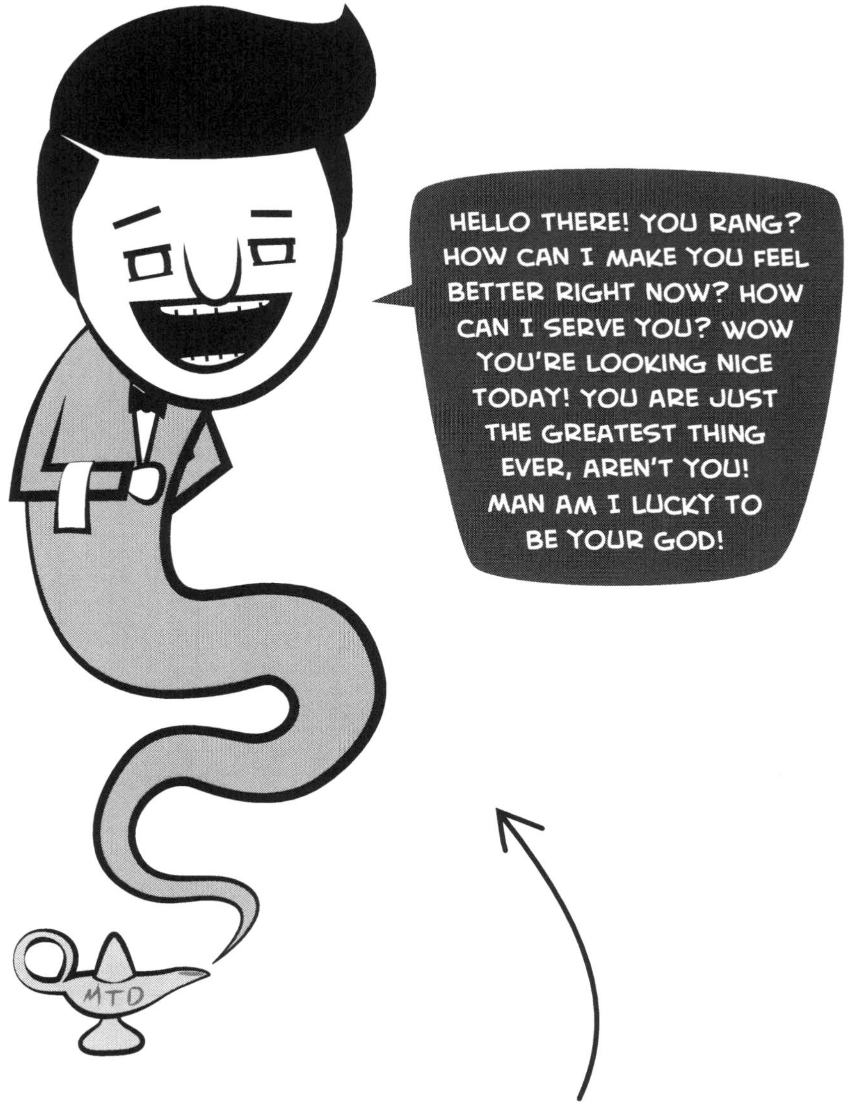
HELLO THERE! YOU RANG? HOW CAN I MAKE YOU FEEL BETTER RIGHT NOW? HOW CAN I SERVE YOU? WOW YOU'RE LOOKING NICE TODAY! YOU ARE JUST THE GREATEST THING EVER, AREN'T YOU! MAN AM I LUCKY TO BE YOUR GOD!
MTD

This is the god of many people who call themselves Christians.

Why is all of this so tragic? Because MTD is not Christianity. It's not even a *version* of Christianity.

Moralistic Therapeutic Deism is a false religion created by and for members of the most rich, catered, defensive, politically-correct, over-protected, over-nurtured, over-fed society the world has ever known, and the fact that it uses the name *Jesus* and various select Christian buzzwords allows it to be passed off as Christianity.

It has nothing to do with biblical Christianity. It's not in the Bible. Jesus didn't teach it. Paul wouldn't recognize it.

And yet it calls itself *Christianity* and it's taught every Sunday by pastors in church buildings all over the place.

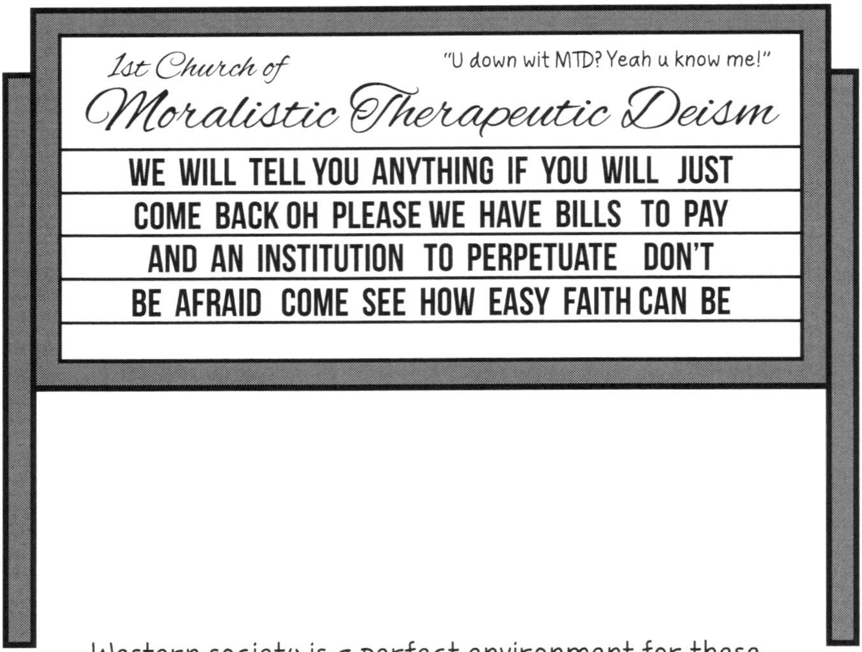
1st Church of
"U down wit MTD? Yeah u know me!"
Moralistic Therapeutic Deism
WE WILL TELL YOU ANYTHING IF YOU WILL JUST
COME BACK OH PLEASE WE HAVE BILLS TO PAY
AND AN INSTITUTION TO PERPETUATE DON'T
BE AFRAID COME SEE HOW EASY FAITH CAN BE

Western society is a perfect environment for these "me-centered" teachings to flourish.

Add to that parents (especially fathers) and churches who fail to teach the truth (especially the harder truths) to the people entrusted to them...

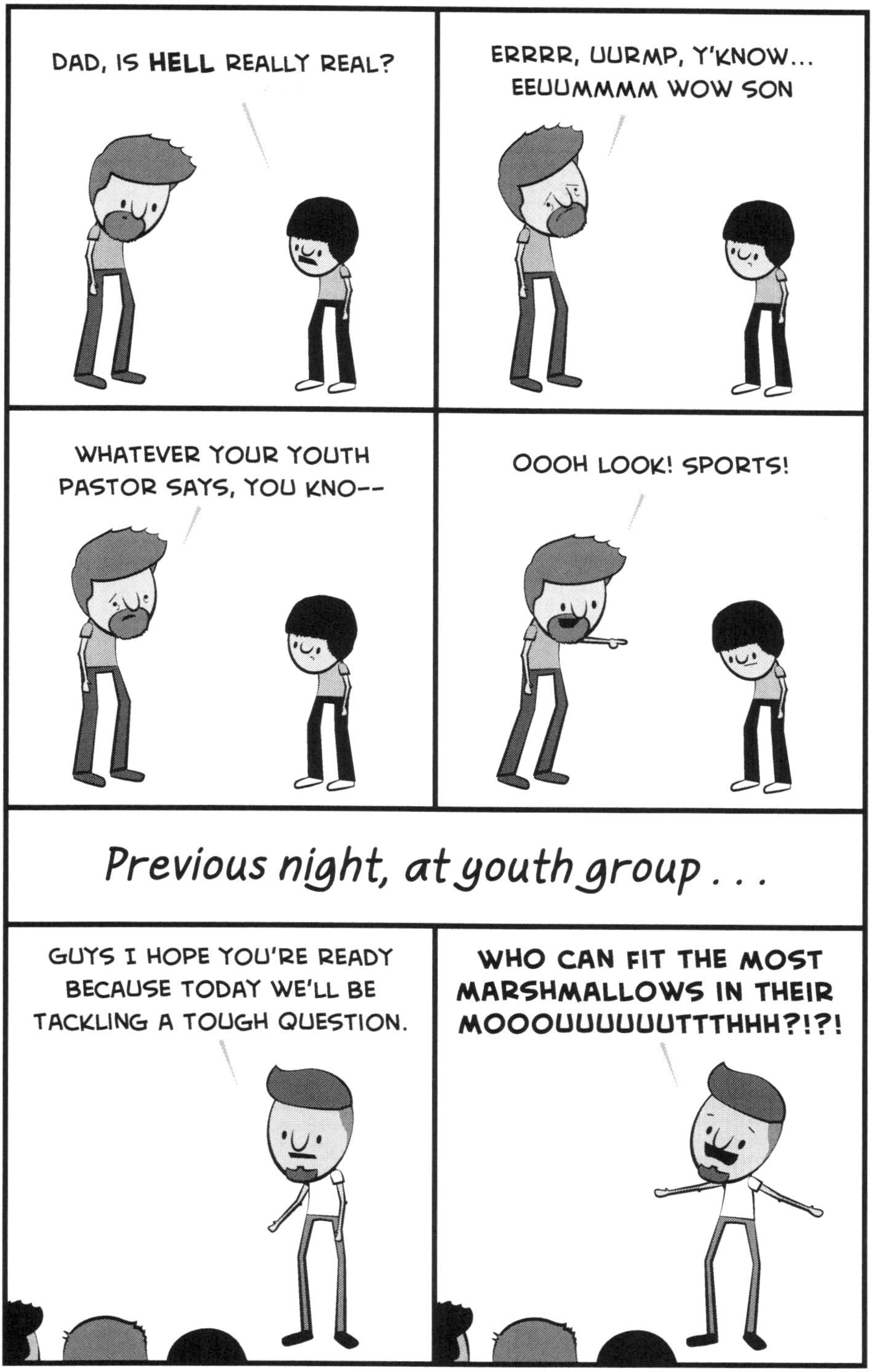
DAD, IS **HELL** REALLY REAL?
ERRRR, UURMP, Y'KNOW... EEUUMMMM WOW SON
WHATEVER YOUR YOUTH PASTOR SAYS, YOU KNO--
OOOH LOOK! SPORTS!
Previous night, at youth group . . .
GUYS I HOPE YOU'RE READY BECAUSE TODAY WE'LL BE TACKLING A TOUGH QUESTION.
WHO CAN FIT THE MOST MARSHMALLOWS IN THEIR MOOOUUUUUUTTTHHH?!?!

...and you've got an epidemic.

And that's exactly what
we have in the West.
An MTD epidemic.

Be honest with yourself.

How many people do you know who check "Christian" yet live as practical Moralistic Therapeutic Deists? Who think God wants them to have everything they want? Who minimize and justify sin – maybe not the sins of others, but the ones *they* like, for sure? Who clearly do not live biblically but would offer a quick, "Judge not!" were someone to question them about that fact? Who can't explain even the most basic biblical theology so many saints have died for in the history of the faith? Who think the extent of following Jesus is to say a prayer one time, "inviting Him into their heart"? Who only call on God when they have a problem or need something? Who assume that because their parents are Christians, or because they grew up in the Bible Belt, or because they pray before meals or attend a church service every now and then, that somehow these things make them Christians, no matter how else they live or what else they believe?

Be honest with yourself.

How many people do you know who subscribe to this fake, watered-down, imposter of a religion?

Be honest with yourself.

Do you?

Abortion logic

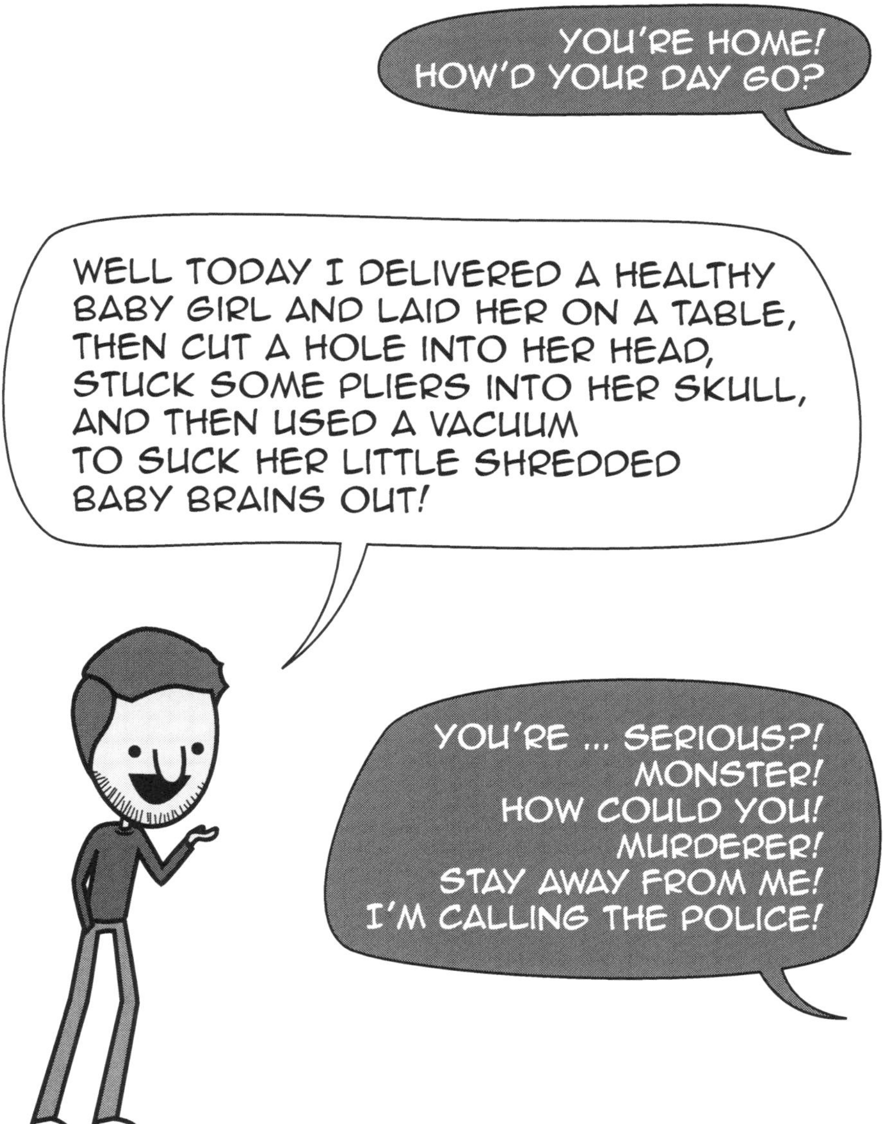
YOU'RE HOME! HOW'D YOUR DAY GO?
WELL TODAY I DELIVERED A HEALTHY BABY GIRL AND LAID HER ON A TABLE, THEN CUT A HOLE INTO HER HEAD, STUCK SOME PLIERS INTO HER SKULL, AND THEN USED A VACUUM TO SUCK HER LITTLE SHREDDED BABY BRAINS OUT!
YOU'RE ... SERIOUS?! MONSTER! HOW COULD YOU! MURDERER! STAY AWAY FROM ME! I'M CALLING THE POLICE!

How religion works vs how the gospel works

HOW RELIGION WORKS

I have obeyed all the rules by knocking on 27 doors this week, giving exactly 9.703% out of this month's pay, praying while facing WNW at 6:17 AM, 12:53 PM, and 6:09 PM (PST) every single day, only eating animals slaughtered on Tuesdays by people named Henry, and punching myself in the face every time I think about how yummy ice cream is.

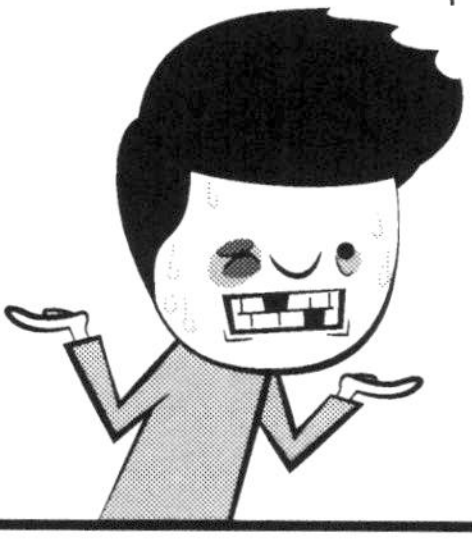

I believe I have obeyed enough for God to love and accept me.

At least I really hope I did enough :(

HOW THE GOSPEL WORKS

I suck :) I am utterly incapable of working my way into God's favor because I am sinful and rebellious to the deepest core of my being. Despite this fact, God loved me and sent Jesus to pay my penalty, so I can be found innocent of my rebellion, even though I didn't deserve His grace.

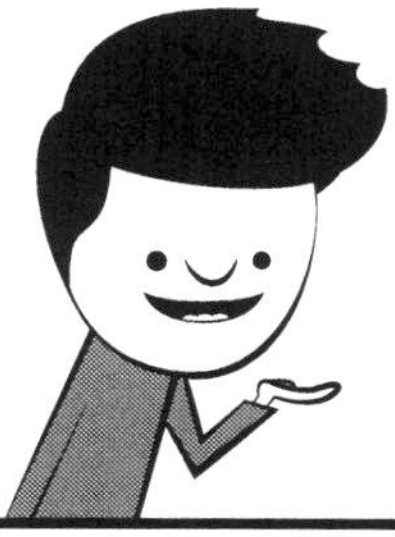

I know God loves and accepts me, so it's my pleasure to follow and obey Him.

Marriage equality

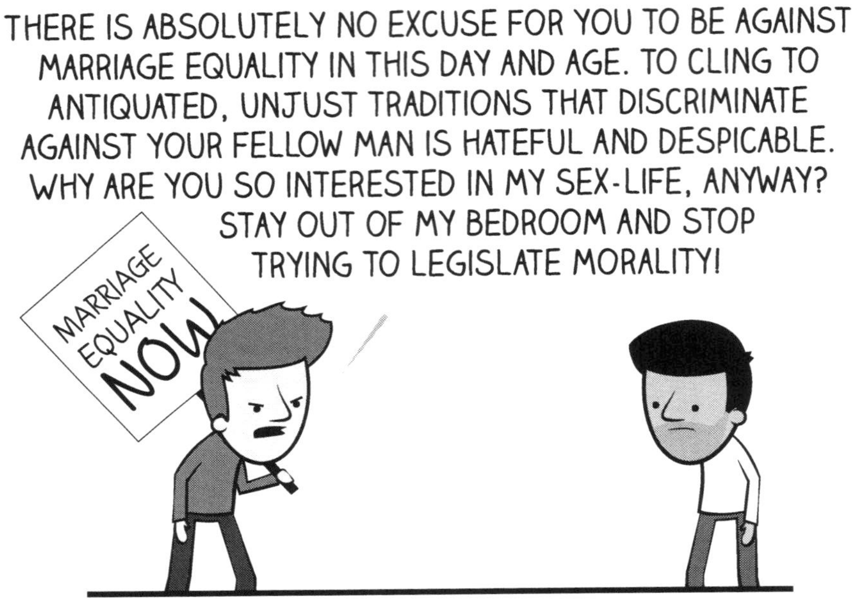
THERE IS ABSOLUTELY NO EXCUSE FOR YOU TO BE AGAINST MARRIAGE EQUALITY IN THIS DAY AND AGE. TO CLING TO ANTIQUATED, UNJUST TRADITIONS THAT DISCRIMINATE AGAINST YOUR FELLOW MAN IS HATEFUL AND DESPICABLE. WHY ARE YOU SO INTERESTED IN MY SEX-LIFE, ANYWAY? STAY OUT OF MY BEDROOM AND STOP TRYING TO LEGISLATE MORALITY!
MARRIAGE EQUALITY NOW

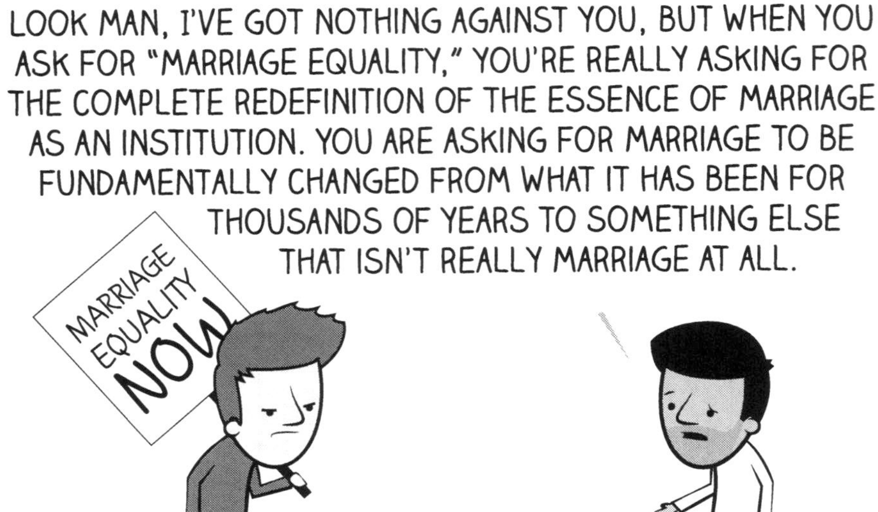
LOOK MAN, I'VE GOT NOTHING AGAINST YOU, BUT WHEN YOU ASK FOR "MARRIAGE EQUALITY," YOU'RE REALLY ASKING FOR THE COMPLETE REDEFINITION OF THE ESSENCE OF MARRIAGE AS AN INSTITUTION. YOU ARE ASKING FOR MARRIAGE TO BE FUNDAMENTALLY CHANGED FROM WHAT IT HAS BEEN FOR THOUSANDS OF YEARS TO SOMETHING ELSE THAT ISN'T REALLY MARRIAGE AT ALL.
MARRIAGE EQUALITY NOW

THE "THAT'S HOW IT'S ALWAYS BEEN" EXCUSE DOES NOT CUT IT ANYMORE! YOU CAN'T NAME ONE RATIONAL REASON WHY YOU SHOULD HAVE THE RIGHT TO MARRY WHO YOU LOVE BUT I SHOULD NOT HAVE THE SAME RIGHT. ALL YOU CAN SAY IS, "THAT'S HOW IT'S ALWAYS BEEN." WELL THE WORLD IS PROGRESSING AND YOU ARE TRYING TO DRAG IT BACKWARDS. YOU ARE JUST A BIGOT!

MARRIAGE EQUALITY NOW

THE GUY ON THE RIGHT IS GAY AND IN A SAME-SEX MARRIAGE.

THE GUY ON THE LEFT IS A POLYGAMIST.

THAT'S HOW YOU READ IT, RIGHT?

IF YOU MEET WITH A SYSTEM OF THEOLOGY
WHICH MAGNIFIES MAN,

FLEE FROM IT

I prophesy that you're ALL THAT!
Uh-just-uh-reach-out and-grab-it-uhhh. Uh-Gawd-uh-sez-uh you-can-have-it-uh.
Create the life you want! Claim your victory today!
I declare it's your time to break out and have your best life now! You can you will! Favor and Fridays!
Didn't get your way? It was the Devil!
FIYAH ON EVERY SINGLE ONE OF YA SINFUL DESIRES! FIYYAAAHHH!!!!

AS FAR AS YOU CAN!

-CHARLES SPURGEON, 1878

The Bible says we should only eat locusts

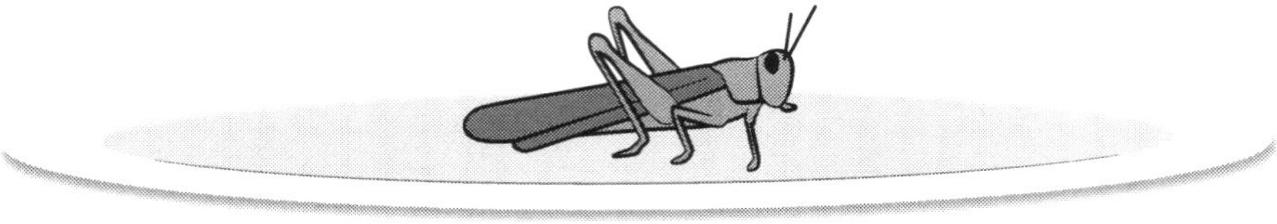

Don't believe me? Take a look:

> The insects you are permitted to eat include all kinds of locusts, bald locusts, crickets, and grasshoppers. –Lev 11:22 NLT

So in the Old Testament God listed four insects His people were allowed to eat.

Do you see which one is listed *twice*?

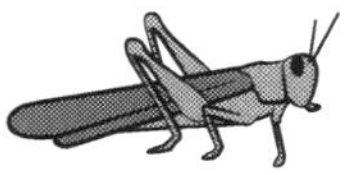 **Locusts.** 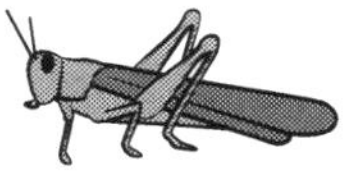

Why would God list locusts **twice** ...*unless He was specifically trying to communicate the great importance of eating locusts?*

You might be thinking:

But this is just outdated Old Testament stuff. Doesn't apply today!

Oh yeah?

Ever hear of a fellow in the New Testament called *John the Baptist?*

Want to guess what *he* ate?

Now John wore a garment of camel's hair and a leather belt around his waist, and his food was <u>locusts</u> and wild honey. —Matt 3:4

So here it's confirmed in the New Testament.

John the Baptist ate only locusts and honey.

Well maybe he was just a weirdo, you know??

Well, let's take a look at that...

What did people say about John the Baptist? Was he just some weirdo?

What did *Jesus* say about him?

I tell you the truth, of all who have ever lived, none is greater than John the Baptist.
—Jesus (Matt 11:11 NLT)

Well OK then!

But how about another one, just to make it crystal-clear?

> I tell you, of all who have ever lived, none is greater than John.
> —Jesus (Luke 7:28 NLT)

Jesus says John the Baptist, who only ate locusts (with honey for seasoning), is the greatest person to ever live.
Put all of this together:

1.) In the Old Testament God clearly highlights the importance of eating locusts.

2.) The New Testament clearly describes John the Baptist's locust-*only* diet.

3.) On more than one occasion Jesus clearly states the fact that John the Baptist is the greatest person to ever live, thus validating his locust-only diet.

It couldn't be any more clear...

The Bible says we should only eat locusts.

Eat me!
Try me with a lil honey

OK, come back to reality with me.

Here, I'll switch to Times New Roman to sober the mood a bit.

So what was the point of that ridiculous Case for a Locust-Only Diet? It was this:

You can make the Bible "say" anything.

You can make the Bible "say" anything – *as long as you're not concerned with what it actually says.*

I don't imagine you were convinced that the Bible really says we should only be eating locusts (obviously it doesn't).

But imagine for a second how much more inclined you would be to believe my justification for the Locust-Only Diet if you came upon it already hoping – like really, really hoping – that it were true.

Or what if I wrote a whole book on the subject? I could do that. What if you really, really wanted to believe that we should eat nothing but locusts and then I published a 224-page book "making that case from the Bible?"

Well, you might just believe me.

Would your desire for it to be true or my deceptive case for its truth make it true, even a little bit? Nope.

But if you want to believe we should only be eating locusts, *you can make that claim and "justify it" using the Bible, even though the Bible clearly does not say that.*

Do you see where I'm going with this?

If you want to believe sin is no big deal, *you can make that claim and "justify it" using the Bible, even though the Bible clearly says that it is.*

If you want to believe hell is not real, *you can make that claim and "justify it" using the Bible, even though the Bible clearly says that it is.*

If you want to believe homosexuality is not a sin, *you can make that claim and "justify it" using the Bible, even though the Bible clearly calls it a sin.*

If you want to believe abortion is OK with God, *you can make that claim and "justify it" using the Bible, even though the Bible clearly says it is not.*

If you want to believe "praying a prayer one time" makes you a Christian, no matter what happens in your life afterward, *you can make that claim and justify it using the Bible, even though the Bible clearly says otherwise.*

You can make the Bible "say" anything as long as you're not concerned with what it actually says...but what we *want* the Bible to say does not have any bearing on what it *actually* says.

Do not believe something is biblical
just because somebody else says it is.

Go, look for yourself!

Study! Work! Read! Learn!

No matter how long it takes!

Nothing is more important than knowing
what the Bible really says.

But if we use Scripture merely to justify
our pre-existing opinions, we're not
getting God's word at all;

we're talking over Him,

correcting Him,

and believing ourselves instead.

What a horrifying prospect.

You're a theologian, too

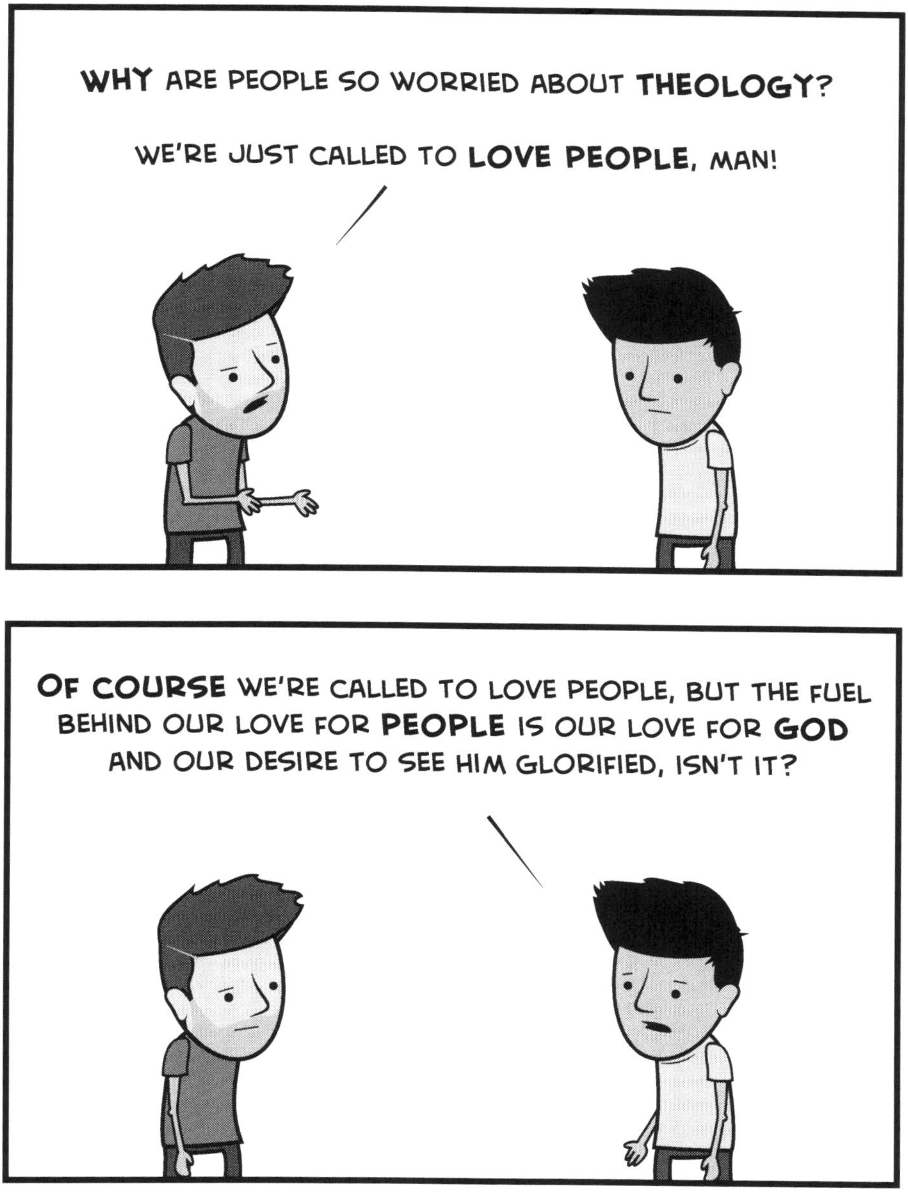
WHY ARE PEOPLE SO WORRIED ABOUT THEOLOGY?
WE'RE JUST CALLED TO LOVE PEOPLE, MAN!
OF COURSE WE'RE CALLED TO LOVE PEOPLE, BUT THE FUEL BEHIND OUR LOVE FOR PEOPLE IS OUR LOVE FOR GOD AND OUR DESIRE TO SEE HIM GLORIFIED, ISN'T IT?

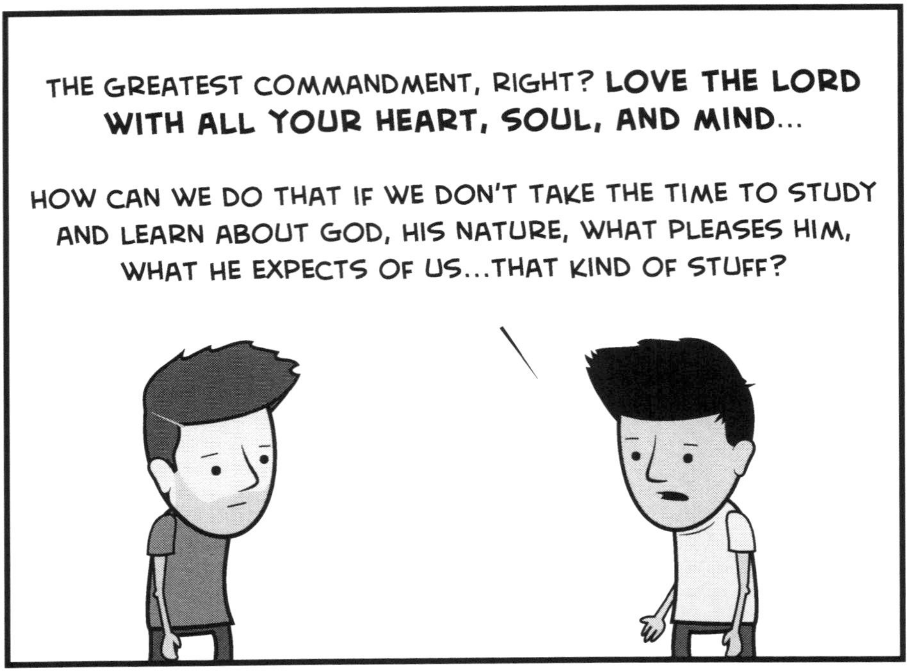
THE GREATEST COMMANDMENT, RIGHT? **LOVE THE LORD WITH ALL YOUR HEART, SOUL, AND MIND**...
HOW CAN WE DO THAT IF WE DON'T TAKE THE TIME TO STUDY AND LEARN ABOUT GOD, HIS NATURE, WHAT PLEASES HIM, WHAT HE EXPECTS OF US...THAT KIND OF STUFF?

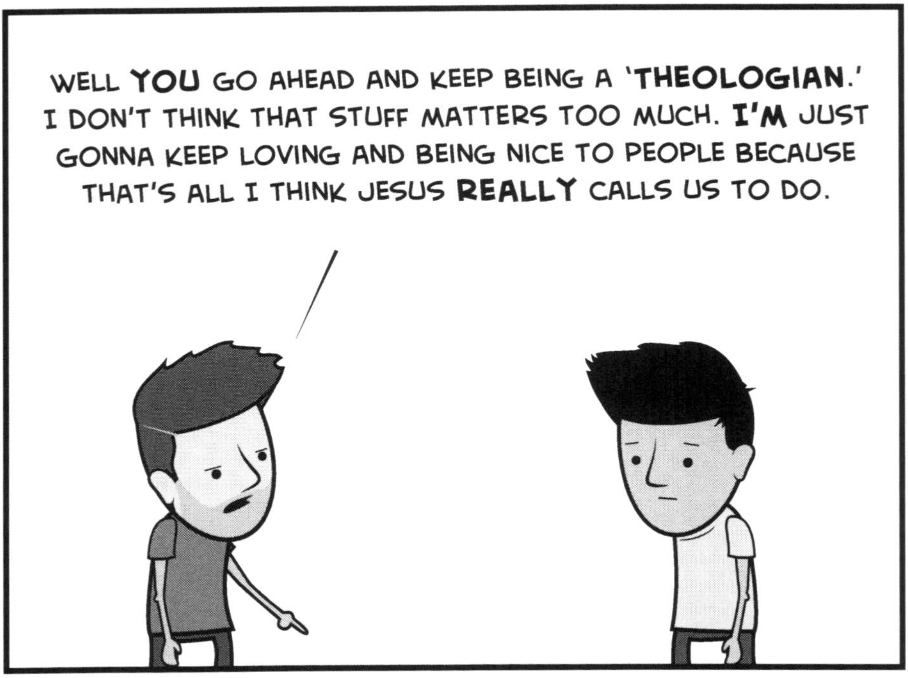
WELL **YOU** GO AHEAD AND KEEP BEING A '**THEOLOGIAN**.' I DON'T THINK THAT STUFF MATTERS TOO MUCH. **I'M** JUST GONNA KEEP LOVING AND BEING NICE TO PEOPLE BECAUSE THAT'S ALL I THINK JESUS **REALLY** CALLS US TO DO.

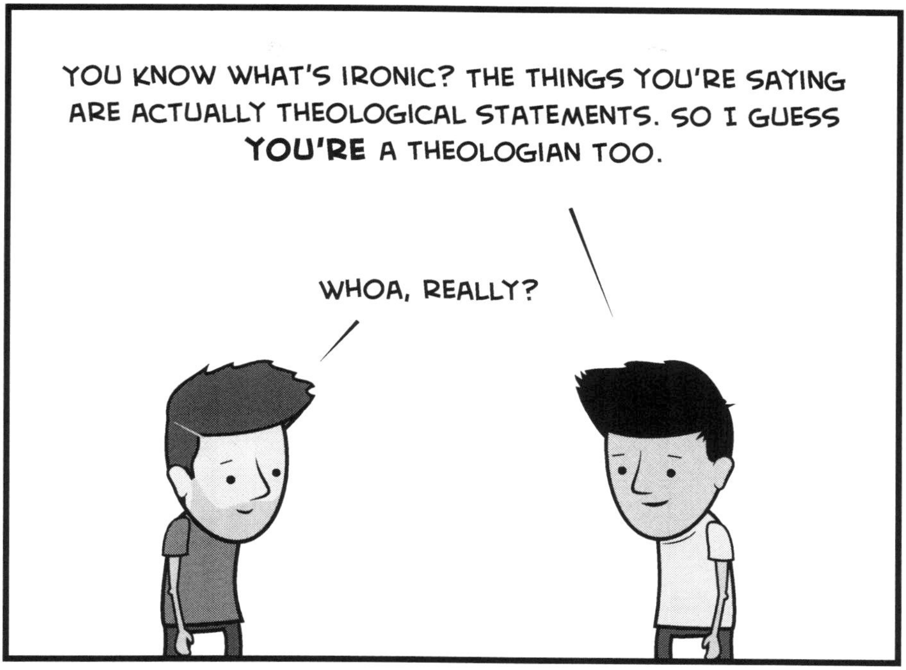
YOU KNOW WHAT'S IRONIC? THE THINGS YOU'RE SAYING ARE ACTUALLY THEOLOGICAL STATEMENTS. SO I GUESS **YOU'RE** A THEOLOGIAN TOO.
WHOA, REALLY?

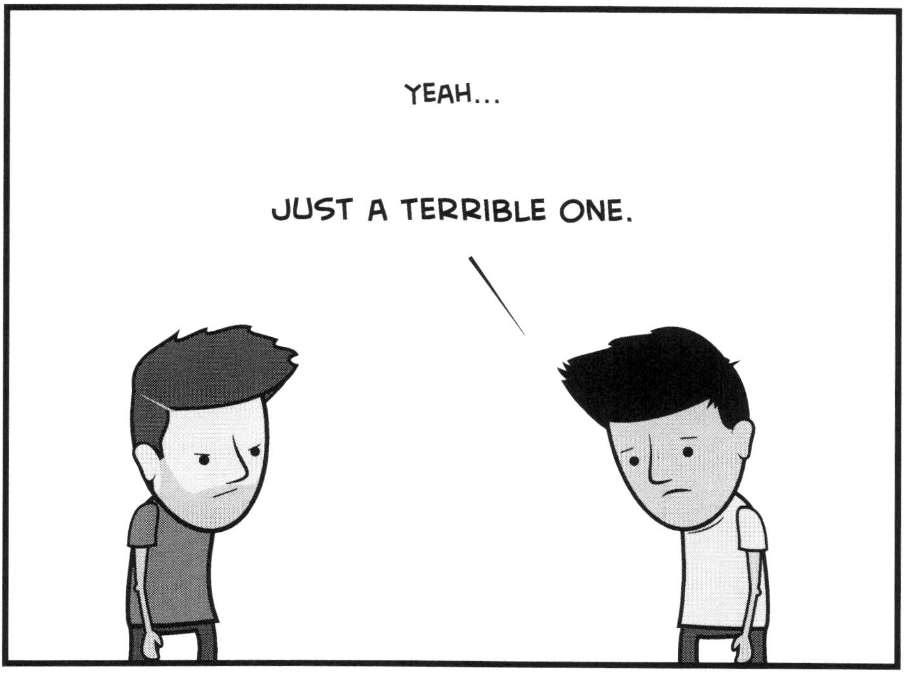
YEAH...
JUST A TERRIBLE ONE.

Pray for your President

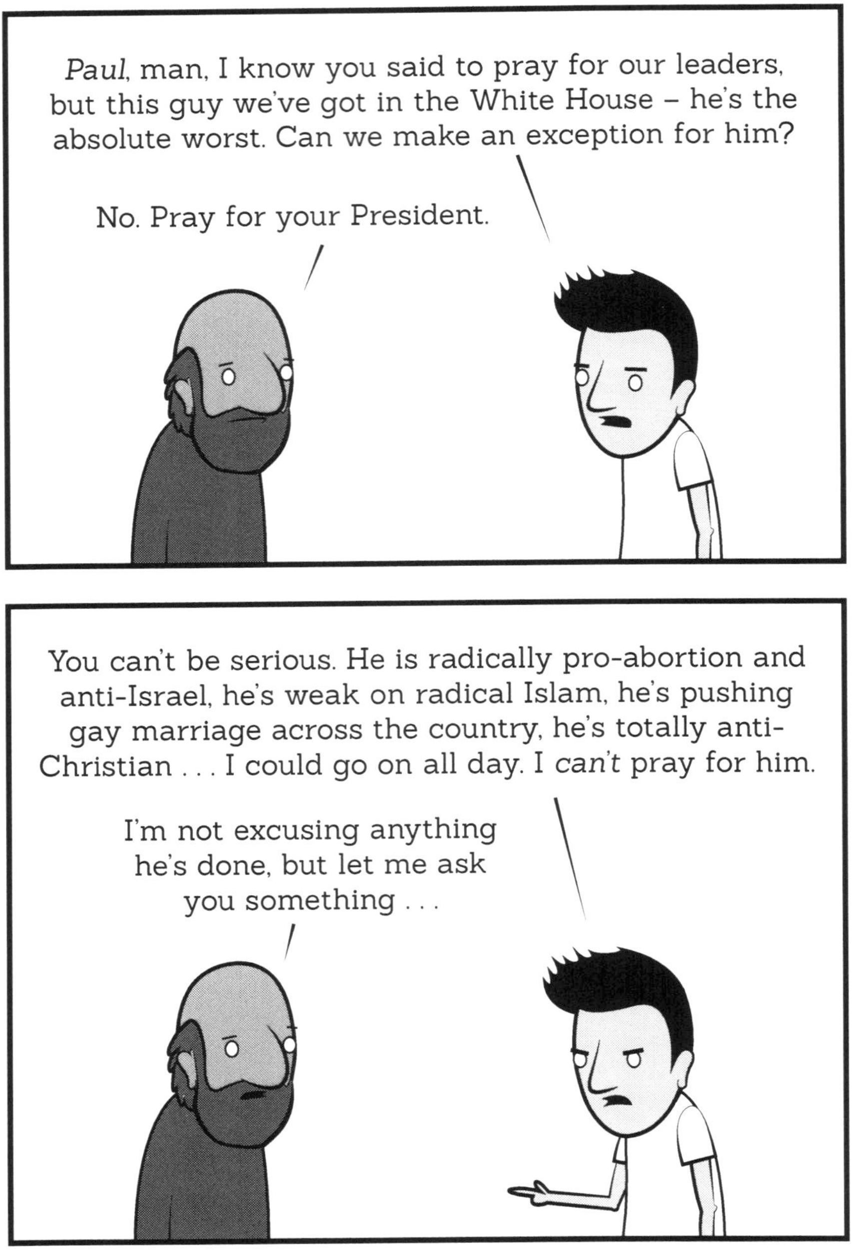
Paul, man, I know you said to pray for our leaders, but this guy we've got in the White House – he's the absolute worst. Can we make an exception for him?
No. Pray for your President.
You can't be serious. He is radically pro-abortion and anti-Israel, he's weak on radical Islam, he's pushing gay marriage across the country, he's totally anti-Christian . . . I could go on all day. I *can't* pray for him.
I'm not excusing anything he's done, but let me ask you something . . .

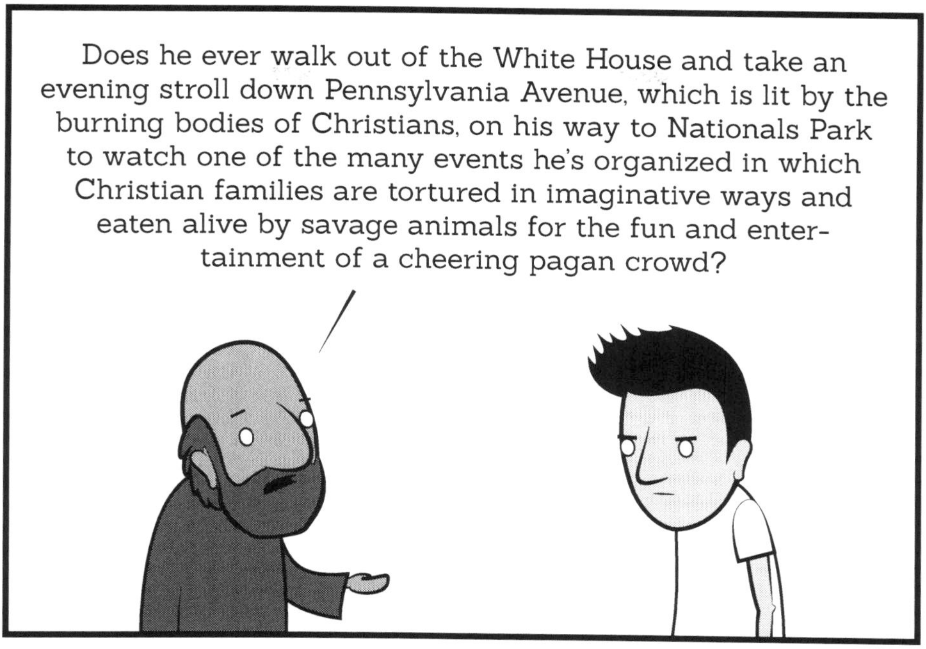
Does he ever walk out of the White House and take an evening stroll down Pennsylvania Avenue, which is lit by the burning bodies of Christians, on his way to Nationals Park to watch one of the many events he's organized in which Christian families are tortured in imaginative ways and eaten alive by savage animals for the fun and entertainment of a cheering pagan crowd?

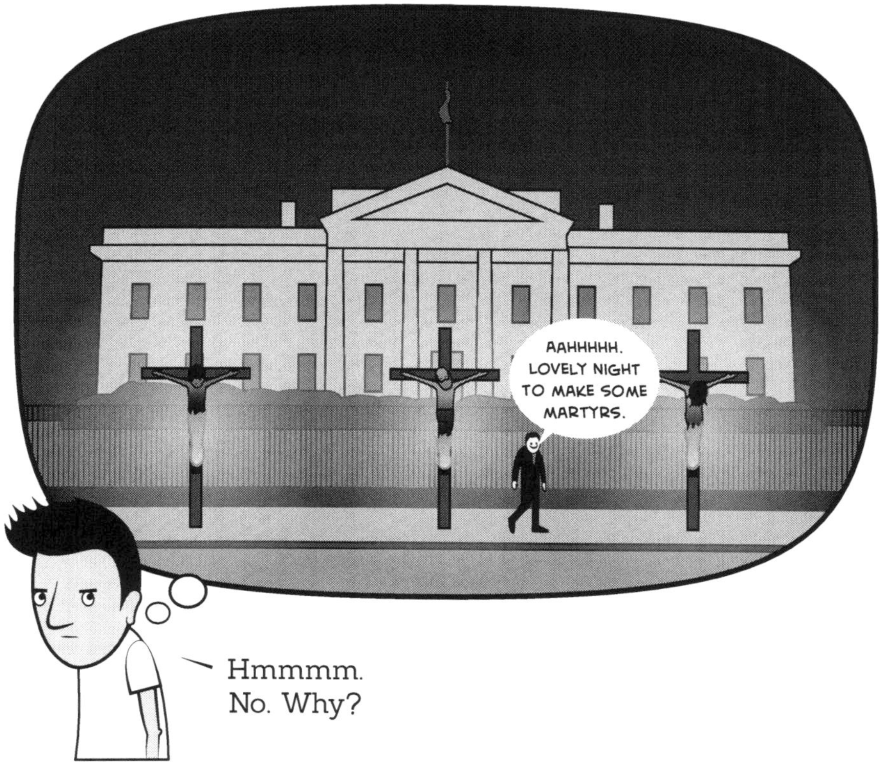
AAHHHHH. LOVELY NIGHT TO MAKE SOME MARTYRS.
Hmmmm. No. Why?

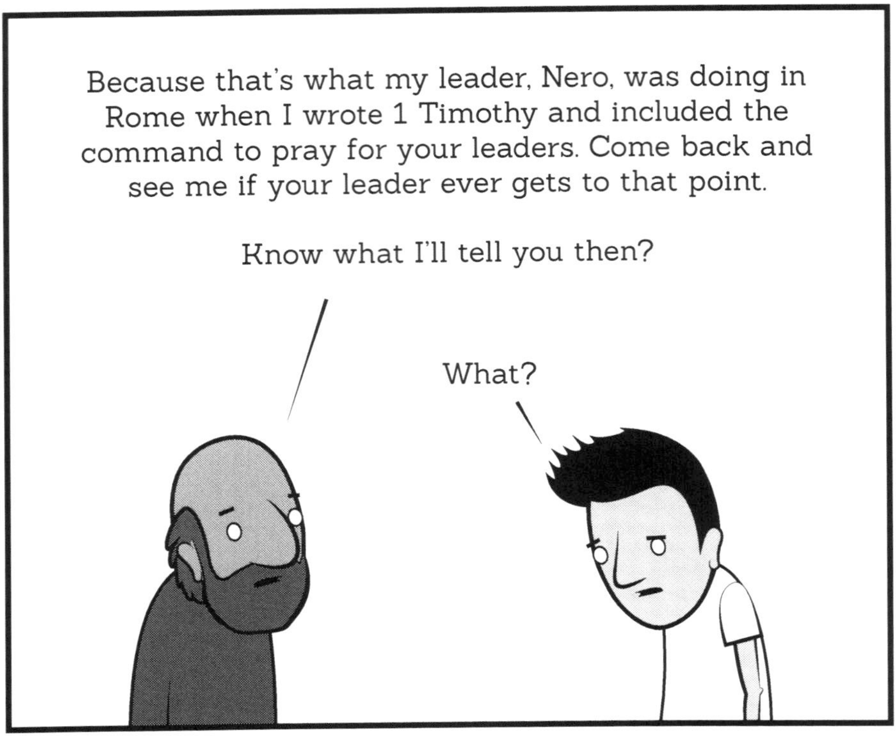
Because that's what my leader, Nero, was doing in Rome when I wrote 1 Timothy and included the command to pray for your leaders. Come back and see me if your leader ever gets to that point.
Know what I'll tell you then?
What?

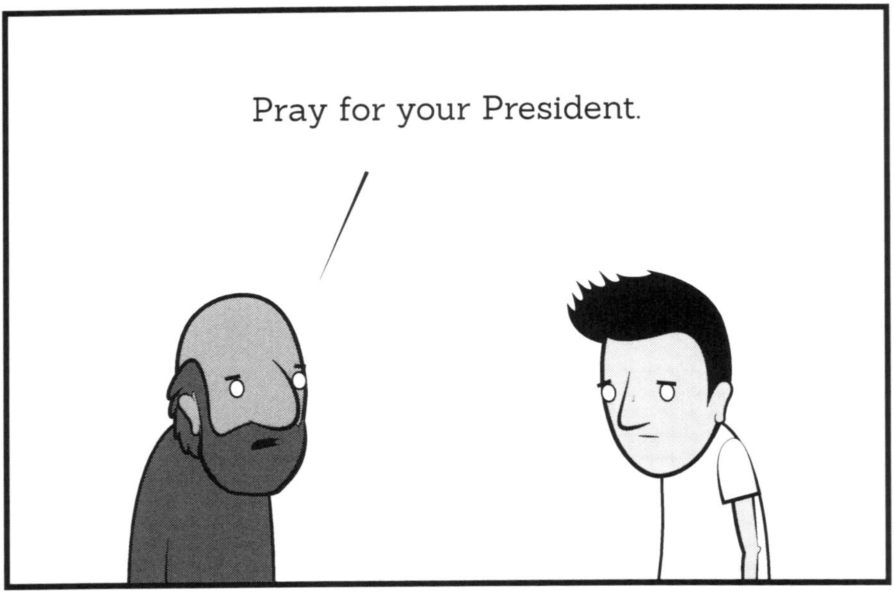
Pray for your President.

Radical Muslim vs radical Christian

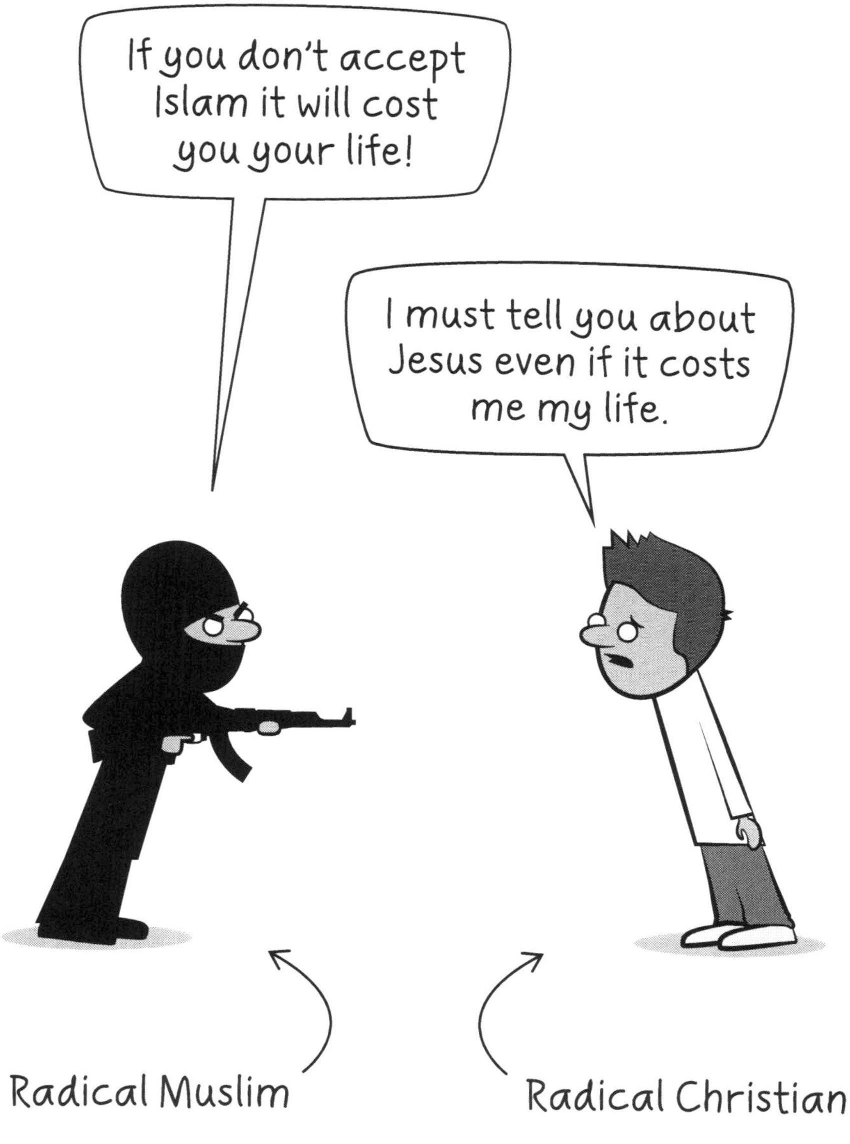
If you don't accept Islam it will cost you your life!
I must tell you about Jesus even if it costs me my life.
Radical Muslim
Radical Christian

Name it and claim it

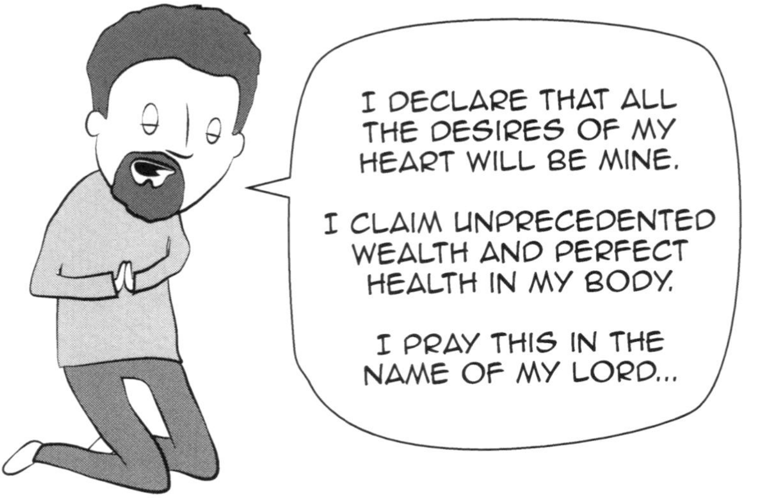
I DECLARE THAT ALL THE DESIRES OF MY HEART WILL BE MINE.
I CLAIM UNPRECEDENTED WEALTH AND PERFECT HEALTH IN MY BODY.
I PRAY THIS IN THE NAME OF MY LORD...

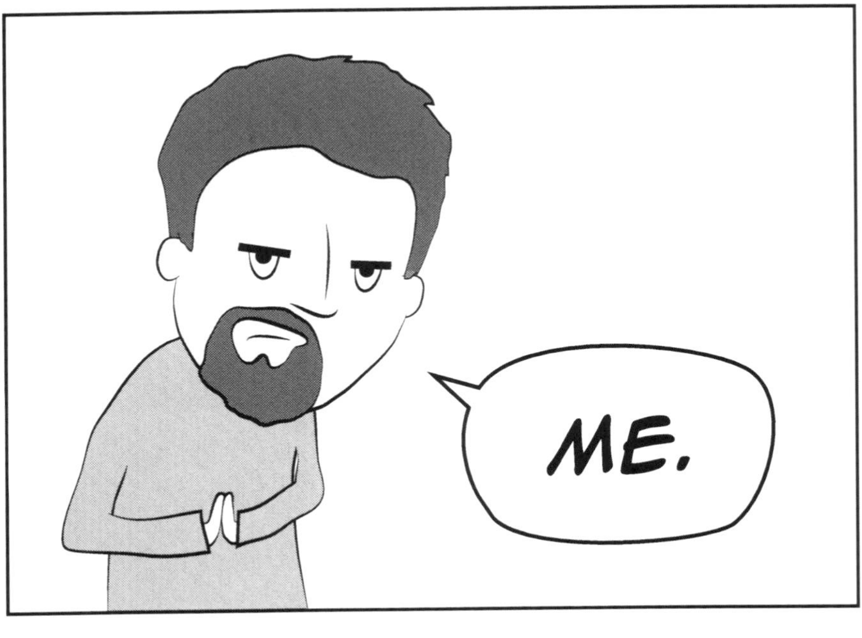
ME.

I have my own ideas about Jesus

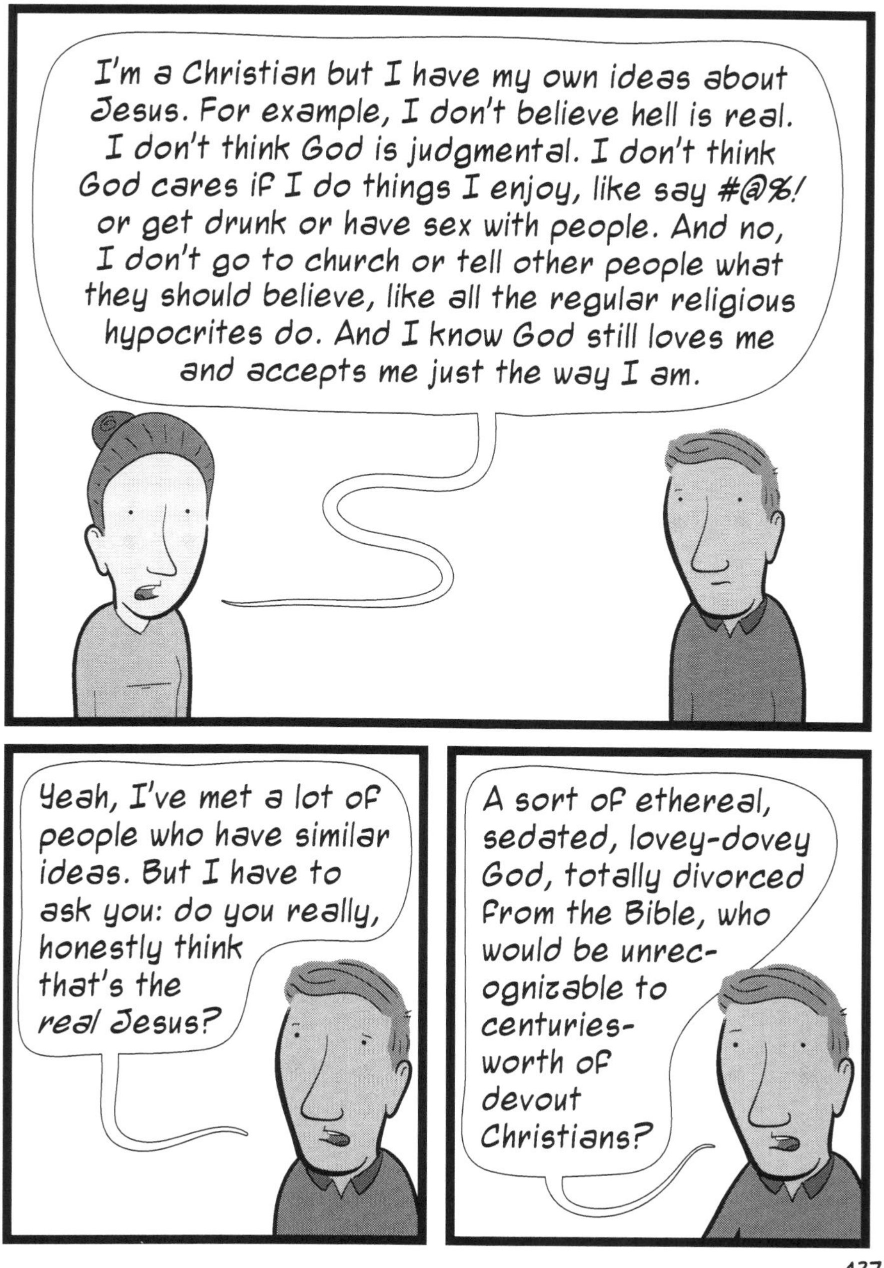
I'm a Christian but I have my own ideas about Jesus. For example, I don't believe hell is real. I don't think God is judgmental. I don't think God cares if I do things I enjoy, like say #@%! or get drunk or have sex with people. And no, I don't go to church or tell other people what they should believe, like all the regular religious hypocrites do. And I know God still loves me and accepts me just the way I am.
Yeah, I've met a lot of people who have similar ideas. But I have to ask you: do you really, honestly think that's the *real* Jesus?
A sort of ethereal, sedated, lovey-dovey God, totally divorced from the Bible, who would be unrecognizable to centuries-worth of devout Christians?

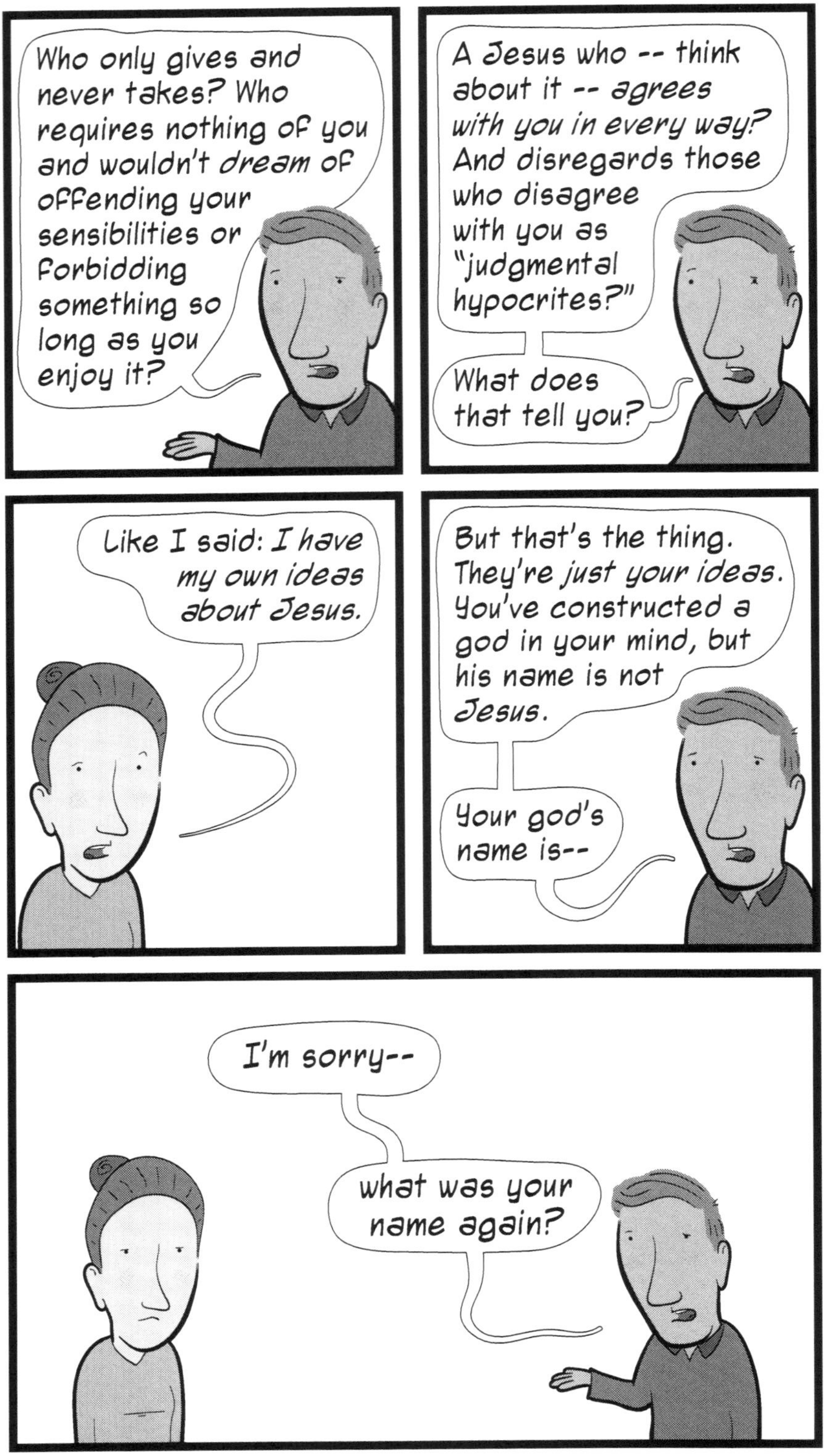
Who only gives and never takes? Who requires nothing of you and wouldn't *dream* of offending your sensibilities or forbidding something so long as you enjoy it?
A Jesus who -- think about it -- *agrees with you in every way?* And disregards those who disagree with you as "judgmental hypocrites?"
What does that tell you?
Like I said: *I have my own ideas about Jesus.*
But that's the thing. They're *just your ideas.* You've constructed a god in your mind, but his name is not *Jesus.*
Your god's name is--
I'm sorry--
what was your name again?

The prayer fairy

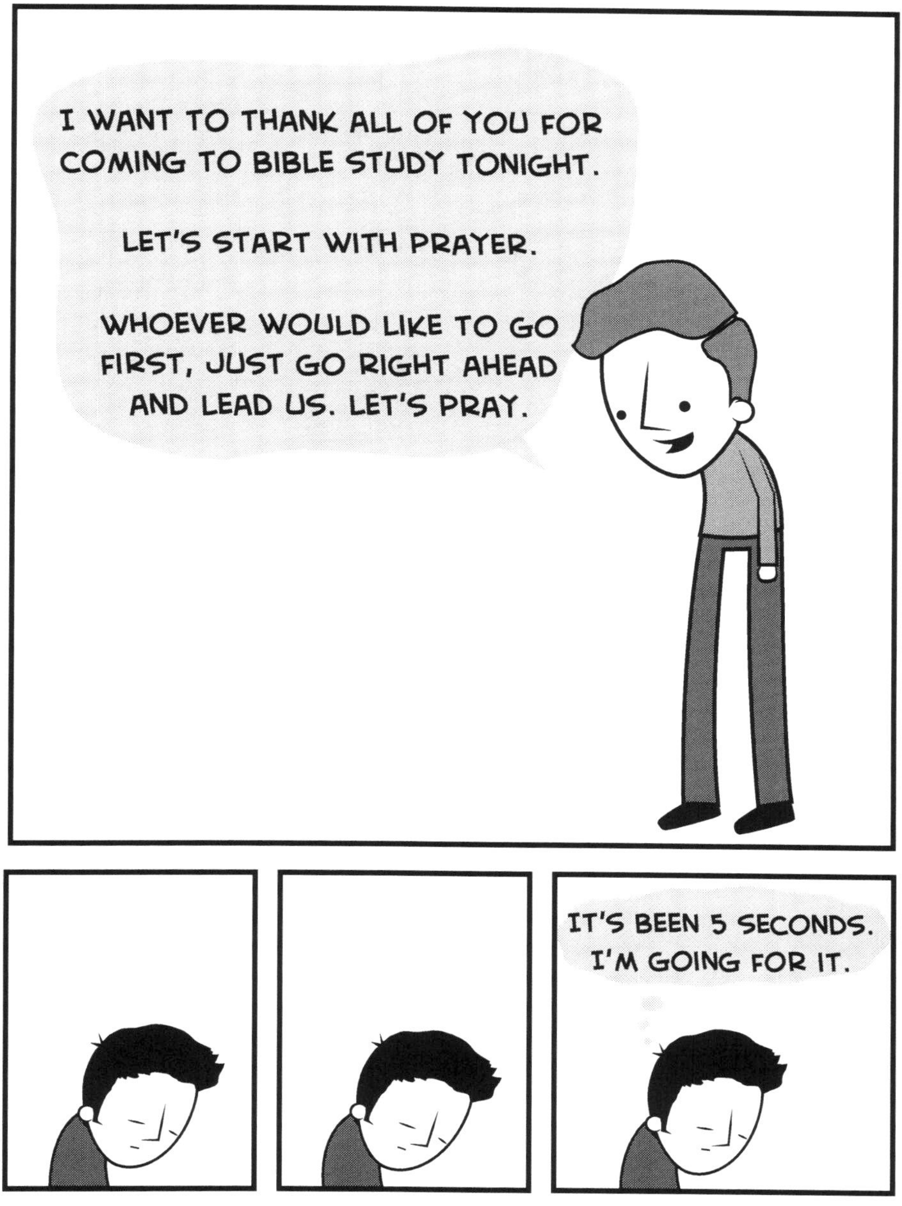
I WANT TO THANK ALL OF YOU FOR COMING TO BIBLE STUDY TONIGHT.
LET'S START WITH PRAYER.
WHOEVER WOULD LIKE TO GO FIRST, JUST GO RIGHT AHEAD AND LEAD US. LET'S PRAY.
IT'S BEEN 5 SECONDS. I'M GOING FOR IT.

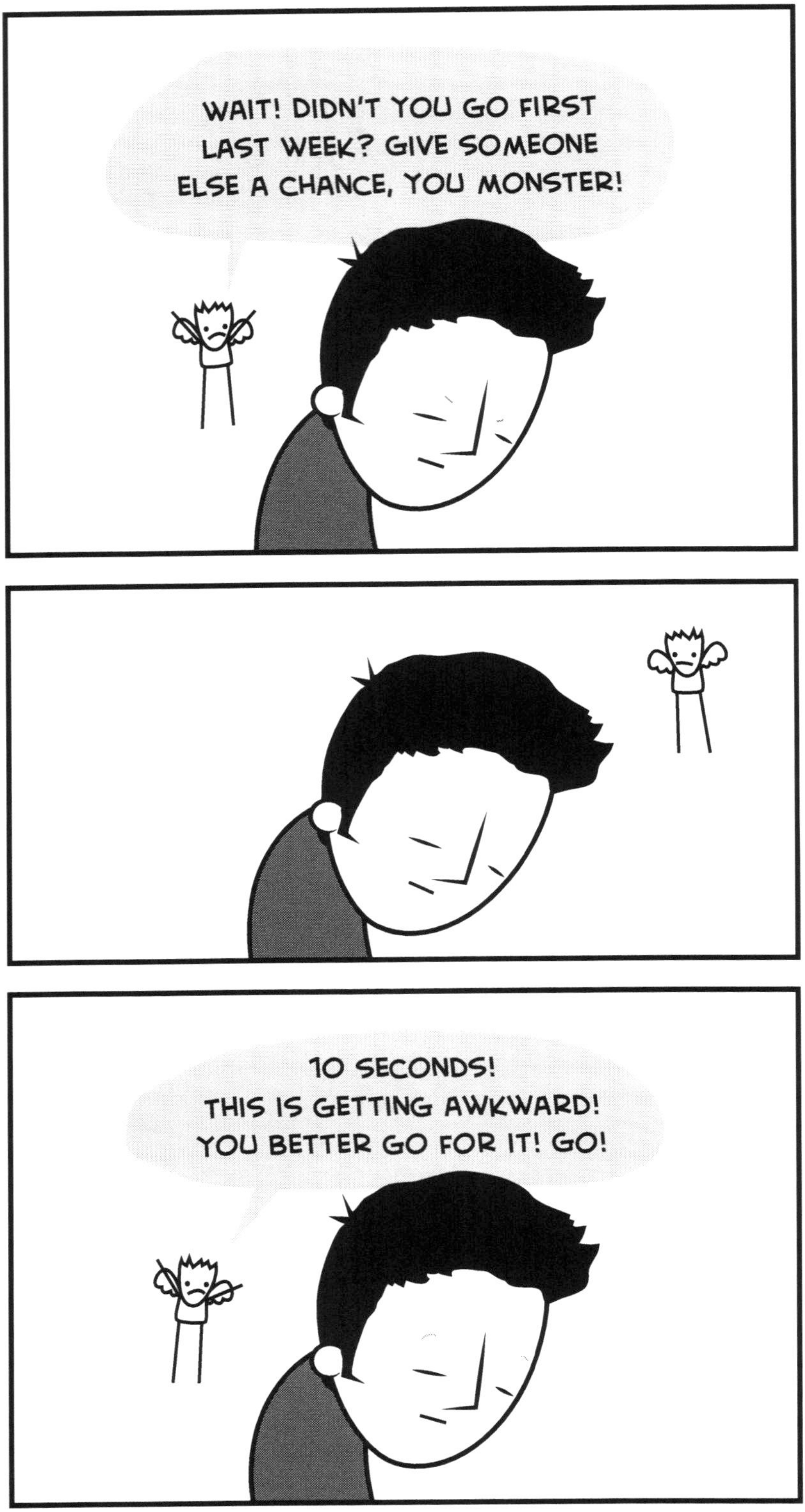
WAIT! DIDN'T YOU GO FIRST LAST WEEK? GIVE SOMEONE ELSE A CHANCE, YOU MONSTER!
10 SECONDS! THIS IS GETTING AWKWARD! YOU BETTER GO FOR IT! GO!

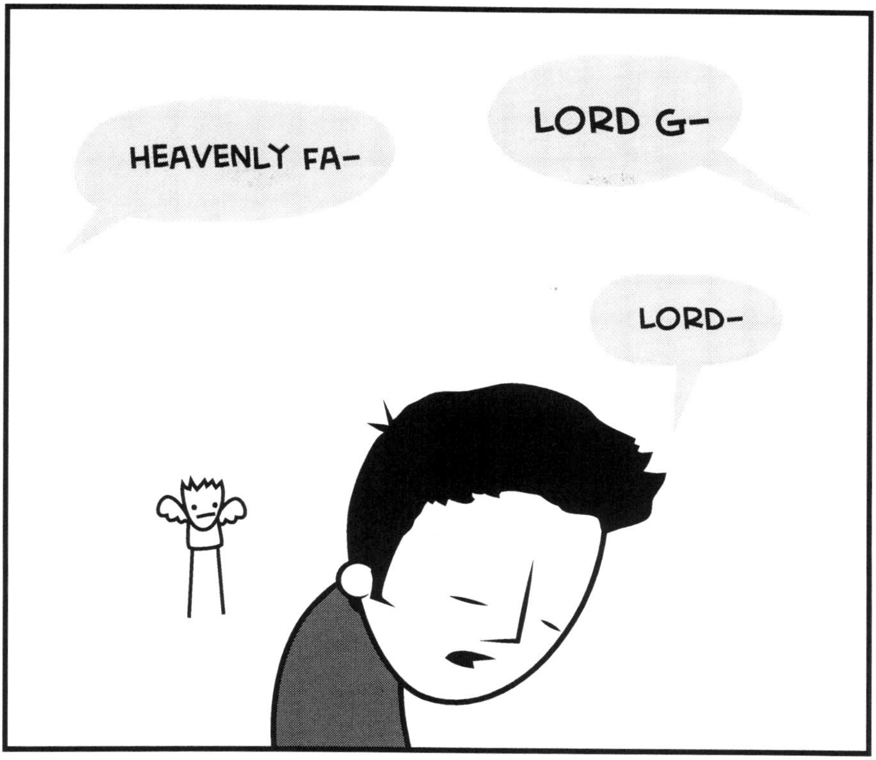
HEAVENLY FA-
LORD G-
LORD-

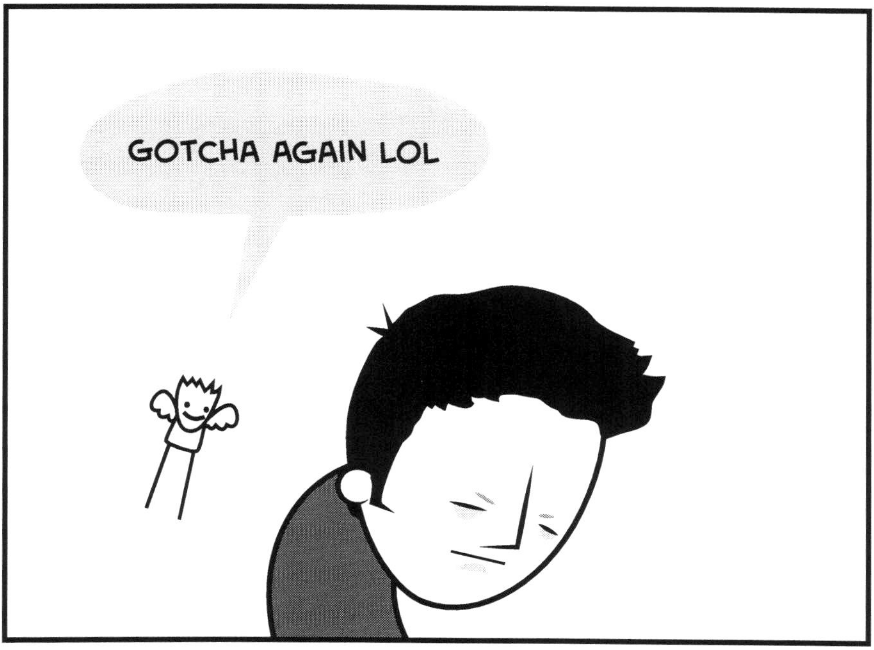
GOTCHA AGAIN LOL

Jesus takes Joel Osteen's advice

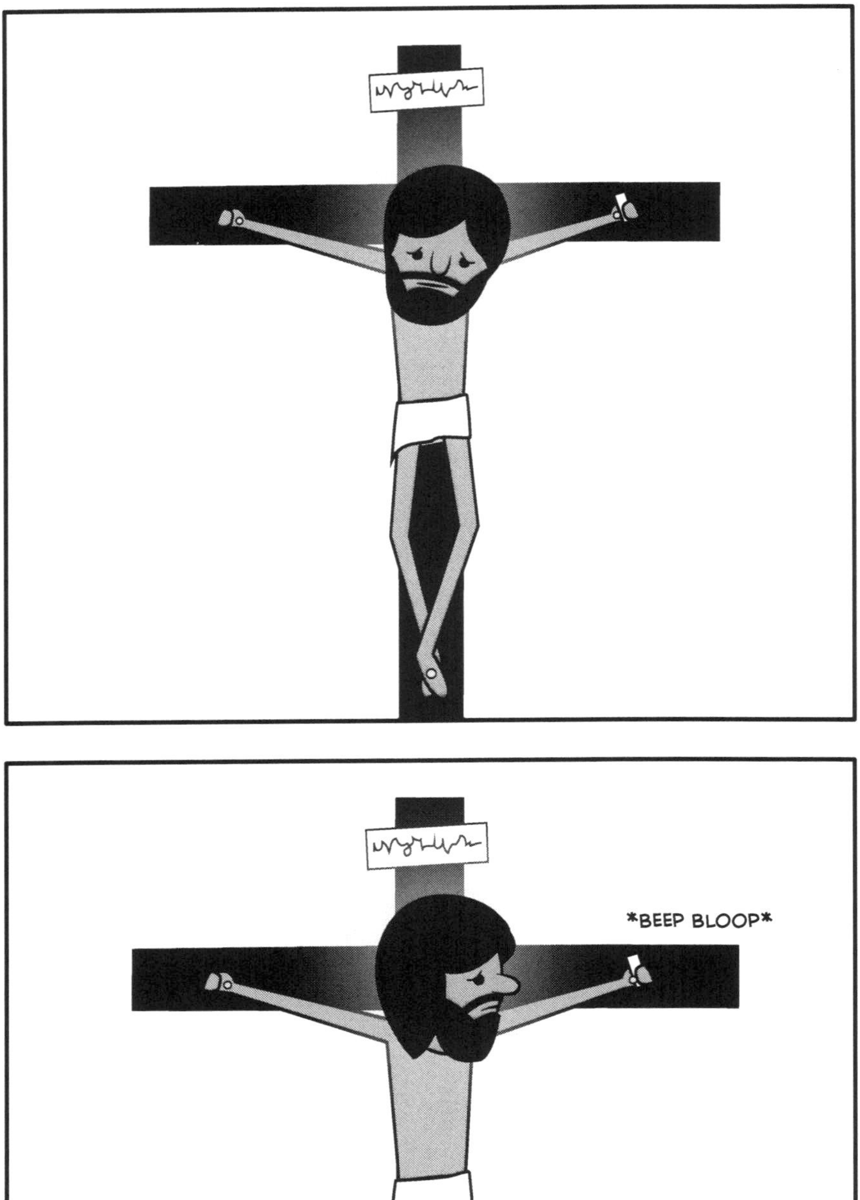
BEEP BLOOP

Joel Osteen
@JoelOsteen
Don't waste time with people who don't appreciate what you have to offer. The people around you should celebrate who you are.
700m RETWEETS 900m LIKES

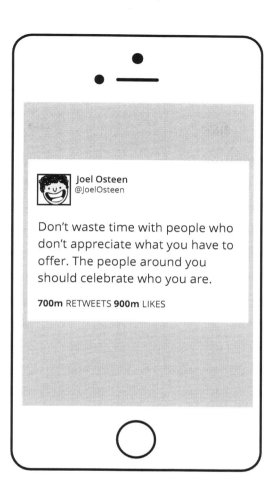

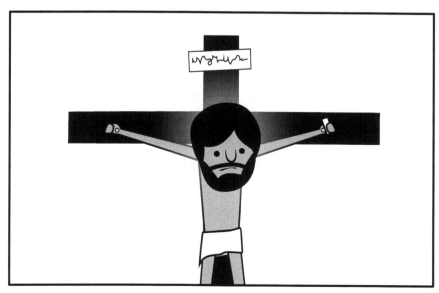

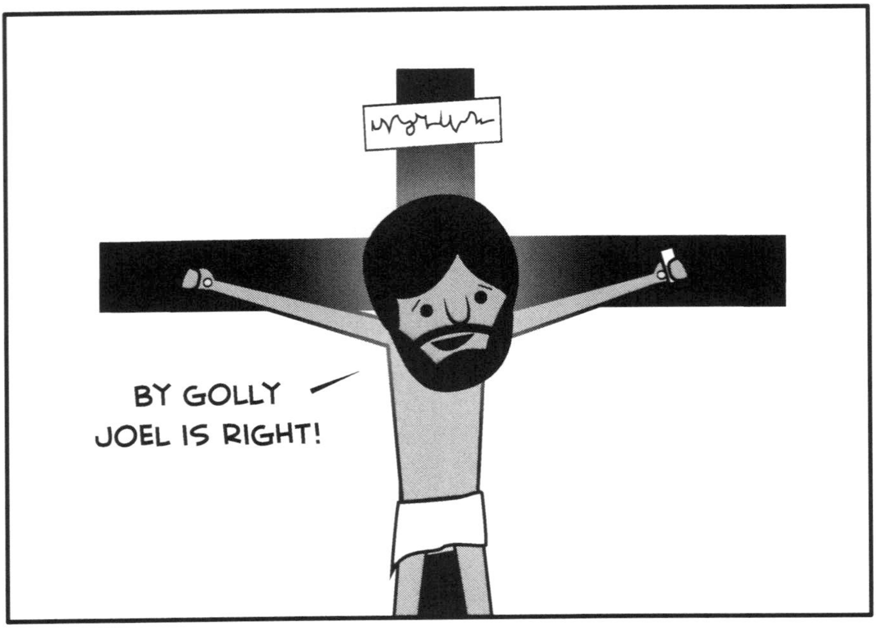
BY GOLLY
JOEL IS RIGHT!

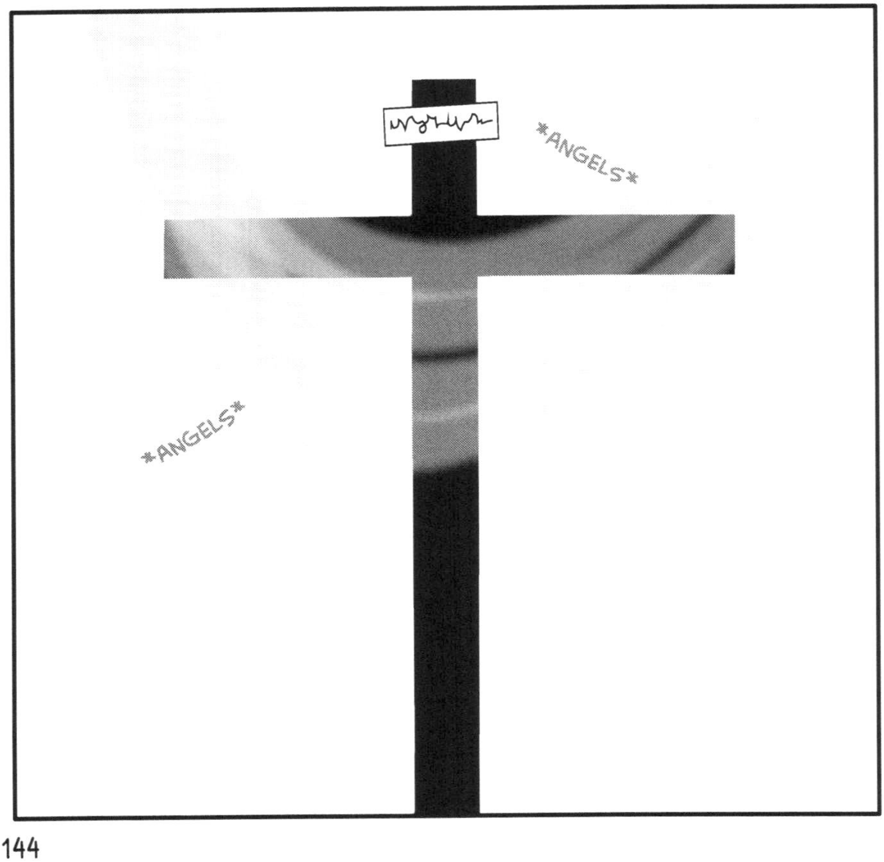
ANGELS
ANGELS

Does slavery ever bother you?

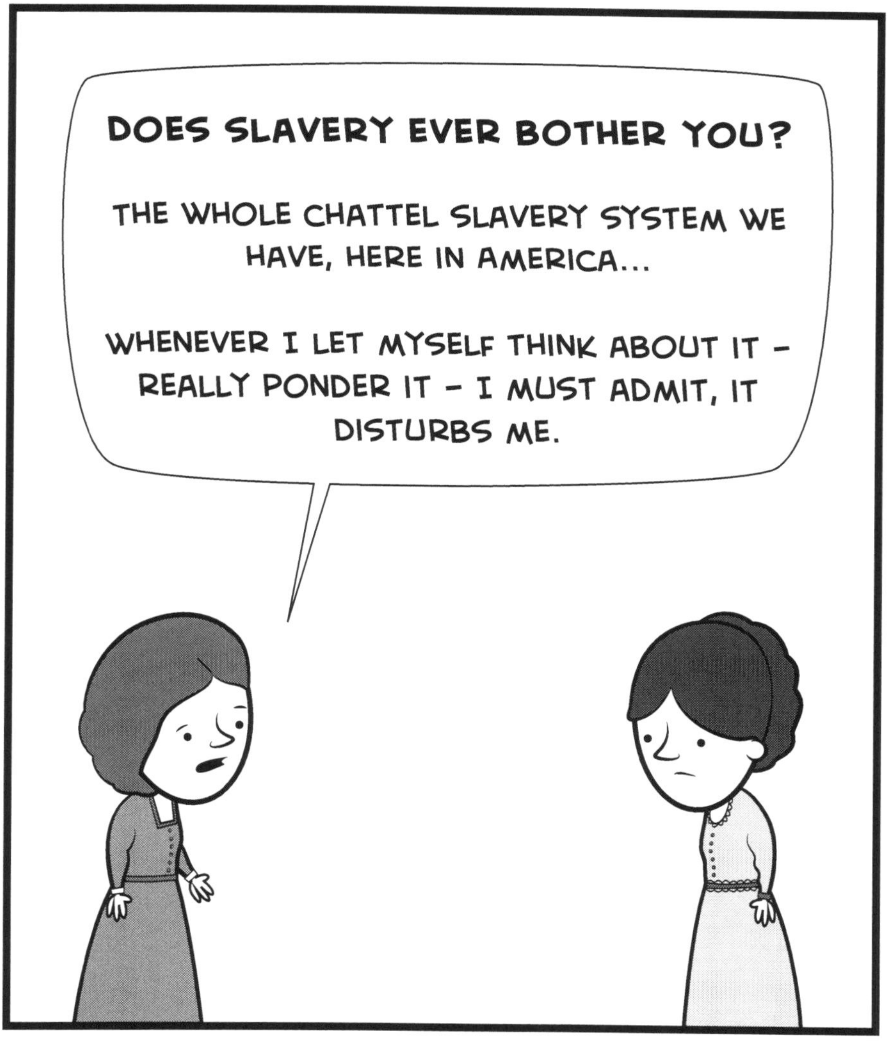

DOES SLAVERY EVER BOTHER YOU?
THE WHOLE CHATTEL SLAVERY SYSTEM WE HAVE, HERE IN AMERICA...
WHENEVER I LET MYSELF THINK ABOUT IT - REALLY PONDER IT - I MUST ADMIT, IT DISTURBS ME.

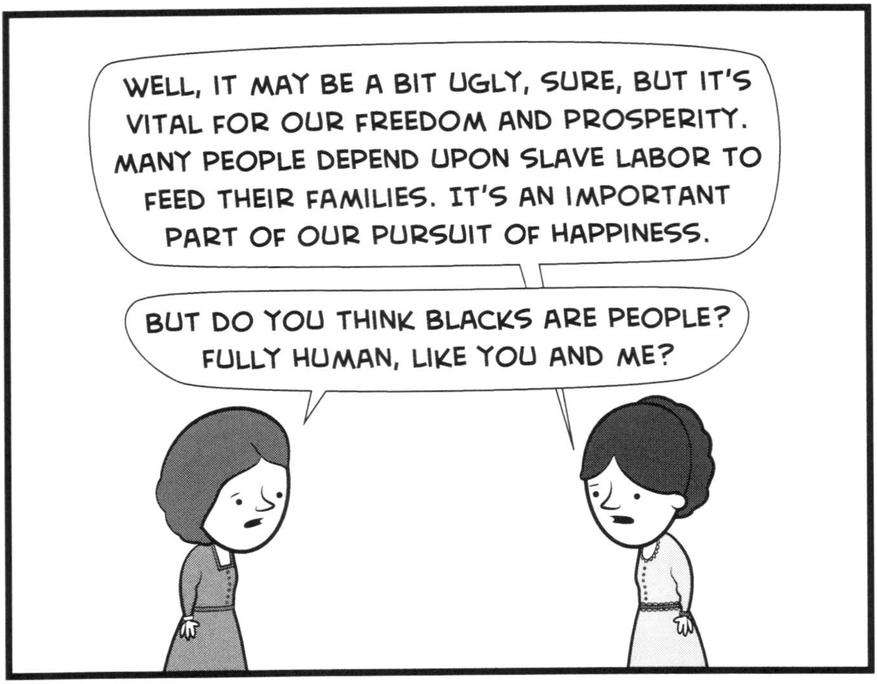
WELL, IT MAY BE A BIT UGLY, SURE, BUT IT'S VITAL FOR OUR FREEDOM AND PROSPERITY. MANY PEOPLE DEPEND UPON SLAVE LABOR TO FEED THEIR FAMILIES. IT'S AN IMPORTANT PART OF OUR PURSUIT OF HAPPINESS.
BUT DO YOU THINK BLACKS ARE PEOPLE? FULLY HUMAN, LIKE YOU AND ME?

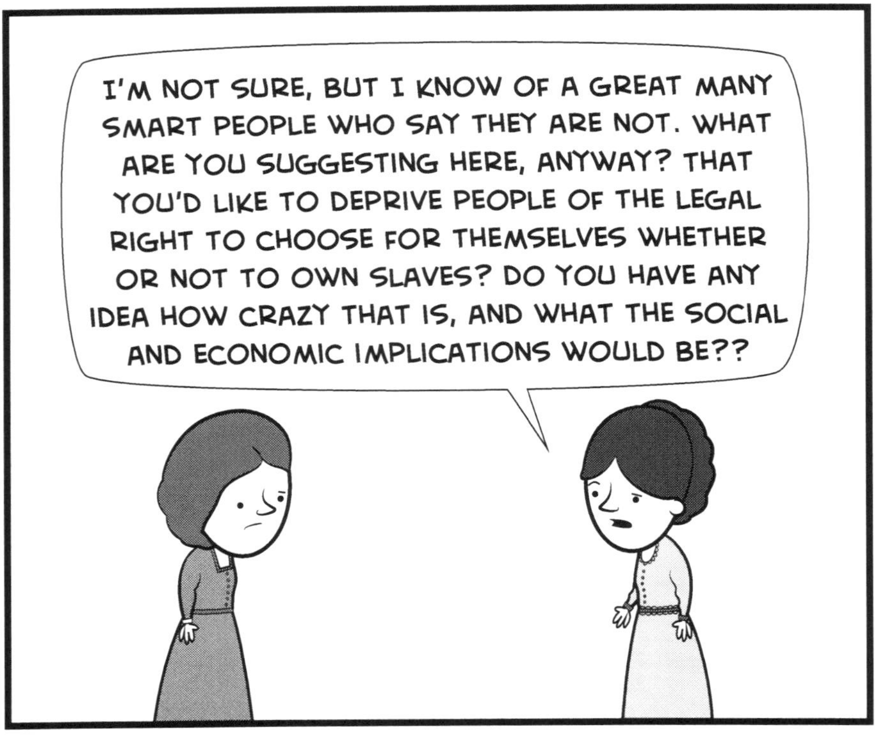
I'M NOT SURE, BUT I KNOW OF A GREAT MANY SMART PEOPLE WHO SAY THEY ARE NOT. WHAT ARE YOU SUGGESTING HERE, ANYWAY? THAT YOU'D LIKE TO DEPRIVE PEOPLE OF THE LEGAL RIGHT TO CHOOSE FOR THEMSELVES WHETHER OR NOT TO OWN SLAVES? DO YOU HAVE ANY IDEA HOW CRAZY THAT IS, AND WHAT THE SOCIAL AND ECONOMIC IMPLICATIONS WOULD BE??

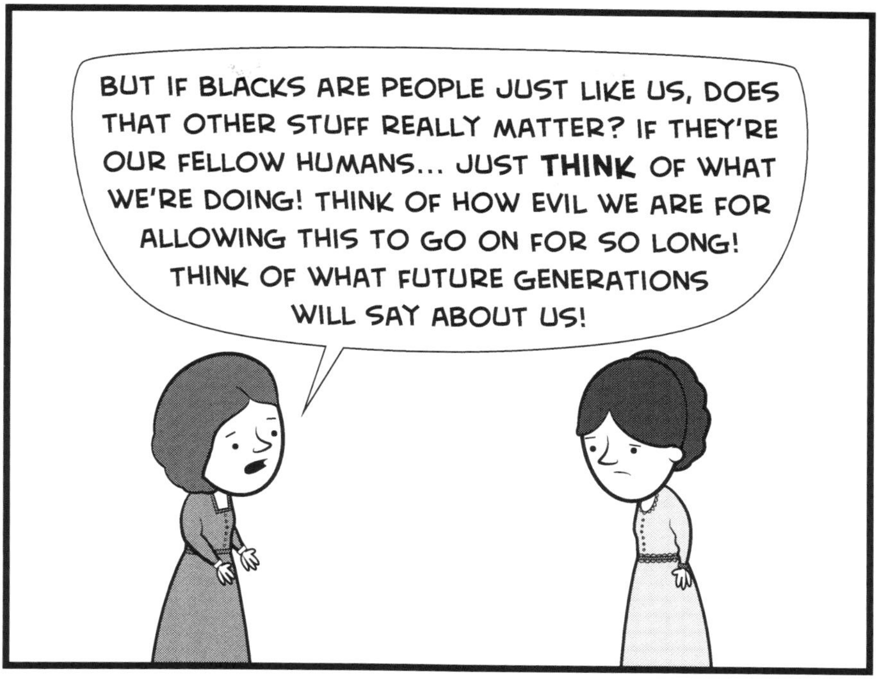
BUT IF BLACKS ARE PEOPLE JUST LIKE US, DOES THAT OTHER STUFF REALLY MATTER? IF THEY'RE OUR FELLOW HUMANS... JUST **THINK** OF WHAT WE'RE DOING! THINK OF HOW EVIL WE ARE FOR ALLOWING THIS TO GO ON FOR SO LONG! THINK OF WHAT FUTURE GENERATIONS WILL SAY ABOUT US!

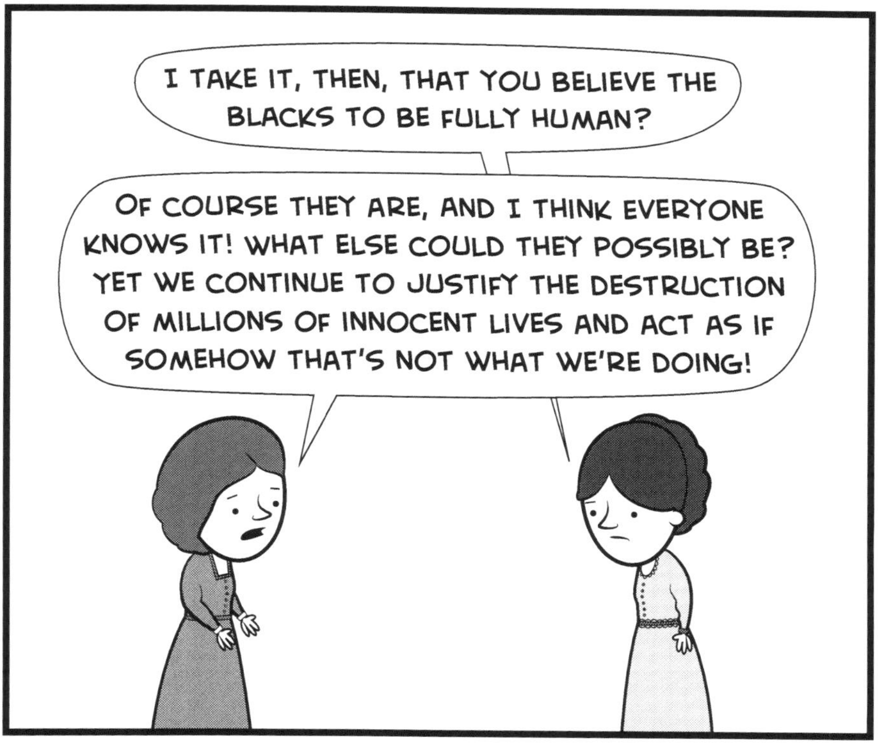
I TAKE IT, THEN, THAT YOU BELIEVE THE BLACKS TO BE FULLY HUMAN?
OF COURSE THEY ARE, AND I THINK EVERYONE KNOWS IT! WHAT ELSE COULD THEY POSSIBLY BE? YET WE CONTINUE TO JUSTIFY THE DESTRUCTION OF MILLIONS OF INNOCENT LIVES AND ACT AS IF SOMEHOW THAT'S NOT WHAT WE'RE DOING!

200 YEARS LATER

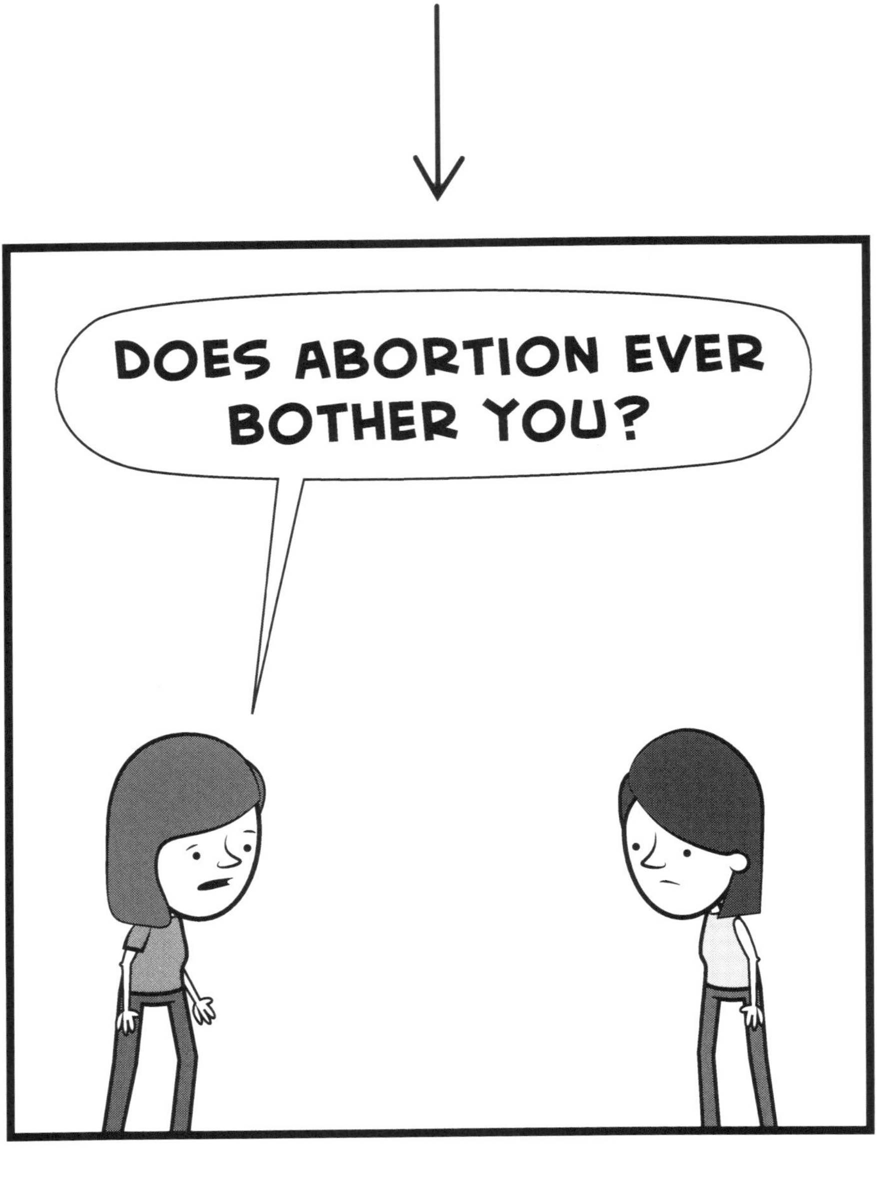
DOES ABORTION EVER BOTHER YOU?

Falling asleep while praying

Sometimes I lay down in bed at night,

begin to pray to God,

and promptly fall asleep.

HELP ME, LORD, TO BE FAITHFUL...
THANK Y... ZzzzzzZzz- *BRMPF*
HELP ME TO GLORI... FY......
ZzzzZz
ZzzzzzzzZz
ZZZZZZZZZZZZZZZZZZZZZZZZZZZ

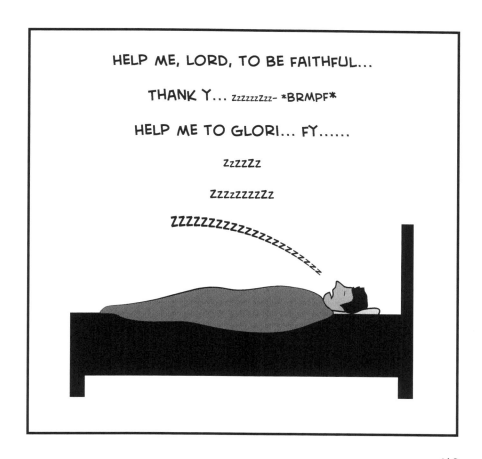

Early in my Christian walk I would feel guilty about this.
I would think about it the next day, like,

Wow, nice, I fell asleep while talking to the
Creator of the Universe.
Way to be sanctified, champ.

Jesus rebuked the disciples for
falling asleep at Gethsemane,

and here I am dozing off before I can finish a little prayer.

(Expectation of what probably
happened shortly thereafter.)

And then one day a wise woman told me something about this:

Drifting off to sleep mid-prayer is not
an affront to God.

It doesn't mean you're lazy or irresponsible or self-centered.

It just means you're a child
falling asleep...

I .... LOVE YOU.

I'M TH...ANK...FUL

FOR...

ZzZzzzZzzzz

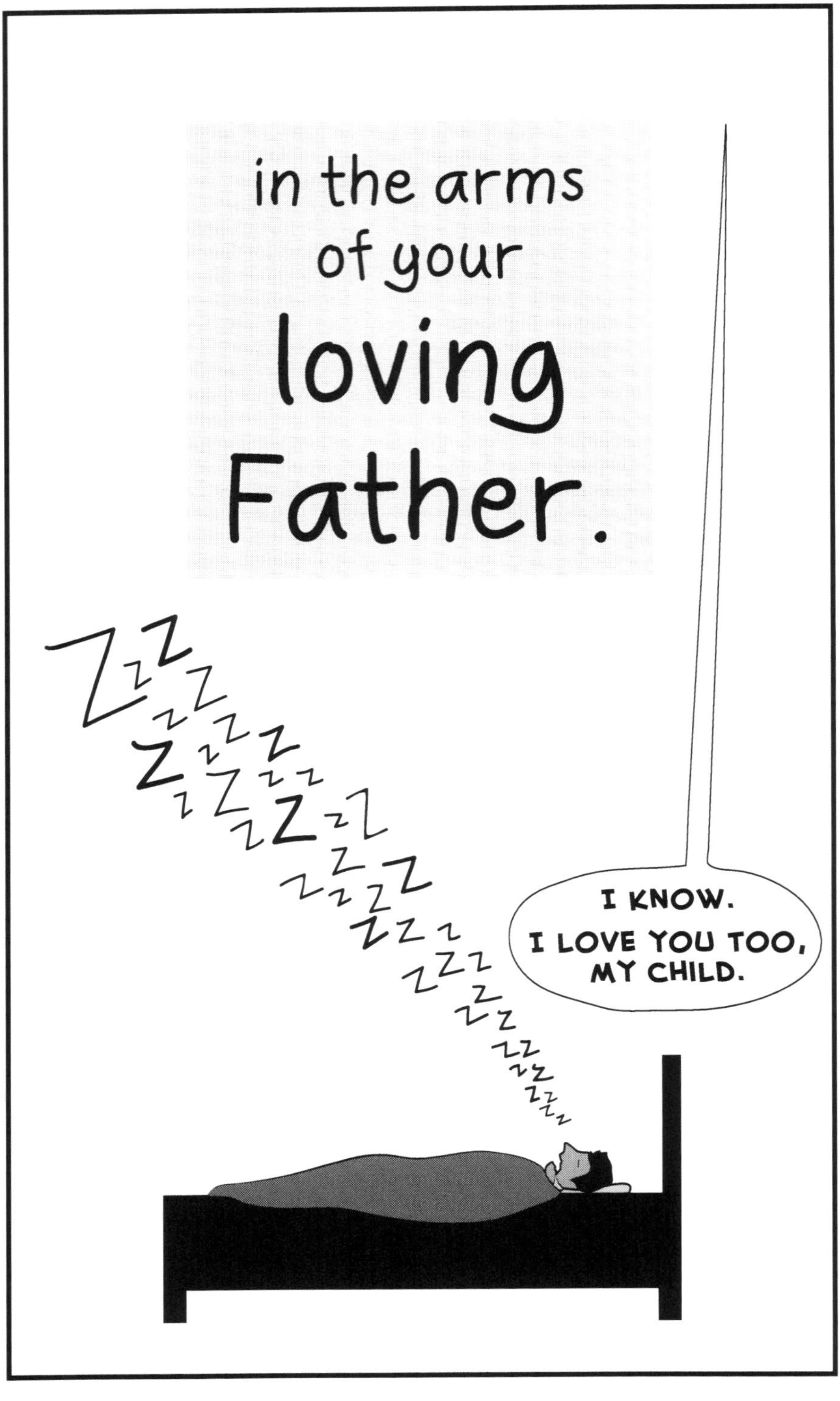
in the arms of your loving Father.
ZZZ
I KNOW.
I LOVE YOU TOO, MY CHILD.

Why don't you ever go to church?

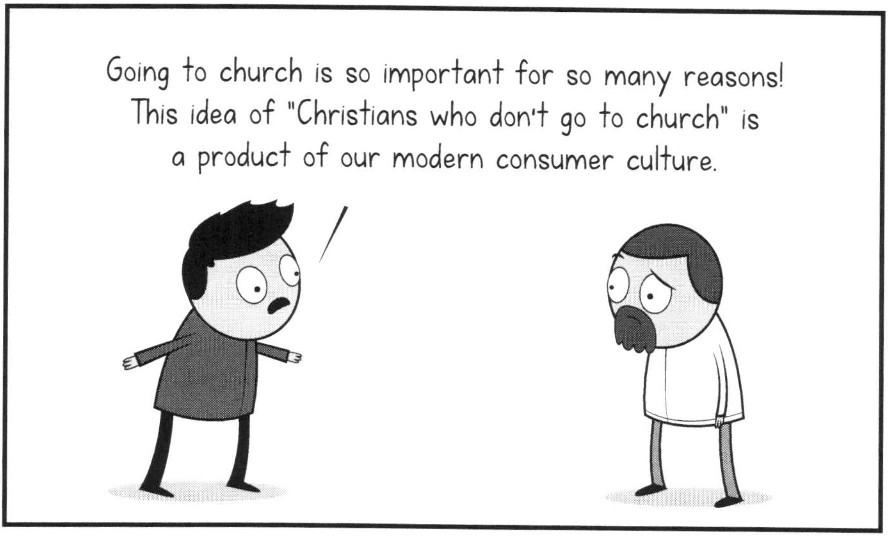
Going to church is so important for so many reasons! This idea of "Christians who don't go to church" is a product of our modern consumer culture.

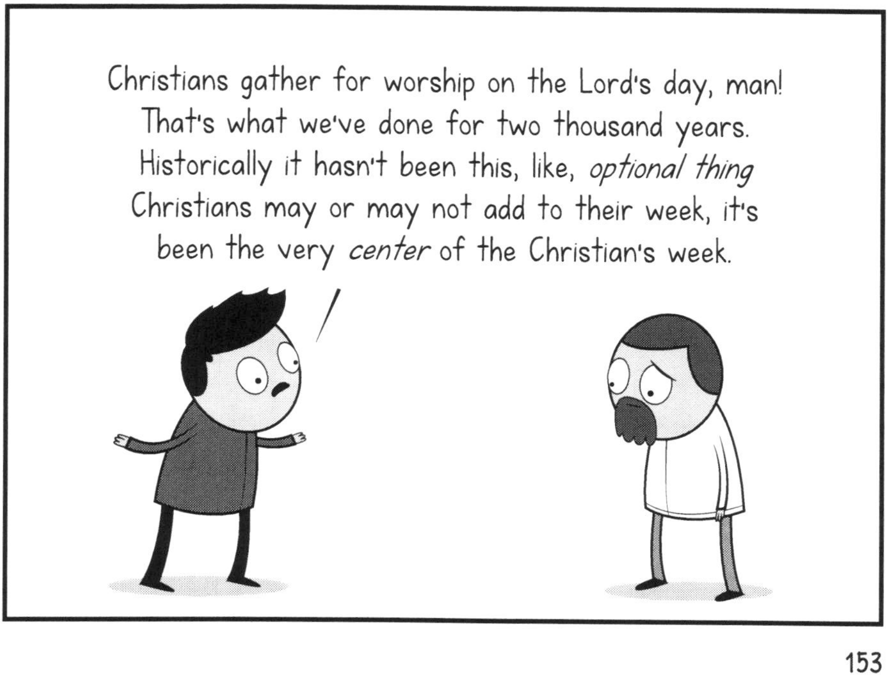
Christians gather for worship on the Lord's day, man! That's what we've done for two thousand years. Historically it hasn't been this, like, *optional thing* Christians may or may not add to their week, it's been the very *center* of the Christian's week.

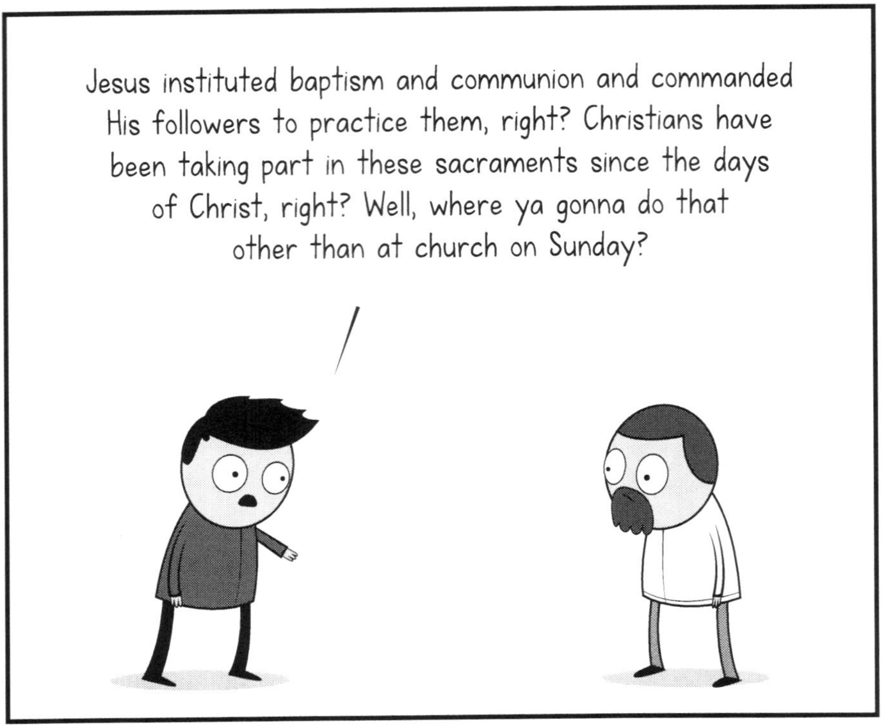
Jesus instituted baptism and communion and commanded His followers to practice them, right? Christians have been taking part in these sacraments since the days of Christ, right? Well, where ya gonna do that other than at church on Sunday?

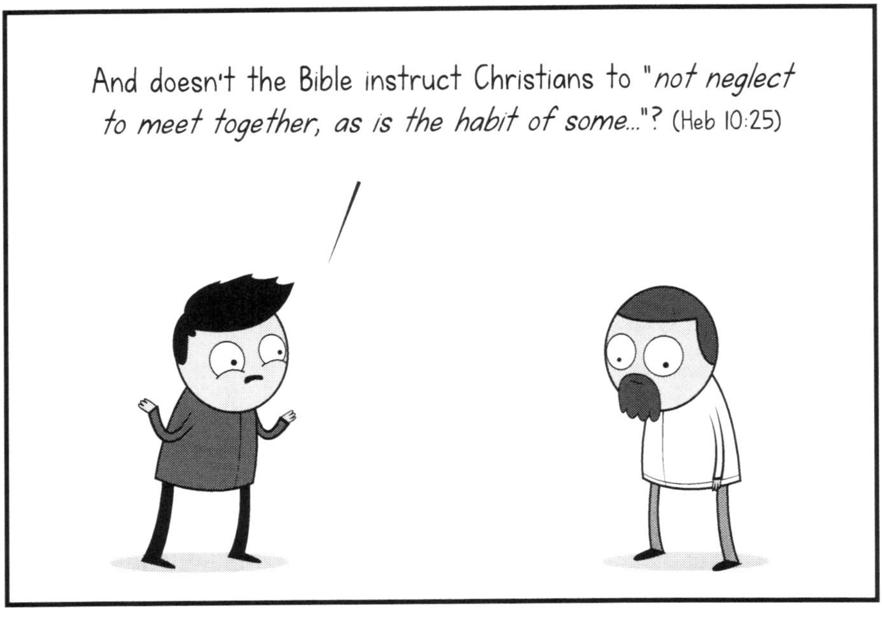
And doesn't the Bible instruct Christians to "*not neglect to meet together, as is the habit of some...*"? (Heb 10:25)

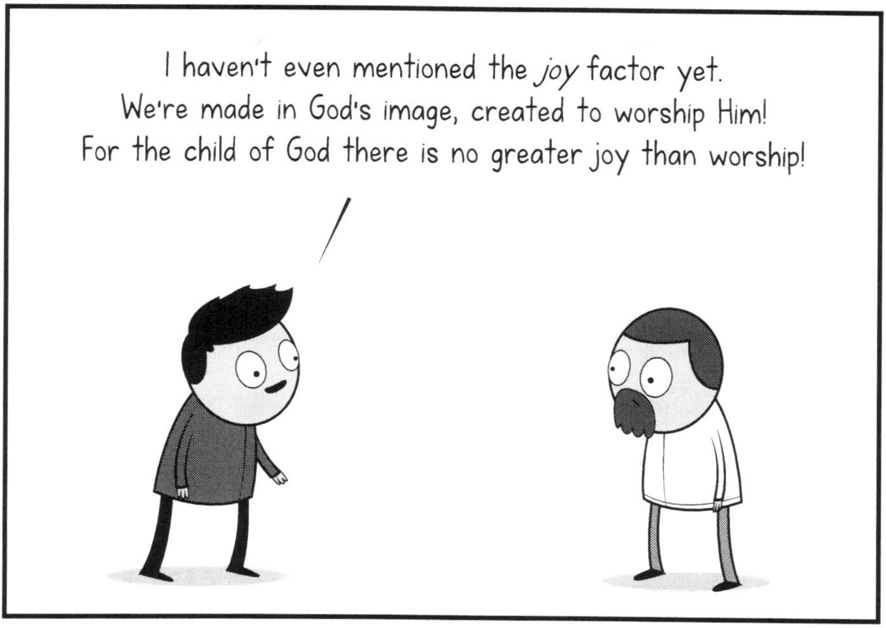
I haven't even mentioned the *joy* factor yet. We're made in God's image, created to worship Him! For the child of God there is no greater joy than worship!

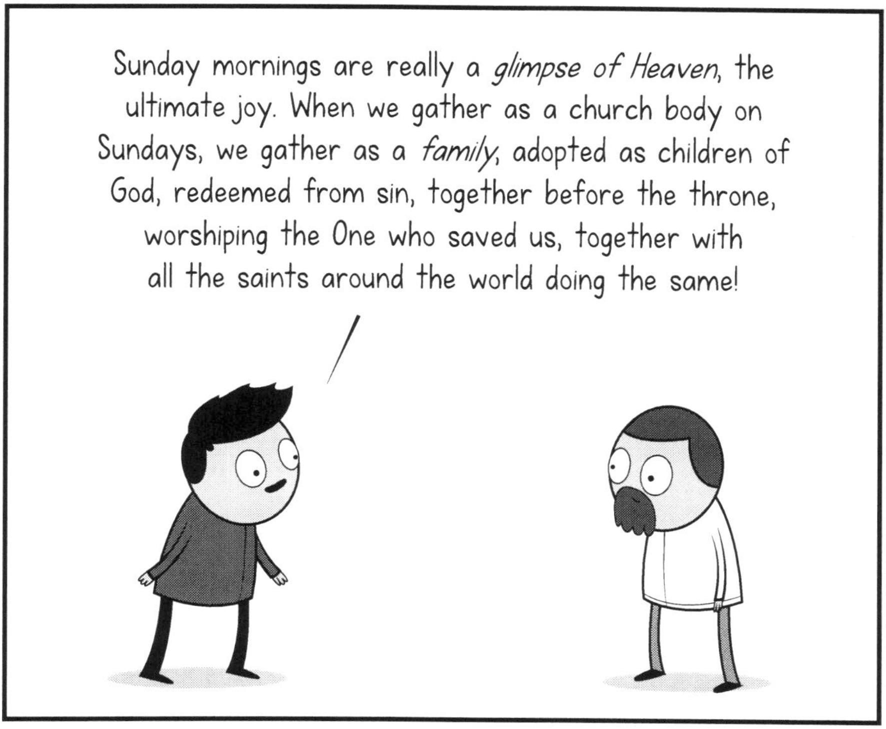
Sunday mornings are really a *glimpse of Heaven*, the ultimate joy. When we gather as a church body on Sundays, we gather as a *family*, adopted as children of God, redeemed from sin, together before the throne, worshiping the One who saved us, together with all the saints around the world doing the same!

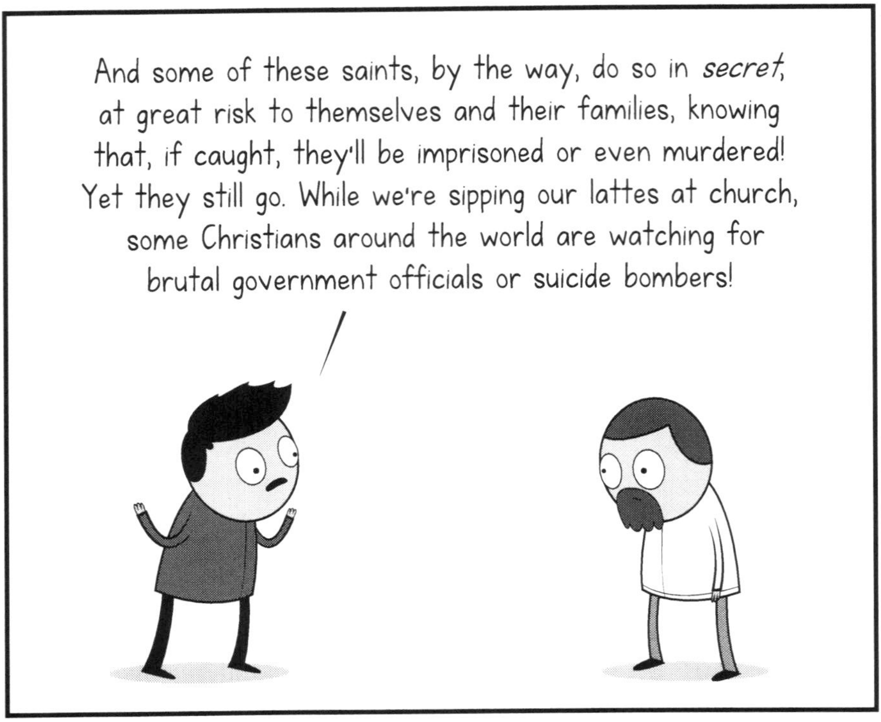
And some of these saints, by the way, do so in *secret*, at great risk to themselves and their families, knowing that, if caught, they'll be imprisoned or even murdered! Yet they still go. While we're sipping our lattes at church, some Christians around the world are watching for brutal government officials or suicide bombers!

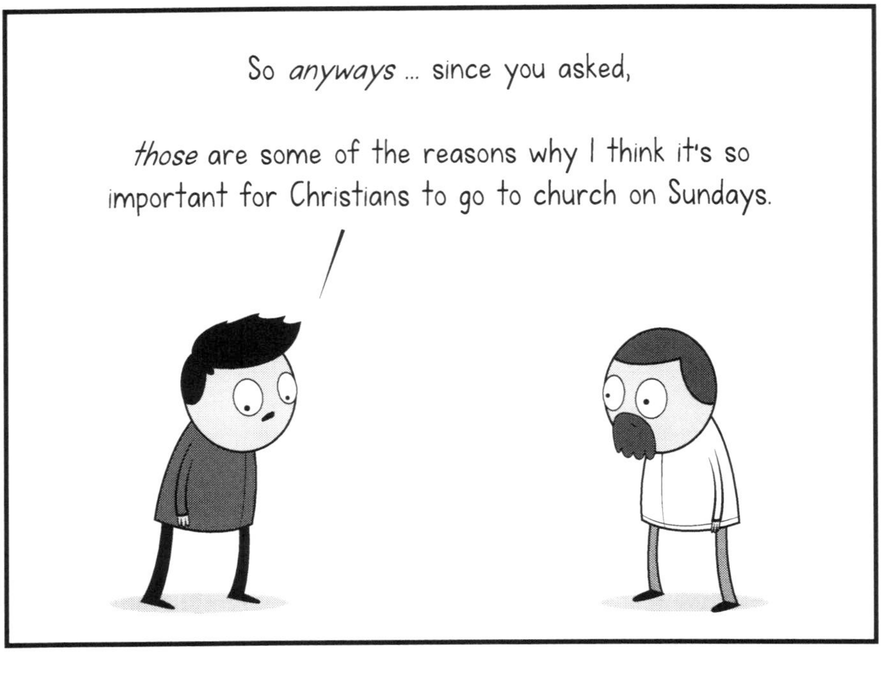
So *anyways* ... since you asked,
those are some of the reasons why I think it's so important for Christians to go to church on Sundays.

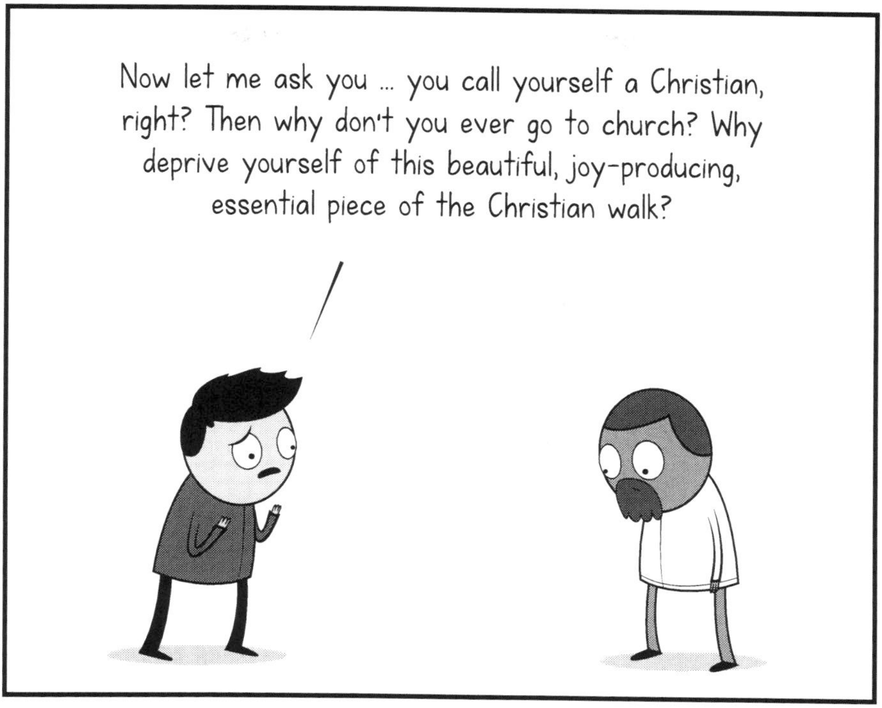
Now let me ask you ... you call yourself a Christian, right? Then why don't you ever go to church? Why deprive yourself of this beautiful, joy-producing, essential piece of the Christian walk?

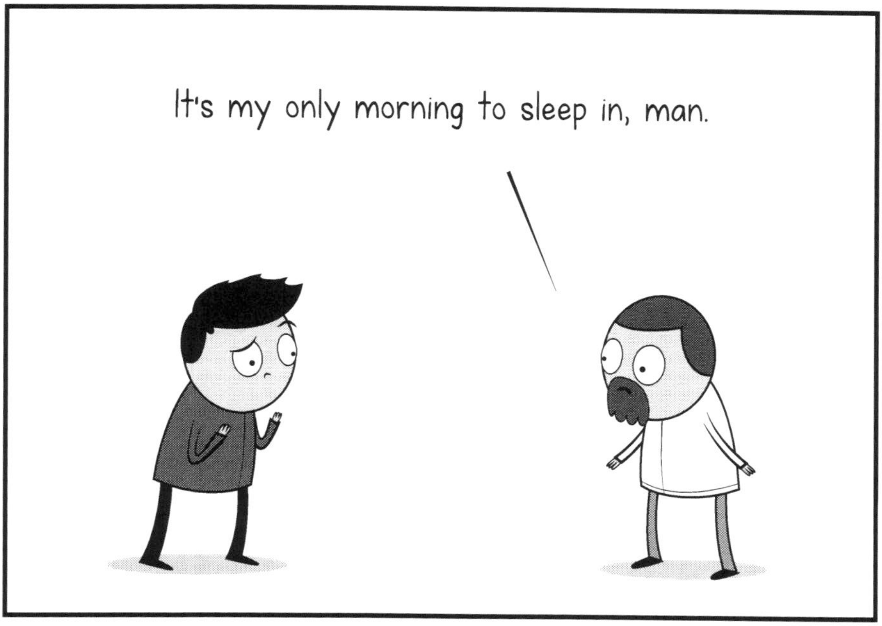
It's my only morning to sleep in, man.

Tolerance police

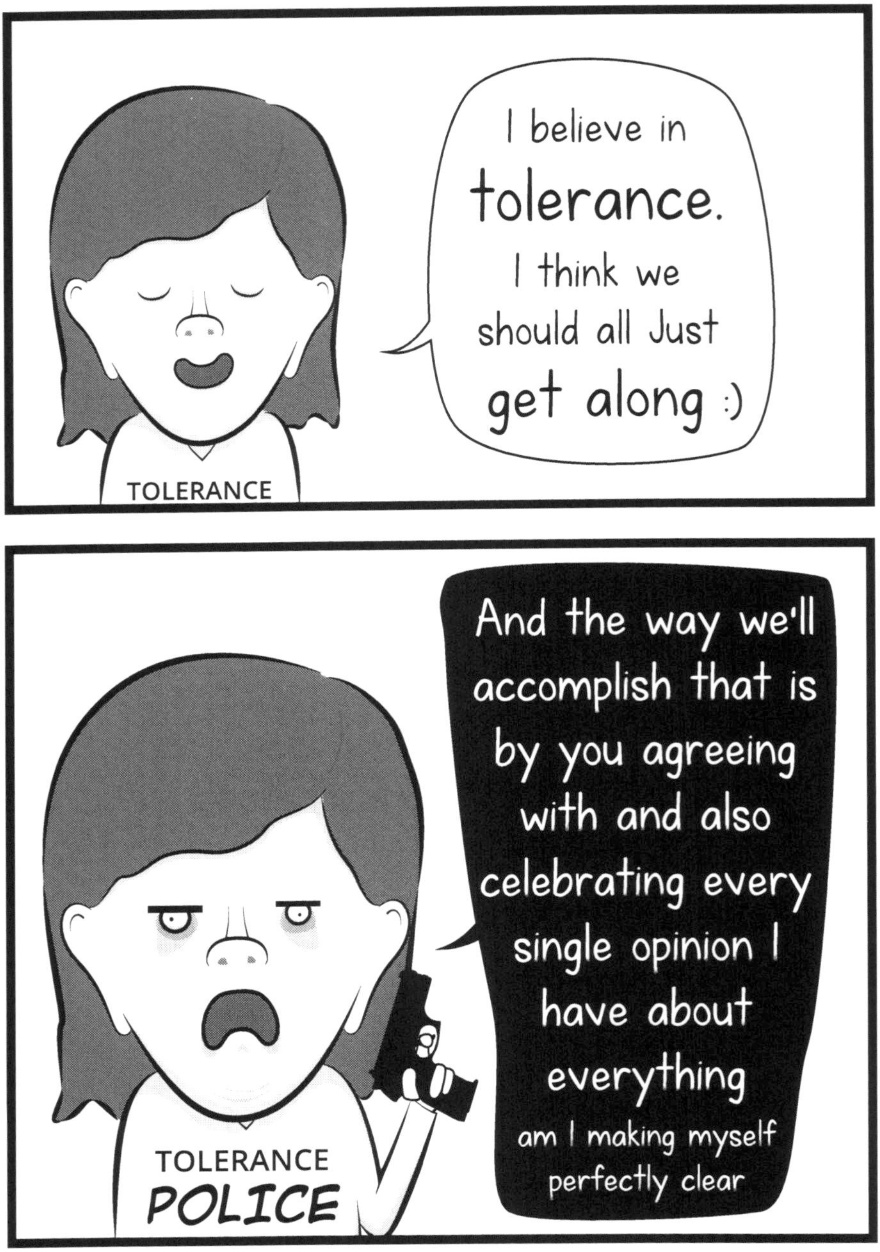

I believe in tolerance. I think we should all Just get along :)
TOLERANCE
And the way we'll accomplish that is by you agreeing with and also celebrating every single opinion I have about everything
am I making myself perfectly clear
TOLERANCE POLICE

Don't be a crazy Christian

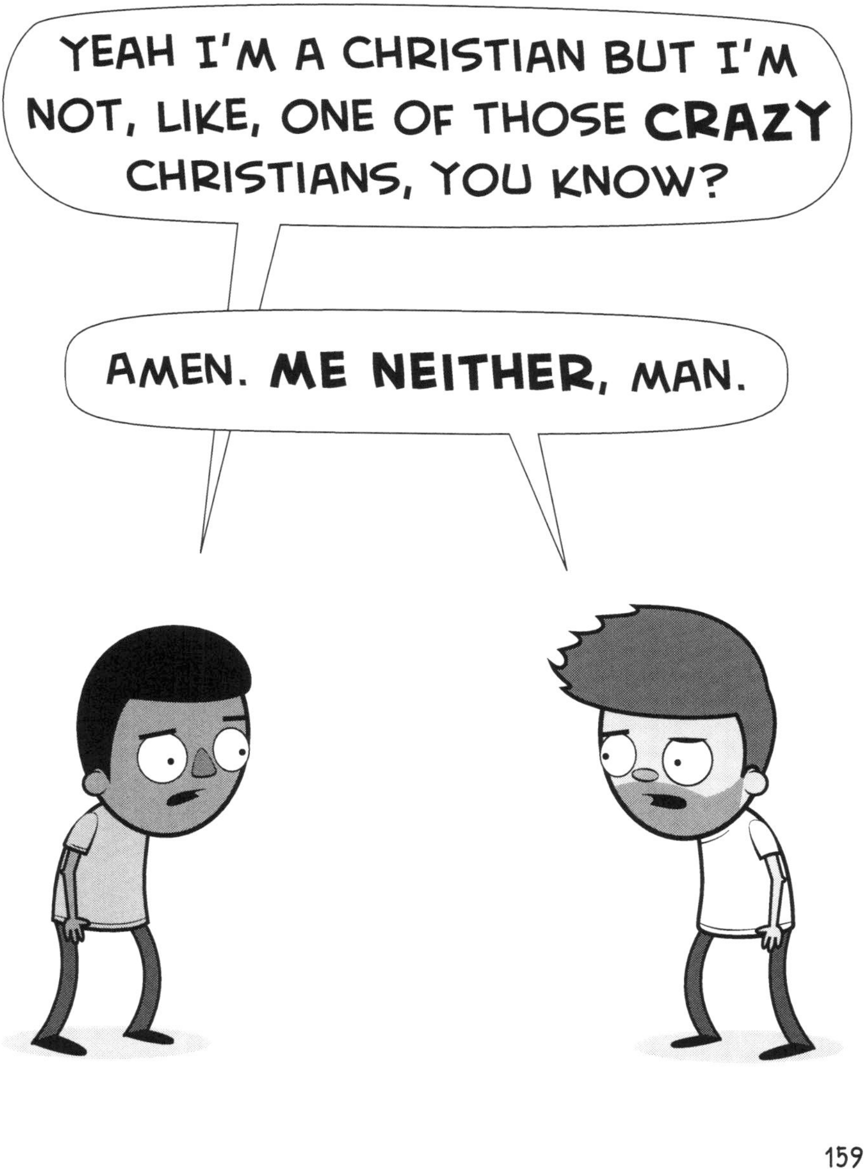
YEAH I'M A CHRISTIAN BUT I'M NOT, LIKE, ONE OF THOSE **CRAZY** CHRISTIANS, YOU KNOW?
AMEN. **ME NEITHER**, MAN.

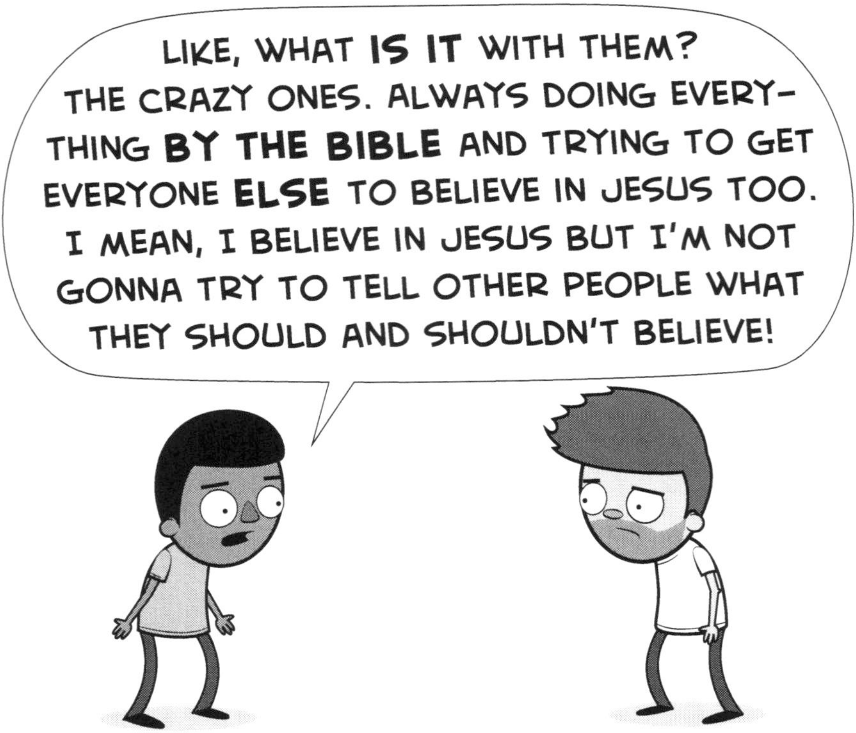
LIKE, WHAT IS IT WITH THEM? THE CRAZY ONES. ALWAYS DOING EVERYTHING BY THE BIBLE AND TRYING TO GET EVERYONE ELSE TO BELIEVE IN JESUS TOO. I MEAN, I BELIEVE IN JESUS BUT I'M NOT GONNA TRY TO TELL OTHER PEOPLE WHAT THEY SHOULD AND SHOULDN'T BELIEVE!

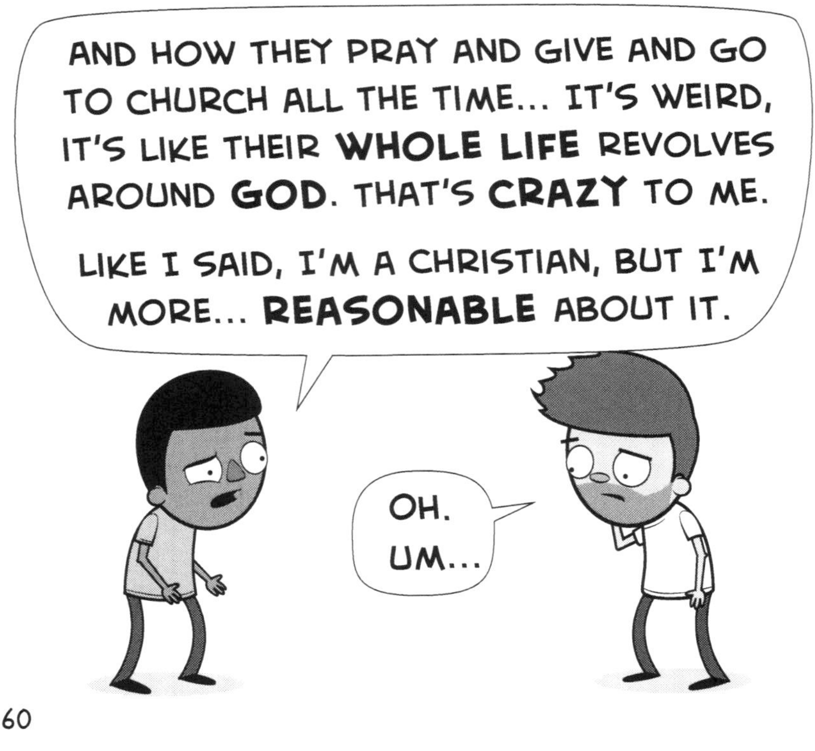
AND HOW THEY PRAY AND GIVE AND GO TO CHURCH ALL THE TIME... IT'S WEIRD, IT'S LIKE THEIR WHOLE LIFE REVOLVES AROUND GOD. THAT'S CRAZY TO ME.
LIKE I SAID, I'M A CHRISTIAN, BUT I'M MORE... REASONABLE ABOUT IT.
OH. UM...

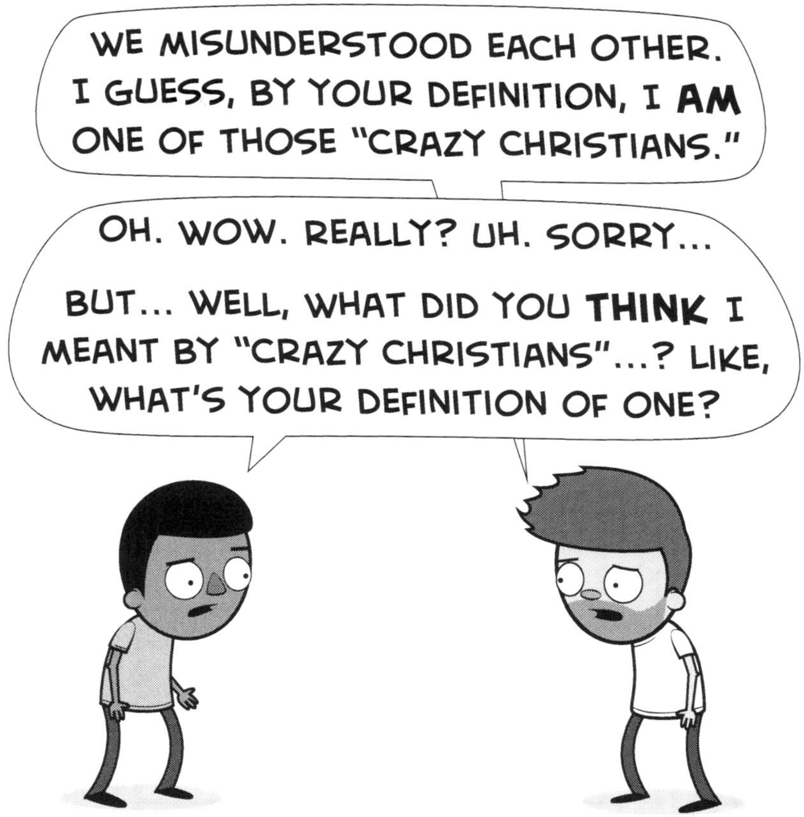
WE MISUNDERSTOOD EACH OTHER. I GUESS, BY YOUR DEFINITION, I **AM** ONE OF THOSE "CRAZY CHRISTIANS."
OH. WOW. REALLY? UH. SORRY...
BUT... WELL, WHAT DID YOU **THINK** I MEANT BY "CRAZY CHRISTIANS"...? LIKE, WHAT'S YOUR DEFINITION OF ONE?

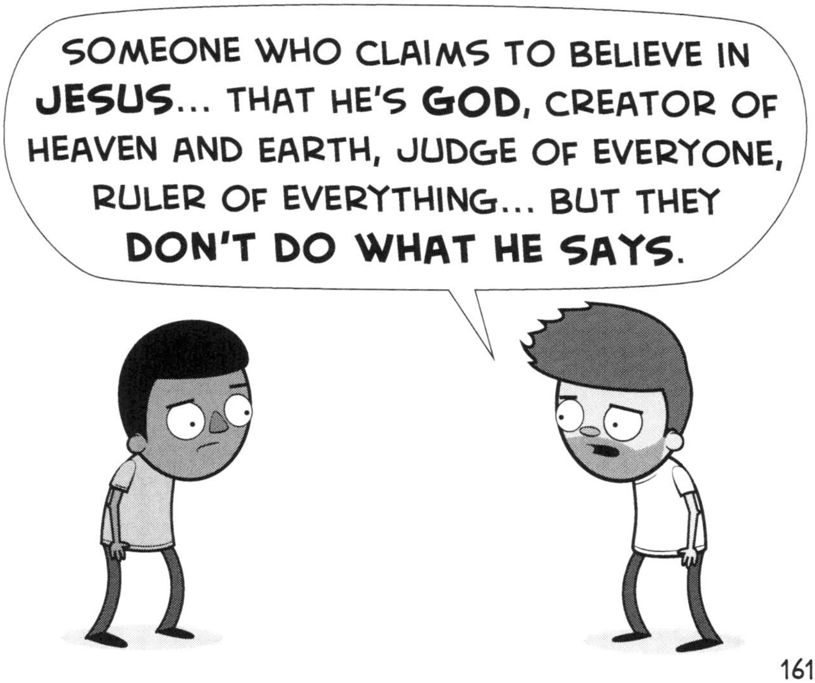
SOMEONE WHO CLAIMS TO BELIEVE IN **JESUS**... THAT HE'S **GOD**, CREATOR OF HEAVEN AND EARTH, JUDGE OF EVERYONE, RULER OF EVERYTHING... BUT THEY **DON'T DO WHAT HE SAYS**.

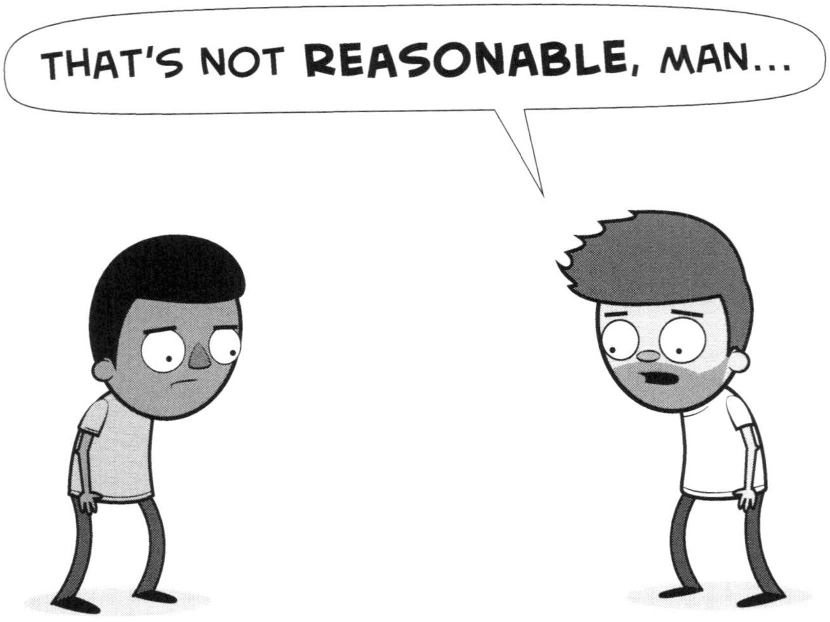
THAT'S NOT REASONABLE, MAN...

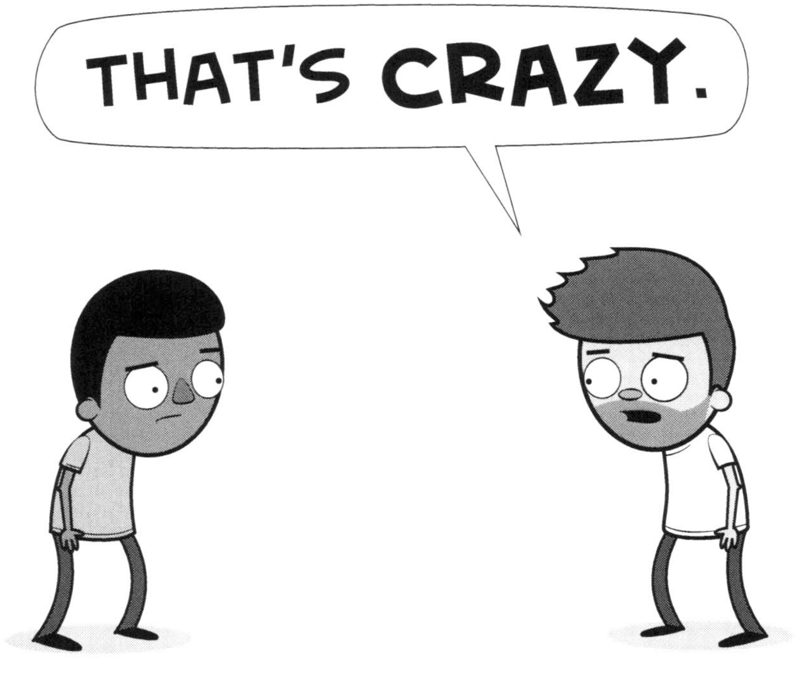
THAT'S CRAZY.

The Bible advocates slavery, polygamy, rape, and genocide!

When someone says this:

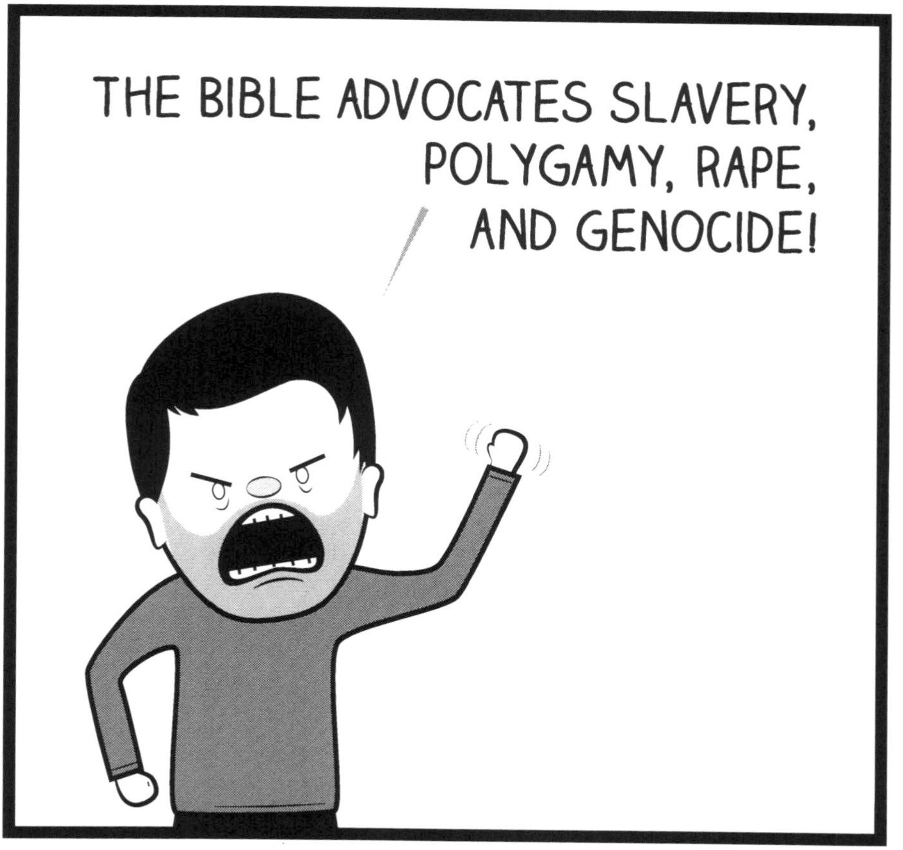
THE BIBLE ADVOCATES SLAVERY, POLYGAMY, RAPE, AND GENOCIDE!

They're really saying this:

IT WOULD TAKE LIKE TEN MINUTES OF MY LIFE TO SEARCH ONLINE AND LEARN FROM PEOPLE WHO ACTUALLY STUDY THE BIBLE HOW FALSE THIS STATEMENT IS AND THEREFORE HOW INTELLECTUALLY DISHONEST IT IS FOR ME TO CLAIM THAT IT'S TRUE, BUT IT IS SO MUCH EASIER JUST TO QUOTE A FEW VERSES FROM THE BIBLE WITH ZERO CONTEXT AND THEN REGUR-GITATE OPINIONS I HEARD FROM SOME MILITANT ANTI-CHRISTIAN!

AND THE BIBLE COMMANDS CHRISTIANS TO KILL GAY PEOPLE TOO BTW!!!!

What changes a "clump of cells" into a baby?

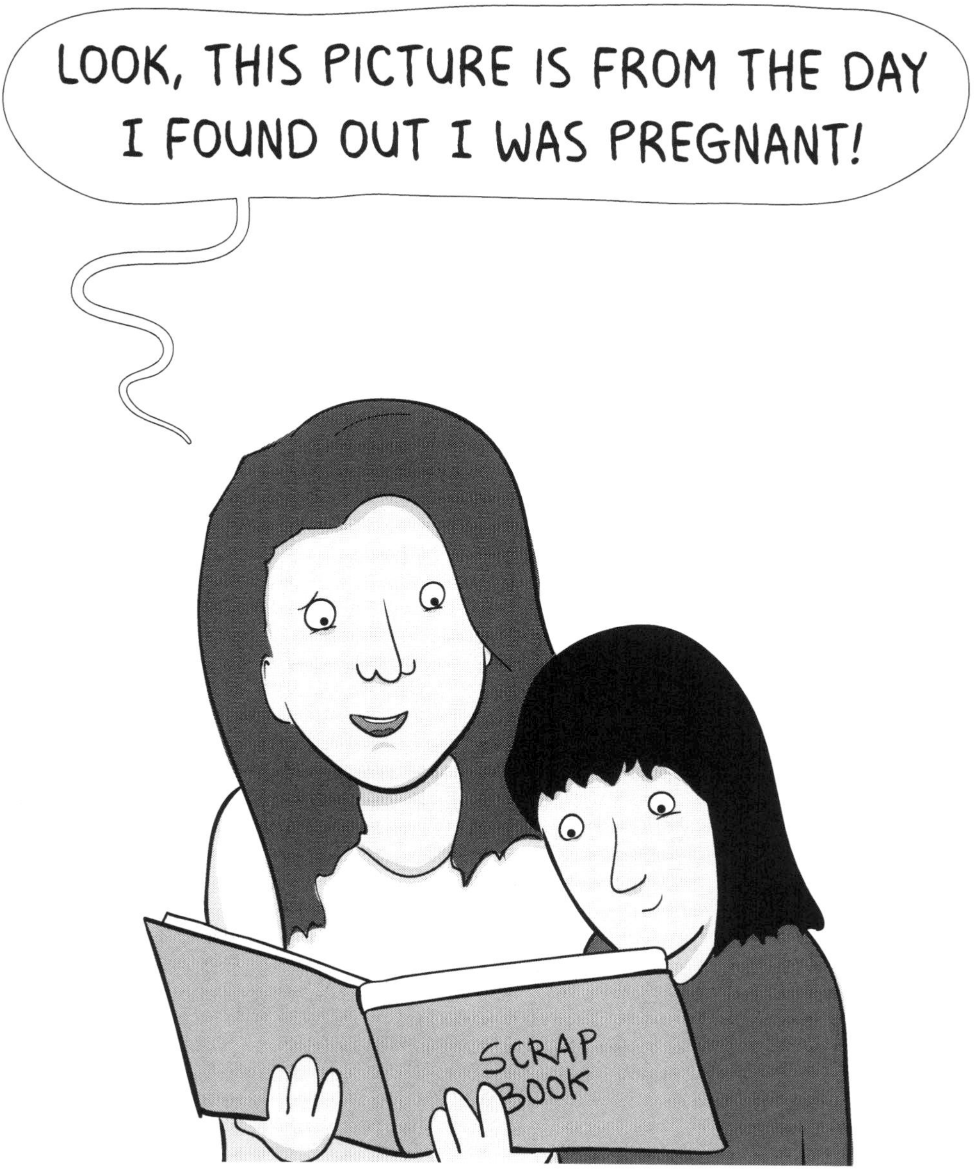
LOOK, THIS PICTURE IS FROM THE DAY I FOUND OUT I WAS PREGNANT!
SCRAP BOOK

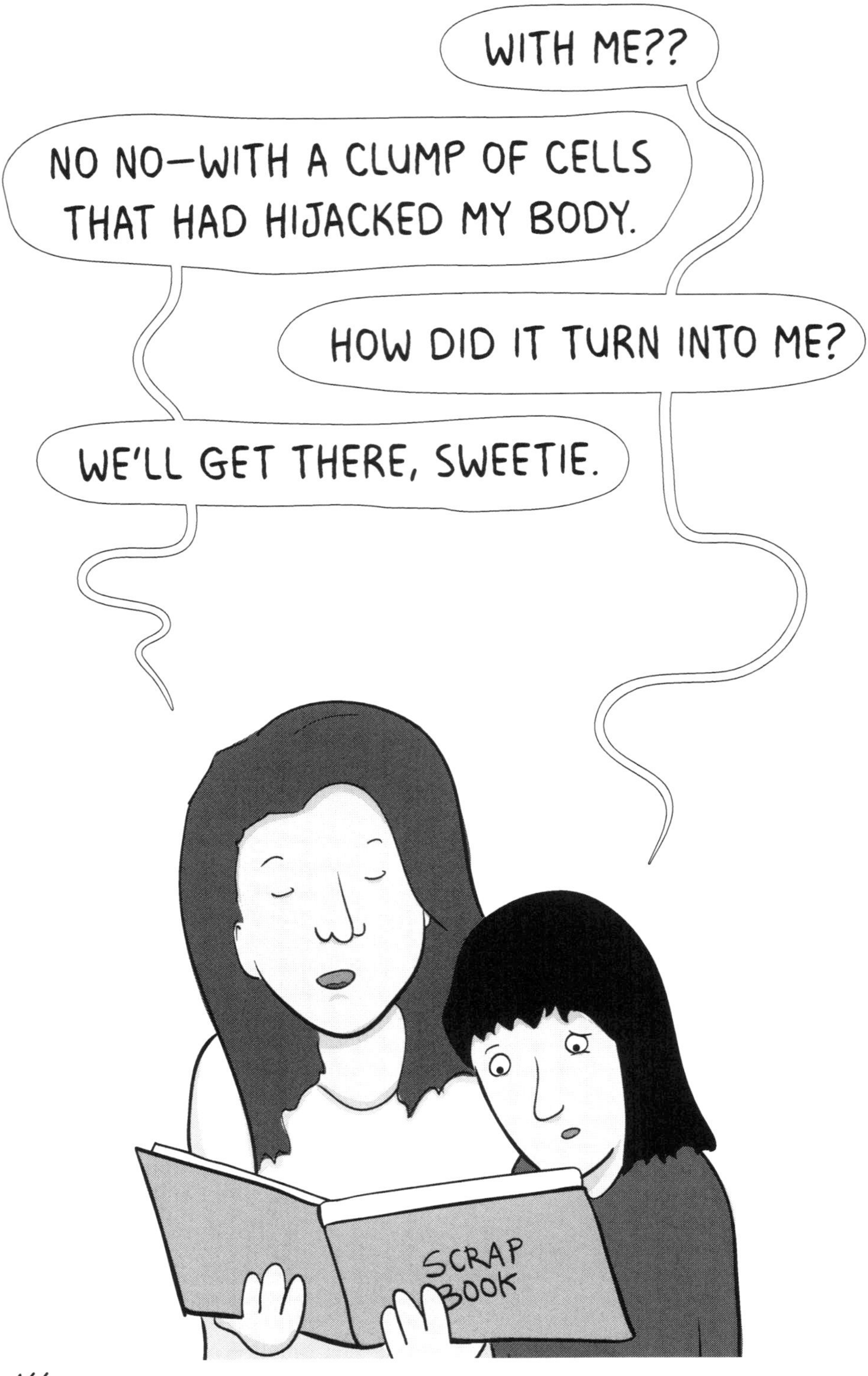
WITH ME??
NO NO—WITH A CLUMP OF CELLS THAT HAD HIJACKED MY BODY.
HOW DID IT TURN INTO ME?
WE'LL GET THERE, SWEETIE.
SCRAP BOOK

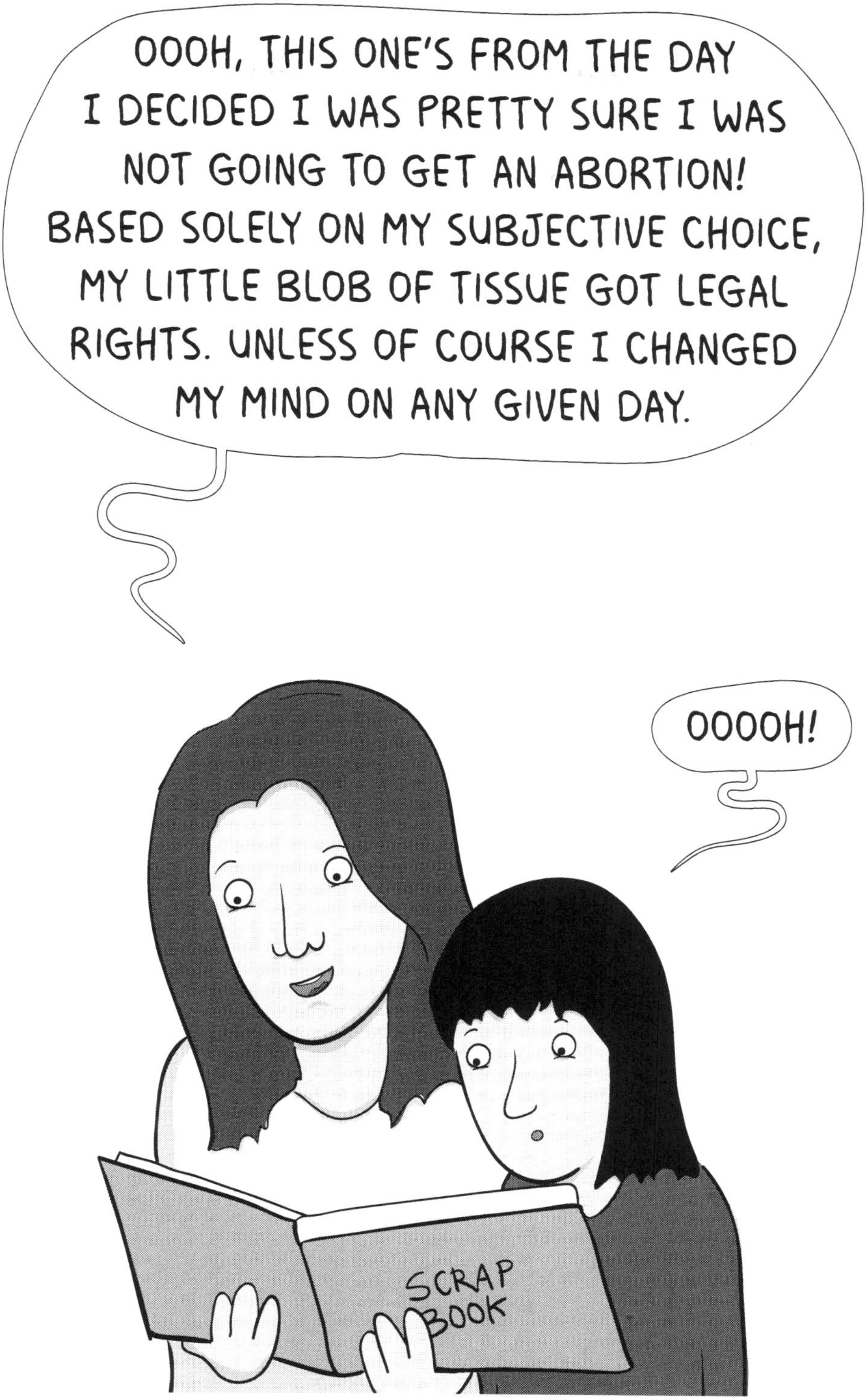
OOOH, THIS ONE'S FROM THE DAY I DECIDED I WAS PRETTY SURE I WAS NOT GOING TO GET AN ABORTION! BASED SOLELY ON MY SUBJECTIVE CHOICE, MY LITTLE BLOB OF TISSUE GOT LEGAL RIGHTS. UNLESS OF COURSE I CHANGED MY MIND ON ANY GIVEN DAY.
OOOOH!
SCRAP BOOK

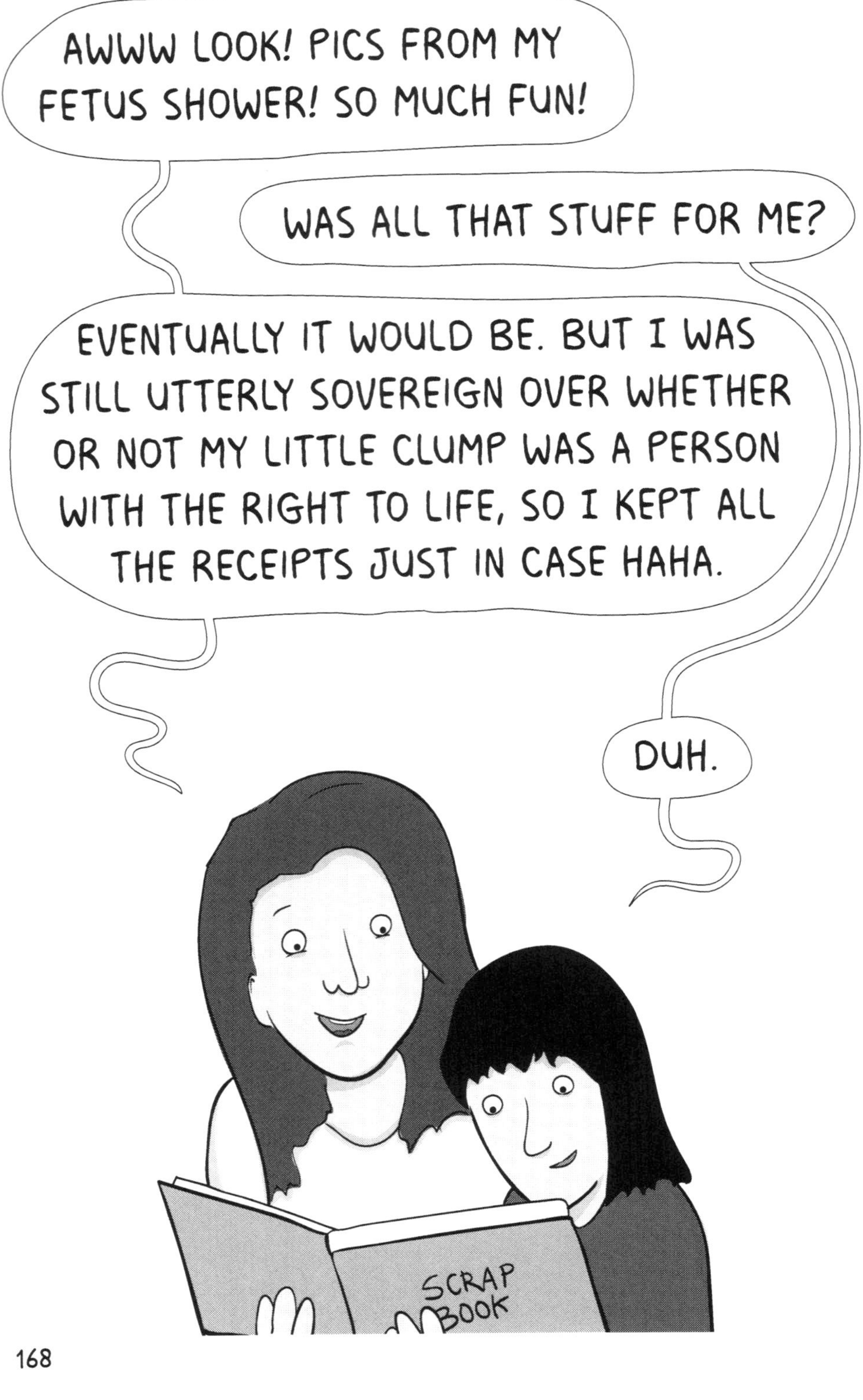
AWWW LOOK! PICS FROM MY FETUS SHOWER! SO MUCH FUN!
WAS ALL THAT STUFF FOR ME?
EVENTUALLY IT WOULD BE. BUT I WAS STILL UTTERLY SOVEREIGN OVER WHETHER OR NOT MY LITTLE CLUMP WAS A PERSON WITH THE RIGHT TO LIFE, SO I KEPT ALL THE RECEIPTS JUST IN CASE HAHA.
DUH.
SCRAP BOOK

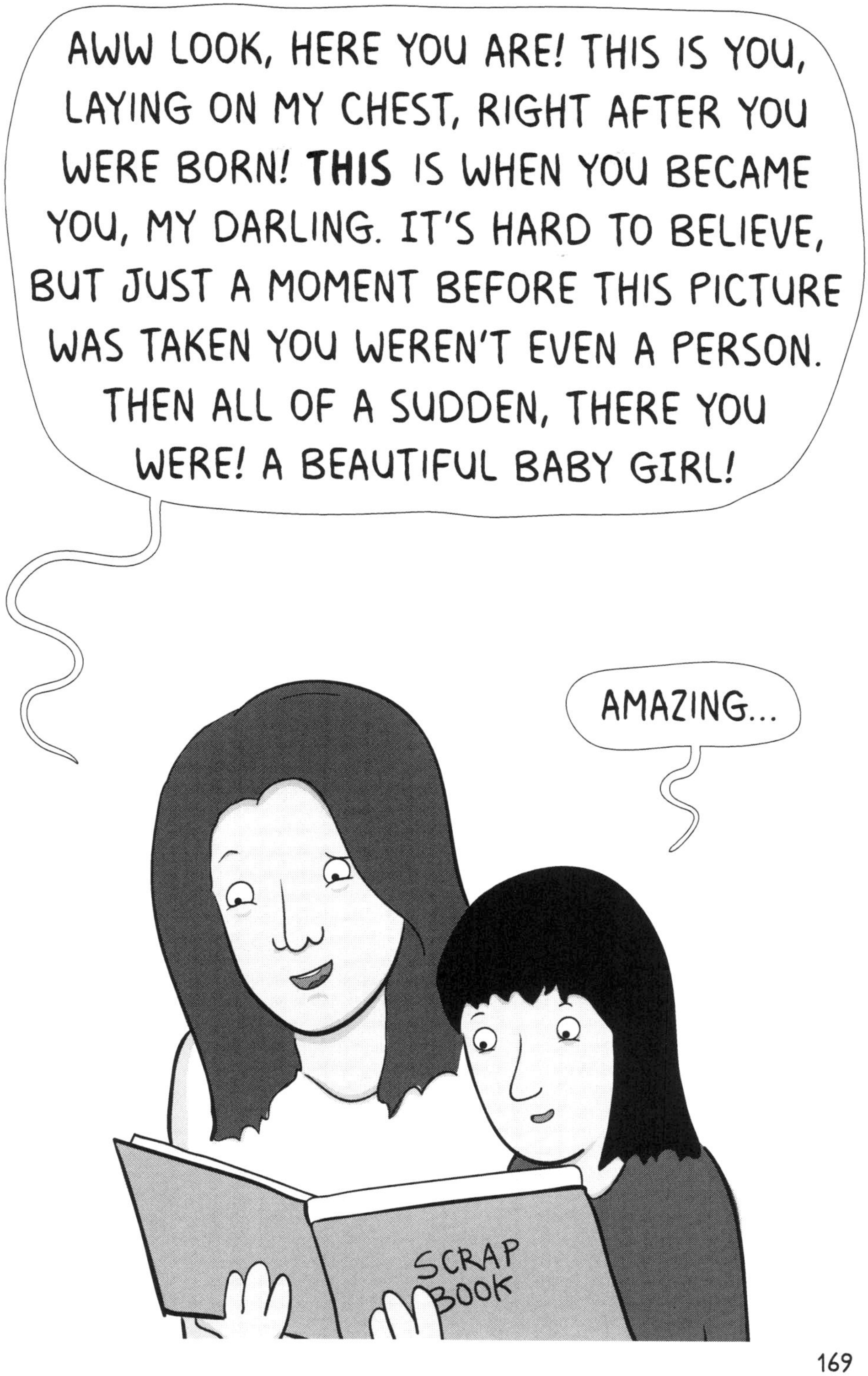
AWW LOOK, HERE YOU ARE! THIS IS YOU, LAYING ON MY CHEST, RIGHT AFTER YOU WERE BORN! **THIS** IS WHEN YOU BECAME YOU, MY DARLING. IT'S HARD TO BELIEVE, BUT JUST A MOMENT BEFORE THIS PICTURE WAS TAKEN YOU WEREN'T EVEN A PERSON. THEN ALL OF A SUDDEN, THERE YOU WERE! A BEAUTIFUL BABY GIRL!
AMAZING...
SCRAP BOOK

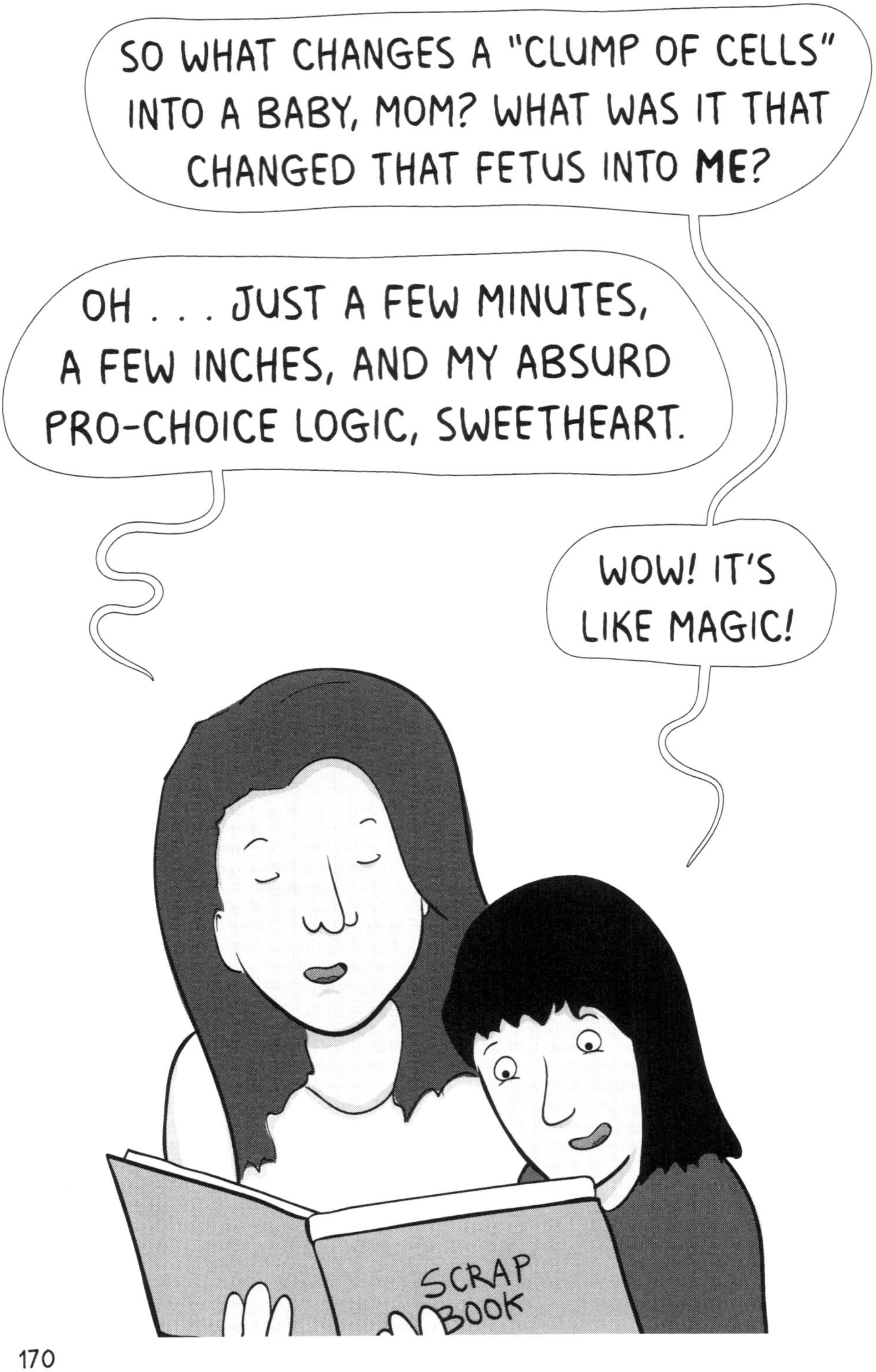
SO WHAT CHANGES A "CLUMP OF CELLS" INTO A BABY, MOM? WHAT WAS IT THAT CHANGED THAT FETUS INTO **ME**?
OH . . . JUST A FEW MINUTES, A FEW INCHES, AND MY ABSURD PRO-CHOICE LOGIC, SWEETHEART.
WOW! IT'S LIKE MAGIC!
SCRAP BOOK

Jesus, Paul, and the theological liberal

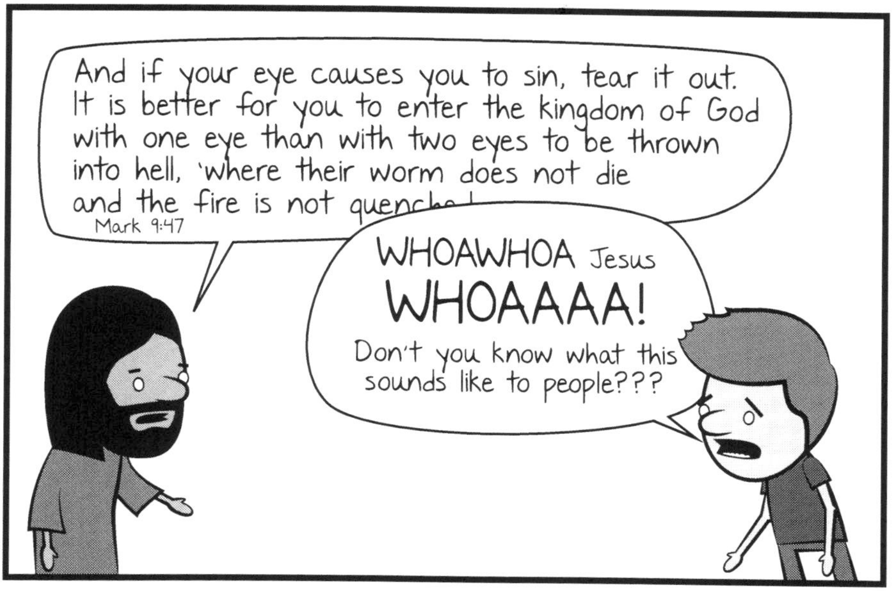
And if your eye causes you to sin, tear it out. It is better for you to enter the kingdom of God with one eye than with two eyes to be thrown into hell, 'where their worm does not die and the fire is not quench
Mark 9:47
WHOAWHOA Jesus WHOAAAA! Don't you know what this sounds like to people???

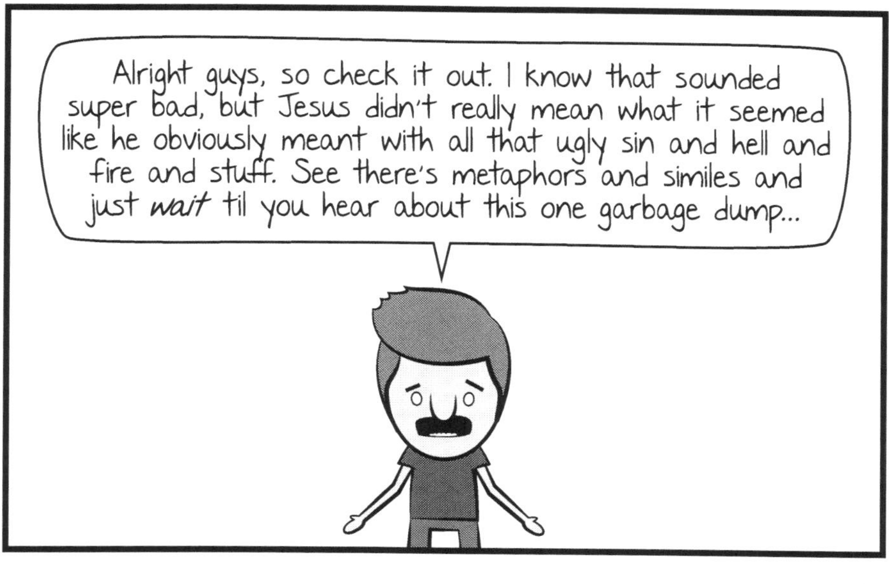
Alright guys, so check it out. I know that sounded super bad, but Jesus didn't really mean what it seemed like he obviously meant with all that ugly sin and hell and fire and stuff. See there's metaphors and similes and just *wait* til you hear about this one garbage dump...

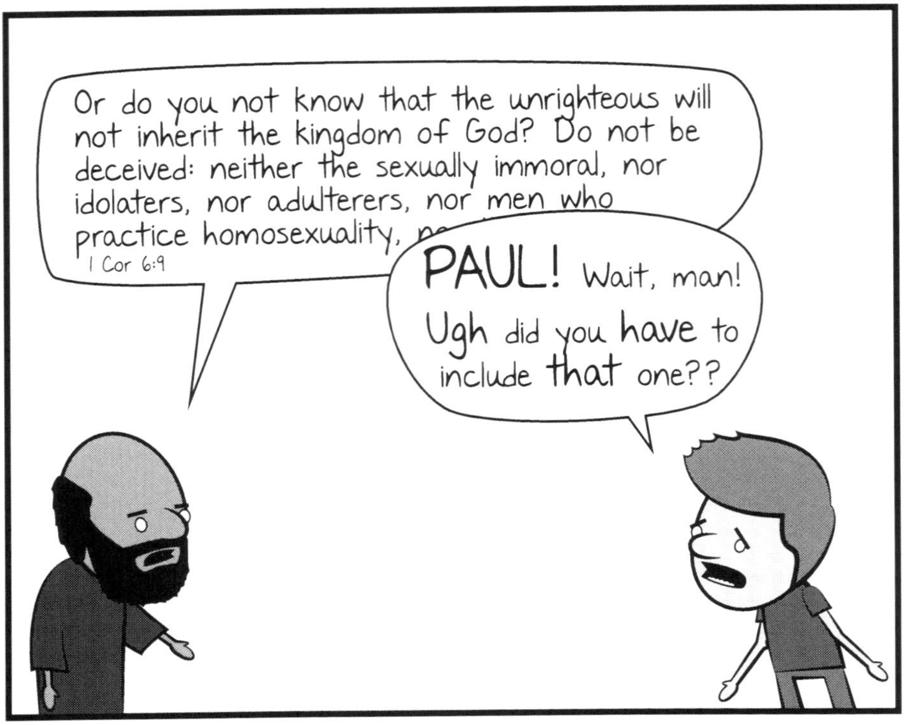
Or do you not know that the unrighteous will not inherit the kingdom of God? Do not be deceived: neither the sexually immoral, nor idolaters, nor adulterers, nor men who practice homosexuality,
1 Cor 6:9
PAUL! Wait, man! Ugh did you have to include that one??

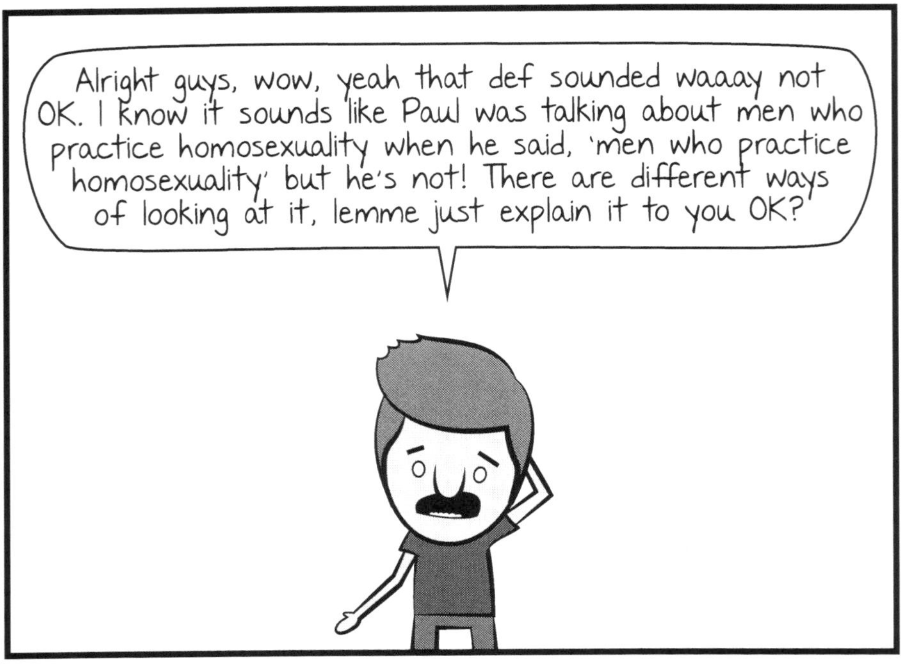
Alright guys, wow, yeah that def sounded waaay not OK. I know it sounds like Paul was talking about men who practice homosexuality when he said, 'men who practice homosexuality' but he's not! There are different ways of looking at it, lemme just explain it to you OK?

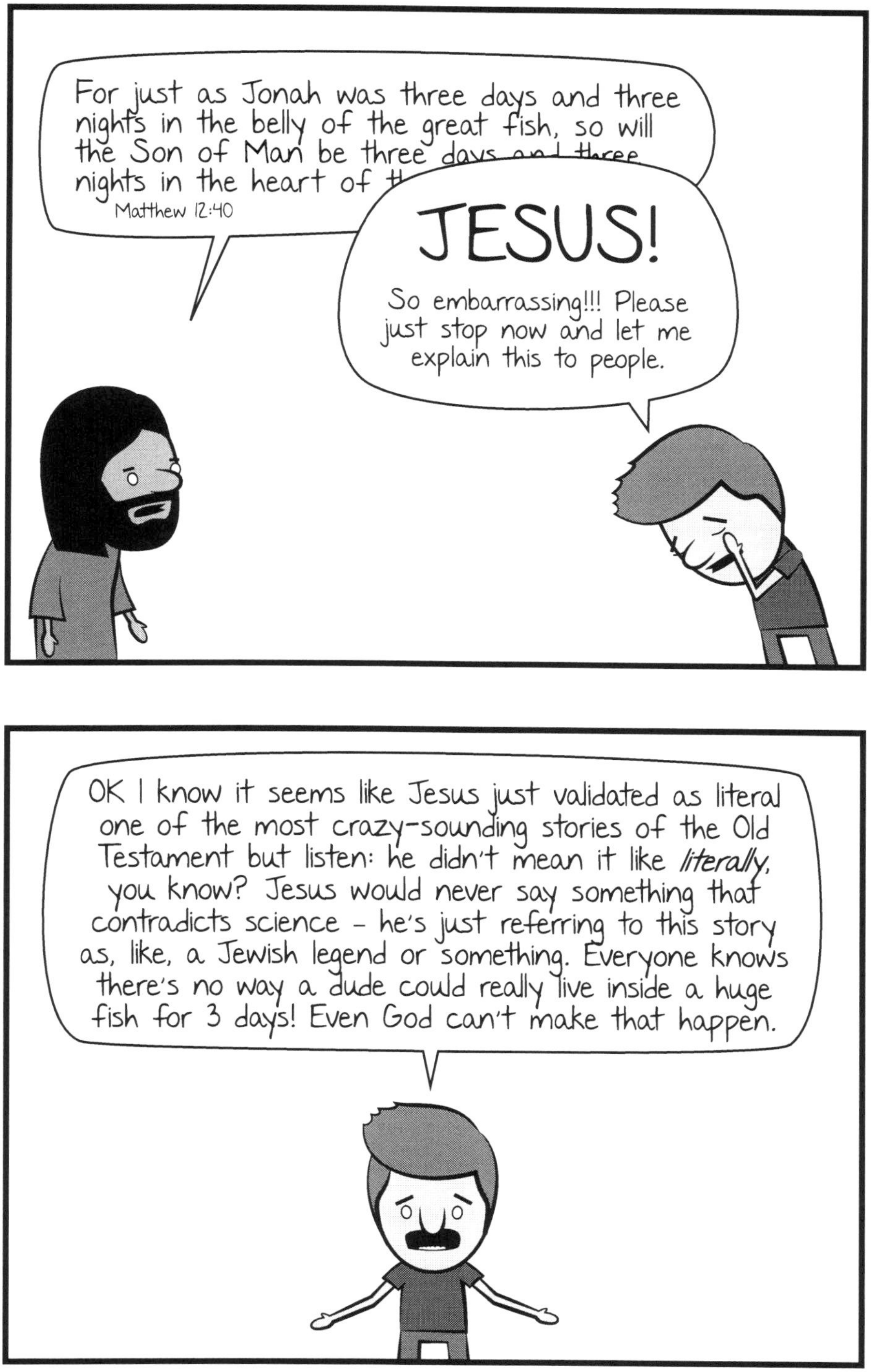
For just as Jonah was three days and three
nights in the belly of the great fish, so will
the Son of Man be three
nights in the heart of
Matthew 12:40
JESUS!
So embarrassing!!! Please just stop now and let me explain this to people.
OK I know it seems like Jesus just validated as literal one of the most crazy-sounding stories of the Old Testament but listen: he didn't mean it like *literally*, you know? Jesus would never say something that contradicts science – he's just referring to this story as, like, a Jewish legend or something. Everyone knows there's no way a dude could really live inside a huge fish for 3 days! Even God can't make that happen.

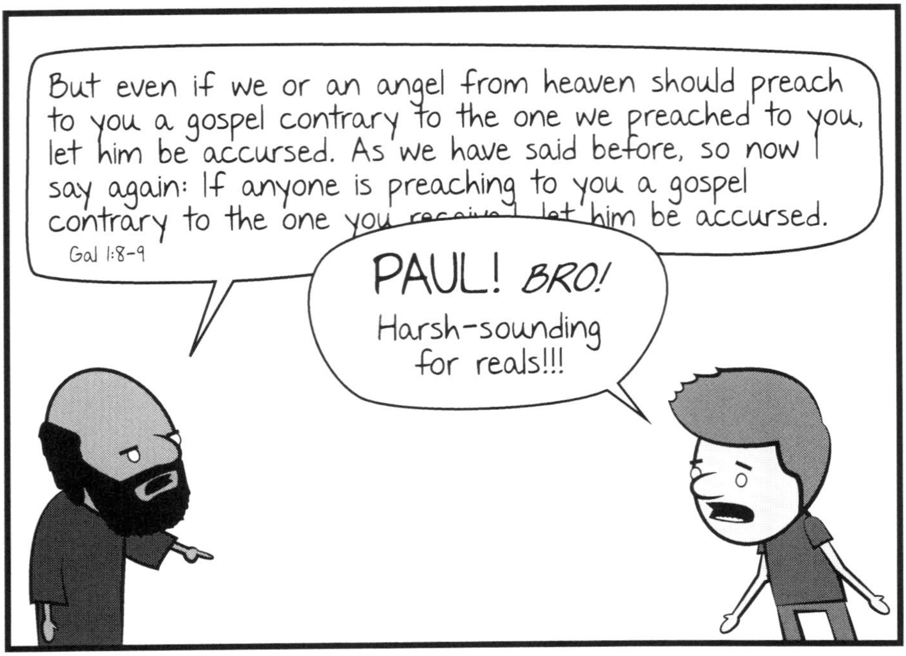
But even if we or an angel from heaven should preach to you a gospel contrary to the one we preached to you, let him be accursed. As we have said before, so now I say again: If anyone is preaching to you a gospel contrary to the one you him be accursed.
Gal 1:8-9
PAUL! *BRO!* Harsh-sounding for reals!!!

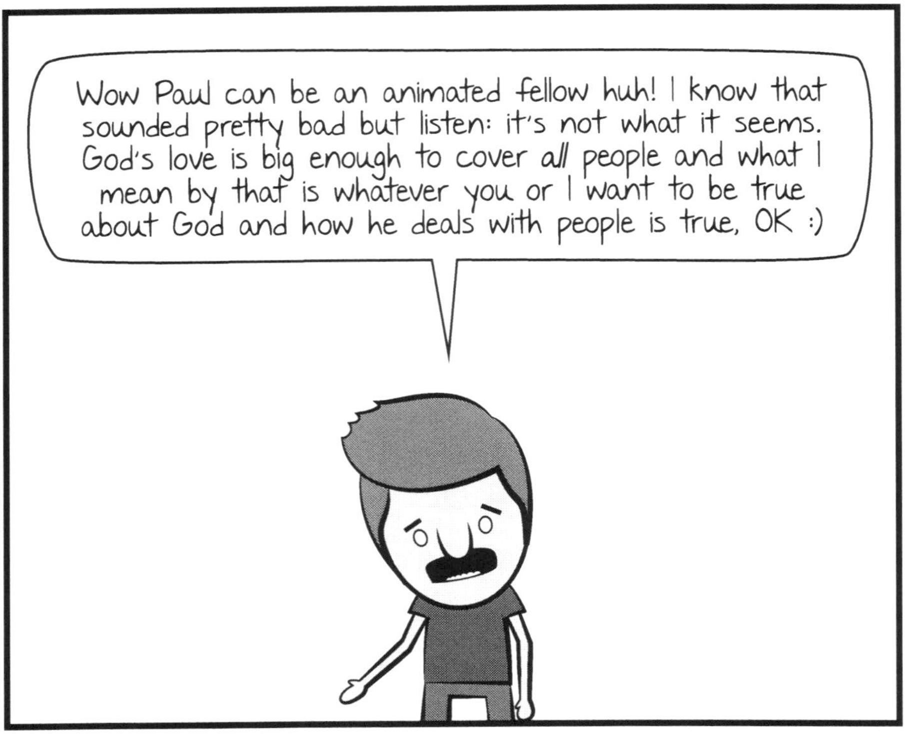
Wow Paul can be an animated fellow huh! I know that sounded pretty bad but listen: it's not what it seems. God's love is big enough to cover *all* people and what I mean by that is whatever you or I want to be true about God and how he deals with people is true, OK :)

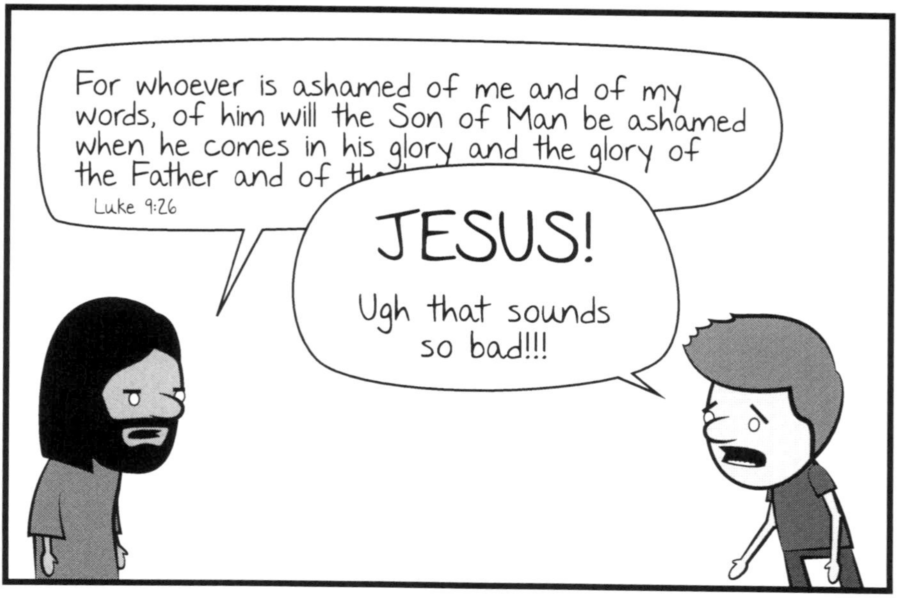
For whoever is ashamed of me and of my words, of him will the Son of Man be ashamed when he comes in his glory and the glory of the Father and of th
Luke 9:26
JESUS!
Ugh that sounds so bad!!!

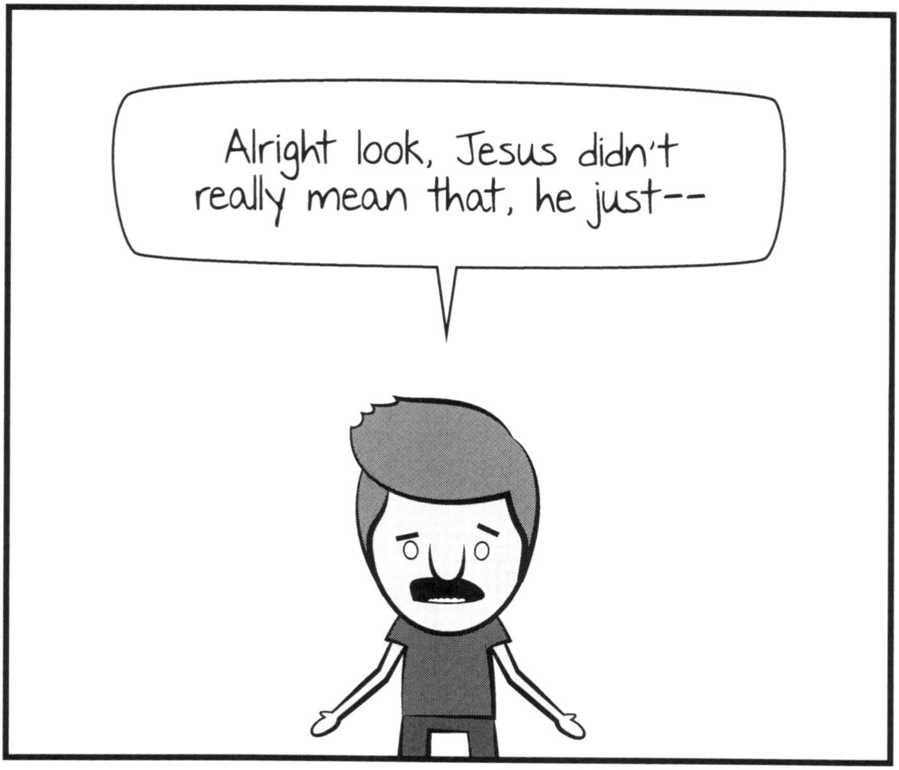
Alright look, Jesus didn't really mean that, he just--

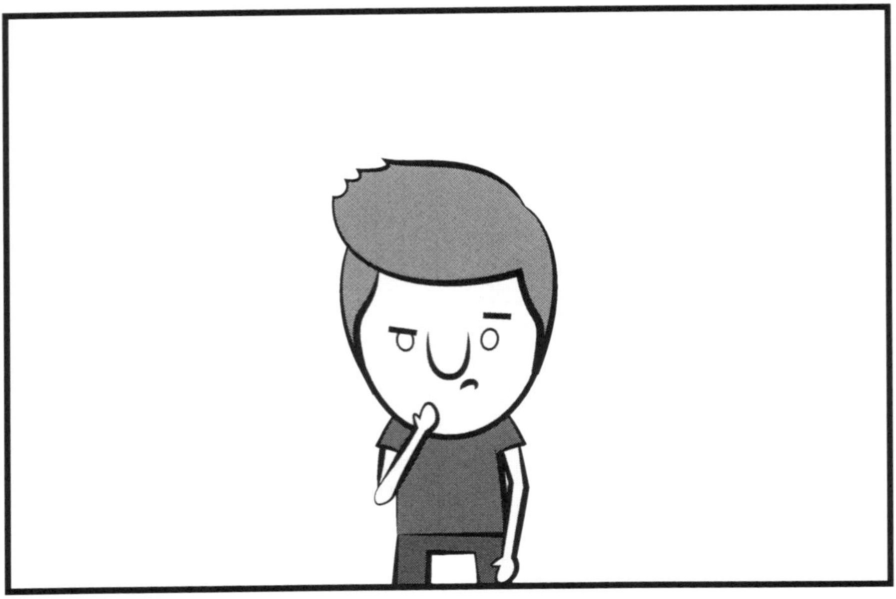

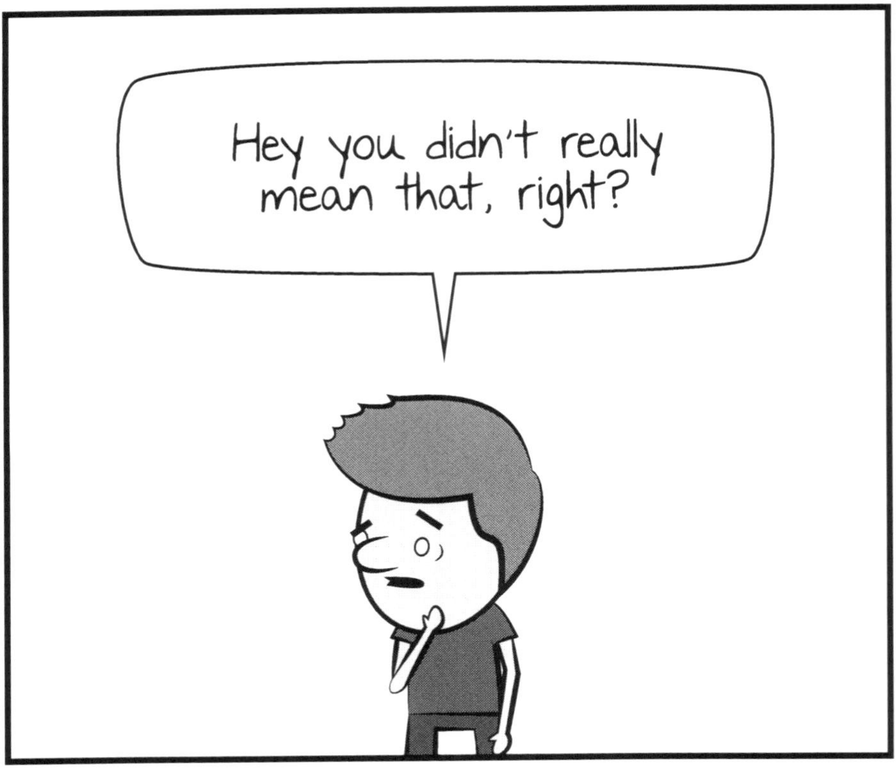
Hey you didn't really mean that, right?

I must believe in God because of all the evil in the world

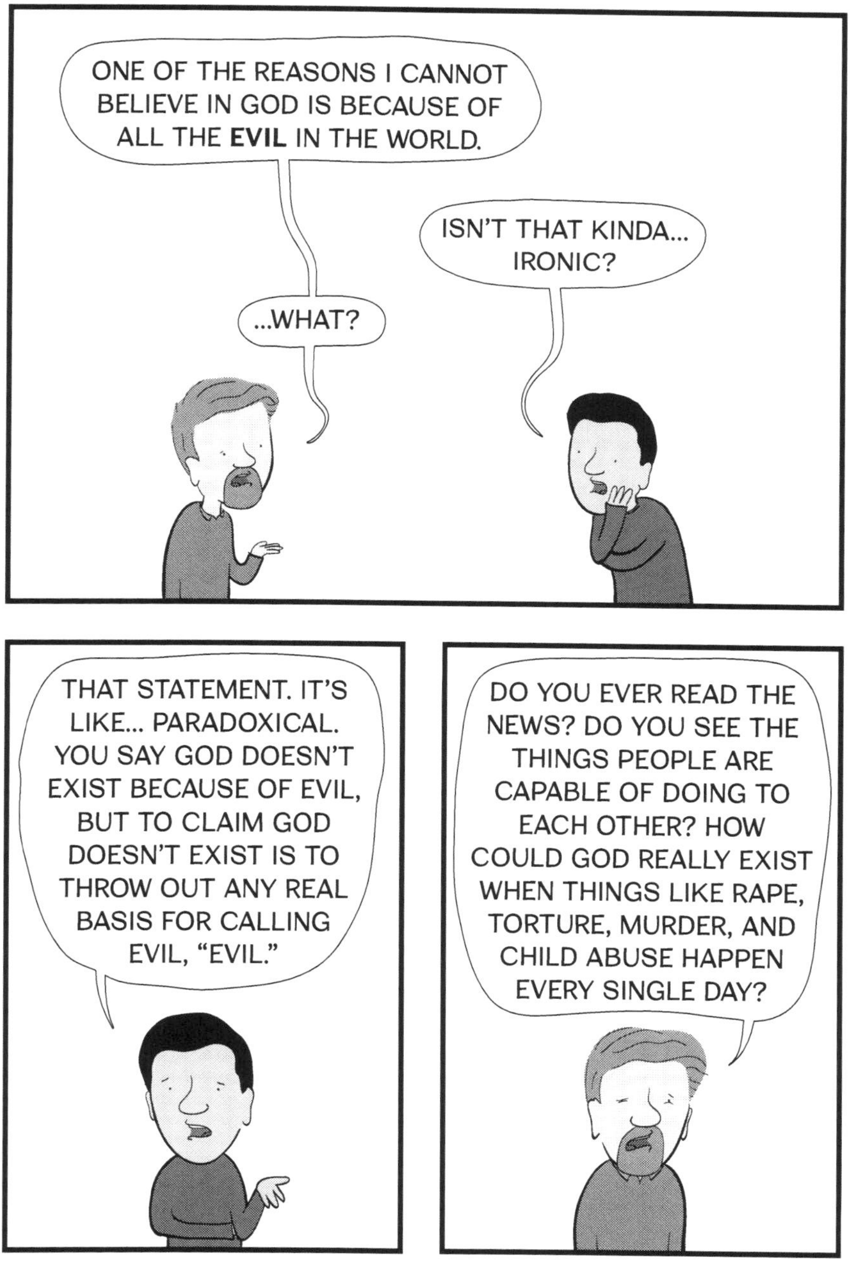
ONE OF THE REASONS I CANNOT BELIEVE IN GOD IS BECAUSE OF ALL THE **EVIL** IN THE WORLD.
ISN'T THAT KINDA... IRONIC?
...WHAT?
THAT STATEMENT. IT'S LIKE... PARADOXICAL. YOU SAY GOD DOESN'T EXIST BECAUSE OF EVIL, BUT TO CLAIM GOD DOESN'T EXIST IS TO THROW OUT ANY REAL BASIS FOR CALLING EVIL, "EVIL."
DO YOU EVER READ THE NEWS? DO YOU SEE THE THINGS PEOPLE ARE CAPABLE OF DOING TO EACH OTHER? HOW COULD GOD REALLY EXIST WHEN THINGS LIKE RAPE, TORTURE, MURDER, AND CHILD ABUSE HAPPEN EVERY SINGLE DAY?

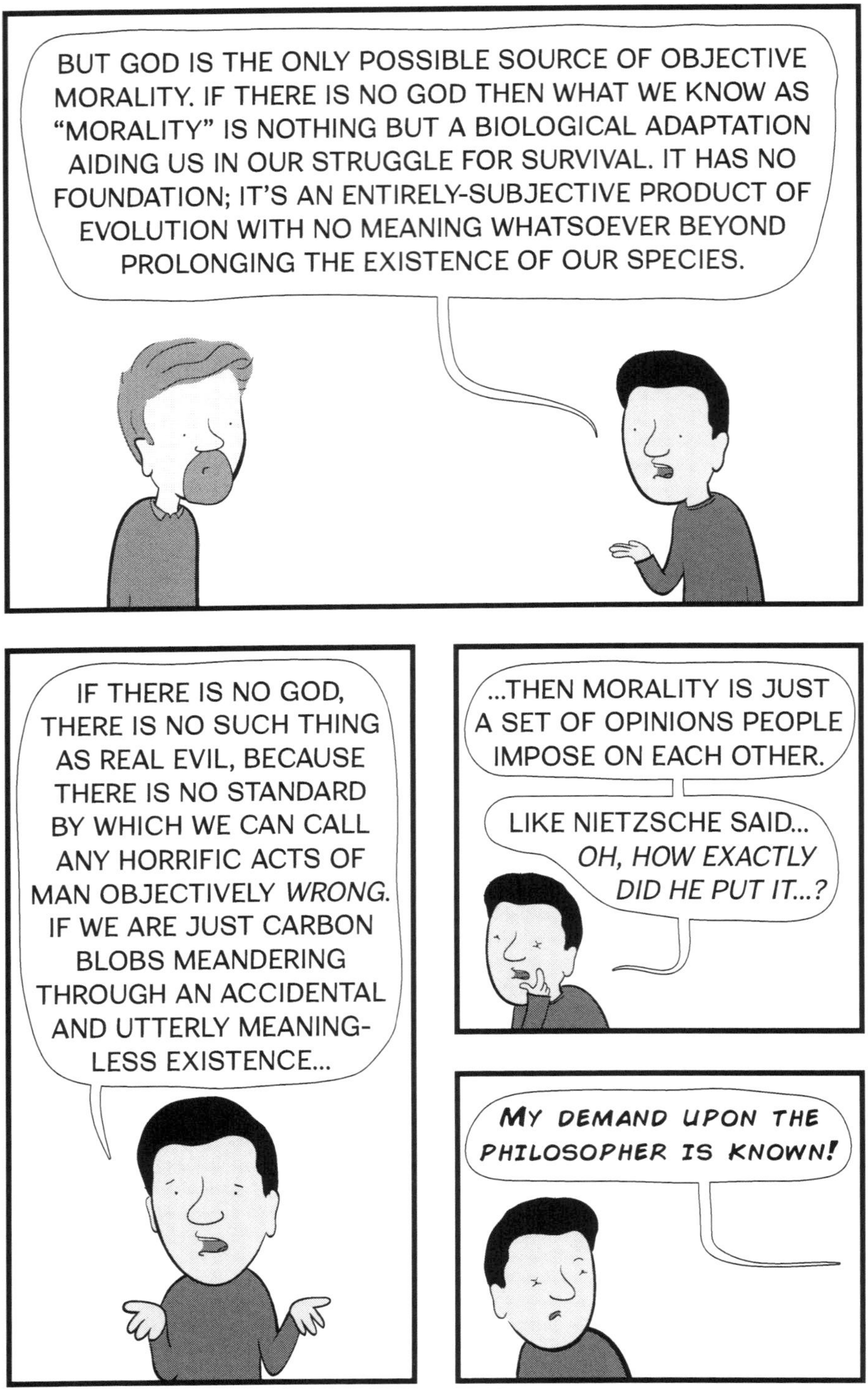
BUT GOD IS THE ONLY POSSIBLE SOURCE OF OBJECTIVE MORALITY. IF THERE IS NO GOD THEN WHAT WE KNOW AS "MORALITY" IS NOTHING BUT A BIOLOGICAL ADAPTATION AIDING US IN OUR STRUGGLE FOR SURVIVAL. IT HAS NO FOUNDATION; IT'S AN ENTIRELY-SUBJECTIVE PRODUCT OF EVOLUTION WITH NO MEANING WHATSOEVER BEYOND PROLONGING THE EXISTENCE OF OUR SPECIES.
IF THERE IS NO GOD, THERE IS NO SUCH THING AS REAL EVIL, BECAUSE THERE IS NO STANDARD BY WHICH WE CAN CALL ANY HORRIFIC ACTS OF MAN OBJECTIVELY *WRONG*. IF WE ARE JUST CARBON BLOBS MEANDERING THROUGH AN ACCIDENTAL AND UTTERLY MEANING-LESS EXISTENCE...
...THEN MORALITY IS JUST A SET OF OPINIONS PEOPLE IMPOSE ON EACH OTHER.
LIKE NIETZSCHE SAID... *OH, HOW EXACTLY DID HE PUT IT...?*
MY DEMAND UPON THE PHILOSOPHER IS KNOWN!

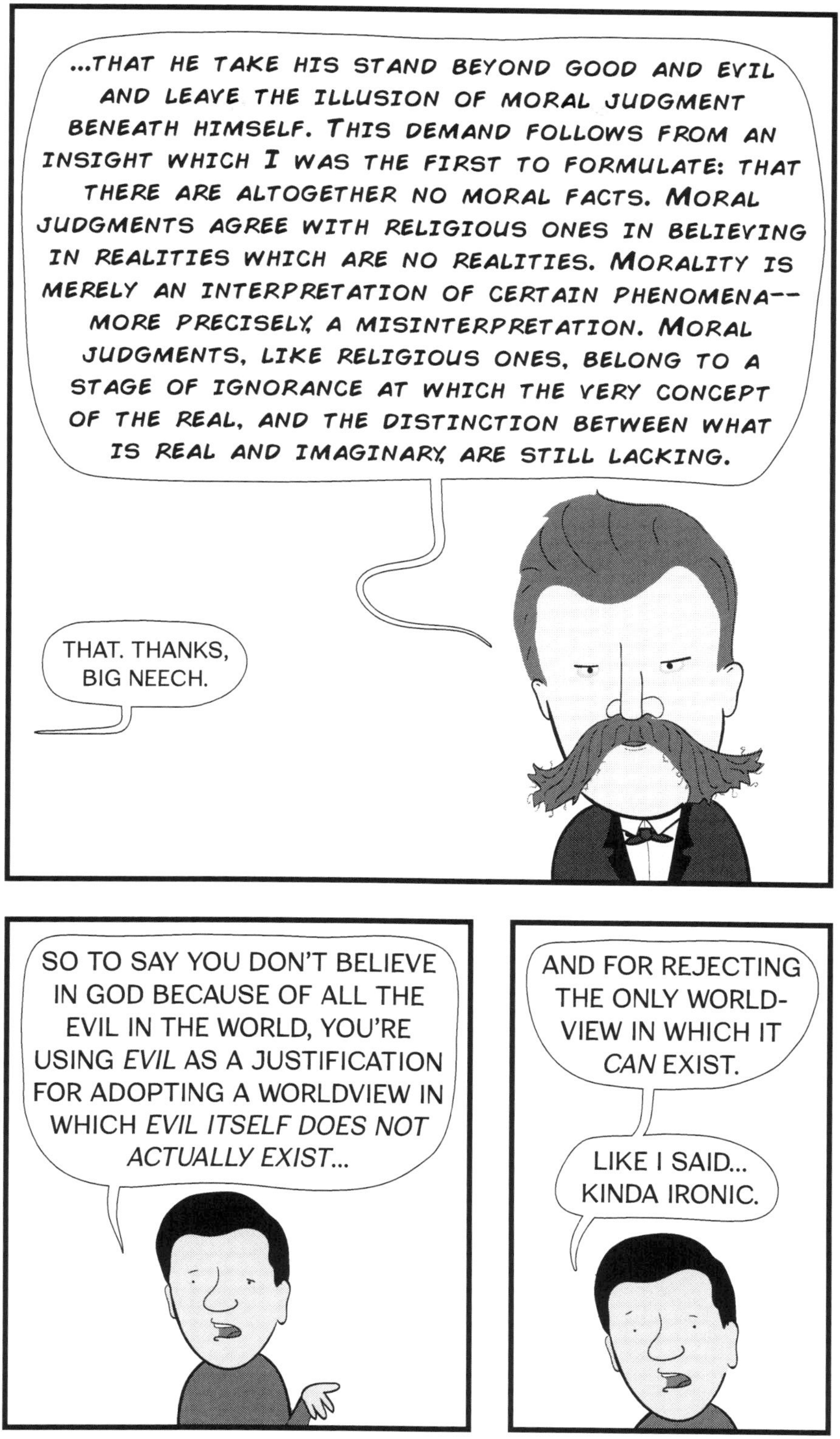
...THAT HE TAKE HIS STAND BEYOND GOOD AND EVIL AND LEAVE THE ILLUSION OF MORAL JUDGMENT BENEATH HIMSELF. THIS DEMAND FOLLOWS FROM AN INSIGHT WHICH I WAS THE FIRST TO FORMULATE: THAT THERE ARE ALTOGETHER NO MORAL FACTS. MORAL JUDGMENTS AGREE WITH RELIGIOUS ONES IN BELIEVING IN REALITIES WHICH ARE NO REALITIES. MORALITY IS MERELY AN INTERPRETATION OF CERTAIN PHENOMENA--MORE PRECISELY, A MISINTERPRETATION. MORAL JUDGMENTS, LIKE RELIGIOUS ONES, BELONG TO A STAGE OF IGNORANCE AT WHICH THE VERY CONCEPT OF THE REAL, AND THE DISTINCTION BETWEEN WHAT IS REAL AND IMAGINARY, ARE STILL LACKING.
THAT. THANKS, BIG NEECH.
SO TO SAY YOU DON'T BELIEVE IN GOD BECAUSE OF ALL THE EVIL IN THE WORLD, YOU'RE USING *EVIL* AS A JUSTIFICATION FOR ADOPTING A WORLDVIEW IN WHICH *EVIL ITSELF DOES NOT ACTUALLY EXIST*...
AND FOR REJECTING THE ONLY WORLD-VIEW IN WHICH IT *CAN* EXIST.
LIKE I SAID... KINDA IRONIC.

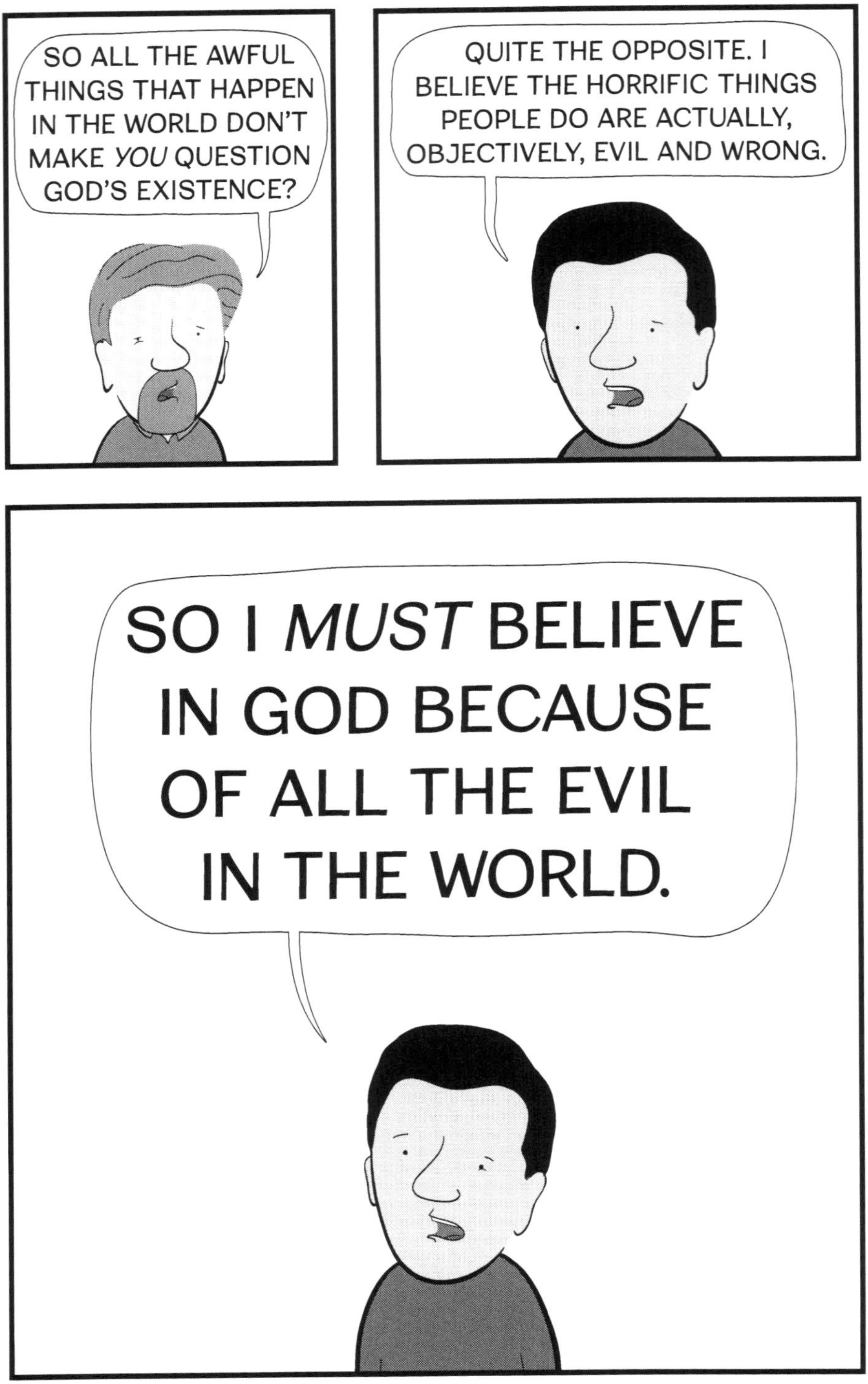
SO ALL THE AWFUL THINGS THAT HAPPEN IN THE WORLD DON'T MAKE *YOU* QUESTION GOD'S EXISTENCE?
QUITE THE OPPOSITE. I BELIEVE THE HORRIFIC THINGS PEOPLE DO ARE ACTUALLY, OBJECTIVELY, EVIL AND WRONG.
SO I *MUST* BELIEVE IN GOD BECAUSE OF ALL THE EVIL IN THE WORLD.

Silence in the face of evil

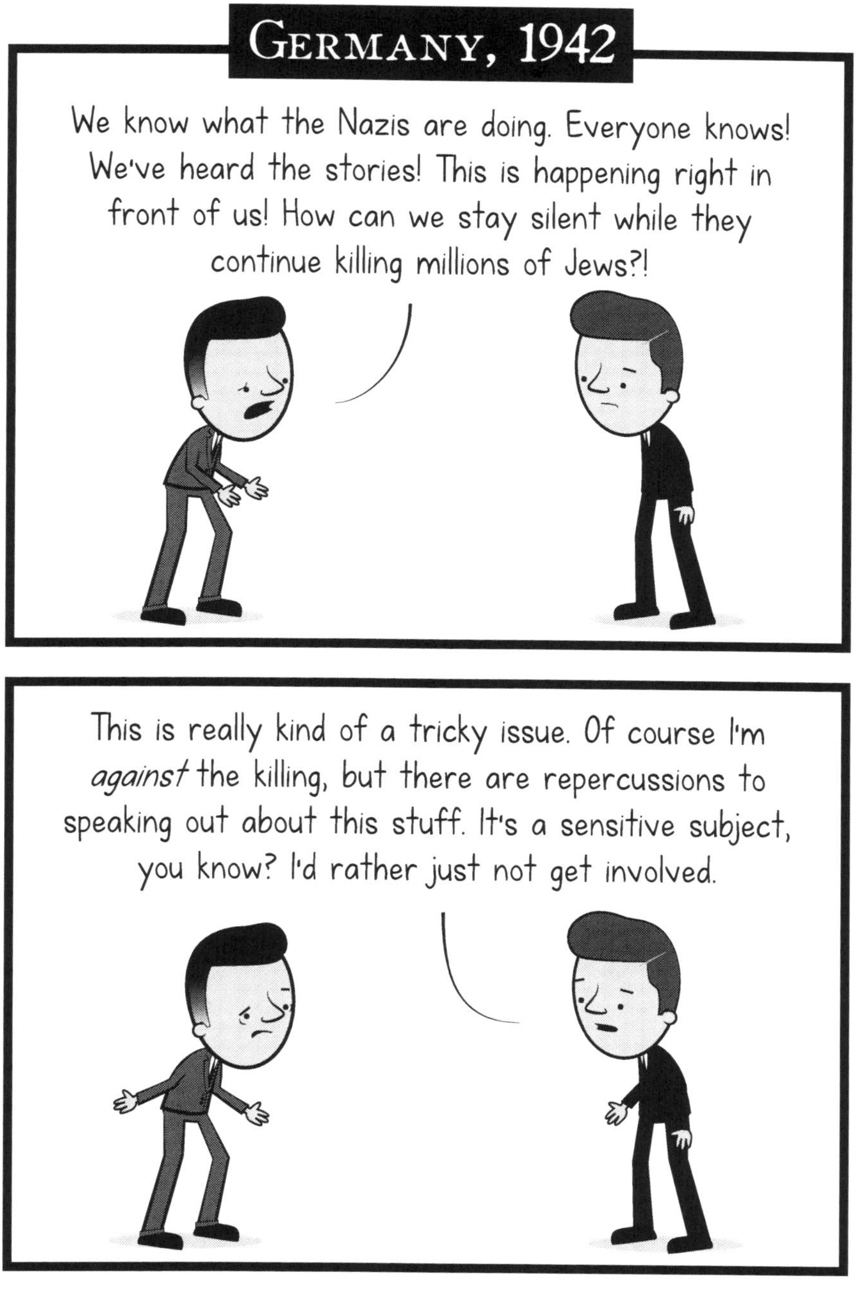
GERMANY, 1942
We know what the Nazis are doing. Everyone knows! We've heard the stories! This is happening right in front of us! How can we stay silent while they continue killing millions of Jews?!
This is really kind of a tricky issue. Of course I'm *against* the killing, but there are repercussions to speaking out about this stuff. It's a sensitive subject, you know? I'd rather just not get involved.

We know what Planned Parenthood is doing. Everyone knows! We've seen the pictures and videos! This is happening right in front of us! How can we stay silent while they continue killing millions of babies?!

This is really kind of a tricky issue. Of course I'm *against* the killing, but there are repercussions to speaking out about this stuff. It's a sensitive subject, you know? I'd rather just not get involved.

SILENCE IN THE FACE OF EVIL IS ITSELF EVIL. GOD WILL NOT HOLD US GUILTLESS. NOT TO SPEAK IS TO SPEAK. NOT TO ACT IS TO ACT. -Dietrich Bonhoeffer, German pastor and theologian, martyred by the Nazis for not being silent.

If you're gay, I want you to know that I don't hate you

Me

You

Amount of hate in this general region: zero

I am a Christian who believes the Bible is the word of God, any homosexual practice is sinful, and marriage will only ever be the life-long union between one man and one woman.

But I promise you, I don't hate you.

Me   You

(Still none)

The world sets us up as polar opposites, though. It says we're bitter enemies in a "culture war," lobbing Molotov cocktails at each other on the front lawn of the White House.

This is not the picture the Bible paints of you and me. The Bible says that in many important ways, we are not all that different, actually.

It says we are both made by God, in His image, with great inherent value.

We are both sinners by birth and by choice. Rebels. We want to choose our own way.

We both have fallen hearts which are bent toward all kinds of sin — including sexual sin.

If you are gay, your fallen heart tells you to lust after people of the same sex.

God calls that sin.

My fallen heart tells me to lust after people of the opposite sex who are not my wife.

God calls that sin.

We are both called by God to turn away from what He calls sin and instead seek after Him.

Because He loves us.
Because He graciously made a way for us.
Because He knows better than we do.
Because Heaven and Hell are real.
Because eternity is forever.
Because God is better than anything.

I am not "super-perfect Christian guy" over here telling you this:

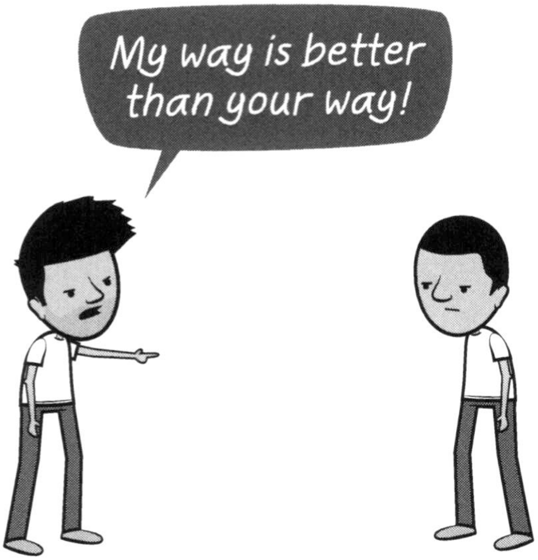
My way is better than your way!

I am a fellow sinner who now knows God for *no reason other than His amazing grace,* who *still screws up all the stinking time,* and I'm with you, telling you this:

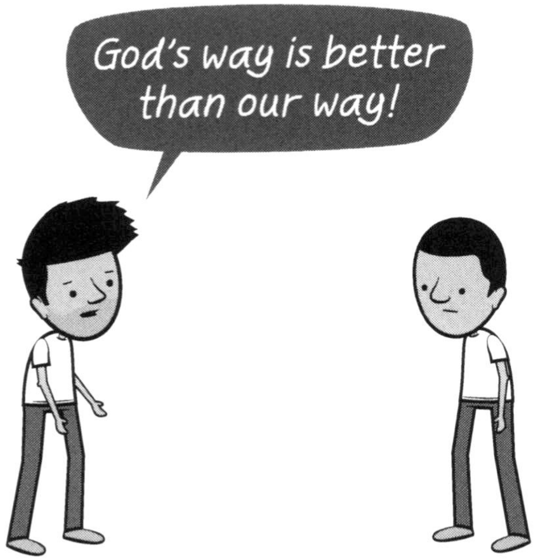
God's way is better than our way!

We tell ourselves to indulge.
Jesus tells us to deny ourselves
and to follow Him. (Luke 9:23)

We tell ourselves to take the easy path.
Jesus tells us to take the difficult path
toward Him. (Matt 7:14)

We tell ourselves to get all the pleasure
we can get out of this life.
Jesus tells us to lose our lives in order
to find Him instead. (Matt 16:25)

We tell ourselves this life is all there is.
Jesus tells us this life is just the blink of an
eye, and then comes eternity. (Luke 12:20)

Jesus tells both of us – *all of us* – to
"Repent and believe the gospel." (Mark 1:15)

To turn from sin and trust in Him.

To believe that He is the Son of God who came
into the world, lived a perfectly sinless life,
died on the cross to absorb the terrible
punishment due to sinners like you and me
for our rebellion against God, and rose from
the grave, defeating death, sin, and Hell.

"Repent and believe," He says to all of us.

Straight, gay, bi, married, single. All of us.

No matter what's in the way.
No matter what we have to give up.

Except sex, right?

No, **even sex**, if that's what it takes.

What is sex compared to **God?**
Jesus is better. Ten billion times better.
Sex is not the path to fulfillment. God is.

And in a world that wants to define you by
and exploit your gayness, God says you are
so much more than your sexuality.

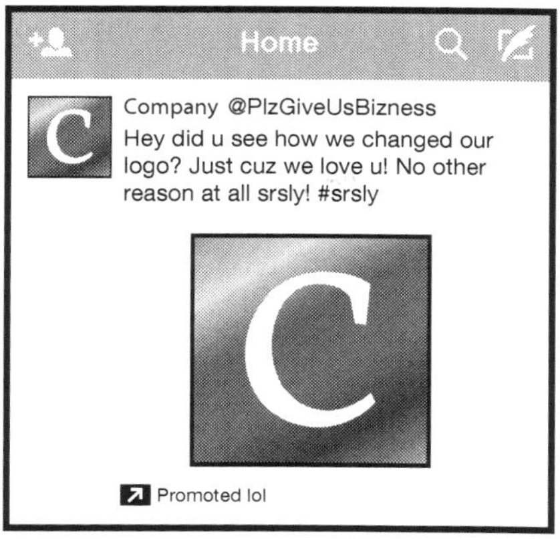
Home
Company @PlzGiveUsBizness
Hey did u see how we changed our logo? Just cuz we love u! No other reason at all srsly! #srsly
Promoted lol

The companies buying promoted tweets to make sure you see their newly-rainbowed logos do not really love you.
They want your business.

The politicians stumbling over each other to tell you how, really, they've always been on your side (even though they voted against gay marriage last term) do not really love you.
They want your vote.

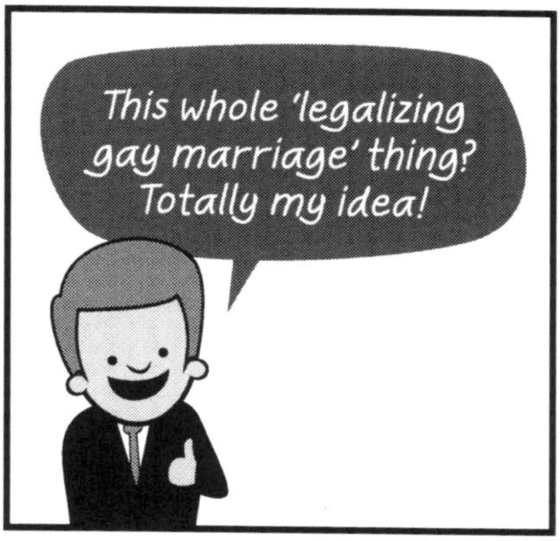
This whole 'legalizing gay marriage' thing? Totally my idea!

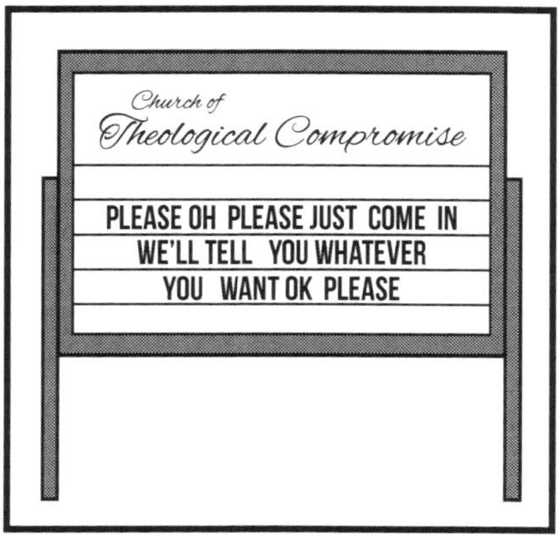
Church of
Theological Compromise
PLEASE OH PLEASE JUST COME IN
WE'LL TELL YOU WHATEVER
YOU WANT OK PLEASE

The liberal "churches" which are now saying, "Oh hey! God changed His mind and is totes cool with the gay stuff now 4 real!" do not really love you.
They want your approval.

But **God**, the Creator of every atom in the universe, the author of life and eternity, *really does love and want you.* (Rom 5:8)

And sexual sin *really does keep people from Him, in this life and in eternity.* (1 Cor 6:9-11)

You must choose one and fight the other.

Not because I say so; because God says so.
(See: entire Bible)

The same charge is in front of you, me, and everyone: **repent and believe the gospel**.

And when you fail and give into temptation, *which happens to every single believer and has happened to me more times than I can count,* do you know what you do then?

Repent and believe the gospel.

Don't celebrate sin, justify it, or rationalize it. Repent, trust God, and *get back in the fight.*

This is the realest stuff I know.

And sharing it with you is not an act of hate,
but an act of love.

That's why I'm sharing it with you.

Not because I hate you. **Because I love you.**

Me

You

There's love here.
Lots actually.

And there are **many** Christians like me.

We do not hate you.

We love you.

We do not want you to be unhappy.

We want you to be supremely and eternally happy.

We do not want to deprive you of rights.

We want you to have every right God so graciously bestows upon His children.

We do not want to keep you from fulfillment.

We want you to have the true fulfillment which is found only in Christ.

We love you, so we must tell you the truth.

Just like a guy loved me ten years ago when I was a devout atheist, hostile toward Christians, and he decided to tell me about Jesus anyway.

Love seeks the highest good of another.

I love you and want the highest good for you:

Eternal life in the presence of the Creator of the universe and only true source of joy, love, hope, pleasure, and fulfillment.

The time is fulfilled, and the kingdom of God is at hand; repent and believe in the gospel.
–Jesus
(Mark 1:15)

What if I could prove it to you?

I SAY CHRISTIANITY IS A FAIRY-TALE. YOU SAY IT'S THE TRUTH AND I SHOULD BELIEVE IN IT. OK THEN, JUST PROVE IT TO ME.

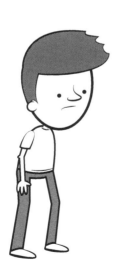

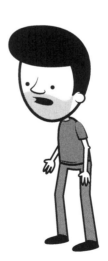

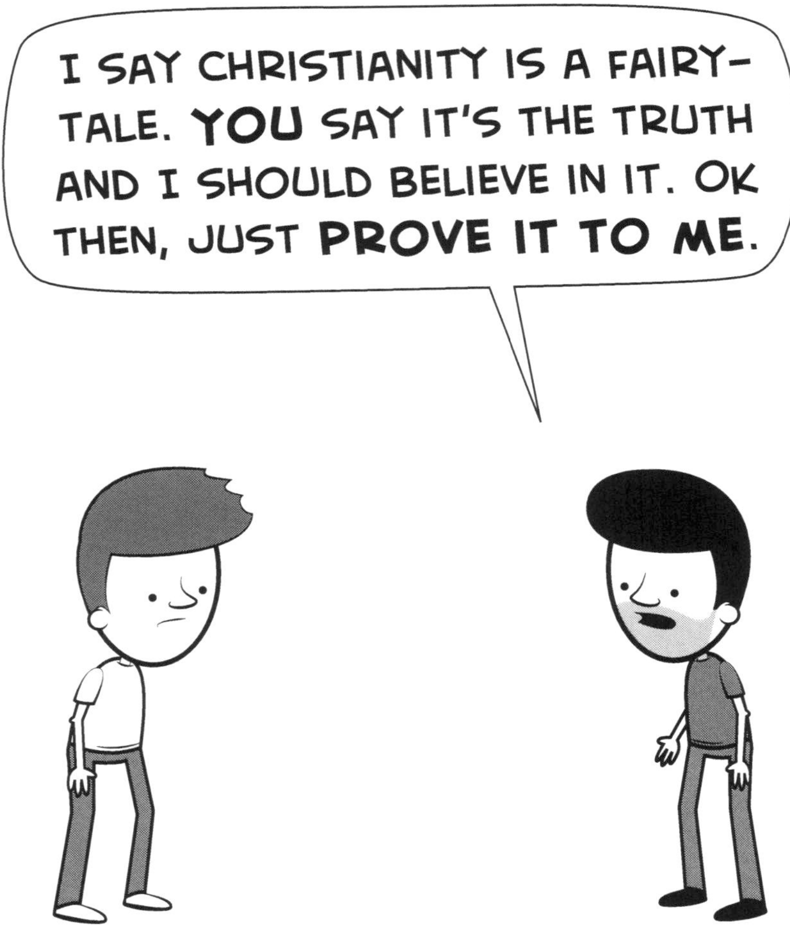

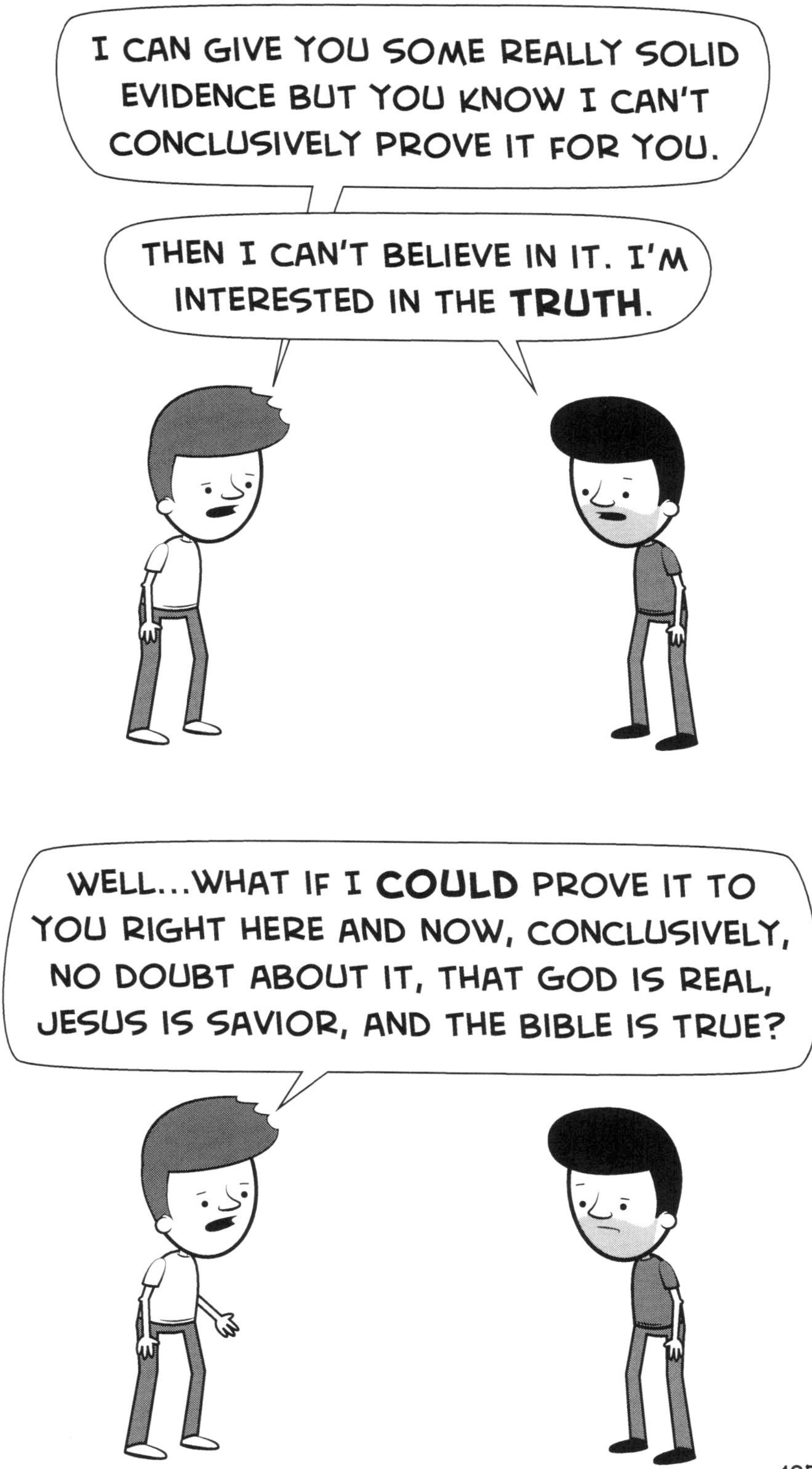
I CAN GIVE YOU SOME REALLY SOLID EVIDENCE BUT YOU KNOW I CAN'T CONCLUSIVELY PROVE IT FOR YOU.
THEN I CAN'T BELIEVE IN IT. I'M INTERESTED IN THE **TRUTH**.
WELL...WHAT IF I **COULD** PROVE IT TO YOU RIGHT HERE AND NOW, CONCLUSIVELY, NO DOUBT ABOUT IT, THAT GOD IS REAL, JESUS IS SAVIOR, AND THE BIBLE IS TRUE?

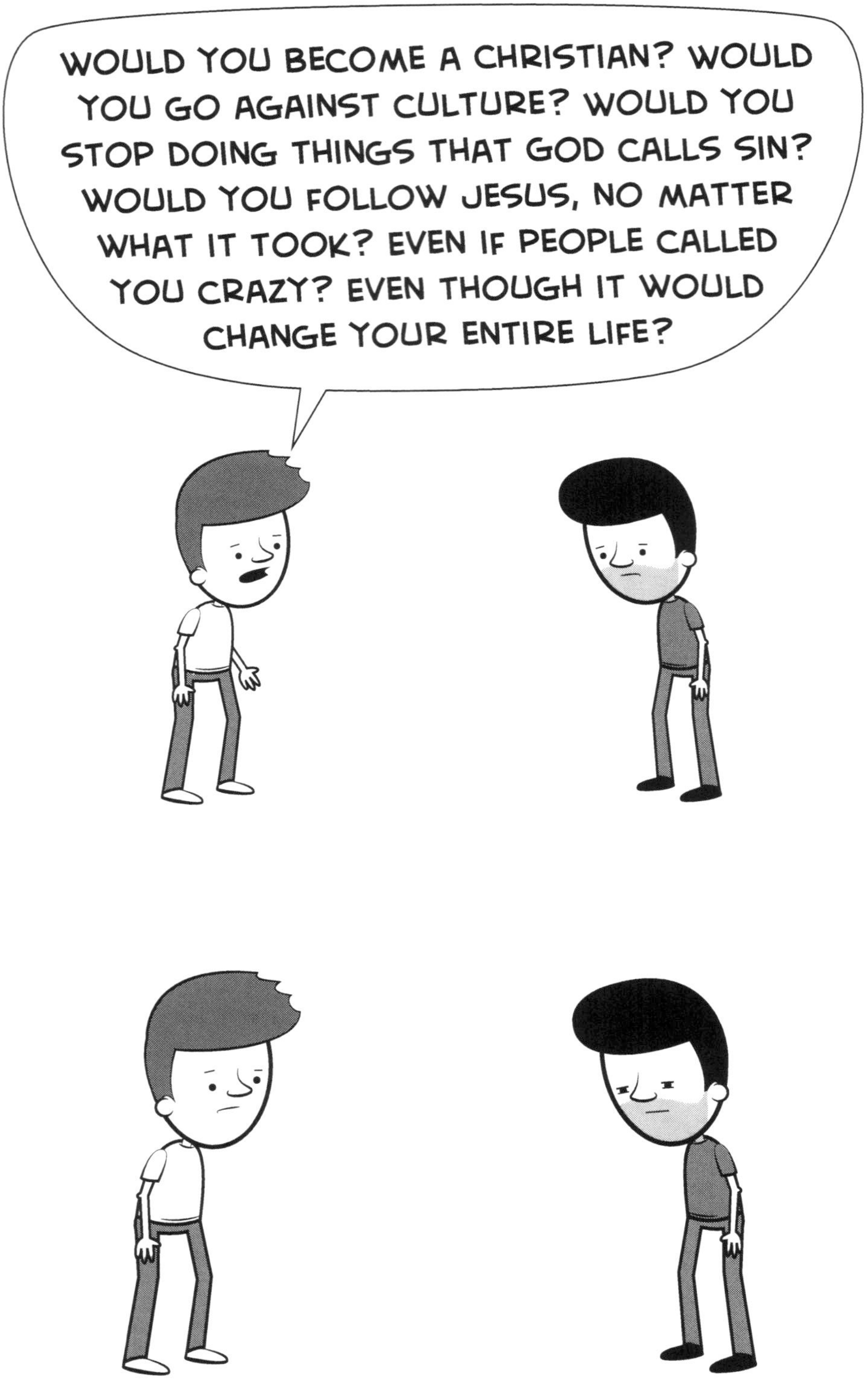
WOULD YOU BECOME A CHRISTIAN? WOULD YOU GO AGAINST CULTURE? WOULD YOU STOP DOING THINGS THAT GOD CALLS SIN? WOULD YOU FOLLOW JESUS, NO MATTER WHAT IT TOOK? EVEN IF PEOPLE CALLED YOU CRAZY? EVEN THOUGH IT WOULD CHANGE YOUR ENTIRE LIFE?

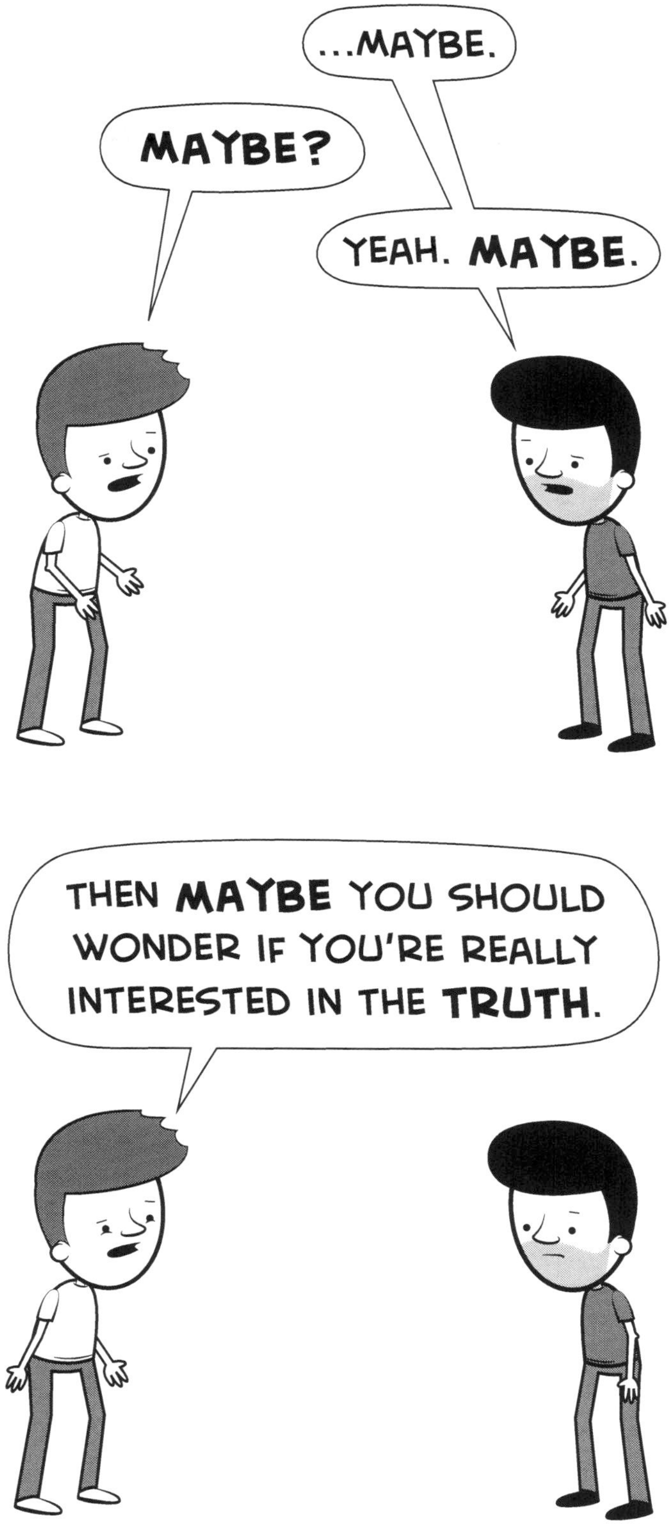
MAYBE?
...MAYBE.
YEAH. MAYBE.
THEN MAYBE YOU SHOULD WONDER IF YOU'RE REALLY INTERESTED IN THE TRUTH.

If you're not sure, don't run it over

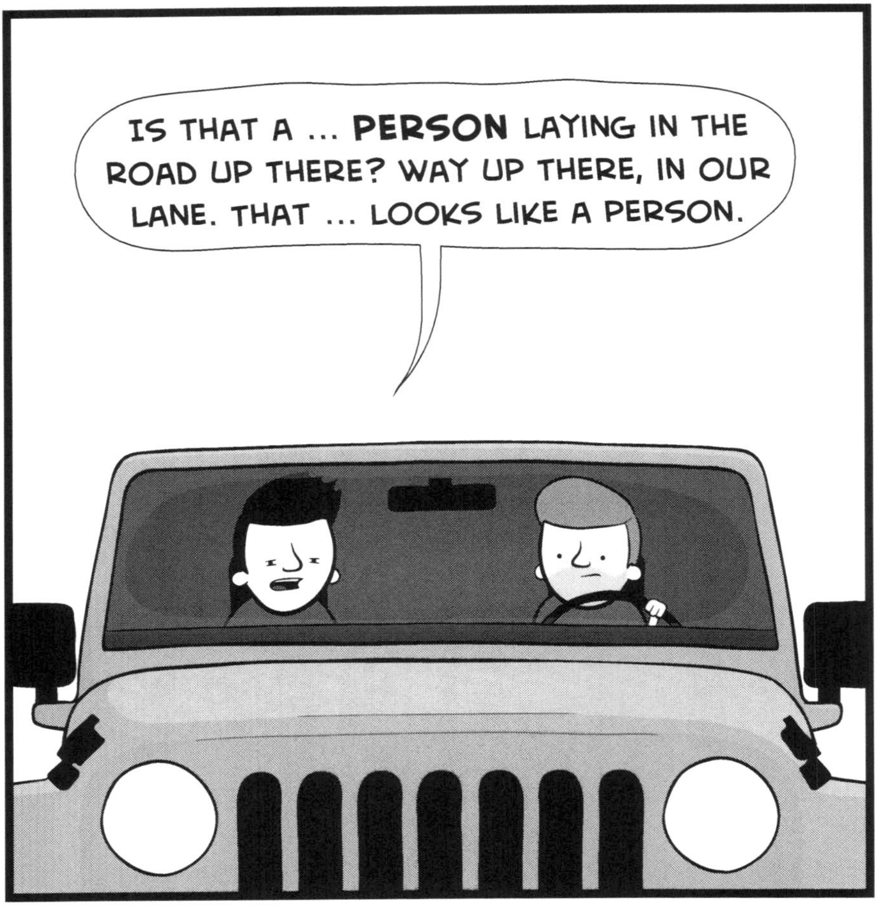
IS THAT A ... PERSON LAYING IN THE ROAD UP THERE? WAY UP THERE, IN OUR LANE. THAT ... LOOKS LIKE A PERSON.

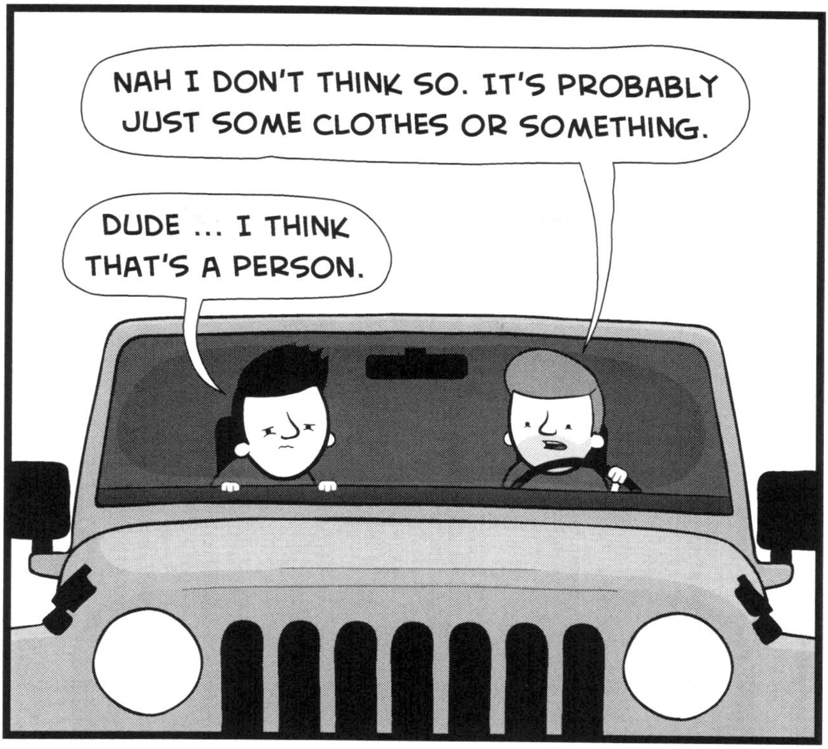
NAH I DON'T THINK SO. IT'S PROBABLY JUST SOME CLOTHES OR SOMETHING.
DUDE ... I THINK THAT'S A PERSON.

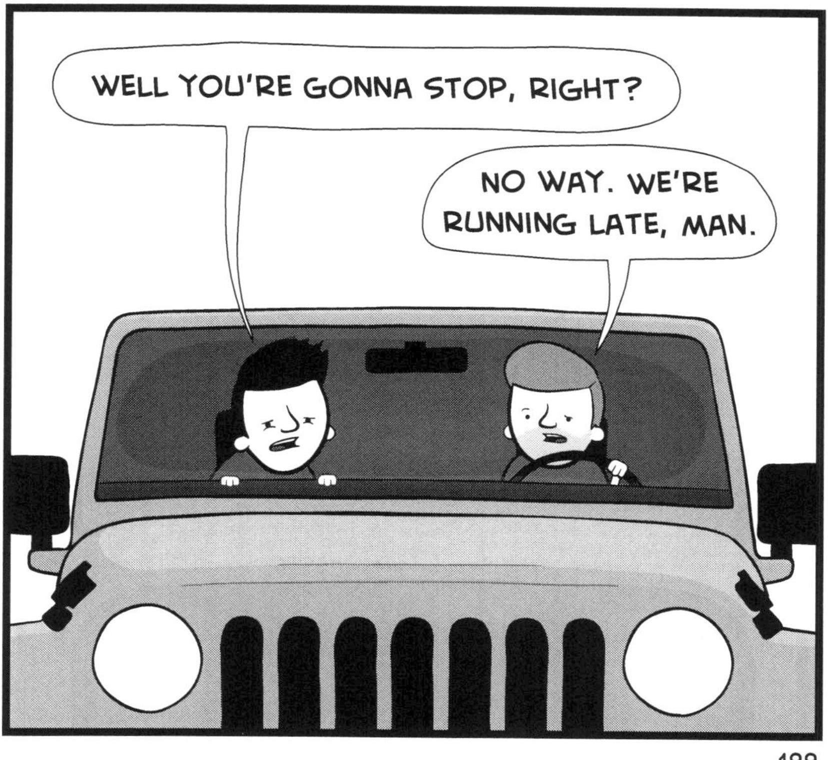
WELL YOU'RE GONNA STOP, RIGHT?
NO WAY. WE'RE RUNNING LATE, MAN.

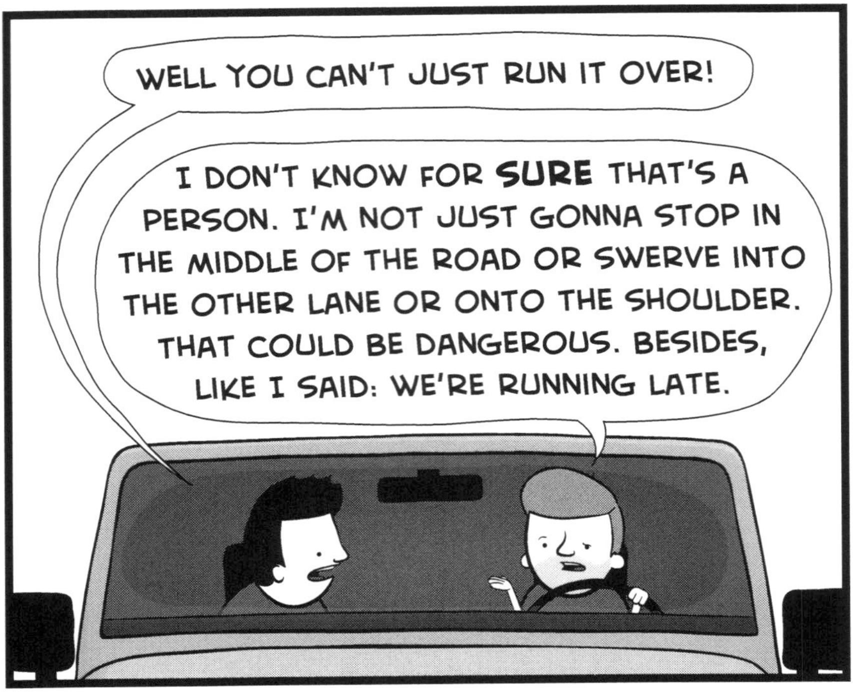
WELL YOU CAN'T JUST RUN IT OVER!
I DON'T KNOW FOR **SURE** THAT'S A PERSON. I'M NOT JUST GONNA STOP IN THE MIDDLE OF THE ROAD OR SWERVE INTO THE OTHER LANE OR ONTO THE SHOULDER. THAT COULD BE DANGEROUS. BESIDES, LIKE I SAID: WE'RE RUNNING LATE.

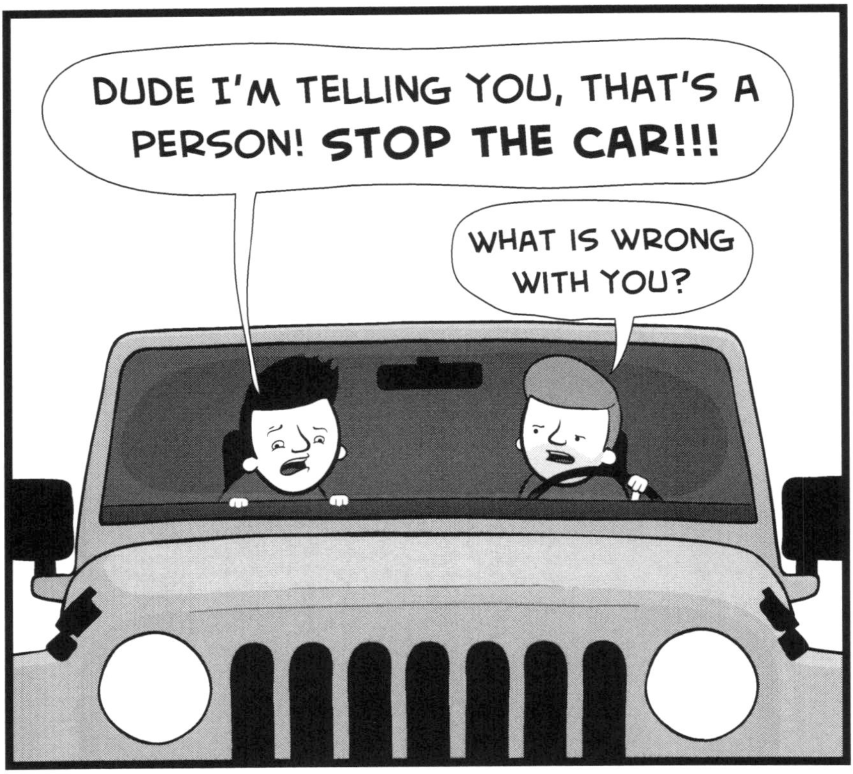
DUDE I'M TELLING YOU, THAT'S A PERSON! **STOP THE CAR!!!**
WHAT IS WRONG WITH YOU?

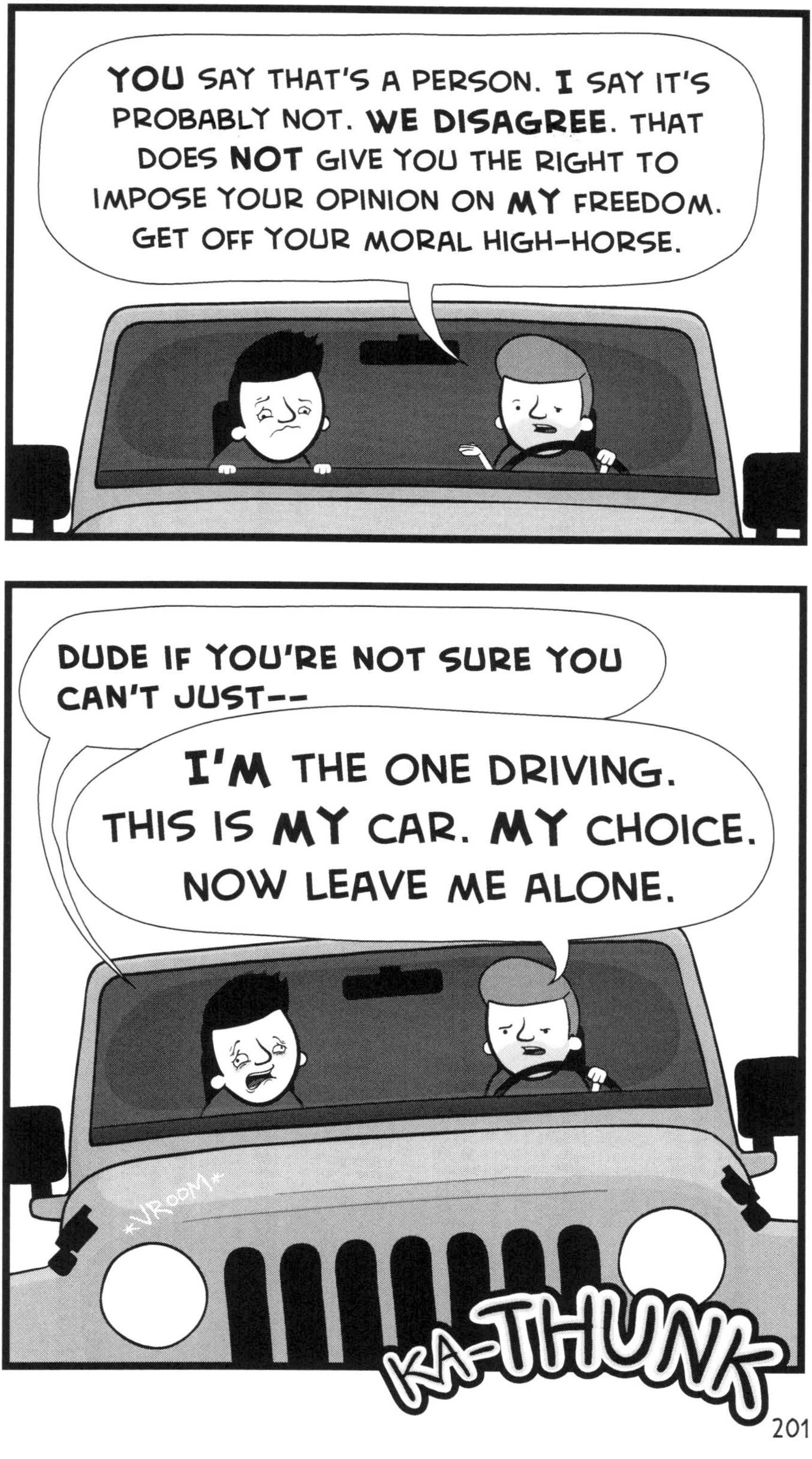
YOU SAY THAT'S A PERSON. I SAY IT'S PROBABLY NOT. WE DISAGREE. THAT DOES NOT GIVE YOU THE RIGHT TO IMPOSE YOUR OPINION ON MY FREEDOM. GET OFF YOUR MORAL HIGH-HORSE.
DUDE IF YOU'RE NOT SURE YOU CAN'T JUST--
I'M THE ONE DRIVING. THIS IS MY CAR. MY CHOICE. NOW LEAVE ME ALONE.
VROOM
KA-THUNK

Unless the driver could somehow be absolutely, 100% sure that the thing in the road was not a person, isn't his decision to run it over morally unconscionable? Yeah, clearly.

If he's NOT sure, he must NOT run it over. He needs to be 100% sure. Not 50%, 75%, or 99% sure. 100%. As in, "I just stopped the car, got out, and held the clothes in my hands. I'm certain they are just clothes and not a person. So I'm gonna drive over them now."

Likewise,

some people say an unborn baby is a person with the same right to life you or I enjoy. And some people disagree.

But unless those who disagree could somehow be absolutely, 100% SURE that an unborn baby IS NOT a person to whom the right to life is naturally due, how can they argue for a default position of, "It's OK to end its life?"

Think about it.

If you're not sure, don't run it over.

And there's NO WAY to be sure.

Yet this is a common pro-choice position:

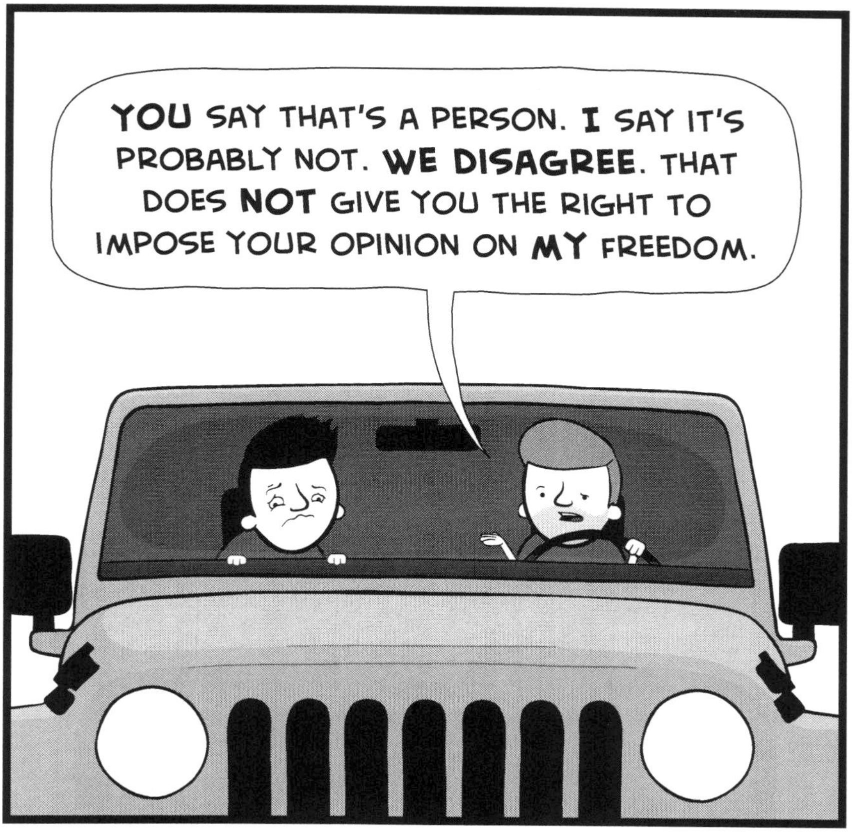
YOU SAY THAT'S A PERSON. I SAY IT'S PROBABLY NOT. WE DISAGREE. THAT DOES NOT GIVE YOU THE RIGHT TO IMPOSE YOUR OPINION ON MY FREEDOM.

The guy driving the Jeep in the comic is clearly wrong for running over the thing in the road while being unsure of whether or not it was a person. We all know that.

Why is it different for abortion?

Help, I'm trapped in a Christian marriage!

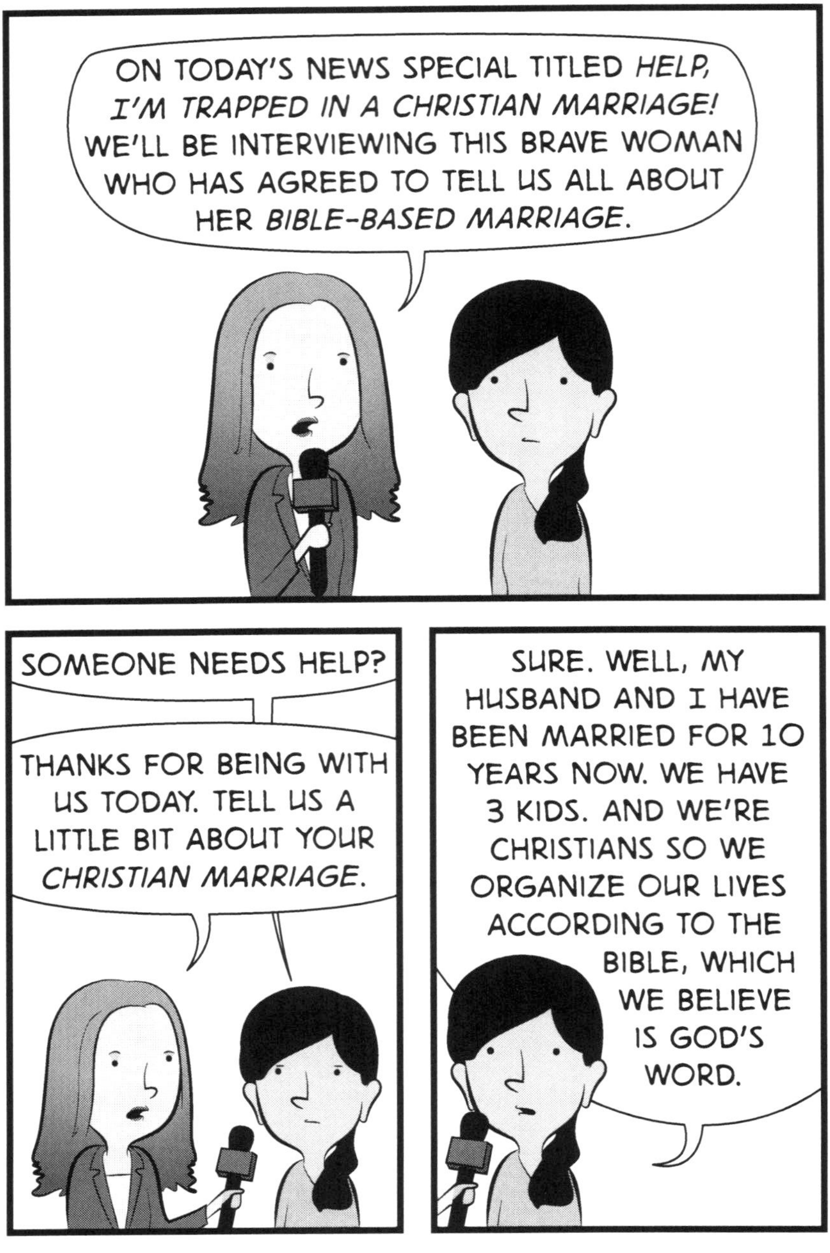

ON TODAY'S NEWS SPECIAL TITLED *HELP, I'M TRAPPED IN A CHRISTIAN MARRIAGE!* WE'LL BE INTERVIEWING THIS BRAVE WOMAN WHO HAS AGREED TO TELL US ALL ABOUT HER *BIBLE-BASED MARRIAGE*.
SOMEONE NEEDS HELP?
THANKS FOR BEING WITH US TODAY. TELL US A LITTLE BIT ABOUT YOUR *CHRISTIAN MARRIAGE*.
SURE. WELL, MY HUSBAND AND I HAVE BEEN MARRIED FOR 10 YEARS NOW. WE HAVE 3 KIDS. AND WE'RE CHRISTIANS SO WE ORGANIZE OUR LIVES ACCORDING TO THE BIBLE, WHICH WE BELIEVE IS GOD'S WORD.

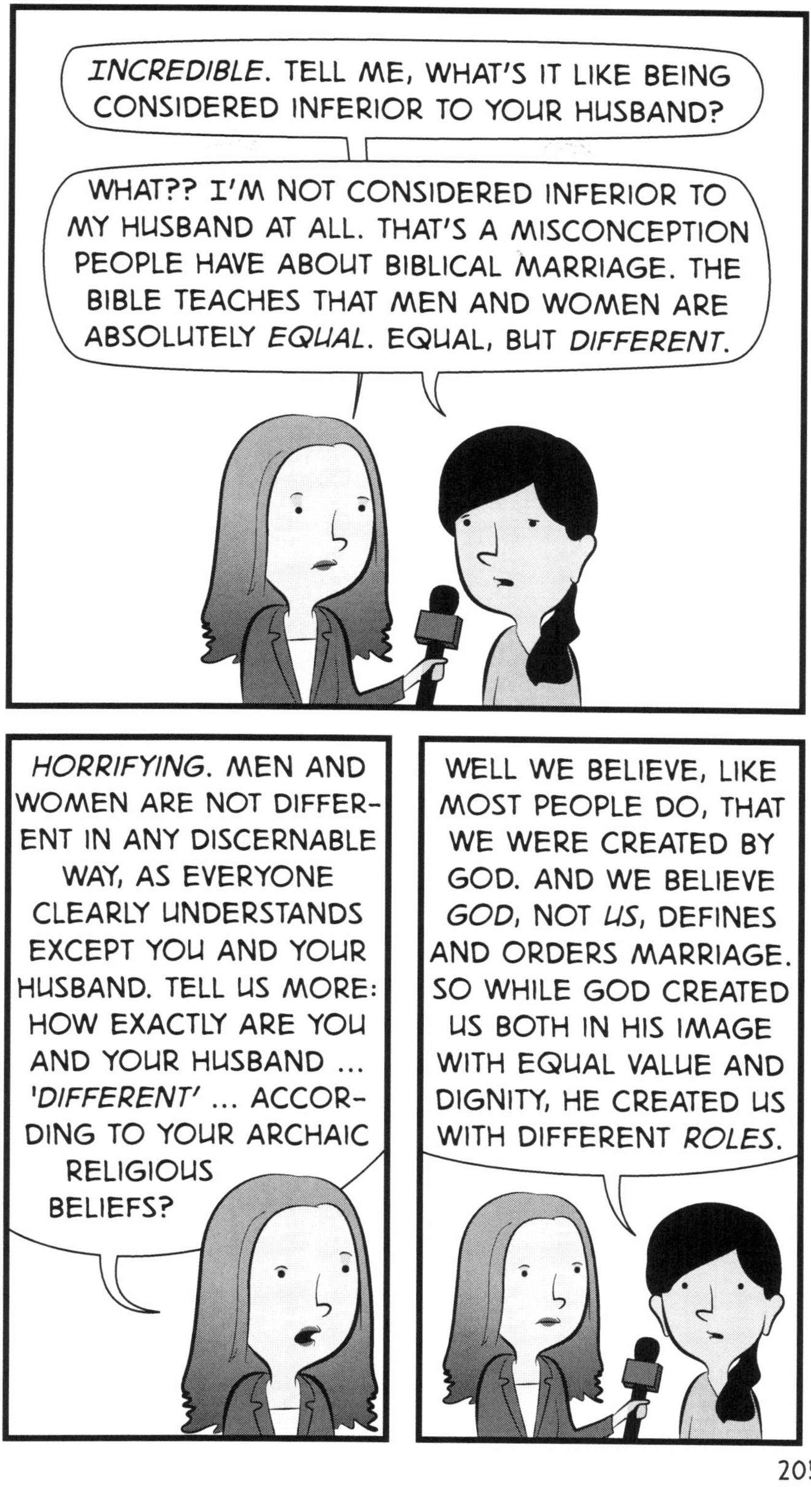
INCREDIBLE. TELL ME, WHAT'S IT LIKE BEING CONSIDERED INFERIOR TO YOUR HUSBAND?
WHAT?? I'M NOT CONSIDERED INFERIOR TO MY HUSBAND AT ALL. THAT'S A MISCONCEPTION PEOPLE HAVE ABOUT BIBLICAL MARRIAGE. THE BIBLE TEACHES THAT MEN AND WOMEN ARE ABSOLUTELY *EQUAL*. EQUAL, BUT *DIFFERENT*.
HORRIFYING. MEN AND WOMEN ARE NOT DIFFERENT IN ANY DISCERNABLE WAY, AS EVERYONE CLEARLY UNDERSTANDS EXCEPT YOU AND YOUR HUSBAND. TELL US MORE: HOW EXACTLY ARE YOU AND YOUR HUSBAND ... '*DIFFERENT*' ... ACCORDING TO YOUR ARCHAIC RELIGIOUS BELIEFS?
WELL WE BELIEVE, LIKE MOST PEOPLE DO, THAT WE WERE CREATED BY GOD. AND WE BELIEVE *GOD*, NOT *US*, DEFINES AND ORDERS MARRIAGE. SO WHILE GOD CREATED US BOTH IN HIS IMAGE WITH EQUAL VALUE AND DIGNITY, HE CREATED US WITH DIFFERENT *ROLES*.

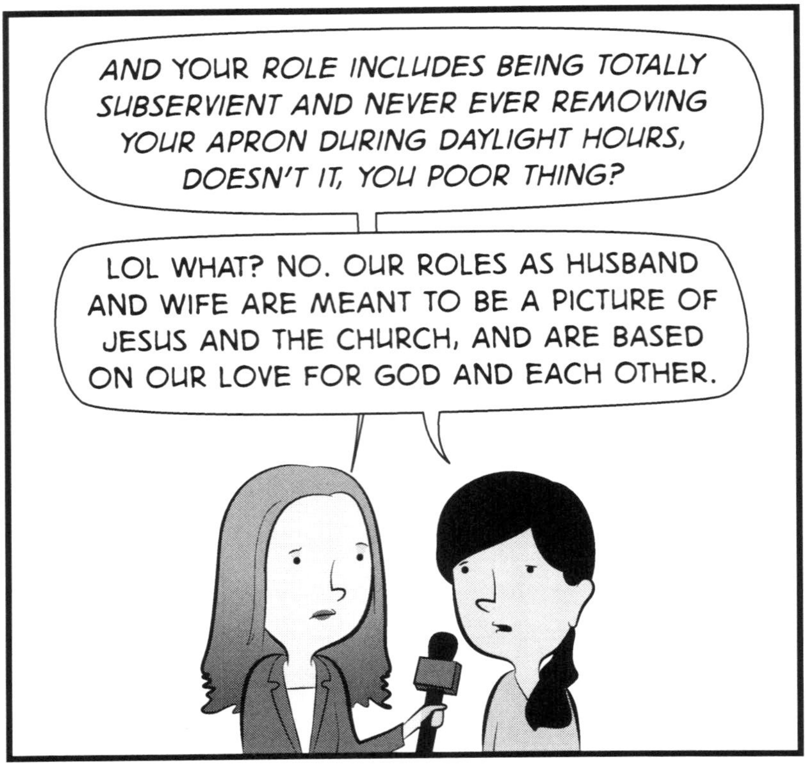
AND YOUR ROLE INCLUDES BEING TOTALLY SUBSERVIENT AND NEVER EVER REMOVING YOUR APRON DURING DAYLIGHT HOURS, DOESN'T IT, YOU POOR THING?
LOL WHAT? NO. OUR ROLES AS HUSBAND AND WIFE ARE MEANT TO BE A PICTURE OF JESUS AND THE CHURCH, AND ARE BASED ON OUR LOVE FOR GOD AND EACH OTHER.

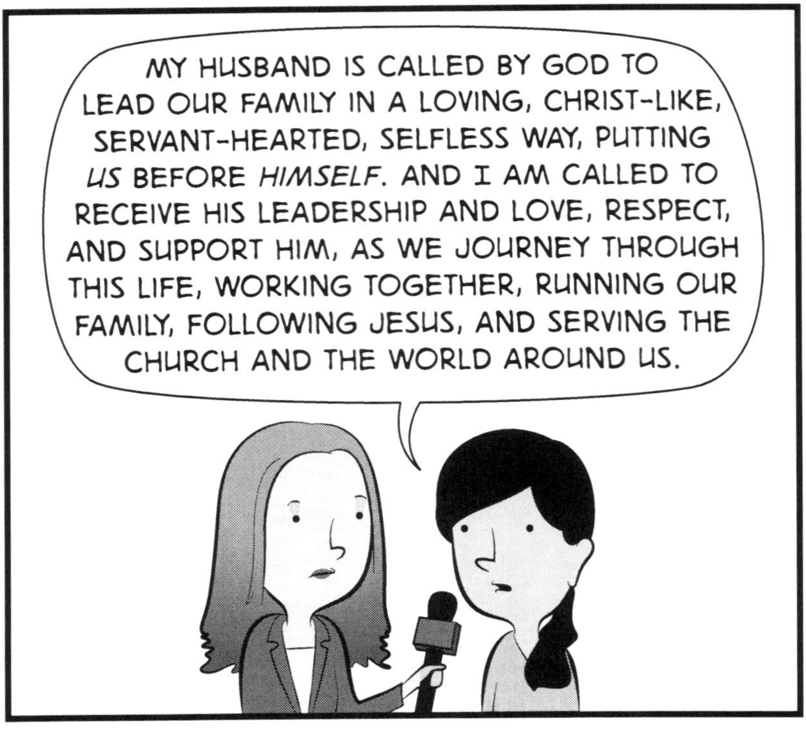
MY HUSBAND IS CALLED BY GOD TO LEAD OUR FAMILY IN A LOVING, CHRIST-LIKE, SERVANT-HEARTED, SELFLESS WAY, PUTTING *US* BEFORE *HIMSELF*. AND I AM CALLED TO RECEIVE HIS LEADERSHIP AND LOVE, RESPECT, AND SUPPORT HIM, AS WE JOURNEY THROUGH THIS LIFE, WORKING TOGETHER, RUNNING OUR FAMILY, FOLLOWING JESUS, AND SERVING THE CHURCH AND THE WORLD AROUND US.

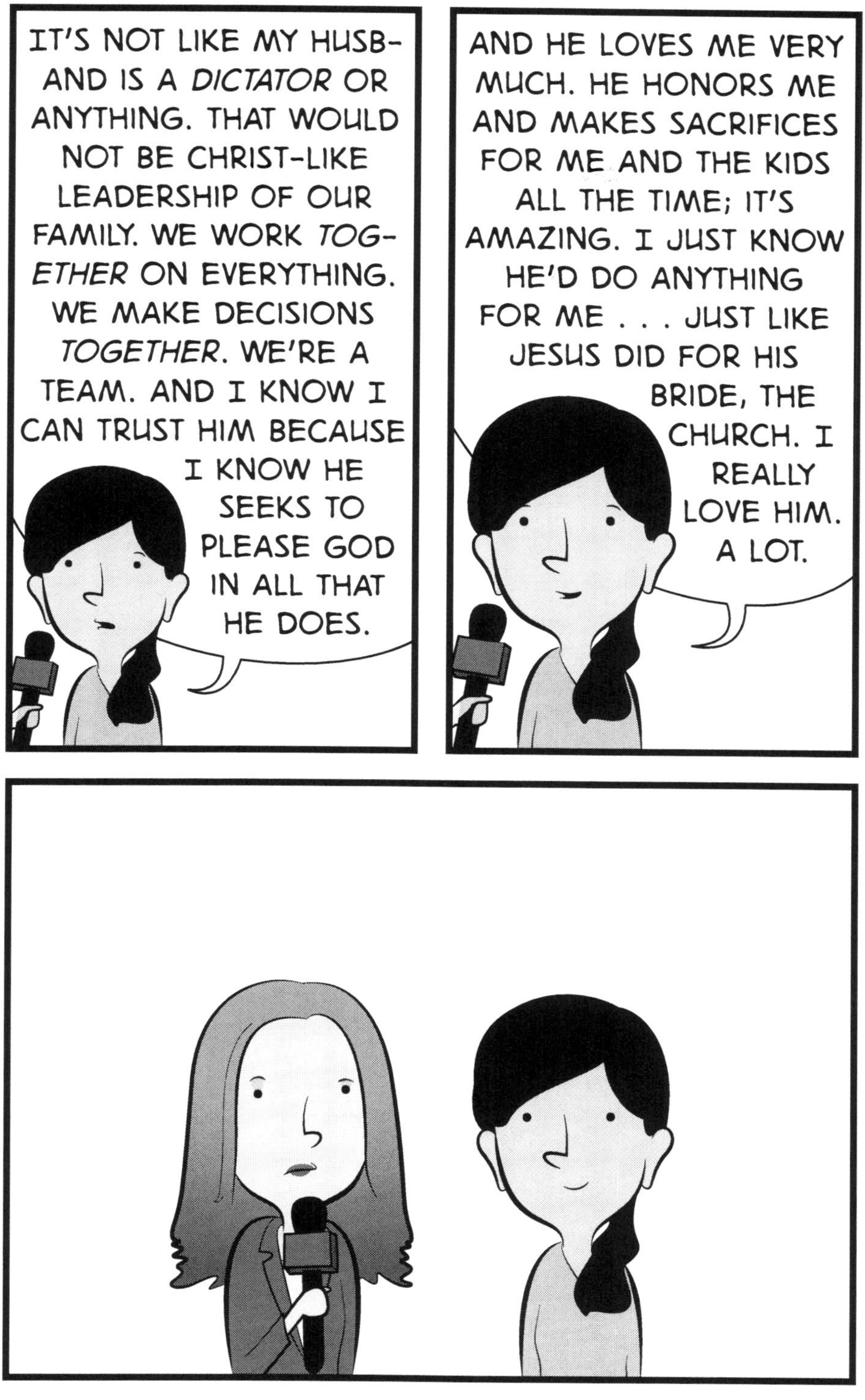
IT'S NOT LIKE MY HUSB-AND IS A *DICTATOR* OR ANYTHING. THAT WOULD NOT BE CHRIST-LIKE LEADERSHIP OF OUR FAMILY. WE WORK *TOGETHER* ON EVERYTHING. WE MAKE DECISIONS *TOGETHER*. WE'RE A TEAM. AND I KNOW I CAN TRUST HIM BECAUSE I KNOW HE SEEKS TO PLEASE GOD IN ALL THAT HE DOES.
AND HE LOVES ME VERY MUCH. HE HONORS ME AND MAKES SACRIFICES FOR ME AND THE KIDS ALL THE TIME; IT'S AMAZING. I JUST KNOW HE'D DO ANYTHING FOR ME . . . JUST LIKE JESUS DID FOR HIS BRIDE, THE CHURCH. I REALLY LOVE HIM. A LOT.

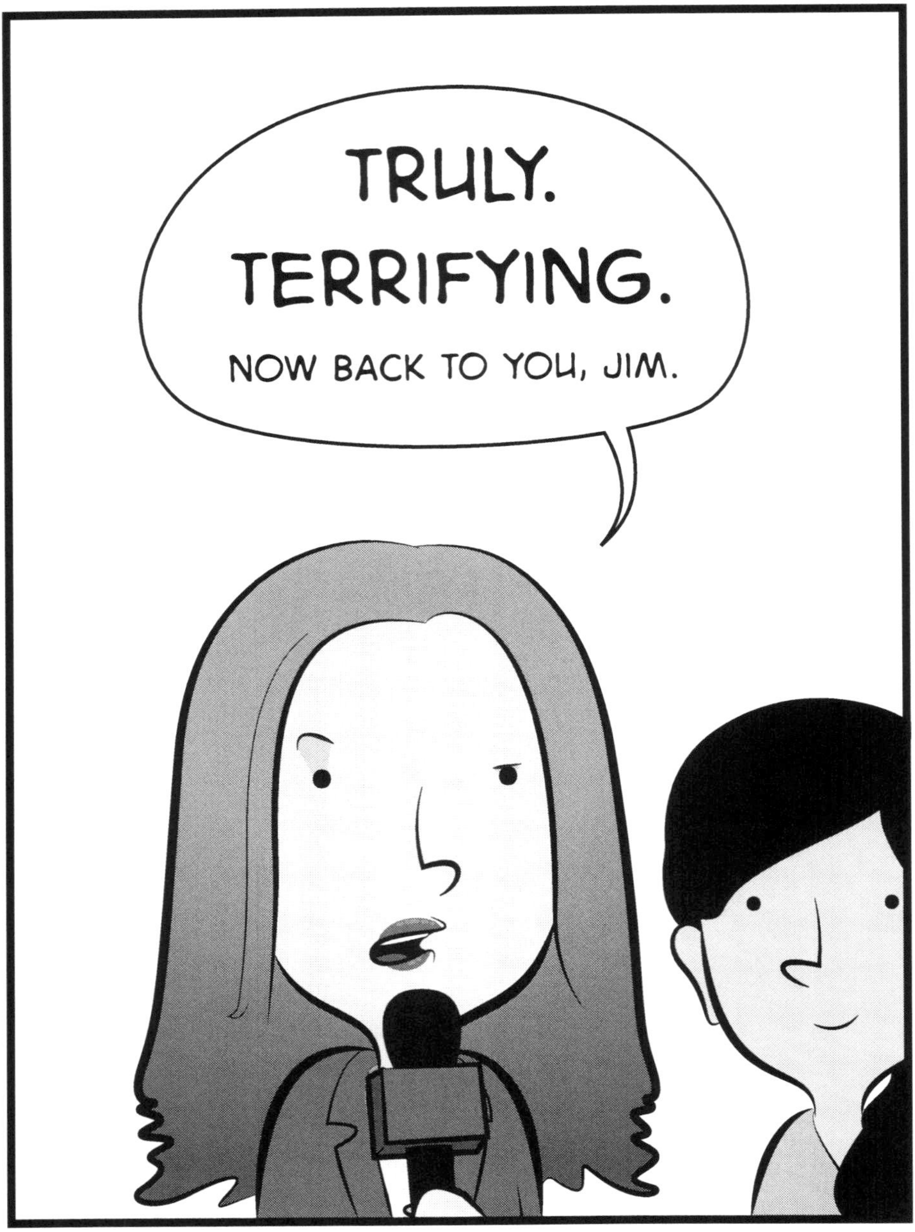
TRULY.
TERRIFYING.
NOW BACK TO YOU, JIM.

Why doesn't God save everyone?

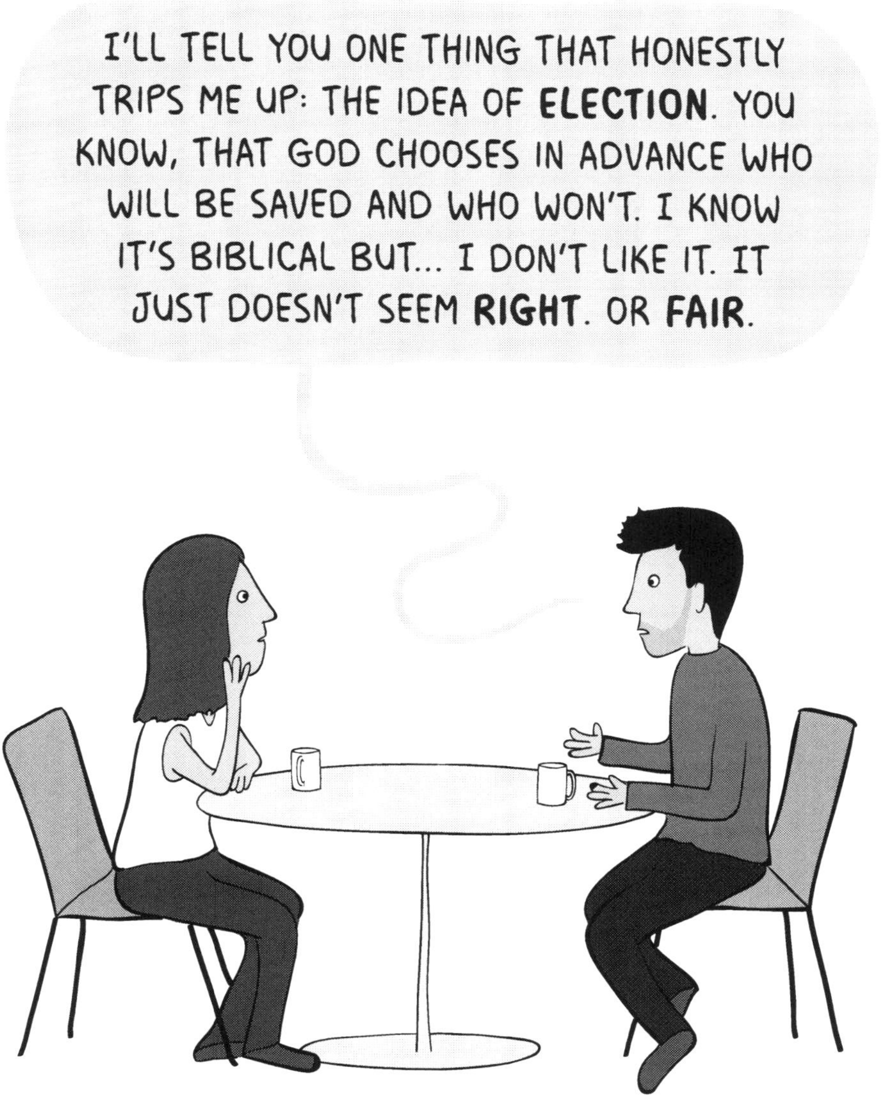
I'LL TELL YOU ONE THING THAT HONESTLY TRIPS ME UP: THE IDEA OF **ELECTION**. YOU KNOW, THAT GOD CHOOSES IN ADVANCE WHO WILL BE SAVED AND WHO WON'T. I KNOW IT'S BIBLICAL BUT... I DON'T LIKE IT. IT JUST DOESN'T SEEM **RIGHT**. OR **FAIR**.

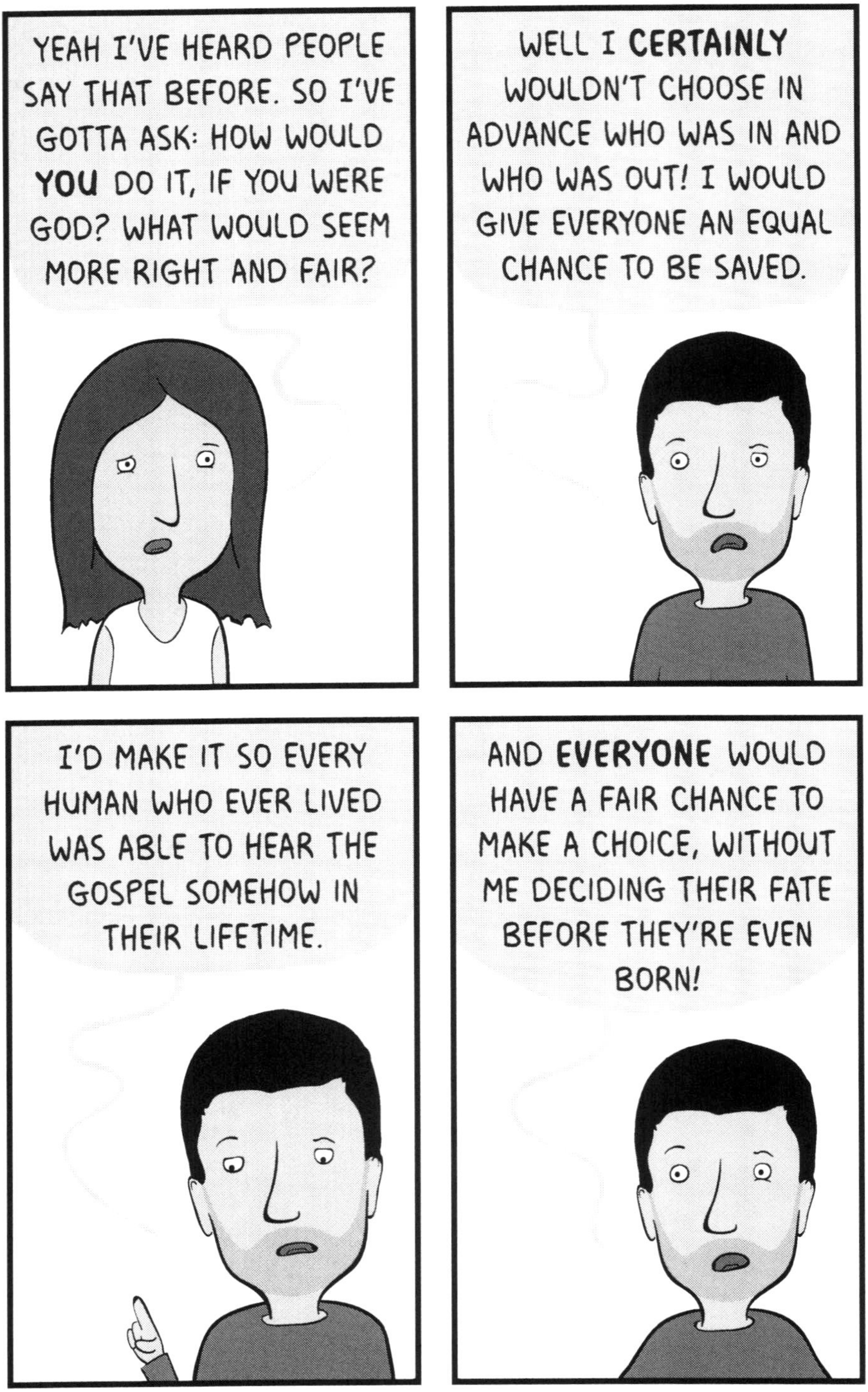
YEAH I'VE HEARD PEOPLE SAY THAT BEFORE. SO I'VE GOTTA ASK: HOW WOULD **YOU** DO IT, IF YOU WERE GOD? WHAT WOULD SEEM MORE RIGHT AND FAIR?
WELL I **CERTAINLY** WOULDN'T CHOOSE IN ADVANCE WHO WAS IN AND WHO WAS OUT! I WOULD GIVE EVERYONE AN EQUAL CHANCE TO BE SAVED.
I'D MAKE IT SO EVERY HUMAN WHO EVER LIVED WAS ABLE TO HEAR THE GOSPEL SOMEHOW IN THEIR LIFETIME.
AND **EVERYONE** WOULD HAVE A FAIR CHANCE TO MAKE A CHOICE, WITHOUT ME DECIDING THEIR FATE BEFORE THEY'RE EVEN BORN!

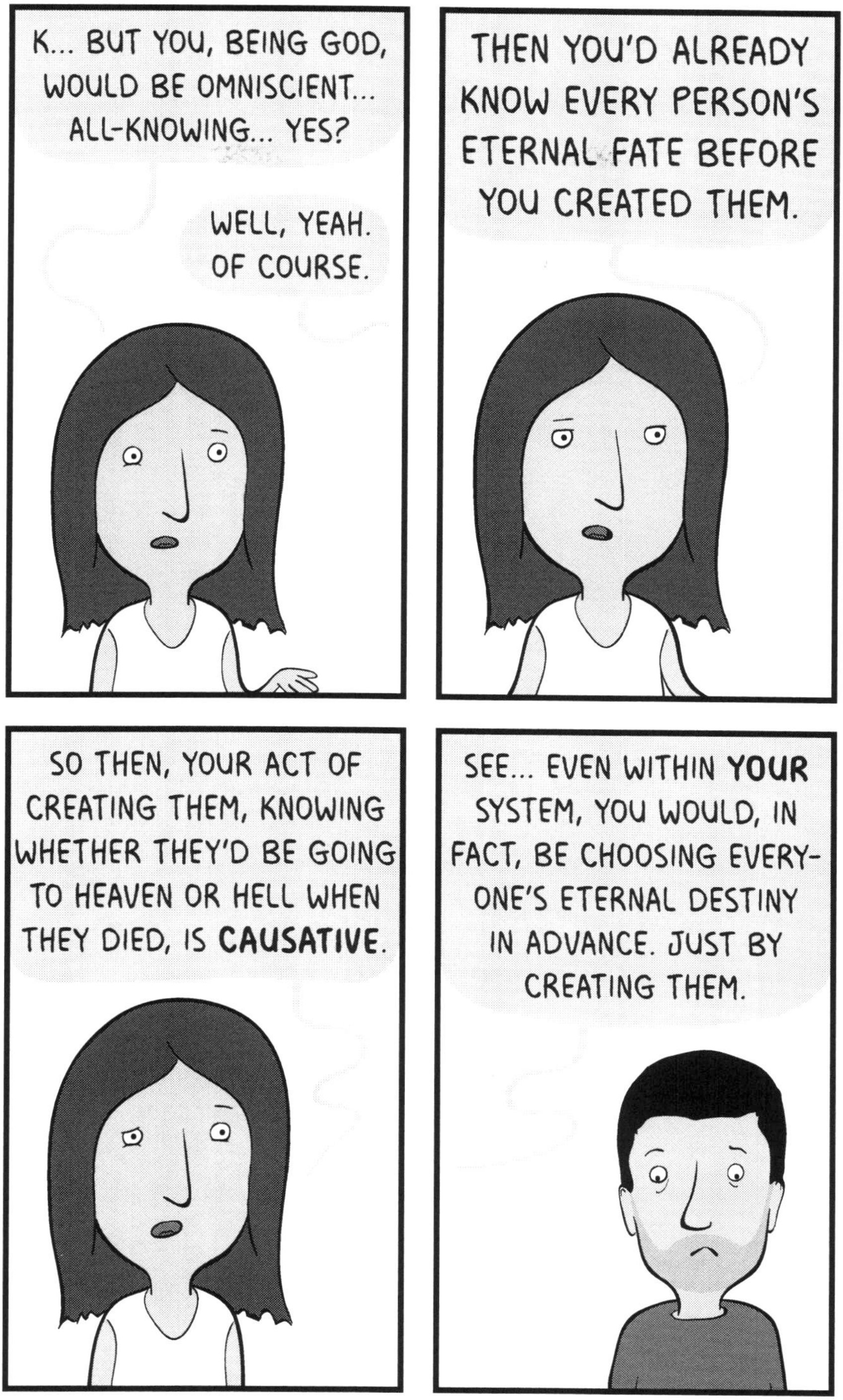
K... BUT YOU, BEING GOD, WOULD BE OMNISCIENT... ALL-KNOWING... YES?
WELL, YEAH. OF COURSE.
THEN YOU'D ALREADY KNOW EVERY PERSON'S ETERNAL FATE BEFORE YOU CREATED THEM.
SO THEN, YOUR ACT OF CREATING THEM, KNOWING WHETHER THEY'D BE GOING TO HEAVEN OR HELL WHEN THEY DIED, IS **CAUSATIVE**.
SEE... EVEN WITHIN **YOUR** SYSTEM, YOU WOULD, IN FACT, BE CHOOSING EVERY-ONE'S ETERNAL DESTINY IN ADVANCE. JUST BY CREATING THEM.

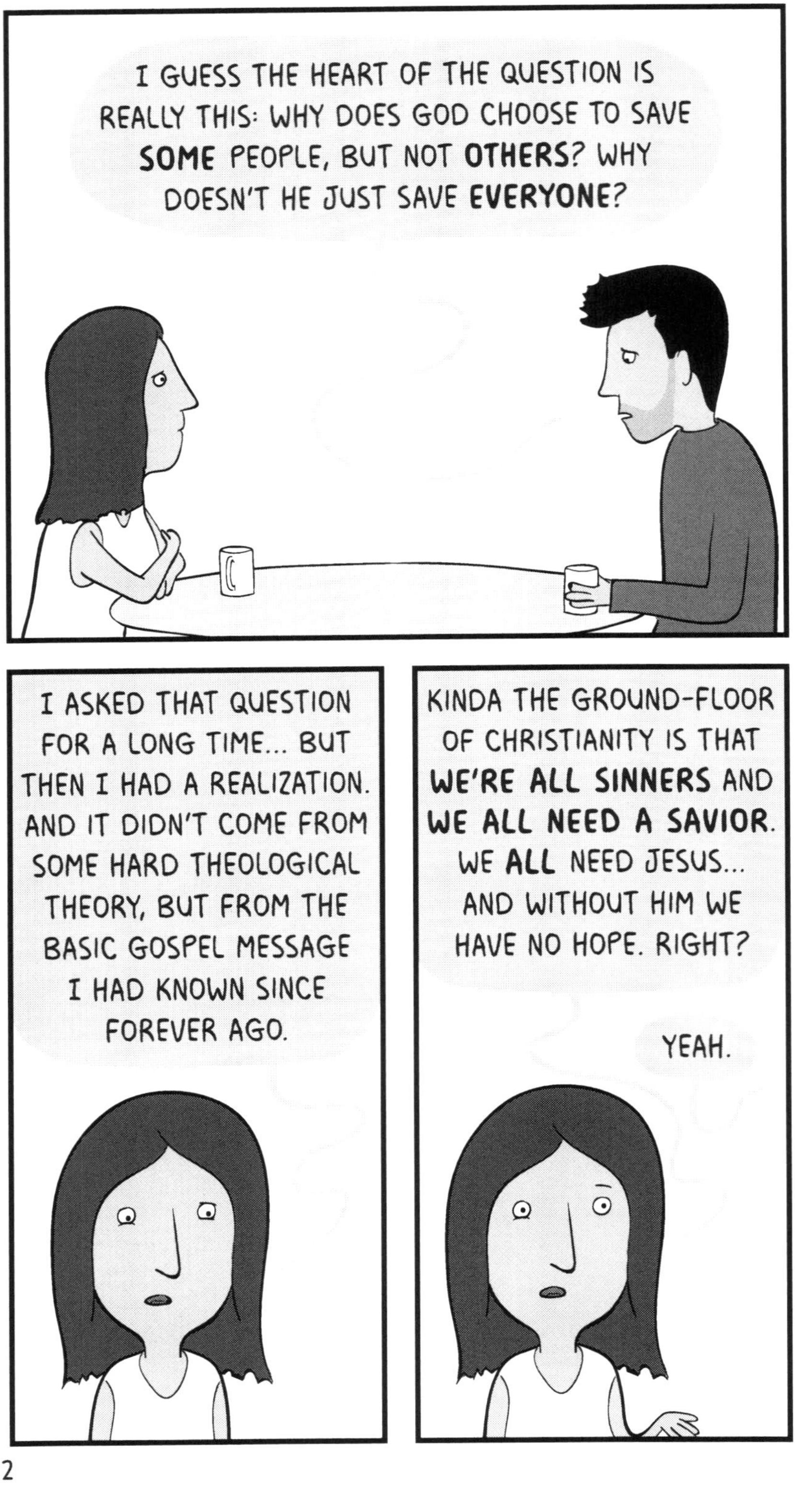
I GUESS THE HEART OF THE QUESTION IS REALLY THIS: WHY DOES GOD CHOOSE TO SAVE **SOME** PEOPLE, BUT NOT **OTHERS**? WHY DOESN'T HE JUST SAVE **EVERYONE**?
I ASKED THAT QUESTION FOR A LONG TIME... BUT THEN I HAD A REALIZATION. AND IT DIDN'T COME FROM SOME HARD THEOLOGICAL THEORY, BUT FROM THE BASIC GOSPEL MESSAGE I HAD KNOWN SINCE FOREVER AGO.
KINDA THE GROUND-FLOOR OF CHRISTIANITY IS THAT **WE'RE ALL SINNERS** AND **WE ALL NEED A SAVIOR**. WE **ALL** NEED JESUS... AND WITHOUT HIM WE HAVE NO HOPE. RIGHT?
YEAH.

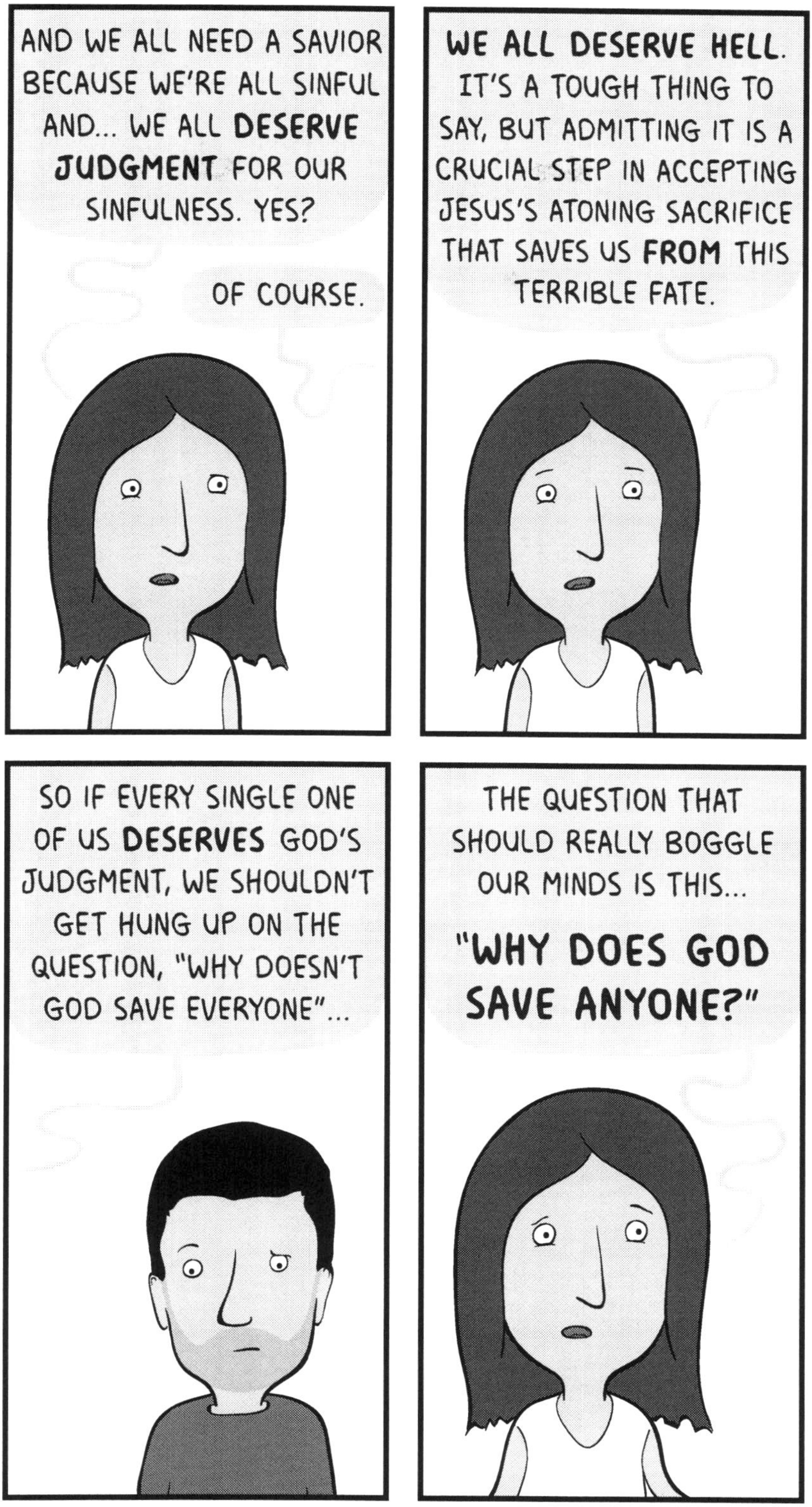
AND WE ALL NEED A SAVIOR BECAUSE WE'RE ALL SINFUL AND... WE ALL **DESERVE JUDGMENT** FOR OUR SINFULNESS. YES?
OF COURSE.
WE ALL DESERVE HELL. IT'S A TOUGH THING TO SAY, BUT ADMITTING IT IS A CRUCIAL STEP IN ACCEPTING JESUS'S ATONING SACRIFICE THAT SAVES US **FROM** THIS TERRIBLE FATE.
SO IF EVERY SINGLE ONE OF US **DESERVES** GOD'S JUDGMENT, WE SHOULDN'T GET HUNG UP ON THE QUESTION, "WHY DOESN'T GOD SAVE EVERYONE"...
THE QUESTION THAT SHOULD REALLY BOGGLE OUR MINDS IS THIS...
"**WHY DOES GOD SAVE ANYONE?**"

How do you know you love Jesus?

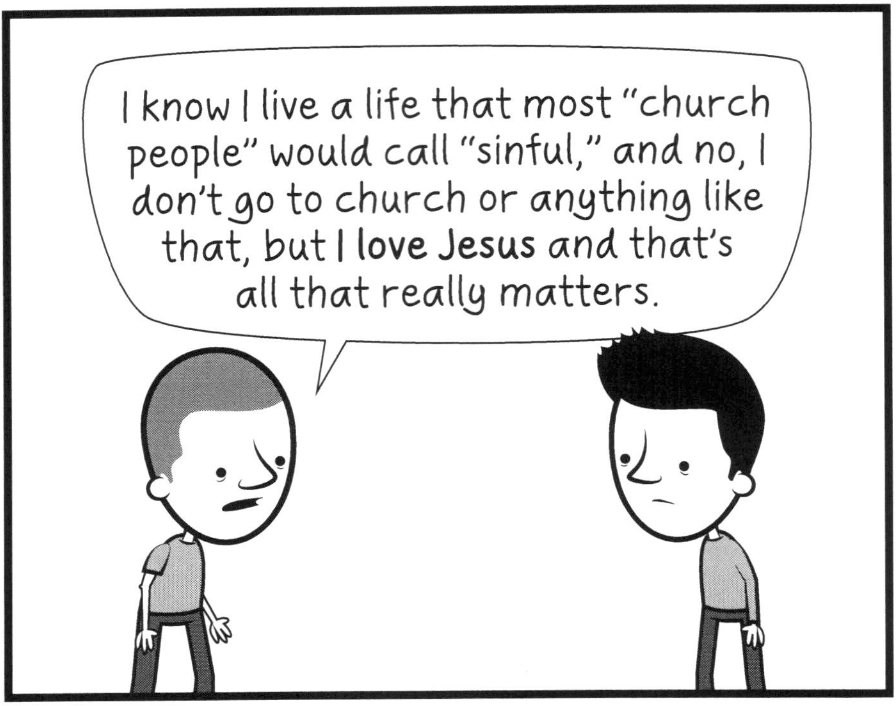
I know I live a life that most "church people" would call "sinful," and no, I don't go to church or anything like that, but I **love Jesus** and that's all that really matters.

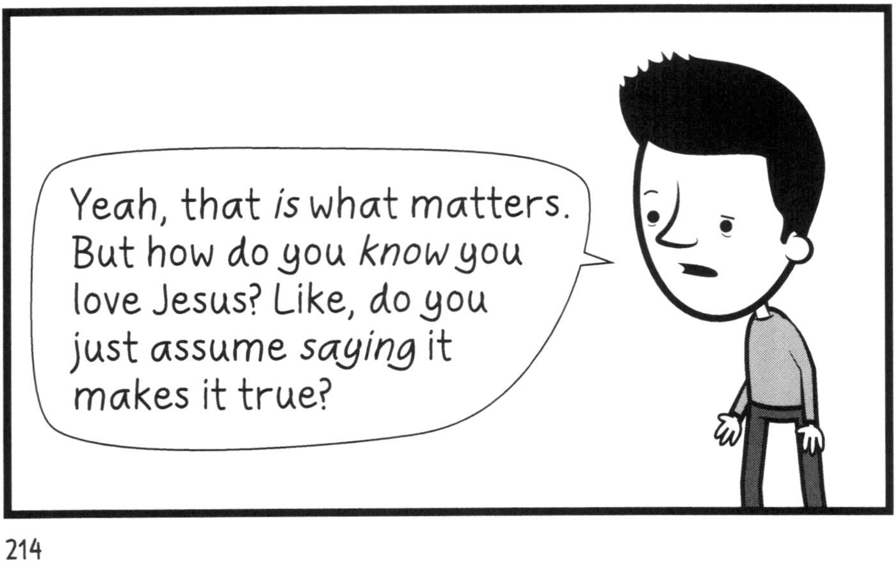
Yeah, that *is* what matters. But how do you *know* you love Jesus? Like, do you just assume *saying* it makes it true?

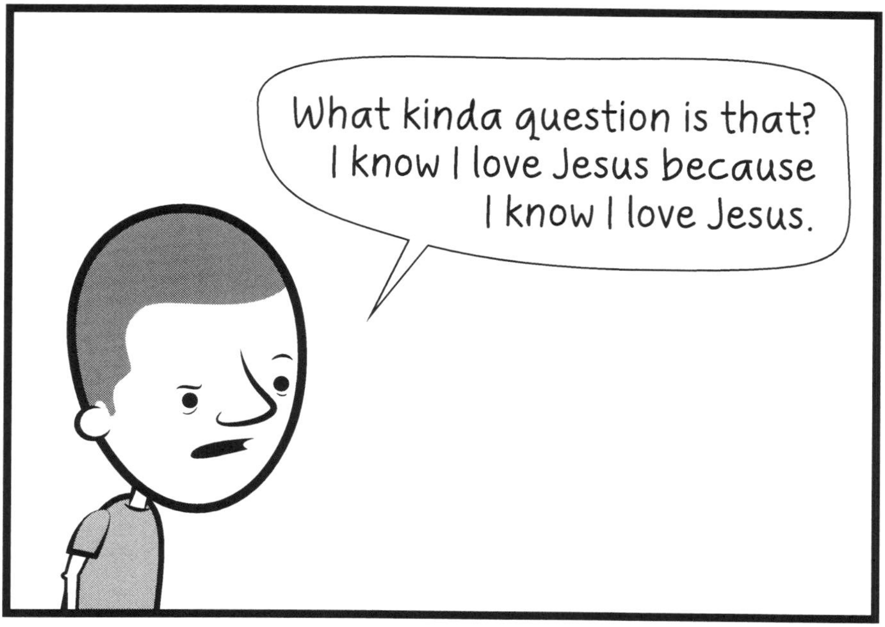
What kinda question is that? I know I love Jesus because I know I love Jesus.

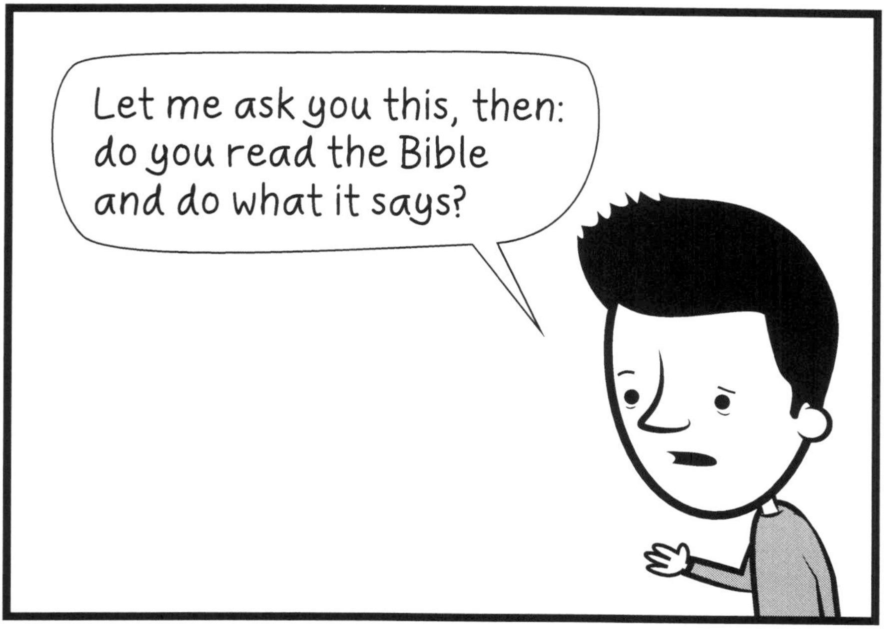
Let me ask you this, then: do you read the Bible and do what it says?

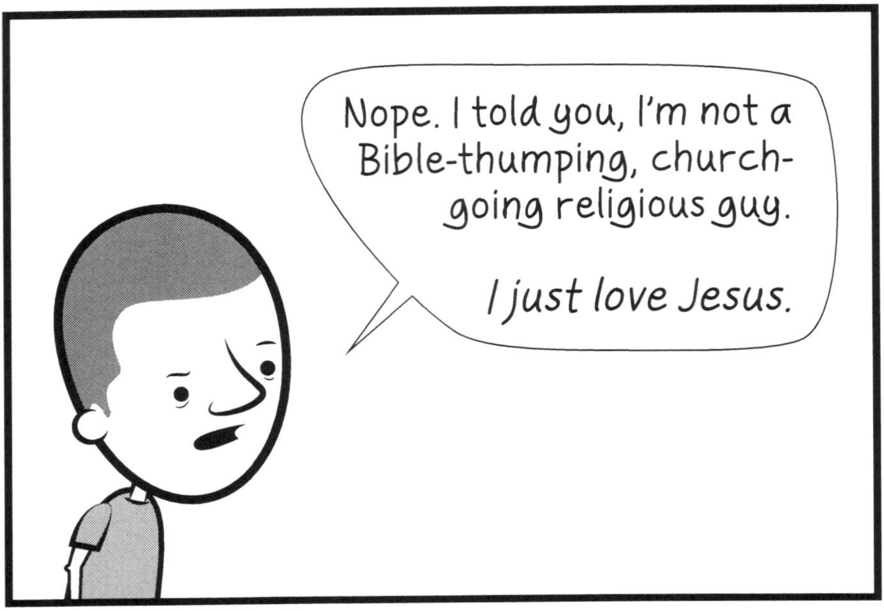
Nope. I told you, I'm not a Bible-thumping, church-going religious guy.
I just love Jesus.

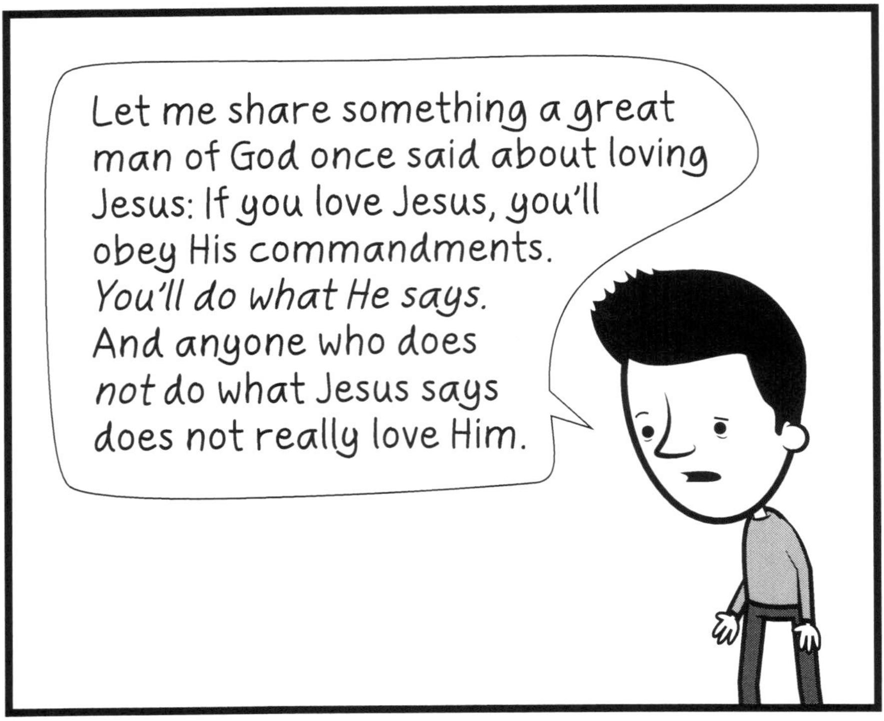
Let me share something a great man of God once said about loving Jesus: If you love Jesus, you'll obey His commandments. *You'll do what He says.* And anyone who does *not* do what Jesus says does not really love Him.

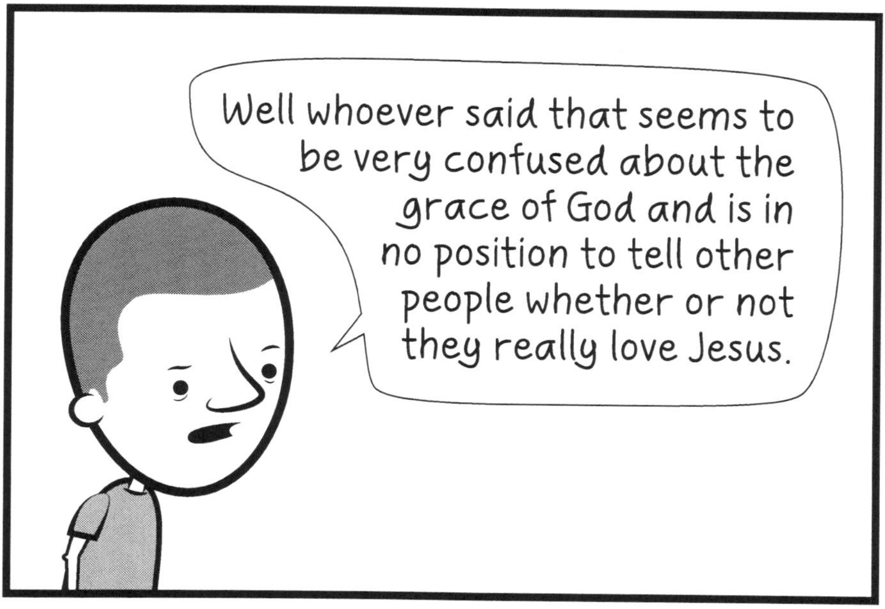
Well whoever said that seems to be very confused about the grace of God and is in no position to tell other people whether or not they really love Jesus.

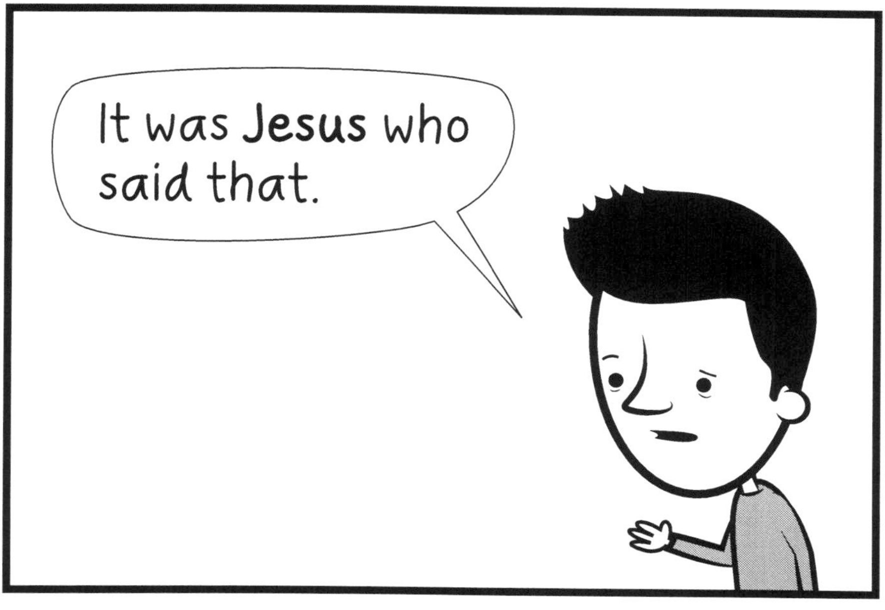
It was **Jesus** who said that.

Five reasons to believe Jesus rose from the dead

DID YOU KNOW THE BIBLE OUTLINES A SPECIFIC SITUATION IN WHICH CHRISTIANS SHOULD ADMIT THAT THEIR FAITH IN JESUS IS STUPID AND WORTHLESS?

MORE ON THAT LATER.

FOR *NOW* I'D LIKE TO OFFER, FOR YOUR CONSIDERATION:

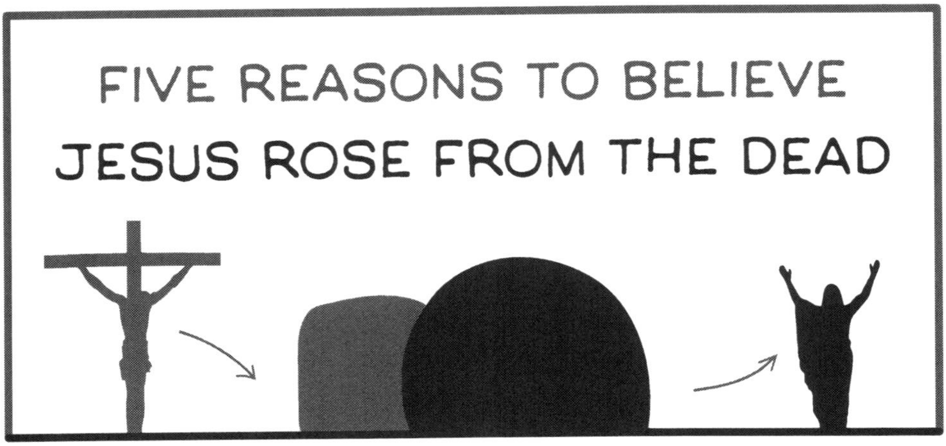
FIVE REASONS TO BELIEVE
JESUS ROSE FROM THE DEAD

FIVE REASONS WHY IT MAKES SENSE TO BELIEVE JESUS OF NAZARETH REALLY DID RISE FROM THE DEAD AFTER BEING EXECUTED ALMOST 2000 YEARS AGO.

1.)
THE EMPTY TOMB

JESUS WAS PUBLICLY EXECUTED BY CRUCIFIXION AND THEN PLACED IN A TOMB BY JOSEPH OF ARIMATHEA, A MEMBER OF THE SANHEDRIN.

THREE DAYS LATER SOME WOMEN CLAIMED **THE TOMB WAS EMPTY.**

IT IS VERY SIGNIFICANT THAT THIS WHOLE CHRISTIANITY THING HINGES ON AN EMPTY TOMB AND A MISSING BODY, BECAUSE THOSE ARE THINGS THAT ARE **PUBLICLY VERIFIABLE AND EMPIRICALLY FALSIFIABLE.**

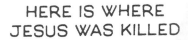

HERE IS WHERE
JESUS WAS KILLED

JERUSALEM

HERE IS WHERE
PEOPLE BEGAN
CLAIMING HE ROSE
FROM THE DEAD

THE PEOPLE IN CHARGE WERE VICIOUSLY
OPPOSED TO JESUS AND ANYONE CLAIMING HE
HAD RISEN FROM THE DEAD, AND THEY COULD
HAVE EASILY SQUASHED THE WHOLE THING BY
PRODUCING A BODY AND PROVING THEM WRONG,
WHICH THEY CERTAINLY TRIED TO DO.

BUT THEY COULDN'T. THE TOMB WAS EMPTY
AND THE BODY WAS NOWHERE TO BE FOUND.

2.)
THE POST-MORTEM APPEARANCES

WHETHER OR NOT ANYONE TODAY BELIEVES JESUS ROSE FROM THE DEAD DOESN'T CHANGE THE FACT THAT A LOT OF PEOPLE IN THE FIRST CENTURY BELIEVED THEY ENCOUNTERED AND INTERACTED WITH JESUS AFTER HIS DEATH.

JESUS APPEARED TO A NUMBER OF PEOPLE, IN DIFFERENT PLACES AND AT DIFFERENT TIMES.

FOR INSTANCE, 1 CORINTHIANS 15:3-8 STATES:

FOR I DELIVERED TO YOU AS OF FIRST IMPORTANCE WHAT I ALSO RECEIVED: THAT CHRIST DIED FOR OUR SINS IN ACCORDANCE WITH THE SCRIPTURES, THAT HE WAS BURIED, THAT HE WAS RAISED ON THE THIRD DAY IN ACCORDANCE WITH THE SCRIPTURES, AND THAT HE APPEARED TO CEPHAS, THEN TO THE TWELVE. THEN HE APPEARED TO MORE THAN FIVE HUNDRED BROTHERS AT ONE TIME, MOST OF WHOM ARE STILL ALIVE, THOUGH SOME HAVE FALLEN ASLEEP. THEN HE APPEARED TO JAMES, THEN TO ALL THE APOSTLES. LAST OF ALL, AS TO ONE UNTIMELY BORN, HE APPEARED ALSO TO ME.

OH SURE, USE THE *BIBLE* AS EVIDENCE THAT *JESUS* CAME BACK FROM THE DEAD . . . LOL

SOMEONE SAYS. BUT PEOPLE SEEM TO THINK OF THE BIBLE AS SOME BOOK THAT MAGICALLY POPPED INTO EXISTENCE, SORTA LIKE THE WAY MANY PEOPLE THINK THE UNIVERSE DID. BUT BEFORE THE CANON WAS COMPILED, THIS BOOK OF THE BIBLE WAS NOT A BOOK OF THE BIBLE-- IT WAS A LETTER FROM A GUY NAMED PAUL TO A GROUP OF FOLKS IN THE CITY OF CORINTH.

THIS SORT OF THING IS ALSO KNOWN AS A
PRIMARY SOURCE.

THIS PRIMARY SOURCE IS STRIKING FOR A
NUMBER OF REASONS, AND THE DATE OF THIS
LETTER IS ALMOST UNIVERSALLY PEGGED AT
ABOUT 20 YEARS AFTER JESUS'S DEATH.

YOU'LL NOTICE THAT PAUL RELAYS INFORMATION
ABOUT JESUS APPEARING TO DOZENS OF
SPECIFIC PEOPLE, INCLUDING HIMSELF, AND TO
HUNDREDS OF OTHER PEOPLE ON TOP OF THEM.

PAUL DID NOT WRITE THIS LETTER IN A VACUUM;
THESE WERE REAL PEOPLE WHO WERE REALLY
LIVING THEIR LIVES IN A REAL TIME AND PLACE.

YOU'LL ALSO NOTICE HE SPECIFICALLY STATES
THAT MOST OF THESE PEOPLE ARE STILL ALIVE.
WHY DO YOU THINK HE MENTIONED THIS . . . ?

READ BETWEEN THE LINES HERE: HE'S SAYING,

"IF YOU DON'T BELIEVE ME, YOU'RE WELCOME TO ASK THEM."

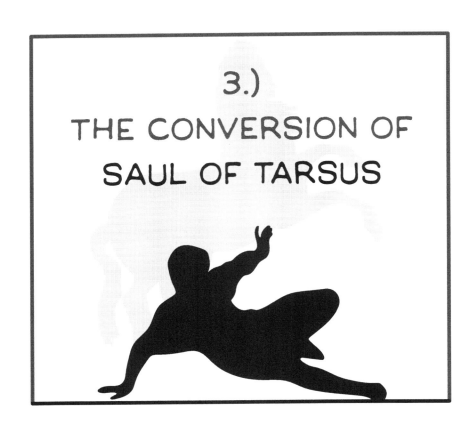

3.)
THE CONVERSION OF SAUL OF TARSUS

SAUL WAS AN IMPORTANT GUY FROM AN IMPORTANT FAMILY IN AN IMPORTANT CITY. HE STUDIED AT THE FEET OF ONE OF THE MOST HIGHLY-REGARDED RABBIS IN THE HISTORY OF JUDAISM, ON HIS WAY TO BECOMING A PROMINENT RELIGIOUS LEADER WHO ENJOYED SABBATH, WALKS ON THE BEACH, AND OVERSEEING THE DETAINMENT, IMPRISONMENT, AND OCCASIONAL KILLING OF THE PESKY NEW JESUS-PEOPLE FOR THEIR AWFUL BLASPHEMIES.

SAUL HAD EVERYTHING A GUY AT THAT TIME AND PLACE COULD'VE WANTED, AND LIKE BASICALLY **HE WAS THAT DUDE.**

THEN ON A WHIM ONE DAY HE DECIDED TO JOIN HIS ENEMIES, THROW AWAY HIS REPUTATION, AUTHORITY, WEALTH, SOCIAL STANDING, AND EVERY OTHER THING HE HAD WORKED FOR HIS ENTIRE LIFE, IN FAVOR OF TRAVELING THOUSANDS OF BRUTAL MILES AND WILLINGLY SUBJECTING HIMSELF TO LASHINGS, BEATINGS TO THE BRINK OF DEATH, STONINGS, SHIPWRECKS, STARVATION, DEHYDRATION, AND YEARS OF IMPRISONMENT, ALL SO HE COULD TELL PEOPLE THAT JESUS IS THE SON OF GOD AND SAVIOR OF THE WORLD.

AND HE DID THIS BECAUSE HE WAS BORED WITH HIS SUPER-NICE LIFE.

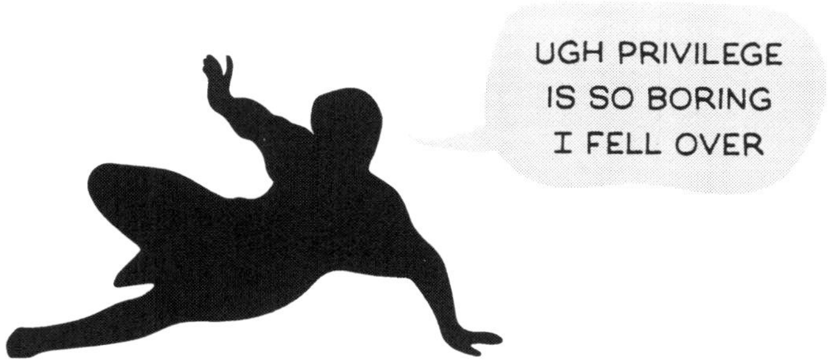
UGH PRIVILEGE IS SO BORING I FELL OVER

OR HE DID IT BECAUSE, AS HE TOLD EVERYONE WHO WOULD LISTEN UNTIL THE MOMENT HIS HEAD WAS LOPPED OFF FOR DOING SO:

HE MET THE RESURRECTED CHRIST.

4.)
THE BOLDNESS OF
THE DISCIPLES

THIS GROUP OF WHINY SNIVELERS WHOM JESUS CHOSE TO BE HIS DISCIPLES HAD TRIED TO BE BRAVE DURING JESUS'S LIFE AND HAD FAILED TIME AND TIME AGAIN.

EVEN **PETER**, THE ALPHA OF THE GROUP AND THE ONE WHO HAD THE SAND TO DRAW HIS SWORD ON THE SOLDIERS WHO WERE ARRESTING JESUS, SOON AFTER **DENIED THREE TIMES THAT HE EVEN KNEW WHO JESUS WAS.**

BECAUSE HE WAS SCARED.

THAT'S PETER ON THE OPPOSITE PAGE, AT THE
END OF HIS LIFE, BEING CRUCIFIED UPSIDE-DOWN
FOR BOLDLY PREACHING THE RESURRECTED
JESUS WHO HE CLAIMED TO HAVE MET.

WITH THE EXCEPTION OF ONE (JOHN), ALL OF THE
OTHER DISCIPLES HAD SIMILAR FATES:

JAMES: EXECUTED BY SWORD
THOMAS: SPEARED TO DEATH
MATTHEW: SPEARED TO DEATH
PHILIP: TORTURED, CRUCIFIED UPSIDE-DOWN
BARTHOLOMEW: SKINNED ALIVE, CRUCIFIED
UPSIDE-DOWN
ANDREW: CRUCIFIED
JAMES: CRUCIFIED
THADDEUS: CRUCIFIED
SIMON: CRUCIFIED

ALL OF THESE MEN CLAIMED TO HAVE INTERACTED
WITH THE BODILY-RISEN JESUS, AFTER HIS DEATH.

WOULD THEY FEARLESSLY PROCLAIM THIS, ALL THE
WAY TO THEIR UNIMAGINABLE DEATHS, KNOWING IT
WAS ACTUALLY JUST SOMETHING THEY MADE UP?

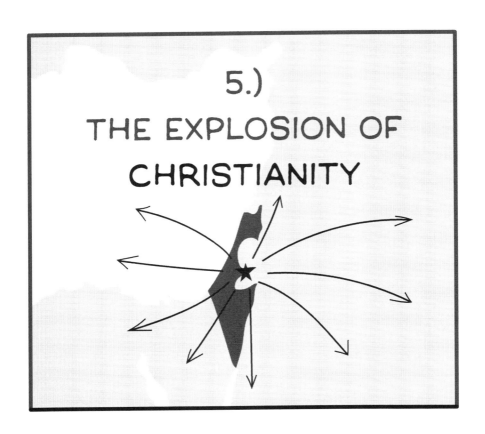

5.)
THE EXPLOSION OF CHRISTIANITY

AS YOU KNOW, **CHRISTIANITY EXPLODED** AFTER THE EXACT THING THAT SHOULD HAVE KILLED IT BEFORE IT WAS BORN: THE DEATH OF JESUS.

THE NUMBER OF CONVERTS MULTIPLIED EXPONENTIALLY, DAY IN AND DAY OUT, AMONG A POPULACE THAT DID NOT BELIEVE PEOPLE CAME BACK FROM THE DEAD AND WOULD HAVE THOUGHT THE IDEA OF WORSHIPING A MAN AS GOD REPREHENSIBLE.

SO WHY DID THAT HAPPEN?
WHAT CAN ACCOUNT FOR IT?

I'LL TELL YOU WHAT CAN ACCOUNT FOR IT:
JESUS'S TOMB BEING EMPTY, HIS BODY MISSING,
AND HUNDREDS OF PEOPLE ENCOUNTERING HIM
AFTER HIS DEATH AND TELLING EVERYONE THEY
KNEW, SWEARING ON THEIR LIVES THAT THEY SAW
HIM WITH THEIR OWN TWO EYES, WILLING TO DIE
RATHER THAN DENY THAT JESUS WAS RISEN.

THAT SORTA THING WOULD GET AROUND, Y'KNOW?

AT THE BEGINNING OF THIS PIECE I MENTIONED A
SPECIFIC SITUATION IN WHICH THE BIBLE SAYS
CHRISTIANS SHOULD JUST GIVE UP THEIR FAITH.

IT'S FROM 1 CORINTHIANS, THE SAME BOOK I
QUOTED IN POINT 2, WRITTEN BY SAUL, THE GUY
FROM POINT 3, WHO BECAME THE APOSTLE PAUL.

HE SAID IF JESUS DID NOT REALLY REALLY RISE FROM THE DEAD, OUR FAITH IS IN VAIN. IT'S FUTILE.

IF JESUS DID NOT REALLY RISE FROM THE
DEAD, THERE IS NO CHRISTIANITY.

BUT IF HE REALLY *DID* RISE FROM THE DEAD,

THEN HE IS WHO HE CLAIMED TO BE.

IF HE REALLY *DID* RISE FROM THE DEAD,

THE IMPLICATIONS FOR YOU AND ME ARE MIND-BLOWING AND MORE IMPORTANT THAN ANY-THING ELSE.

THIS LITTLE LIST PROVIDES FIVE REASONS TO BELIEVE JESUS REALLY ROSE FROM THE DEAD.

AS I SAID FROM THE GO, IT'S DEFINITELY NOT AN EXHAUSTIVE LIST.

BUT IT IS A SUFFICIENT LIST.

Why'd you give me this, God?

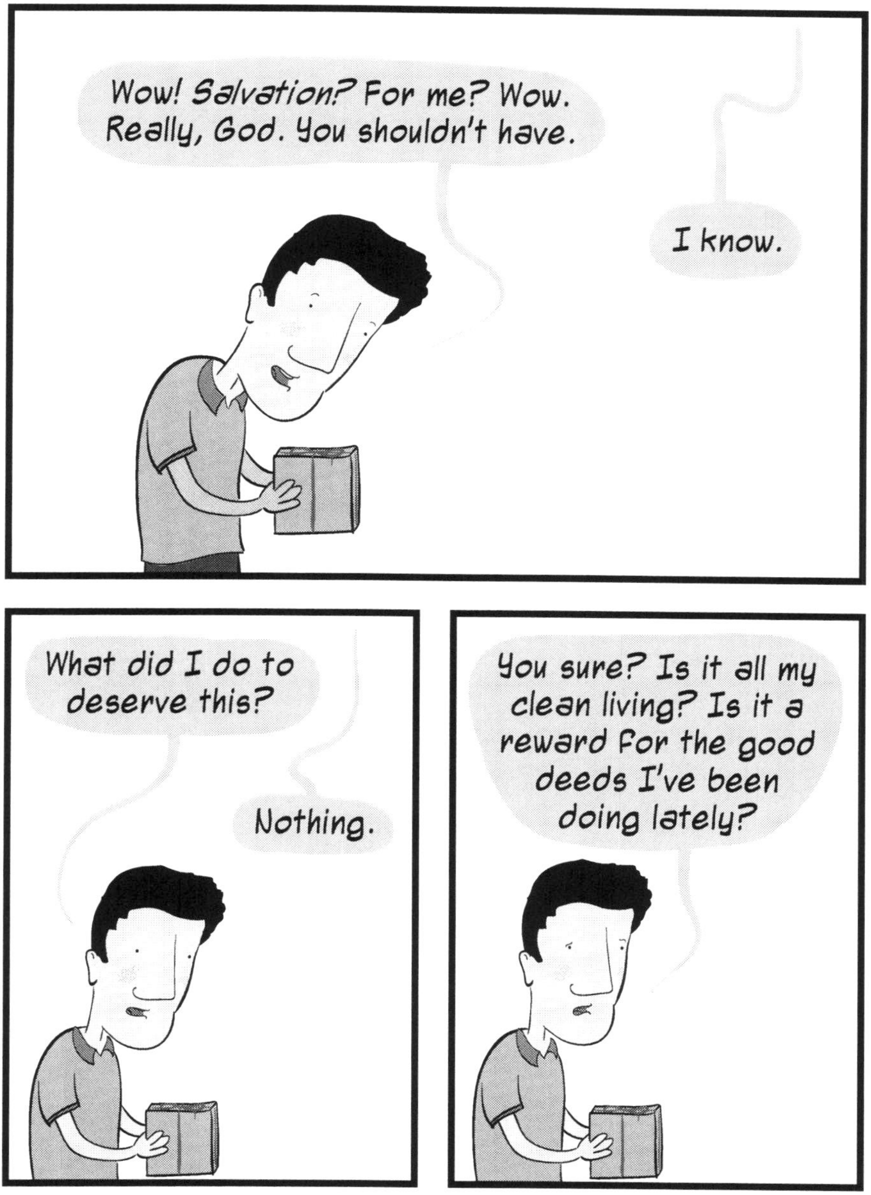
Wow! Salvation? For me? Wow. Really, God. You shouldn't have.
I know.
What did I do to deserve this?
Nothing.
You sure? Is it all my clean living? Is it a reward for the good deeds I've been doing lately?

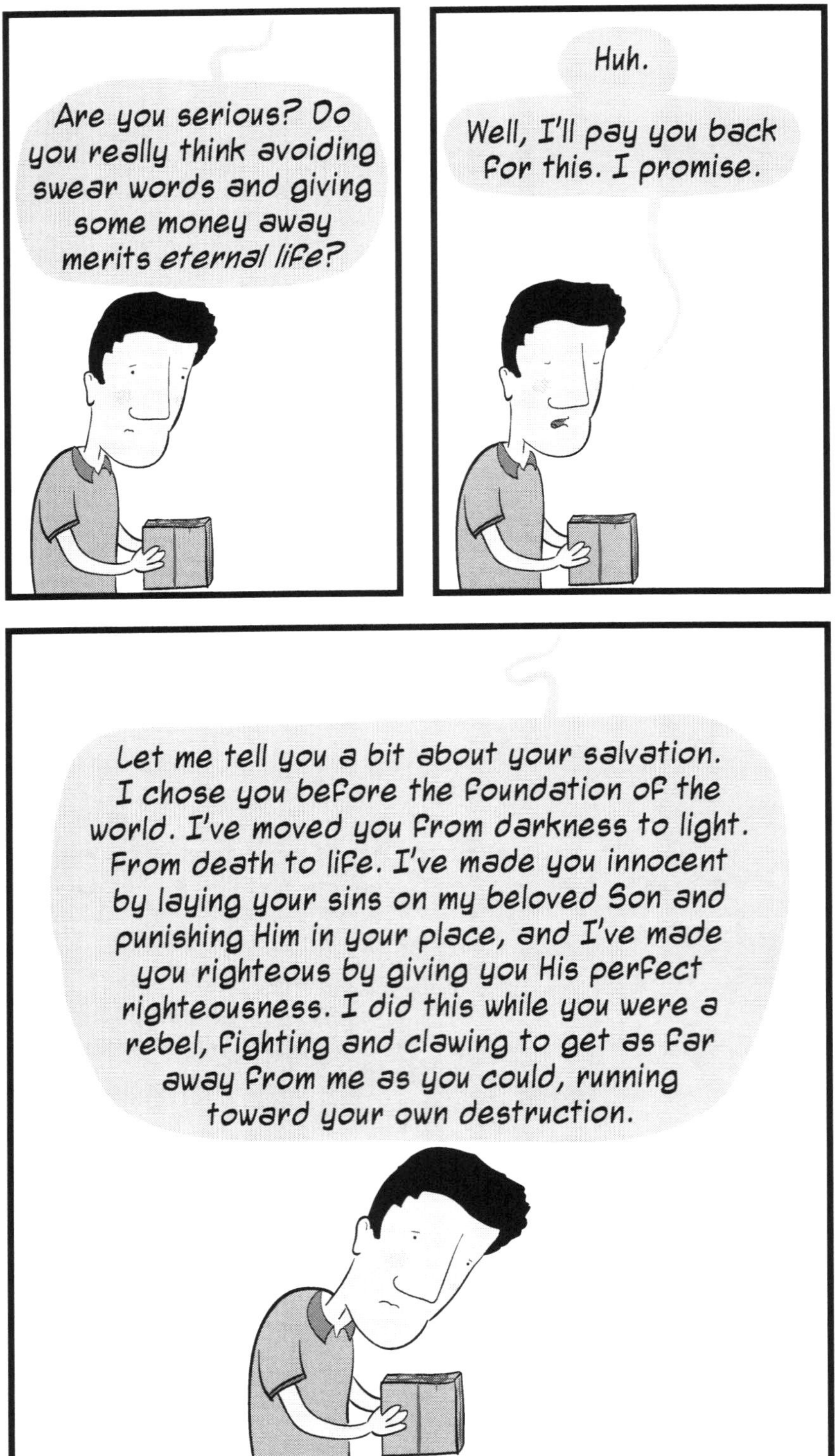
Are you serious? Do you really think avoiding swear words and giving some money away merits *eternal life*?
Huh.
Well, I'll pay you back for this. I promise.
Let me tell you a bit about your salvation. I chose you before the foundation of the world. I've moved you from darkness to light. From death to life. I've made you innocent by laying your sins on my beloved Son and punishing Him in your place, and I've made you righteous by giving you His perfect righteousness. I did this while you were a rebel, fighting and clawing to get as far away from me as you could, running toward your own destruction.

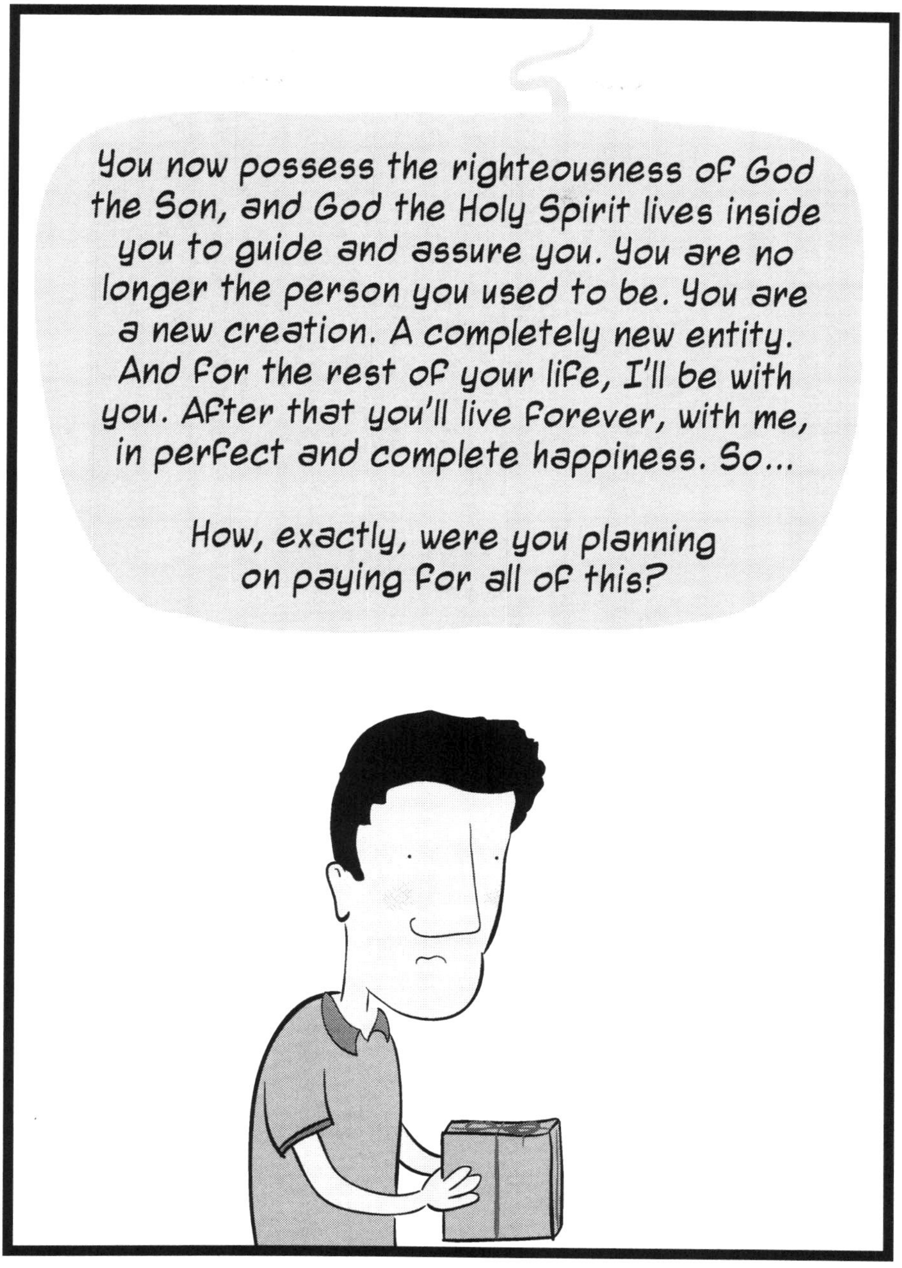
You now possess the righteousness of God the Son, and God the Holy Spirit lives inside you to guide and assure you. You are no longer the person you used to be. You are a new creation. A completely new entity. And for the rest of your life, I'll be with you. After that you'll live forever, with me, in perfect and complete happiness. So...
How, exactly, were you planning on paying for all of this?

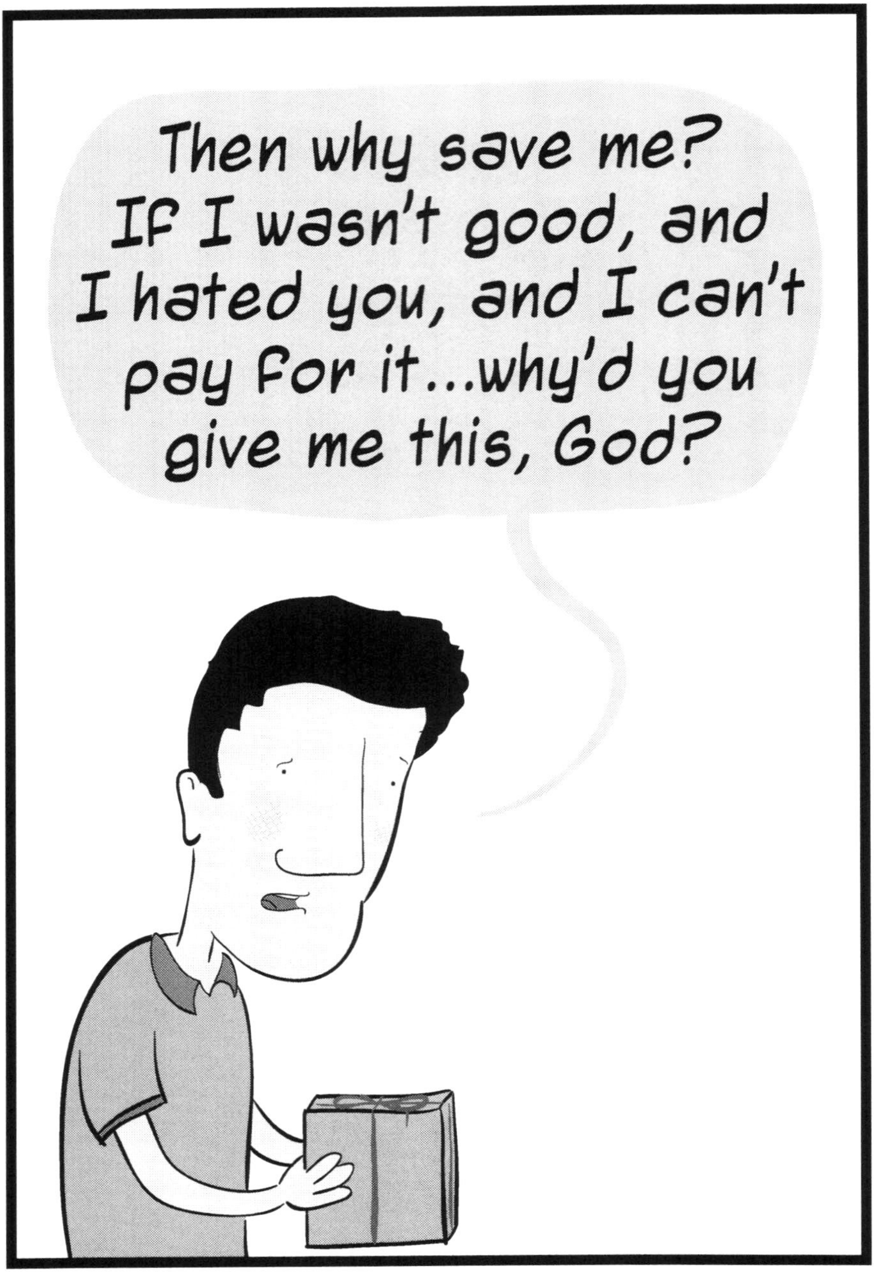
Then why save me? If I wasn't good, and I hated you, and I can't pay for it...why'd you give me this, God?

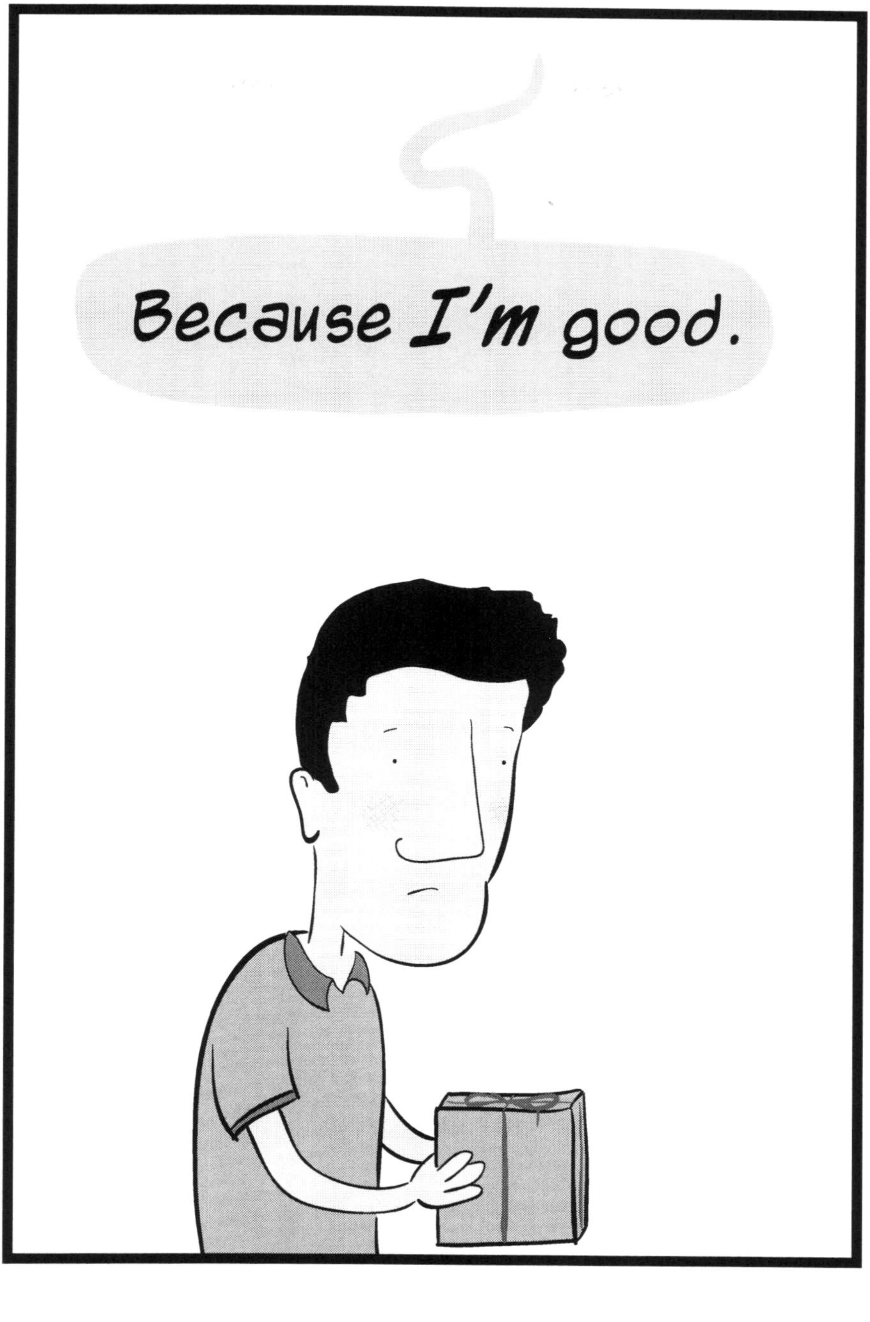
Because I'm good.

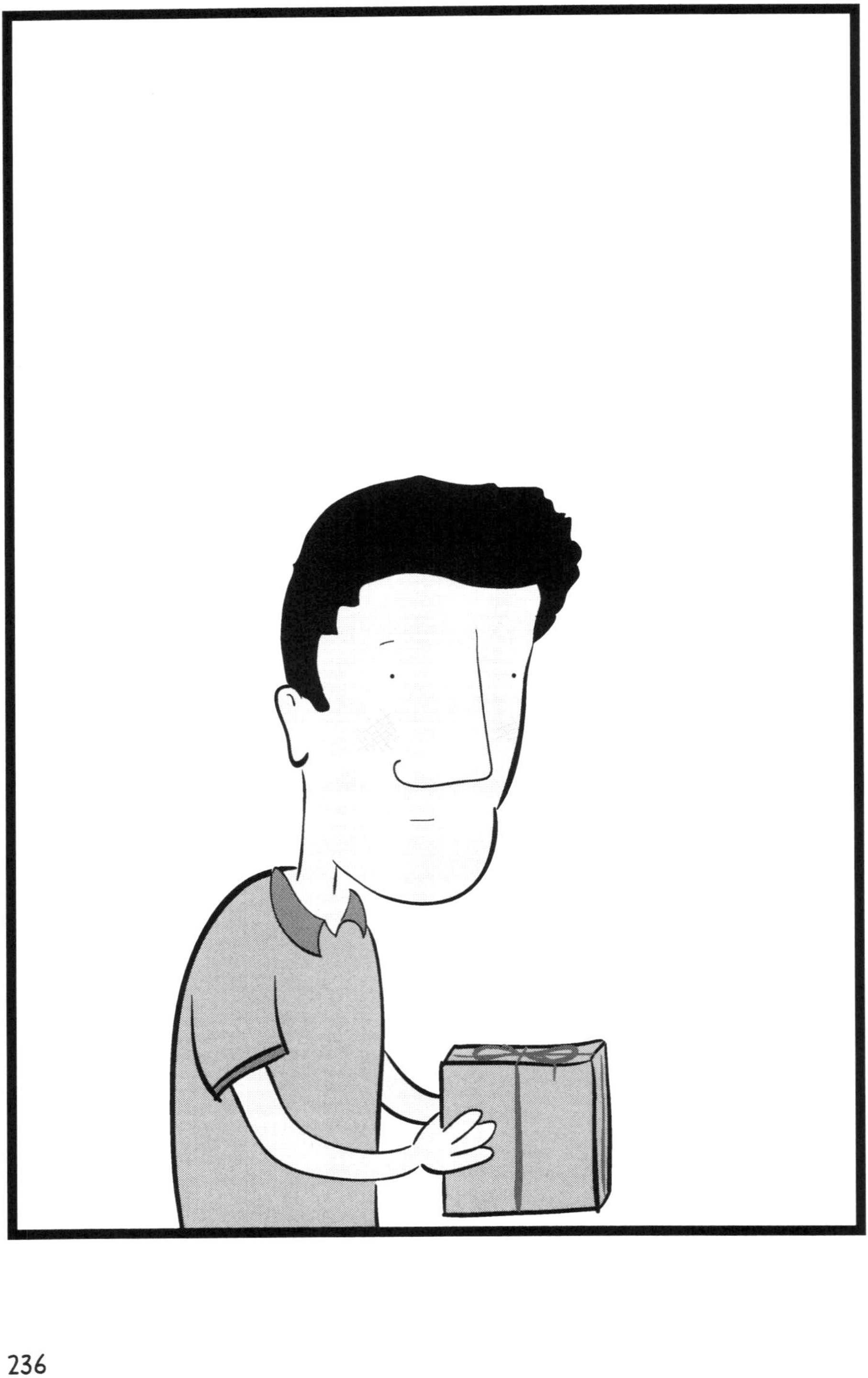

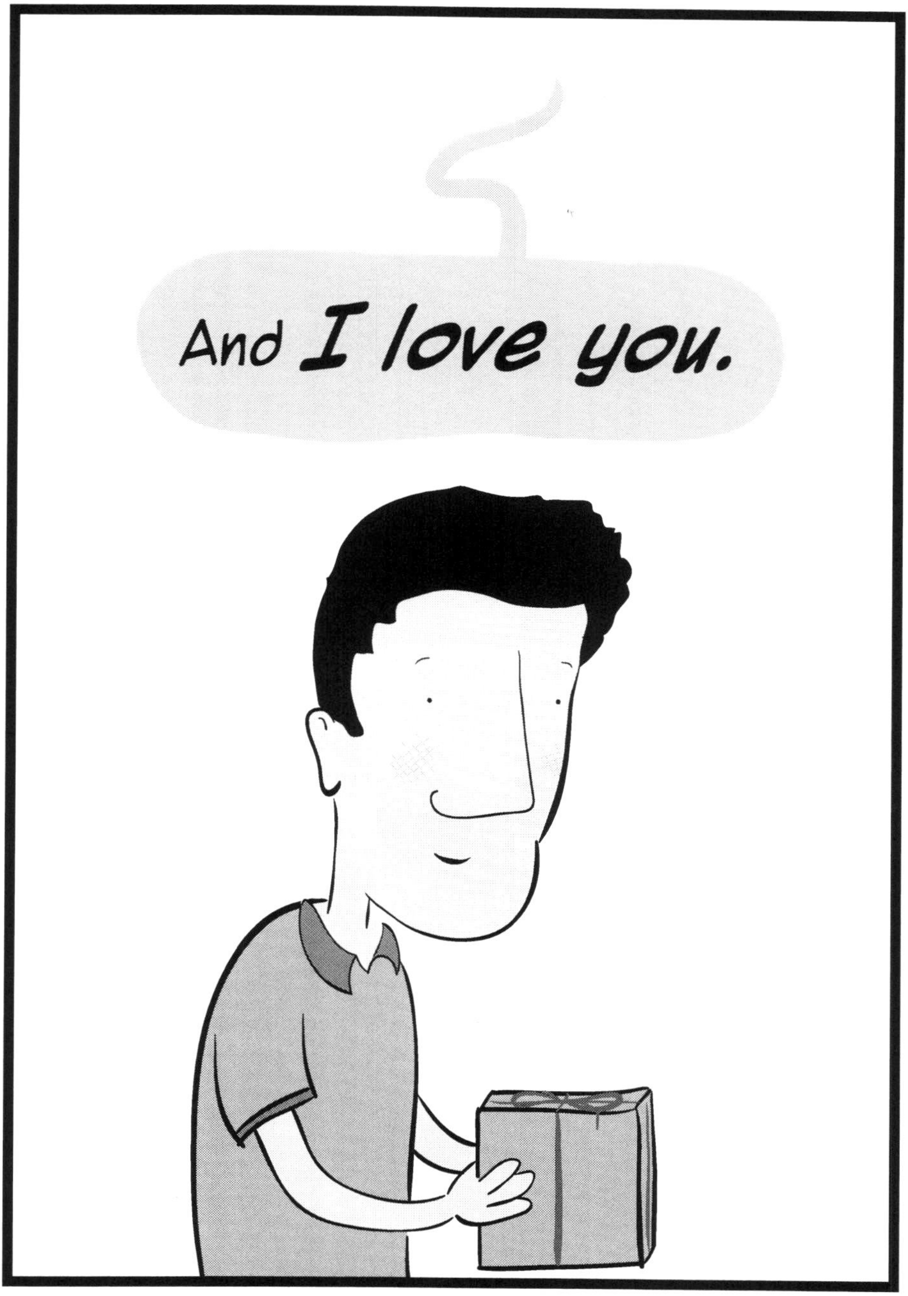
And I love you.

Made in the USA
San Bernardino, CA
19 December 2016